Henry Buckley was the *Daily Telegraph*'s correspondent in Spain during the Spanish Civil War. He arrived in Spain in 1929, six years before the outbreak of the conflict, and left Spain with the remnants of the Republican forces that fled over the Pyrenees following their defeat by Franco in 1939. After covering the Second World War, during which he was wounded at Anzio, Buckley returned to Spain in 1949, living there until his death in 1972.

'The overwhelming value of this wonderful book is that it provides an objective picture of a crucial decade of contemporary Spanish history, based on an abundance of the eye-witness material that only a really assiduous resident correspondent could garner. For Hemingway, Hugh Thomas and others, [Henry Buckley] was a living archive of the [Spanish Civil] war. Fortunately for those who could not consult him personally, he left *The Life and Death of the Spanish Republic*, a worthy monument to a great correspondent.'
                              – Paul Preston, author of *The Spanish Holocaust*,
                                        from the Introduction to this book

'Henry Buckley was one of the best of a top array of foreign correspondents of the 1930s and after, the only first-hand observer to write an account of the entire history of the Spanish Republic. The book is a classic, written with great personal honesty.'
                              – Stanley G. Payne, author of *The Spanish Civil War*

'*The Life and Death of the Spanish Republic* is a compelling account of one time-locked country's bid for democratic change, and of the human and structural obstacles to it. Henry Buckley, the war correspondent's correspondent who mentored Hemingway, already knew Spain before the Nazi- and Fascist-backed military coup sent it spiralling into civil war in 1936; Buckley's writing encapsulates the hugeness and implacability of 'History' in the fresh and direct detail of ordinary people's hopes and fears. A clear-headed, humane assessment – with an almost unbearable immediacy – of hopes raised and dashed. One of the best books ever written on the subject in any language.'
                              – Helen Graham, author of *The Spanish*
                                        Civil War: A Very Short Introduction

'The Spanish Civil War was the central element of twentieth-century Spanish history. Throughout the almost eighty years since that summer of 1936, novelists, poets and historians have attempted to explain its causes and its consequences, the most bitter conflicts and the politics that drove them. *The Life and Death of the Spanish Republic* presents a clear, sharply defined first-hand portrait of this conflict. It is an exceptional testimony.'
                              – Julián Casanova, author of *A Short*
                                        History of the Spanish Civil War

THE LIFE AND DEATH OF THE SPANISH REPUBLIC

A WITNESS TO THE SPANISH CIVIL WAR

HENRY BUCKLEY

INTRODUCTION BY PAUL PRESTON

I.B. TAURIS

LONDON · NEW YORK

New edition published in 2013 by I.B.Tauris & Co Ltd
6 Salem Road, London W2 4BU
175 Fifth Avenue, New York NY 10010
www.ibtauris.com

Distributed in the United States and Canada
Exclusively by Palgrave Macmillan
175 Fifth Avenue, New York NY 10010

First published in 1940 by Hamish Hamilton
Copyright © 2013 Patrick, Ramón and George Buckley

ISBN: 978 1 78076 429 0

A full CIP record for this book is available from the British Library

A full CIP record is available from the Library of Congress

Library of Congress Catalog Card Number: available

Printed and bound by TJ International Ltd, Padstow, Cornwall

MIX
Paper from
responsible sources
FSC
www.fsc.org FSC® C013056

CONTENTS

CONTENTS — *continued*

LIST OF ILLUSTRATIONS

Photos taken by Henry Buckley, courtesy of the Arxiu Comarcal de l'Alt Penedès (ACAP) Fons Henry Buckley

THE HUMANE OBSERVER: HENRY BUCKLEY

PAUL PRESTON

IT is said that when Hemingway returned to Madrid after the Civil War, he would always turn to Henry Buckley to find out what was really going on in Franco's Spain. When Hugh Thomas published his monumental history of the Spanish Civil War, he thanked Buckley for allowing him 'to pick his brains remorselessly'. William Forrest, who was in Spain during the war, representing first the *Daily Express* and later the *News Chronicle*, wrote that 'Buckley saw more of the Civil War than any foreign correspondent of any country and reported it with a scrupulous adherence to the truth that won the respect even of those who sometimes might have preferred the truth to remain uncovered'. Henry Buckley may not have written any of the most famous chronicles of the war like Jay Allen's account of the massacre of Badajoz or George Steer's account of Guernica. Nevertheless, in addition to his sober news items throughout the war and to the help freely dispensed to less experienced colleagues, he produced this book, one of the most enduring records of the Spanish Republic and the Civil War, a monumental testimony to his work as a correspondent.

Henry Buckley's *Life and Death of the Spanish Republic* constitutes a unique account of Spanish politics throughout the entire life of the Second Republic, from its foundation on 14 April 1931 to its defeat at the end of March 1939, combining personal recollections of meetings with the great politicians of the day with eye-witness accounts of dramatic events. It lucidly explains a complex period in vivid prose laced with humour, pity for human suffering and outrage at those whom he considered to be responsible for the tragedy of Spain. It summed up his work as a correspondent during the Spanish Civil War representing the *Daily Telegraph*. It was an ironic commentary on the experiences recounted in the book that, not long after it had been published in 1940, the warehouse in London containing stocks of the book was hit by German incendiary bombs and all the unsold copies were destroyed. Thus, this classic history of the war has been unavailable ever since.

Henry Buckley was born in Urms near Manchester in November 1904 and, after stints in Berlin and Paris, he had come to Spain to represent the now defunct *Daily Chronicle*. Henry Buckley was a devout Roman Catholic, with radical social instincts. It was human empathy, rather than ideology, that accounted for his support for the struggles of the industrial workers and the landless peasants in the 1930s. That is clear throughout the book. As befitted a conservative, he was an admirer of the benevolent dictator General Miguel Primo de Rivera, whom he described as 'a national Father Christmas'. Buckley was a determinedly honest man. He liked the dictator's son, José Antonio, although he was disturbed by the paid thugs who belonged to the Fascist party that he created, the Falange.

Buckley was disappointed by his first sight of Spain, and by the shabbiness and poverty of the peasants, yet was also fiercely self-critical about the audacity of reporting on a country of which he knew nothing in 1929. He writes throughout with a humorous awareness of his own deficiencies, describing himself, on leaving Paris for Madrid, as 'a rather crotchety and thin-blooded virgin'. Buckley may have been ignorant on his arrival but he set out to learn and learn he did. He disliked Madrid as 'bleak and draughty and monotonous' and was outraged by a situation in which 'one million Spaniards live at the expense of the rest of the nation'. Yet, as is shown by his account of the siege of the capital during the war, he came to love the city and admire its inhabitants. It seemed like a conservative Englishman speaking when he said, 'I feel that the democratic system adopted by the Republic when King Alfonso left the country was in no small part responsible for Spain's tragedy', but it was soon apparent that his view was based on the rather radical belief that the Republicans were insufficiently dictatorial to engage in a thorough reform of the country's ancient economy.

The overwhelming value of his wonderful book is that it provides an objective picture of a crucial decade of contemporary Spanish history, based on an abundance of the eye-witness material that only a really assiduous resident correspondent could garner. Perceptive and revealing anecdotes abound. With Republican crowds surging the streets of Madrid, Buckley, waiting in the bitter cold on the night of 13 April outside Palacio de Oriente, asks a porter what the Royal Family was doing. 'I imagined its members in anxious conclave, calling up friends, consulting desperately. The answer was calm and measured: "Their Majesties are attending a cinematographic performance in the salon recently fitted up with a sound apparatus."' The next day, he witnesses the future war leader but then unknown Dr Negrín calming an impatient crowd by arranging for a Republican flag to be draped on a balcony of the Royal Palace. In Chicote's bar in the Gran Vía, 'a polished British-public-school-educated son of a Spanish banker tells him "the only future the Republicans and Socialists will have will be on the gallows or in gaol"'.

One of the greatest joys of Buckley's prose is to be found in his immensely perceptive portraits of the major political and military figures of the day which have profoundly coloured the later judgements of historians. On Julián Besteiro, the President of the Cortes whose misguided judgements stood in the way of agrarian reform, he wrote with morbid irony: 'he showed fine tolerance, quick to hurry to the support of the weak—in this case the representatives of feudalism who had ridden rough-shod over their opponents for many a century.' In the aftermath of the massacre by security forces of anarchist peasants at Casas Viejas in the province of Cádiz on 8 January 1933, Buckley describes Carlos Esplá, then Under-Secretary for the Home Ministry, as a 'superlatively inefficient and muddle-headed Republican' and goes a long way to explaining the weakness of the Republic because of its politicians' inability to deal with the high-handed brutality of the Civil Guard. Despite a lack of sympathy for his politics, Buckley admired the political efficacy of the CEDA leader, José María Gil Robles – 'truculent, forceful, an excellent executive and with considerable judgement in men and politics'. In contrast, he saw the revolutionary rhetoric of the Socialist leader Francisco Largo Caballero as utterly false and describes in satirical terms the vacuous oratory of Niceto Alcalá Zamora, the President of the Republic.

Henry Buckley knew every politician of note in 1930s Spain. He particularly admired Dr Juan Negrín, the wartime Socialist premier, but he was utterly bowled over by 'Pasionaria', the Communist orator Dolores Ibárruri. After meeting her in Valencia in May 1937 and being subjected to a passionate harangue, he wrote: 'But what a woman! She was, I think, the only Spanish politician I ever met; and I think I know most of those who have any call on fame during this generation, and she is the only one who really did impress me as being a great person.' He liked the moderate Socialist Indalecio Prieto and admired his untiring work as a minister during the Civil War, but was aware that not all of his feverish work was as productive as it might have been since he insisted on dealing with every minor detail even to the extent of personally examining journalists' applications for visits to the front.

Of the illiterate peasant who became a general in the war, Valentín González, 'El Campesino', Buckley's view confirms that of other observers: 'He had the strangely magnetic eyes of a madman.' Writing of Campesino's great rival, the brutal Stalinist Enrique Líster, Buckley noted that he appreciated the importance of good food: 'He had a cook who had been with Wagon-Lits restaurant cars before the war and in the various times in various retreats in which I managed to pick up a meal at Líster's headquarters I do not think I ever had a bad one.' Buckley could also describe Líster 'handling the remains of an Army corps with coolness and considerable skill'. The greatest admiration is reserved for Negrín, not only for his dynamism but also for his essential kindness:

> My chief impression of him was of his strong pity for human suf-
> fering. He would look at the newsboy from whom he was buying
> an evening paper and say 'Having those eyes treated, sonny? No?
> Well go to Dr So-and-So at such-and-such a clinic and give him this
> card and he'll see that you get treated right away.' Or out in the
> country, he would stop in small villages and talk to the peasants,
> look in at their miserable homes, peer behind the easy mask of pic-
> turesqueness which veils so much disease and suffering in Spain.
> Before leaving he would slip some money or a card which would
> ensure free medical treatment into the hand of the woman of the
> house. That was Negrín as I knew him.

This eye for the telling detail brings the politics of the Second Repub-lic to life. During the run-up to the November 1933 elections, Buckley visited CEDA headquarters and noted the lavish quality of the posters used in Gil Robles's campaign. On 21 April 1934, he attended the rain-soaked rally of the Juventud de Acción Popular at El Escorial. The parading, saluting and chanting led Buckley to see it as the trial for the creation of Fascist shock troops. A turn-out of 50,000 had been expected, but, despite the transport facilities, the giant publicity cam-paign and the large sums spent, fewer than half that number arrived. Besides, as Buckley observed, 'there were too many peasants at El Esco-rial who told reporters quite cheerfully that they had been sent by the local political boss with fare and expenses paid'. On the eve of the min-ers' insurrection in Asturias, on the night of 5 October, Buckley was with the Socialists Luis Araquistain, Juan Negrín and Julio Álvarez Del Vayo in a bar in Madrid discussing the wisdom of Largo Caballero's revolutionary rhetoric. He describes how, during the siege of the capital, the luxurious Hotel Palace was turned into a military hospital. After the Battle of Guadalajara, he interviews captured Italian regular troops who, far from being volunteers, were in Spain under formal military orders. At the end of May 1937, he hastens to Almería to examine the damage done by the German warship *Admiral Scheer* on 31 May 1937 in reprisal for the Republican bombing of the cruiser *Deutschland* two days earlier, and produces a grim description of the destruction of the working-class districts of this undefended port.

As a witness to such scenes, Buckley is overcome with moral indignation, although his sympathies for the poor of Spain were engaged as early as 1931. Reflecting on the situation of Alfonso XIII on the night before his departure from Madrid, he asks rhetorically: 'Where are your friends? Can anyone believe that this fine people of Spain have hearts of stone? No. If you had ever shown generosity or comprehension of their aches and struggles they would not leave you friendless tonight. You never did.' Although a practising Catholic throughout his life, Buckley wavered in his Catholic faith because of right-wing Catholic hostility to the Republic, commenting that, 'Much as I disliked the mob violence and the burning of churches I felt that the people in Spain who professed most loudly their Catholic faith were the most to blame for the existence of illiterate masses and a threadbare national economy.' His humanity was brought into conflict with his religious faith, as can be seen in his vivid accounts of the daily lives of near-starving *braceros* in the south.

To some degree, the greatest object of Buckley's indignation is the role of the British government and the diplomatic corps. He comments that, 'When I did talk to any of our diplomatic officers I found them very complaisantly disposed towards the Spanish Right. They looked upon them as a guarantee against Bolshevism, much preferable to have them in power than either Socialists or Republicans for this reason, and they would gently pooh-pooh any suggestion that the Spanish Right might one day side with Germany and Italy and we might suddenly find our Empire routes in danger.' After the bombing of the German battle-cruiser *Deutschland*, the German crew members killed were buried with full military honours in Gibraltar. After the German revenge attack on an undefended Almería, Buckley witnessed the funeral of one of the victims. Looking at the worn faces and gnarled hands of those who followed the coffin, he wondered 'how it is that so few people care how much the working masses suffer'. He was appalled that while the port of Gandía was bombed by German aircraft and British ships were destroyed, the Royal Navy destroyer standing nearby in Valencia was ordered to do nothing. Effectively, the picture painted by Buckley is one of the British establishment putting its class prejudices before its strategic interests. In this regard, he quotes a British diplomat who says that 'the essential thing to remember in the case of Spain is that it is a civil conflict and that it is very necessary that we stand by our class'.

While working for the *Daily Telegraph*, Henry Buckley established friendships with many of the most prominent war correspondents who worked in Spain, including Jay Allen, Vincent Sheehan, Lawrence Fernsworth, Herbert Matthews and Ernest Hemingway. Quietly spoken—one Spanish journalist commented that his speaking voice was 'almost a sigh'—Buckley was extremely popular among his colleagues, who called him 'Enrique'. The young American reporter Kitty Bowler made a trip to Madrid in October 1936 which she described as 'a nightmare', but it was made bearable by Henry Buckley. He rescued her from the unwelcome attentions of men in her hotel and she later wrote of him as 'the sweetest reporter in Spain. His everyday banter acted like a welcome cocktail.' The novelist Josephine Herbst met him in April 1937 and remembered him as 'a wonderful fellow, and with more background about Spain's past than any other correspondent in Spain'. Constancia de la Mora, in charge of liaison with the Republic's Foreign Press Bureau, described Henry Buckley as 'a little sandy-haired man, with a shy face and a little tic at the corner of the mouth which gave his dry humour a sardonic twist'.

Yet his quiet manner belied the courage which saw him visiting every front at considerable risk to himself. In the latter stages of the Battle of the Ebro, on 5 November 1938, he crossed the river in a boat with Ernest Hemingway, Vincent Sheean, Robert Capa and Herbert Matthews. He commented later:

> We were sent out to cover the news on Líster's front—Hemingway was then reporting to the North American Newspaper alliance. At that time, virtually all the bridges across the Ebro had been smashed by the fighting and a series of treacherous spikes had been sunk in the river to discourage all navigation on it. However, since there was no other way of getting to the front, the five of us set out in a boat with the idea of rowing along the shore until we got to the deepest part of the river, then crossing, and rowing back to the opposite shore. The trouble was that we got caught in the

current and started drifting into the centre. With every moment that passed, the situation became more menacing, for, once on the spikes, the bottom of the boat was certain to be ripped out; almost as certain was that we would drown once the boat had capsized. It was Hemingway who saved the situation, for he pulled on the oars like a hero, and with such fury that he got us safely across.

Buckley was, of course, playing down his own bravery. Hemingway described him during the war as 'a lion of courage, though a very slight, even frail creature with (or so he says in his book) jittery nerves'. The eternally cynical Cedric Salter, who occasionally accompanied him in the last stages of the war, commented that Buckley 'was always quietly gay when things looked bad, but perhaps because he is made in a more sensitive mold than the others I always felt that in order to do the things he did required more real moral courage for him than from the others'. Salter's insight is substantiated by Buckley's own account. He recalled a conversation with several colleagues after a visit to the front. With considerable understatement, he wrote:

> Our dangers came from long-distance shelling and from the constant bombing and machine-gunning of the roads behind the lines. The risk was actually not very great. I had no hesitation in saying that I always felt highly nervous when getting near the front. Nor had I any shame in confessing that when I lay in some field and watched bombers coming towards the point where I was lying and heard the 'whur-whur-whur' as the bombs came speeding down, was I ever anything but thoroughly frightened. Even more terrifying, I think, is being machine-gunned. You know that a bomb must practically fall on top of you in an open field in order to hurt you. But it is only rarely that any shelter against machine-gunning can be found when one dives haphazard from a car with the planes coming over and minutes or even seconds in which to throw oneself into the best shelter available.

After the capture of Catalonia by the rebel forces at the end of January 1939, Buckley, along with Herbert Matthews, Vincent Sheean and other correspondents, had joined the exodus of refugees. He and Matthews established themselves in a hotel in Perpignan and devoted themselves to reporting on the appalling conditions in the concentration camps improvised by the French authorities into which the refugees had been herded. They managed to intervene to rescue people that they knew from the groups being taken to the camps.

Although he says little of his own role, Buckley's pages are alive with fury when he reaches his horrendous account of refugees arriving at the French frontier. He was outraged that Britain and France did not do more:

> The whole world was excited about the rescuing of some 600 chefs d'oeuvres of Spanish and Italian art which were being guarded near Figueras after their long odyssey. But we cared nothing about the soul of a people which was being trampled on. We did not come to cheer them; to encourage them. To have taken these half million and cherished them and given them work and comfort in Britain and France and their colonies, that indeed would have been culture in its real sense of the word. I love El Greco, I have spent countless hours just sitting looking at the Prado Titians and some of Velázquez's works fascinate me, but frankly I think that it would have been better for mankind if they had all been burnt in a pyre if the loving and warm attention that was lavished on them could have been devoted to this half-million sufferers. Better still if we had hearts big enough to cherish both, but since apparently we have not, it would at least have been a happier omen if such drops of the milk of human kindness which we still possess could have gone to the human sufferers. Yet while men well known in Catalan and Spanish cultural life in addition to tens of thousands of unknown persons were lying exposed to the elements and an average of sixty persons a week were dying of sickness and disease among the refugees in and around Perpignan, the art treasures left for Geneva in 1,842 cases on February 13; they were well protected from wind and rain. Women and children and sick and wounded men could sleep in the open air, almost uncared for. But the twenty trucks of Prado pictures had great tarpaulin covers and the care of a score of experts.

In the summer of 1938, accompanied by the artist Luis Quintanilla and the American reporter Herbert Matthews, Buckley had gone to Sitges. Quintanilla introduced him to the Catalan painter Joaquim Sunyer. He in turn presented Buckley to a Catalan girl, María Planas. They fell in love and quickly decided to marry. Despite the fact that the Catholic Church was still proscribed in Republican Spain, Constancia de la Mora used her influence to permit them to be married in a chapel used by the Basques exiled in Catalonia. After the Spanish Civil War, Buckley was posted to Berlin where he worked until two days before the outbreak of the Second World War when he was obliged to leave

8

by the Nazis. After a brief time in Amsterdam covering the German invasion, he spent a year and a half in Lisbon before becoming a war correspondent for the *Daily Express*. Thereafter, he and María were able to see each other just once a year in Gibraltar. As a correspondent for Reuters, he landed with British forces at the Anzio beachhead and was very badly wounded when a German shell exploded near a jeep in which he was riding on the drive on Rome. As a consequence, he was left with shrapnel in his right side and was in acute pain for the rest of his life. Immediately after the war, he was attached to the Allied forces in Berlin and later was Reuters correspondent in Madrid and, during 1947 and 1948, in Rome before returning to Madrid.

In 1949 he came back to Madrid as director of the Reuters office, and he remained there until September 1966 apart from brief assignments to Morocco, Portugal and Algeria. On 11 January 1961, along with other members of the board of the Foreign Press Association, he was received by General Franco. In 1962, he covered the last stand of the OAS in Oran. He maintained his friendship with Hemingway and they would meet whenever the American novelist visited Madrid. After thirty years in Spain, the Spanish Government marked his retirement in 1966 with the award of Spain's highest civilian honour, the Cruz de Caballero de la Orden de Isabel la Católica, which was given to him by the then Foreign Minister Fernando María Castiella. In January 1968, Queen Elizabeth II of England appointed him Member of the Order of the British Empire, which was conferred upon him by the then British Ambassador Sir Alan Williams.

After 1966, Henry Buckley retired to live in Sitges but continued to work for the BBC as an occasional correspondent. He died on 9 November 1972. He was much loved and admired by his professional colleagues, Spanish and foreign, for his honesty and gentleness of manner. The Spanish journalists who knew him knew little of his experiences during the Civil War or of his friendship with Negrín. For Hemingway, Hugh Thomas and others, he was a living archive of the war. Fortunately for those who could not consult him personally, he left *Life and Death of the Spanish Republic*, a worthy monument to a great correspondent.

FOREWORD

You, the reader, may wonder why in the midst of the vast international conflict in which we are involved I feel it worth while to write of Spain. The book was in fact already finished when war broke out on September 3 but it is clear that its publication could have been relegated to more peaceful times if its sole value consisted in the record contained in these pages of the sad history of the Spanish Republic which was born with such high hopes and so peacefully on April 14, 1931, and which ended with the proclamation of General Franco on April 1, 1939, that the entire territory of Spain was now under the control of his totalitarian régime.

Yet I feel that it is tremendously important that we study the brief history of the Spanish Republic. Because I hold the opinion that the democratic system adopted by the Republic when King Alfonso left the country was in no small part responsible for Spain's tragedy. Democracy was tried and found wanting. Why did it fail? Surely now more than ever we who to-day are engaged in what is perhaps the greatest struggle ever entered on by our Empire should analyse and study the reason for Democracy's failure? Only a few weeks before we once again found ourselves at war with Germany, Lord Baldwin sounded a warning note to Democrats in a speech made in New York. He pointed out that Democracy could only survive as a system if it were constructive in character. In saying this the former Prime Minister stated a fact which however obvious it may seem to be, is only too often overlooked. A political system is not good just because the principles behind it are good. It is only good if it resolves the political and economic problems with which the nation which uses it is faced.

The men who took control of Spain when King Alfonso left his throne were on the whole capable and honest men. They were all, or nearly all, soaked in the Liberal doctrines of the nineteenth century. Their whole outlook was based on democratic concepts. They at once organised elections and submitted themselves immediately to the will of the Parliament elected by the people of Spain. This Parliament was a worthy body. In so far as four hundred and seventy men of vastly different ideas and up-bringing can work expeditiously as a body, that first national chamber of the Republic worked hard and intelligently in the preparation of the nation's future.

The task of the Republic was to convert a nation in a state of political collapse and which in so far as it had any economic system remained in its essentials a feudal régime, into a progressive twentieth-century nation with an economy founded on the possibilities of the land in relation to the swift march of science with its revolution in transport, manufacture of goods, agricultural methods and in the education and enlightenment of the individual.

Now Democracy did not come of its own easy accord in England. Oliver Cromwell dealt the final blow to feudalism amid a certain amount of upheaval. The French Republic of to-day is the child of the French Revolution. We have been through the mill in our time. If the British and French Democracies in 1931 had been alert and progressive they would have warned the young Republic behind the Pyrenees that it must rid itself of the feudal elements before it could hope to build something new. Then they would have pointed out that with feudalism expelled and with no strong middle class to take its place the Spanish State must at once plan a new economy on a national basis, leaving private initiative where this could give useful help, suppressing this when feeble capitalistic enterprise merely clogged all efforts of reform. All this would have cost much disturbance, probably also a certain amount of bloodshed, but it would have enabled the foundations to be laid for a new nation preparing to take its place in the European confraternity.

But no such advice as this came across the Pyrenees. The fat of our prosperity affects also the brains of Democracy. The Gods have been too kind. If there was any advice at all given from Britain and France to the youthful Spanish Republic it was to the effect that as little as possible should be changed. In Spain, as elsewhere, we hoped and wished not that much should happen but that nothing should happen.

So the Spanish Republicans failed. They modelled their young State on a nineteenth-century Liberal pattern without regard to the fact that certain defects were already very evident in the functioning of Democracy in places where it was long-established and ignoring the not inconsiderable feudal foundations on which they now proceeded to erect a structure of a very different character from that which the foundations were designed to carry.

I watched the process year by year. I could see that something essential was missing but it cost me many years before some inkling of the fundamental wrong began to dawn on my mind.

The question now is whether we will see the danger signals in time. It is no use sitting back and throwing the blame on Fascism. We have to realise quickly and definitely that Democracy cannot be interpreted as meaning the indefinite maintenance of a status quo, of an existing state of political or economic affairs. If we accept this interpretation then Democracy will surely be pushed aside or at least adapted by force to new existing conditions, for history knows no status quo. It is vital and urgent that we overhaul and analyse our concept of Democracy. On the foundations of this creed we must evolve a new system—or systems, for the solution suitable to one nation will need much variation for some other land with different economic problems—which will enable the nation adopting such a new system to face effectively, and cope with, the dramatic economic changes brought about by the scientific discoveries which are revolutionising mankind and his world at a speed which few of us appreciate.

I hope that my presentation of Spanish happenings as I witnessed them from the fall of General Primo de Rivera onwards may cause others to reflect on the reasons for the tragic fate of the Spanish Republic. In searching for the reasons for the failure of the Republic we may perhaps stumble on truths which if applied to our own political and economic system may come at the right moment in order to help us to render the structure of the British Commonwealth impervious to the many attacks now being made upon it.

HENRY BUCKLEY.

London, December 1939.

12

Life and Death of the Spanish Republic

CHAPTER I

THE SPAIN I FOUND

NOTHING had prepared me for the grim aspect of the Castilian uplands in November, for the shabbiness and poverty of the peasants, for the smell of rancid olive oil at wayside stations. I felt bitterly disillusioned as the train crept slowly across the Peninsula from Irun to Madrid.

I have spoken to many travellers who have suffered from similar loss of illusion on their first visit to Spain. Such notions of Spain's geography as patient schoolmasters inculcate are heavily outweighed by a mass of songs and books which describe in detail love affairs apparently permanently afoot in orange groves to the soft strumming of guitars. Most northern Europeans become sentimental when Spain is mentioned and the Germans wax particularly effusive about 'Das Land wo die Zitronen bluehen. . . .' Perhaps it is in the nature of world affairs that while we enthuse about orange groves, the Germans become fervent on the subject of lemon trees. It is somewhat disconcerting to find that a very great portion of Spain is treeless and rugged; splendid in its wilderness and colouring—but not what one expected.

Moreover I have since discovered that an orange grove is singularly unsuited to flirtation; for orange trees are low bushy affairs and in walking among them it is no small task to keep twigs and branches out of one's eyes. Nor in nine years in Spain did I ever hear a guitar played in an orange grove.

However, such knowledge as this came later. On the particular afternoon in November 1929 as I made my first trip across Spain, disillusion saddened me greatly. As a practising Catholic with a moderate amount of fervour I regarded with distaste two very stout friars who occupied my compartment and who not only were unable, or unwilling, to understand my stuttering Spanish, but who had not shaved for several days. That seemed particularly important to my somewhat intolerant Anglo-Saxon mind which found it difficult to reconcile spiritual fervour with a greasy and unshaven jowl.

Outside Madrid the rain poured down steadily and a mist which might have come straight off those Derbyshire Moors where I spent my boyhood, swirled in through the window. The train stopped for five minutes outside the terminus with the platform lights winking tantalisingly in the near distance.

This was my first introduction to an old Spanish custom formally observed at important termini such as Madrid and Barcelona. Each train must pass so to speak a period of quarantine before being allowed to enter. I can see that the system has its points. I presume that an office boy trots around to the stationmaster's office and tells him with fine Spanish courtesy and the compliments of the signalman that the 8.15 from Irun is here and please may it enter the station. Doubtless this functionary gives his consent and then proceeds to don his best uniform coat and hat. In this way an important train cannot catch the station staff in its shirt-sleeves, but the remedy is not one which appeals to the British traveller. Years later I lay in a ditch just near the point where the train stopped while shells crashed noisily and unpleasantly near and time seemed unimportant, but now I was anxious to reach Madrid and to recover quickly those lost illusions.

And in certain measure I did so. Plumed sentries on motionless horses loomed out of the night in front of the Royal Palace and small infantrymen in scarlet and blue with fixed bayonets guarded the entrance to the residence of Don Alfonso, whose picture I had seen hundreds of times in the Press and of whom my impression, picked up haphazardly from newspaper reports, was that he was a good fellow who did his best with a rather fractious nation. There seemed to be colour and romance after all in Spain. Ten minutes later I found that an excellent hotel room with telephone, private bathroom and two and a half meals daily cost but ten shillings. It seemed to me that Madrid had many good points.

When I look back I am amazed at the blithe way in which

14

I arrived in Spain and promptly commenced to report happenings there with but the vaguest knowledge of what was going on. But that is the way things are done in our imperfect world. I suppose that if Europe survives the present efforts of well-meaning statesmen which seem unlikely to lead to anything other than complete disaster, then a day will come when the most learned men of the nations will be employed in diagnosing the financial, political and moral health of Europe's component states. It will then be as unlikely for war, revolution or economic crisis to catch the world by surprise as it would be if a building regularly passed as sound by a competent architect were to collapse suddenly.

I imagine that in the year A.D. 2000 the young journalist who arrives in Madrid will glide into the Norte Station in a luxurious motor-train which will have whirled him down from the frontier in four or five hours. Or he will land at Barajas Airport after a speedy stratosphere flight from London. He will arrive primed with data on Spain prepared by the learned men to whom I have referred above and the study of which will enable him to judge with fair accuracy the conditions in the country even before his arrival. Doubtless my young colleague of the future will have been examined and certified by some international body as a fit and competent person to undertake the highly delicate work which reporting on international affairs comprises if it is done intelligently and honourably. Such at least are my hopes for a future which seems very distant indeed in these days when Europe is in a fair way to return to the Stone Age in its customs.

However in 1929 here was I in my clean and comfortable hotel room complacently prepared to report Spain to the world. I had just worked for two years as a reporter in Paris.

Looking back on those two years in Paris I think that I could hardly have got less out of them. Religious prejudice prevented me even from obtaining a sexual education and I left Paris as I came, a rather crotchety and thin-blooded virgin. My work was very intense and exacting and left me with little energy to study literature, art, theatre and all the things Paris offers us with such generous open hands.

In Spain I ate better, big solid meals of good food. I worked

15

less; read more. Life is completely different if you have two well cooked, substantial meals of good wholesome food daily. I put on weight and looked at Madrid. Philip II, who was responsible for the Armada, was equally responsible for Madrid. He chose as bleak and draughty and monotonous a spot as could well be found in Spain. There are now one million people there. The Good Lord only knows why. I hope that some wise Government will decree that Madrid shall not exceed 500,000 inhabitants. I was flabbergasted to find that the largest factory in Madrid employed 700 workers —imagine that in a city of one million. There is nothing productive there. One million Spaniards live at the expense of the rest of the nation; all on the strength of this being the capital. Washington, I believe, rules the United States with some 600,000 inhabitants to keep the bureaucratic machine functioning. Canberra has, I understand, only some 40,000 inhabitants but Canberra is apparently not a great success. Madrid bureaucrats lived, or existed, in shoals because a seat for the school lavatory in an obscure village near Cadiz could not be installed without a commission coming to Madrid to petition and negotiate said seat.

Absentee landlords built houses instead of growing wheat; prostitutes, pimps, abounded. Honest peasants without labour because the landlord had put his money into a great block of smart flats past which he could walk each day and feel a man of substance, flocked in looking for work of any kind. Madrid bled Spain in those days. Since then Madrid has bled heavily to save Spain; but God forbid that it ever achieve such bloated proportions again, for there can be no economic well-being in Spain with one million beings in Madrid feeding unproductively from the slender national income.

Do not, however, get the idea that I dislike Madrid. I am fond of it. Streaks of it are eighteenth and nineteenth century with much dignity and the rest is rather slap-dash twentieth century with many baby skyscrapers. I found in 1929 that central heating was general and that all the comforts even only now obtainable at high prices in London, such as lifts, electric refrigerator in the flat, could be had for little money there. Of course it was all wrong. All this money should have been returning to the soil instead of going into blocks of flats. But it was civilised living and heavenly after the primitive homes of Britain and France.

Life seemed so much more interesting in Madrid than in Paris, which is against all theories. Perhaps the altitude, over 2,000 feet, gives stimulation to the body. On the whole I think my new zest came principally from eating like a prince and working relatively little. I liked a drink, new to me, named Manzanilla, a light dry Sevillan wine. Each glass is accompanied by a 'tapa', or snack, which may be anything from tripe to boiled snails and a different 'tapa' should be taken with each glass. I learned that Spaniards wear themselves out sexually at an early age and for the rest of their lives wander about remedying their deficiencies by murmuring 'Beautiful . . .' to almost anything with skirts which passes them by on the streets. I wondered whether excess was as uncomfortable in results as chastity. I hoped not.

One night while strolling down the broad Calle de Alcalá, a friend drew my attention to a cloaked figure strolling past, leaning somewhat on his cane, a tired but still debonair man around the sixties. It was Primo de Rivera. I liked his looks and afterwards was sorry that I did not have a chance to talk with him before he fell, but events were moving quickly and in these troubled days for the Dictator there was no longer 'open house' for foreign journalists. It pleased me to see a Dictator who could stroll alone along the main street like a normal human being. I suppose he was duly shadowed but there was no obvious protective force and it was pleasant to see that he did not need to be surrounded by myriads of hulking, gun-swinging bodyguards as is the case with most of Europe's 'strong men' when they venture out in public.

Primo was a finished Dictator when I arrived in Madrid. Almost everybody, except Primo himself, knew this. Just before I reached the capital there had been a shooting party in the mountains given by Don Alfonso with the object of persuading Primo, during quiet walks, of the necessity of standing down and giving place to the aristocratic Duke of Alba. Primo behaved as you would expect a good-natured, elderly general to behave who has had enormous success in governing a nation single-handed for six years, who is worn down to breaking point by overwork and who cannot believe that the credits he has obtained almost without asking for are no longer forthcoming. He refused to hear of resignation.

Perhaps the comparison is not altogether nice but Primo in these moments reminded me of a bull near the end of the fight, stabbed by an incompetent 'torero' and with the latter's assistants or 'monaguillos', fluttering capes around its head so that it will move its head and neck and open one of the partial wounds which may then prove fatal. It is described in Spanish as 'making the bull dizzy' and it is an unpleasant spectacle to see a fine animal streaming with blood and surrounded by taunting, fluttering capes which it no longer has the strength to charge. Poor Primo answered his taunters in more and more stupid notes, poured gold out in an attempt to bolster the declining peseta, and continued blindly to believe that there must be a way out and that some day he would be less tired and then the solution would come in a flash.

There was no Balbo or Goering waiting around the Spanish dictatorial corner. Primo tried to form a Spanish Fascist Party with his Patriotic Union. It became an efficient machine for milking the Treasury and distributing the money thus obtained, but nothing more.

General Primo in September 1923 merely fulfilled the wish of every Spanish general to be the saviour of his nation; preferably not on a battle-field. He found the banks full of gold, the World War had been profitable to this distinguished sitter on the fence, political parties quarrelling among themselves and with Spain's leading politician, Don Alfonso. A disgruntled working class disliked all politicians, including the leading figure, and an aristocratic class completely out of touch with national life was of no importance to anyone.

With Spanish gold as backing, and with the United States bursting to lend money to anyone who would take it, Primo launched out on a great policy of spending. Roads, railways, reservoirs, sprang up over-night. Primo was intelligent; he cared for the workers, gave them high wages, collective contracts, paid holidays—all this for the town workers only, however. He co-operated with the French to hustle the

18

troublesome Abd-El-Krim out of Morocco. Spain was El Dorado for some years.

But enormous international bills began to come home to roost. There is quite a considerable time lag between the execution of a work of public utility and the repayment to the Treasury of the money expended in the form of new created national wealth which brings in increased taxation or an improved volume of interior or exterior commerce.

Primo had foreseen this coming shortage of money. He decided to take the Spanish State into business—and he selected the oil business. He turned the petrol and oil trade into a national monopoly. This made a great deal of money for the State and a great deal of trouble for Primo. The oil kings of the world do not take expulsion lightly. It would be foolish to say that they brought about Primo's downfall but we can have little doubt that when around 1928 the first effects of tremendous spending began to be felt, Primo had bitter enemies in powerful financial circles as a result of his ejection of the private petrol firms from Spain just at the moment when they were looking forward to bumper trade from the new motor roads Primo was laying out far and wide.

Rather than a Dictator, Primo was a national Father Christmas. It may be asked why the politicians, rarely in disagreement when there are large sums to be spent, had not used the available credits for which there was obviously profitable employment available. The answer, I think, lies in the fact that although feudalism had been dying for some centuries it still remained at the bottom the only economic system in Spain. The ABC of Spanish politics still remained Army, Bishops and Crown. The middle class had no strength. It ran Spain politically but with little vigour and always hemmed in by the ABC which prevented new solutions without having anything to offer suitable for twentieth-century acceptation. Universal suffrage and Parliament were in large part fictitious. Docile peasants suitably organised by expert political bosses returned this or that faction to Parliament. It meant nothing. There was a bloodless bourgeoisie at the Spanish helm, buried in innumerable and unimportant internal conflicts. To obtain executive action became almost impossible because each tiny faction leader wanted this or that concession before he would vote the issue in question. Primo could take a decision and put it into action and have an important work completed before Parliament would even have managed to get it on to the agenda paper. This was the secret of his success.

Moreover the ease of his accession to power, his relatively bloodless and moderate rule, inspired confidence abroad which bolstered up still further the national credit.

This very great Andalusian gentleman—in the best and only acceptable application of this word—had in synthesis seen that there was money available and he had spent it more or less in the national interests. Now much money had gone and credits suddenly disappeared with the swiftness of a May snowfall in England. There is nothing so volatile as credit. In one moment it is present in thick, rich layers. Hey presto, another moment, and not a trace is left.

To foreign eyes the financial situation did not appear tragic. The peseta had fallen from twenty-nine to the pound to thirty-four during 1929. This seemed unimportant. It is only when one understands that General Primo's whole success had been based on wide expenditure and that now retrenchment was necessary that his difficult situation becomes clear.

The old politicians, disgruntled at the way in which Primo had taken the reins of power and spent billions of pesetas without their intervention, agitated lustily. The working classes and petite bourgeoisie were relatively prosperous in the towns following the new high wages, with work available and six years of social and political peace. They now demanded that they have a say in affairs. The Army-Bishops-Crown combination had disliked Primo's independent way of doing things; it was rather frightened by the general discontent and falling peseta and inclined to throw Primo overboard. These were the principal contributory causes expressed in a very general way; it would need a whole and lengthy book to study the Dictatorship thoroughly.

Primo was a very tired old man, sick with diabetes, with enemies plotting everywhere against him, not overlooking the hand of the oil kings pulling strings on the international money markets. Even his youthful Minister of Finance, José

Calvo Sotelo, turned against him.   Primo had taken him up
when he was only thirty and made him a Cabinet Minister.
Now, even though he might disagree with the Dictator's financial policy, it was hardly a loyal act to abandon the tired old
man to whom he owed everything and who obviously had not
more than a few weeks of office before him.

CHAPTER II

DEATH OF A DICTATOR

I WENT back to the Norte Station early one morning of March 1930. The waiting-room was full of flowers, candles flickered, and on a draped catafalque in the centre lay the mortal remains of General Primo de Rivera, just returned from their last journey. Kneeling before the coffin was King Alfonso XIII in the blue and scarlet uniform of a colonel of the Spanish Army. I could see his face in the candlelight and it is an ugly face to look on. This seemed to me a moment for emotion, but Don Alfonso showed none. His face was a mask; the face of a man trained to hide what he thinks: showing cleverness, cunning perhaps, but not intelligence. He strode out in his hasty, jerky manner and there was more breathing space in the improvised chapel as a shoal of plain-clothes men disappeared also.

Primo was neatly ejected with threats of violence at the end of January and he went to Paris unheeded by anyone and died of exhaustion just as might happen to anyone of Primo's age who worked steadily eighteen hours a day on a responsible job without ever taking even a day off and with no recreations and at the end of six and a half years suddenly stopped work altogether. I know many cases of business-men who have retired and have died shortly afterwards. Naturally reports were circulated that he had been poisoned and similar non-sense.

The way of Primo's going was inelegant and reflected little credit on those involved. There was every evidence that General Manuel Goded was preparing a *coup d'état* against the Dictator in Cadiz and people saw in this a Palace intrigue. It may or may not have been, but Goded was made Under-Secretary for War in the Government formed to replace Primo so you may draw your own conclusions. Primo, pressed to go from every side, friendless, turned desperately to the Army and sent a circular message to the twelve Captain-Generals of the various military zones of the Peninsula in which these generals were a species of Chinese mandarin, asking if they still approved of his Dictatorship. All except the fiery General Sanjurjo replied formally that they were loyal to the King and to any Government he named. This appeal to the Army and its negative response gave Don Alfonso a chance to accuse Primo of having made the Army the arbiter of the nation's destinies instead of this power being invested in the King and to insist vigorously on his resignation. This time it was forthcoming. But it was all rather sordid and somewhat childish, for obviously it was the Army which supported General Primo in 1923 and the King had not complained then about it taking on itself the supreme power to decide concerning the national welfare.

World attention was now focused on Don Alfonso of Bourbon. Would he survive the fall of his Dictator? In the early days he associated himself ostentatiously with him. He presented him to King Victor Emmanuel of Italy with the words: 'This is my Mussolini.' It is said that the Duce was displeased. In the last years there was much friction. A phrase of Primo's to one of his friends: 'The King must not think that he can play his Bourbon tricks on me and succeed. . . .' was whispered about town.

On the day of Primo's downfall the old political leaders such as Count Romanones, Sr. Sanchez Guerra, Sr. Alcalá Zamora and others waited for a call from the Palace. They were as disappointed as was Lord Curzon of Kedleston on a famous occasion when he waited in expectation of a premiership which went to Mr. Baldwin. The King did not seek their advice either directly or indirectly. He appointed the Head of his Military Household, General Damaso Berenguer, as Prime Minister. The Minister of Education—later of Foreign Affairs—was the Duke of Alba. The Cabinet list was completed with friends of the King or friends of friends of the King.

In other words, Don Alfonso was going to rule himself and he could scarcely have chosen a worse moment.

I have never been able to understand the motives which

induced Don Alfonso to scorn the politicians at a moment when he needed them more than ever in his life. He had abandoned them to their fate in 1923 and had given his blessing to the *coup d'état*. For six and a half years General Primo had ruled with the Army. The weak middle class of Spain had on the whole been aloof. It had profited but it disliked the usurping of what it considered its right to govern the nation. In previous moments of national crisis the King had always known that he had the Army behind him. Even that was not so sure now. The Army had become involved in the dictatorial adventure and disliked this on the whole very much. Primo had tried to introduce reform in the Artillery Corps and had found himself face to face with a mutiny.

The Church, of course, continued actively on the side of Don Alfonso but its capacity for giving active physical support was not great. Seven or eight hundred years of monopoly of religion in Spain had not left it a great deal of red blood. It had a certain amount of financial power for the seizure of the landed properties of the Church during the last century had led the clergy to invest their money in stocks and shares. Most of this was done indirectly, and always with the property registered in the name of a third party so as to avoid expropriation and to make it almost impossible to assess the property of this or that order or of any given diocese. So we now had the Church in Spain an active partner in shipping companies, railways, newspapers, broadcasting. In Madrid, Jesuit money played a part in the tram company, gas and electricity corporations, and the water company; according to reliable reports.

The lack of any strong bourgeoisie in Spain or of any large-scale industry prevented the existence of strong financial groups such as form what we call 'The City' at home or 'The Two Hundred Families' in France. The two richest individuals in Spain were believed to be Count Romanones and Don Juan March. Both belonged more or less to the middle-class circles which were now so offended at Don Alfonso's failure to hand back to them the executive control of national affairs.

As for the landed aristocracy, the Dukes of Fernan-Nuñez, of Alba, and such families who had written their names large

24

in Spanish history, their power in modern Spain was little. The Duke of Alba was the one figure among the old aristocracy who made some show of interest in national affairs. The remainder were decadent families, almost all absentee land-lords leaving control of their estates to managers and bailiffs. The British aristocracy does at least get occasional doses of good coarse red blood when some lordling weds a chorus girl. In Spain the lordling would never dream of marrying the chorus girl or the typist. Such children as they might have would go to swell the working classes or petite bourgeoisie, while the lordling would in due course marry some daughter of an equally ancient family. These old families controlled vast areas of Spain but represented nothing in the national life.

At this critical moment also very few people had much idea as to what the working masses were thinking. Previously, no one in Spain worried much about this. The peasants either voted in the political machine as their local boss told them to or they had a very rough time for the green-clad Civil Guard could make life a most unpleasant affair for any peasant with independent ideas. The town workers were not quite so easy to handle and Madrid and Barcelona had on various occasions returned Republican or, in the case of the latter town, autonomy-supporting members of Parliament. But Madrid and Barcelona were two drops in the Spanish electoral ocean.

General Primo altered greatly the status of the Spanish working man as far as the towns were concerned. When he tried to extend some of the benefits to the landworkers he ran up against the opposition of the landed families and had to drop the matter. But the town workers with good wages and paid holidays—I think the only workers in Europe at the time to have this—were now a force to reckon with even outside Madrid and Barcelona. Primo worked together with the Socialists, or at least with some of the Socialists. Francisco Largo Caballero, a stolid trade unionist leader, even took office on the Council of State, a body largely concerned with social reform. It was one of the childish incidents so frequent in Spain that Primo had to give him special permission not to visit the King on appointment, as was the custom. Caballero would have compromised himself with the workers if he had gone to the Palace. And there is really little evidence that Alfonso ever tried to get into touch either directly or indirectly with the representatives of the workers. As far as I can learn, he never spoke with Pablo Iglesias, the pioneer of Spanish Socialism, nor with Caballero, nor Prieto. It was considered a great event and an act of almost extreme tolerance when the King and Queen on one occasion went to see a play by the great playwright and writer, Perez Galdós, and received this writer in the royal box. Because Perez Galdós was Republican in sentiments.

But although Caballero very sensibly worked with the Dictatorship some of the Socialists such as Indalecio Prieto, who had close contacts with middle-class interests and who were really Liberals in political sympathies, objected strongly. They foresaw Primo's downfall and did not wish to compromise the Socialist Party.

The new status of the town worker and the effect on the peasants of the building of thousands of miles of roads and railways were bound to have a great effect on the future. Roads meant motor-buses, this meant more movement and freedom for the country people. It meant also that they would want a higher standard of living. A peasant living in a lonely hamlet may accept philosophically conditions which appear intolerable to his brother living on or near a motor road along which luxurious motor-cars come and go and on which for a few pesetas he can go by bus in a short time to a market town which previously was a long journey on donkey-back.

Nothing could be the same in Spain again after General Primo fell. He had launched great schemes of modernisation in a feudal country and there would be much political fruit in addition to economic changes.

Bearing all this in mind it may be seen that Don Alfonso faced a very critical situation and that he made things much worse by offending the politicians. These gentlemen either openly or in private spared Don Alfonso not at all in their criticisms. The leader of the Conservative Party, the elderly Don José Sanchez Guerra, who staged a one-man revolt against Primo but had always been most loyal to the Crown, made a public speech in which he likened the King to a worm and announced that henceforth he could not serve him. Don Niceto Alcalá Zamora, a middle-aged politician and one of the leaders of the Liberal Party, announced that he had become converted to Republicanism. The more discreet pointed out in private conversations the risk the King was taking in attempting to liquidate the Dictatorship without political help. Naturally, it may be argued that as political incompetence had to a great extent provoked and made possible the *coup d'état* of 1923 it would be turning back the Spanish clock to call in the politicians again. But I think the chief arguments weigh the other way. Possibly Don Alfonso might still have fallen but he would have had more chance of staying on the throne if he had frankly given back control to the politicians and submitted to the result of elections. Even if he had had to go the Monarchy might still have been saved under a Regency.

The King's choice of premier was singularly unfortunate because General Berenguer along with Don Alfonso himself was very much involved in the disaster of Annual in Morocco in 1921 when General Silvestre and 10,000 men were massacred by Moors. General Berenguer was the High Commissioner and superior officer in Morocco at that time. The disaster was investigated with considerable slowness by a Parliamentary Commission which was to have presented its findings to Parliament in October 1923. The *coup d'état* of September 1923 rendered signal service to Don Alfonso and some Army chiefs by closing Parliament. How far General Berenguer was responsible or was a victim is not clear. What happened was that General Sylvestre in the eastern zone acted practically autonomously and, there is some reason to believe, was encouraged to do so by Don Alfonso. But now when people were again speaking of this scandal and public opinion was being reminded of the coincidence that the *coup d'état* had occurred but two weeks before Parliament was to investigate Annual, it seemed rather bad politics to make one of the principal figures in that unpleasant affair the Prime Minister. Don Alfonso had never showed much regard for public opinion; he showed less than ever now.

CHAPTER III

JACA—A SUCCESSFUL FAILURE

IN December 1930 I was sent to Saragossa en route for Jaca where I was supposed to see two officers executed and report this event for a British news agency. I did not reach Jaca because at the Gran Hotel in Saragossa I found a telegram instructing me to return to Madrid where it seemed that even more important happenings than the shooting of two officers might be expected. I obediently boarded a train again and arrived at Madrid to find that the important happenings were over; so I had missed two excellent stories.

On the whole I was glad that I did not have to watch an execution. Especially such a foolish execution as this one. Cold-blooded killing is an unpleasant and repugnant act. Nothing was going to be gained by the killing of Captains Fermin Galan and García Hernández.

Since General Primo fell in January Spain had progressed to the stage of open revolt against feudalism as represented tangibly by Don Alfonso of Bourbon. On August 17, 1930, Republicans of all shades of opinion met in San Sebastian and signed the Pact of San Sebastian in which they agreed to work together for the overthrow of the Monarchy. The Catalan Autonomists also signed the Pact, with the exception of Sr. Cambó's Catalan League. The Socialist Party sent an observer, Sr. Prieto. The meeting and the Pact were, of course, kept secret at the time. Sr. Alcalá Zamora, who had only embraced Republicanism in April, led the revolt supported by other newcomers to this creed, the old guard Republicans, Socialists, Anarchists and a few military men who were sympathetic. This revolution began in Jaca on December 12.

Captain Galan was the most active of these sympathetic military men; so active in fact that he appears to have doubted the sincerity of his fellow-conspirators and he revolted two days before the appointed moment, apparently because he felt that in this way the others would be forced to join in and would have no chance of drawing back at the last minute. Galan was afterwards described as a Communist. Actually he was a very highly strung young man, violently rebellious against the injustice of modern Spain but with no background to guide him or to help him to discipline his emotions. If he was anything he was an Anarchist. As a suspect he had been sent to the frontier garrison of Jaca; Spain in those days being so carefree of foreign complications as to be able to regard frontier posts as the best place to send unreliable officers and men. He dragged his men into the revolt by his personality and also his fellow-officer García Hernández who was a pleasant well-meaning young man dominated by his friend. The revolt was easily suppressed by the military commander of the Huesca zone, General García de las Heras, who was himself one of the few casualties and who died some days later. There is reason to believe that this general was also implicated in the revolt but like the remaining officers supposed to rise he failed to do so.

Galan and García Hernández were shot on a Sunday afternoon after a court-martial held the same morning. This was against Spanish tradition which ruled firstly that executions should take place the day after summary trial and that in no case should a man be executed on a Sunday. A telephone engineer on duty in the Saragossa exchange whom I knew well told me that General Berenguer had called up Jaca several times during the morning and had spoken with the officer in charge of the court-martial. According to this engineer, the Prime Minister had insisted on the trial being concluded with the greatest speed and he also emphasised the necessity for exemplary punishment and the immediate carrying out of the sentence.

I mention this because after they were shot and the Government realised that this was a mistake, great pains were taken officially to emphasise that the court-martial had been carried out normally and that the Prime Minister and the King had limited their part to merely confirming the sentence. It was, however, well known that the matter was discussed at a Cabinet Meeting and that the Duke of Alba and several other

Ministers protested strongly. But apparently General Berenguer insisted on a death sentence and immediate execution. And General Berenguer was merely the mouthpiece of Don Alfonso.

In theory, of course, Galan and Hernández were mutineers and must therefore expect the death penalty. But there were several angles to the situation. For instance, what was General Berenguer's position? He was the successor of a successful mutineer, General Primo. Berenguer's Cabinet had no legal standing, except in so far as the King had named it to liquidate the Dictatorship and to hold elections. It was now governing dictatorially and after ten months in office there was no mention of elections. So when General Berenguer accused a fellow-officer of mutiny he was rather in the position of the kettle which accused the frying-pan of blackness.

Anyway the men were shot and maybe it saved the conflagration spreading but what it certainly did was to give the Republican cause two martyrs and for the next weeks there was an enormous sale of pictures of the two men which made their way on to the walls of hundreds of thousands of humble dwellings and could even be seen in many middle-class homes.

The important event which I arrived too late to witness in Madrid, after missing the execution in Jaca, was confined mainly to an aerial demonstration by one Ramón Franco, pilot of the Jesus del Gran Poder, the first aeroplane to fly the South Atlantic. This young man, not to be confused with his brother General Francisco Franco who at this time was head of the Saragossa Military College and who since has achieved some publicity, accompanied by an excitable and irascible officer named General Queipo de Llano, seized the aerodrome known as Cuatro Vientos. He took off in a bombing aeroplane and circled over the Royal Palace for some time. Afterwards Franco said that the sight of little children playing in the Palace grounds deterred him from bombing the royal residence. Whatever it was that stopped him from doing so there is no doubt that a severe set-back to the Republican cause was thus avoided. To have dropped bombs on the Palace would have been a wanton and criminal act which would have aroused Spanish and world opinion in favour of the King and

Queen. The aviators in the neighbouring military aerodrome of Getafe were asked by General Berenguer to chase their colleagues out of the sky. They declined politely but firmly. Sage aviators these. Before intervening they wished to see who would win. Finally several planes did go up in time to see Franco, Queipo and their friends winging their way towards Portugal.

The Jaca rising was over and after a week of skirmishing in the leading towns, where general strikes prevailed—except Madrid where it was not declared—Spain settled down again. The Government brought over from Morocco the Foreign Legion, mainly composed of Spaniards and not of the best kind of Spaniard at that, so they pretend that it is a foreign affair in order to excuse its excesses. This Legion dealt with customary toughness with some villagers on the Mediterranean coast who tried to impede their progress by pulling up the railway lines, and then was sent back to Africa.

On the surface it looked like a triumph for the King. But only on the surface. Very few people went to the Palace to show their sympathy. The middle class did not stir. The Army was more surly and divided than ever. But long queues formed outside the Model Prison on visiting days to show sympathy for that newcomer to Republicanism, Sr. Alcalá Zamora, and his fellow-conspirators. Showing a flair for doing the right thing which later on he seems to have lost, Sr. Alcalá Zamora on being arrested in his home asked to be allowed to attend Mass at his parish church before going to gaol. So he solemnly went to Mass with two plain-clothes men kneeling behind him and then off to the Model Prison. This was excellent propaganda for the Republicans and the unskilful Berenguer Government was handling things very clumsily by laying the blame of the rising on Moscow gold. The Duke of Alba told a British journalist that one Communist agitator had been caught near the frontier with 2,000,000 pesetas 'hidden on his person'. This quick-witted reporter suggested that to 'hide' two million pesetas on one's person would involve some physical difficulties. In the most favourable conditions it would mean secreting no less than 2,000 of Spain's large and relatively thick one-thousand peseta notes. This answer bewildered the noble Duke, obviously accustomed to use a cheque book rather than notes, and he hastened to change the subject.

I went to the Model Prison, which no doubt was a very modern affair when built in 1860 or thereabouts, and looked through the iron bars of the visiting-room at the various celebrities, who seemed quite pleased with life. They were so sure of success that they announced quite openly that they were busy drawing up plans for governing. The principal members of the revolutionary committee in gaol were:

Niceto Alcalá Zamora: Ex-Minister, violently pro-German in the World War, leading campaigner against Catalan autonomy, leader of a small parliamentary faction of the Liberal Party and thus one of the small group leaders who made government almost impossible in the days preceding 1923.

Francisco Largo Caballero: Principal figure of the Socialist trade union movement known as the General Union of Workers.

Fernando de los Rios: Professor of Philosophy of Granada University, a Socialist.

Miguel Maura: Son of Don Antonio Maura and a passionate young man who like Sr. Alcalá Zamora became converted to Republicanism after the fall of Primo and the failure of the King to call in the politicians.

The leading spirit was obviously Sr. Alcalá Zamora, though why this should be the case was a mystery to me. His previous record was against his present highly democratic and progressive attitude.

The situation seemed to me then that the Monarchy had not much chance of survival but I still did not see how it could be overthrown. I had not realised the great wave of pent-up feeling surging up in the land.

In my own little life, the Jaca rising brought me back into journalism and thus was helpful. For I had been teaching in a Language School since the *Daily Chronicle*, whose correspondent in Spain I was, had been absorbed by the *Daily News*, and believe me it is not funny to sit hour after hour asking pupils: 'Is this chair black?' and having them answer: 'No,

32

the chair is white.' I did not, however, dislike the work violently; many of the students were pleasant and intelligent. One class I had included both an hotel porter and a colonel of the Civil Guard who was frequently in attendance on the King and Queen and wished to speak English fluently. A sentimental friendship with a German girl made the months fly easily by. The only hitch in the romance was her penchant for fainting dead away in my arms when kissed: a result due I am afraid to her weakness of heart and not to my prowess in this direction. One night when this occurred near her home I carried her to what I thought was a chemist's shop but which proved to be an undertaker's establishment.

During this romance I found that Madrid had excellent German restaurants where all kinds of wurst dishes could be had and capped by wonderful apple tart and cream.

C

CHAPTER IV

CURTAIN TO A RÉGIME

MUFFLED in a heavy overcoat I kept chilly and lonely vigil outside the Royal Palace on Don Alfonso's last night in Spain.

Occasionally, very occasionally, the big wooden doors swung open and a motor-car came out or went in. The exterior sentries had been withdrawn and I and a little Spanish reporter alone stamped our feet on the cobble-stones by the door and hoped for something sensational to happen. But nothing did happen; which in itself seemed to me the most remarkable thing of all.

I asked a grey-haired, long-coated porter who swung open the door on one occasion what the Royal Family was doing. I imagined its members in anxious conclave, calling up friends, consulting desperately. The answer was calm and measured: 'Their Majesties are attending a cinematograph performance in the salon recently fitted up with a sound apparatus.' If he had told me that the King and Queen in night attire were playing leap-frog up and down one of the long stone corridors of the Palace I could not have been more astonished. It was an amazing situation. The King's position and even his personal safety were in grave peril as a result of the previous day's municipal elections. As I walked down to the Palace I passed through the nerve-centre of Spain, the Puerta del Sol, where a turbulent crowd was cheering the Republic. The police were looking on. Some of the mounted men were off their horses and were exchanging cigarettes with members of the crowd. The Palace was cordoned off except to persons with some legitimate pretext for going there. Yet here in this lonely, isolated Palace the Royal Family was at the cinema.

Where are Spain's four hundred Generals? Where are the two hundred Grandees? What of this Spain which we are told is so catholic; where are Bishops, friars and faithful to-night?

These were the questions which ran through my head. I still do not know where they were that night. Since then most of these elements have deplored the loss of the Monarch; few of them did anything practical to attempt to save him or even to show their sympathy.

This night indeed Don Alfonso learned in full measure the truth that the harvest depends on the sowing. It was easy to see Canalejas expelled from the Cabinet just after your accession; it had been fun to see how Maura became furious and resigned just because you wanted to put a friend of the family into the post of Captain-General of Castile; how easy it was to see that Army demands were fulfilled after patriotic young officers had taught Catalan Democrats a lesson by wrecking the offices of *Cu-Cut*; and those days when you intrigued with Moret to overthrow Romanones and then intrigued with Romanones to overthrow Moret; and so through nearly thirty years finally winding up with the dismissal with very small show of gratitude indeed of old General Primo. To-night is harvest night, Don Alfonso of Bourbon. Where are your friends? Can anyone believe that this fine people of Spain have hearts of stone? No. If you had ever shown generosity or comprehension of their aches and struggles they would not leave you friendless to-night. You never did. You intrigued, you spent every ounce of your energy defending feudalism and not even feudalism respects you. It would still use you if it could, but it despises you. The politicians need you still. But they despise you too. They know you through and through and you know them through and through and you despise each other. And you never thought that this feudal Army which you helped so manfully to triumph over timid democratic attempts would abandon you without a sign of sorrow. It is hard indeed to be King of a nation for twenty-nine years, to have so many chances to incur gratitude, and to find that at the crisis there is not even a single officer or man who will break his sword and follow you into exile; not a woman of these great-hearted women of Spain who will come to your Palace to recite a rosary for your sake before its doors. Your moment of trial has come, Don Alfonso, and you are alone, judged and justly judged by a great people.

35

Municipal elections had been held on the day previously, April twelfth. They had been conducted by a Cabinet of politicians such as Count Romanones, Sr. La Cierva—who in the old days used to send out horsemen to round up the villagers to vote and to drive them to the polls like so many sheep, all this in his political feud of Murcia—and there was Sr. García Prieto who was Prime Minister in 1923 and who announced twelve hours before Primo's *coup d'état* that a Dictatorship could triumph only over his dead body and the whole was presided over by Admiral Aznar who had been called from his naval base of Cartagena to become Prime Minister for some reason not clear to anyone. He told the Press quite cheerfully in later days how he spent the fateful evening of April 13, when his King was at the cinema, reading a French novel, *Rocambole*. It was, he said, a very interesting novel and he could recommend it.

It had taken Don Alfonso nearly fourteen months to realise that it would be hard to hold elections without the politicians; so he had handed over power to them. On Count Romanones's recommendation the original plan to hold parliamentary elections was set aside and municipal elections were called, in order, said the Count, that the Ministers might see which way the wind was blowing. They soon found out. The worthy Admiral Aznar, with the blunt ways of the quarter-deck, told the journalists the morning after elections: 'You want news? Well, what greater news do you want than the fact that a nation which went to bed Monarchist wakes up Republican?'

Since then innumerable typesetters have profited by discussions in books as to whether or not these elections really proved that Spain was Republican. The only figures I saw showed about 60,000 Monarchist councillors returned and some 14,000 Republican representatives. So if you have a mathematical mind you may say that the Monarchists won easily and that Alfonso ought never to have gone and that he was stampeded. What the actual final figures were, nobody can say. Some months later my inquisitive self was conducted into a dusty room in the Ministry of the Interior and a functionary showed me hundreds of brown paper bundles. These contained the final telegraphed returns of the elections. I asked why they had never been sorted out and counted. I was told that this would need the employment of a considerable number of clerks for some days and that unless some Minister gave the order there was no chance of this being done. I wonder if those bundles have escaped Franco's bombs and shells and whether anyone will ever have the curiosity to sort out and tabulate the returns.

Personally I do not care either way. I think that the elections showed that Spain wished to overthrow the Monarchy. In all the provincial capitals of Spain, except Cadiz, the Republican-Socialist coalition triumphed. It did not triumph in thousands of small villages. Because there was no liberty of vote in most of these villages. The peasants lived under the shadow of the landowners and woe betide the rebellious soul; he might well seek work in some distant place. Not only that but if he tried to indulge in political activity of any Left-Wing type he would be taken to the Civil Guard post and beaten with rifle butts.

Later, under the Republic, a British resident of Seville confided to me over manzanilla: 'Conditions are impossible down here nowadays. The Guardia Civil is not allowed to beat up the subversive elements among the peasants and it is hopeless to try to keep order here unless the police has a free hand.' This testimony is not strictly speaking necessary in order to convince investigators of the kind of conditions that prevailed in Spanish villages and hamlets before the Republic. The peasants voted docilely as part of the great political machine inaugurated under universal suffrage in 1890 and which functioned until 1923. In all that time there is no record of a single Government which carried out elections not receiving a majority. The Home Minister who inaugurated universal suffrage told his Cabinet colleagues cheerfully: 'What I did was only to use two-thirds of the votes and to keep one-third in reserve in case of necessity.'

The political machine was not functioning well now. Much had changed under General Primo. New ideas, as well as motor-cars, raced along these fine broad roads which now intersected Spain. In many villages the peasants voted Republican-Socialist despite the frowns of the local landowners and the

Civil Guard. Emilio, an acquaintance of mine who was the village jeweller in Egea de los Caballeros in Aragon and a Republican, told me: 'It was the most imposing thing I have ever seen. The peasants and field workers came in to vote and announced loudly that they were voting for the Republic. The local political bosses were writing their names down and the Civil Guards on duty were taking note. If the Republic had not triumphed many of these men would have been discharged by their employers and would have been persecuted terribly.'

Since April 1931 there has been a spate of argument from Right-Wing sources to the effect that the municipal elections were never meant to have a constitutional issue. Possibly not. But remember that Count Romanones held them to 'find out which way the wind was blowing'. I think that it was due to this fact that the change-over from Monarchy to Republic was so smooth. Parliamentary elections would have been more bitter. There would have been the delay necessary to prepare the meeting of Parliament. I think that the forces which still held on to feudalism as a lifebelt would have had time to organise and prepare resistance. Whether this would have been in the long run a disaster I do not know. Possibly a little bloodshed at that time would have saved a great deal later on.

The municipal electoral results presented great difficulty if any attempt at repression were made. In the scores of towns and villages where Republican-Socialist councillors had a majority, these men were all taking possession and hoisting the Republican flag over the town halls. Some local, isolated outbreak could have been repressed. But for the Government after holding elections to have ordered the Civil Guards to bar the doors of the town halls and to have fired on the angry crowds which would have protested would have been too illogical a proposition. The Prime Minister summed the matter up when he said that 'Spain woke up Republican this morning.' It was impossible to think of trying to repress the popular movement in so many places simultaneously and people who write that Don Alfonso could have subdued the trouble by using force but that he did not wish to do so, may be right but I fail completely to see how it could have been done. Elections had been held and in the important places where there was to some extent, and only a limited extent at that, freedom for voters to vote as they pleased, Republicans and Socialists had triumphed and these results were everywhere greeted with great enthusiasm.

In addition to the impossibility of taking any steps to crush the sweeping tide of Republicanism there also remains the fact that reaction against the Monarchy was very strong indeed. When the Buenavista district in Madrid, which composes mainly a middle-class and aristocratic section of Madrid, returned a Republican majority then there was obviously deep feeling running. And when Guadalajara, for many decades a feud of the Romanones family, returned a Republican city council with a sweeping defeat of the Romanones candidates then indeed few could question the fact that fundamental changes were going on in Spain.

There was much to think of as I walked through the now deserted streets of Madrid at three o'clock in the morning with the bitter wind from the Sierra Guadarrama driving hard. A policeman with a rifle stopped me and asked me for a light. We chatted for a few minutes and he said: 'All we need to do now is to get rid of that monkey on the throne and then things will be better. I and my wife have had a picture of Galan and Hernández on our bedroom wall since they were shot.' When Spain's hard-boiled and highly militarised and disciplined policemen talked this way it was obvious that even if orders were given for repression they were unlikely to be effective. This policeman told me, and I afterwards confirmed his story from other sources, that a young police officer had ordered his men to charge the crowd cheering the Republic, using sabres. His men declined to do so and a sergeant escorted the officer back to barracks. This incident took place in the Puerta del Sol. Next day, or rather to-day, for the night was far advanced, promised to be interesting. The date was April fourteenth.

CHAPTER V

A REPUBLIC IS BORN

Don Alfonso is one of the few people I have heard of who have made an intimate personal friend of their dentist. The Count of Casa Valencia had much personality and had used it so successfully as to rise from an obscure tooth-drawer to become Madrid's leading dentist, royal dentist, count, personal friend of the King and secretary of the great University City fund with which what was destined to be Europe's most modern university was already in the course of construction. This university was to mark twenty-five years on the throne of Spain for Don Alfonso and was a laudable effort continued under the Republic until various generals, friends of King Alfonso, set to work to destroy the part constructed with great expenditure of shot and shell. I met the Count on several occasions and found him a bustling little man with a great liking for publicity.

On the morning of April fourteenth he was dispatched as bearer of bad news to the King. He bore a letter from Count Romanones suggesting that it would be advisable for Don Alfonso to absent himself from the country for some time.

The Cabinet Ministers after passing a comfortable night in bed, the Prime Minister's sleep as I have recorded having been induced by the reading of *Rocambole*, met to discuss matters; and found them unpleasant. They called in General José Sanjurjo, head of the green-clad Civil Guards, a corps resembling somewhat the old Royal Irish Constabulary, but infinitely tougher in its methods. Now undoubtedly Sanjurjo as a very intimate friend of General Primo was bitter against Don Alfonso. Most of Primo's friends were. They felt that he dropped him overboard almost without any display of regret or of gratitude for his services. But I do not think that Sanjurjo would have allowed this bitterness to have outweighed his undoubted loyalty to all that the Monarchist

40

régime stood for if he had seen any practical way of preventing its fall. But for all the reasons explained in the last chapter the technical problem of suppressing the flood of sentiment flowing in the country and of interfering with the accession to their posts of the legally elected councillors which was going on now through the length and breadth of Spain, was virtually insurmountable. He told the Cabinet frankly that he did not think that the Civil Guard could suppress the movement and he seemed doubtful as to whether it would wish to attempt this. Numerous street incidents had already shown how the ordinary police force felt and how little it could be relied on.

General Berenguer, who had remained as War Minister in the Aznar Cabinet, a quiet cultured man with a fund of common sense, had already, twenty-four hours earlier, sent a circular message to Army chiefs recalling the necessity for garrison commanders to refrain from any intervention in what he described as political issues. This circular was much criticised at the Cabinet Meeting by Don Juan La Cierva. This man was at one time known as the 'man of iron' of Spanish politics and he achieved some indirect fame from the achievements of his son who invented the La Cierva autogyro and who was later killed in a smash in one of those unsafe, ordinary aeroplanes which he sought to make more secure for mankind. He now demanded that the Army intervene to suppress the Republican movement. The other ministers shrugged their shoulders. How were they to order the Army to prevent the results of elections held by themselves from taking their course?

The night before it looked as if Don Alfonso and his family by calmly watching an American film were giving a tremendous demonstration of sangfroid. But it seemed now that in royal circles the real situation had not been realised. The King and his family were quite out of touch with national feeling.

Don Alfonso felt that Count Romanones might have come personally on such an important mission instead of sending the royal dentist. Finally the Count went to the Palace. Actually the Prime Minister himself should have gone but poor Admiral Aznar would in normal times have been out of his depths in political tangles and at this critical moment he was virtually useless. No wonder he sought forgetfulness in French literature. The King asked the Count to suggest to the Republicans that elections for a constituent Parliament be held in order that the nation might decide for itself on the kind of state it wished. The King would abide by the decision and leave the country at once if the result were adverse.

The negotiations were carried on in the elegant salons of the house of Dr. Gregorio Marañon, a specialist on glands and at one time a close personal friend of the Monarch. Recently Marañon had shown strong Liberal and Near-Republican views and I think that he had not seen the King for several years. There Count Romanones met his former protégé and political henchman, Niceto Alcalá Zamora, who with his fellow-conspirators had received a trifling sentence which implied immediate release after a spectacular trial.

Alcalá Zamora was quite adamant. There could be no neutral or constitutional period. The King must leave Madrid before sunset. As the evening drew on the factory and office workers would join the vast crowds already thronging the streets and he and his colleagues could not answer for what might happen if Don Alfonso were still in the Palace.

The Count went back to the Palace and gave the drastic message to his Sovereign. The latter suggested that at least he might withdraw in favour of a regent and suggested his cousin, Infante Don Carlos, who was credited with Liberal views and with having been an opponent of the Dictatorship. The Count gave his opinion that this was quite impossible; earlier on it might have been attempted but that it was hopeless to try this now. Conversation then turned to the manner in which Don Alfonso should depart. The usual route to Irun was ruled out because there were already disturbances in San Sebastian. There was a proposal to leave by way of Portugal but it was finally decided that King Alfonso XIII should leave his country on a battle cruiser from the naval base of Cartagena.

After this decision had been taken Romanones and the King walked out into an ante-chamber where various Cabinet Ministers, Grandees and other personalities were gathered. A dashing cavalry officer, General the Marquess of Cavalcanti, said: 'Sire, I offer you the full support of my troops to defend your throne.' General Berenguer immediately cut in with a sharp: 'Prove what you say; prove that it is possible to restore order by bringing out troops before making such sweeping statements!' Cavalcanti was about to answer back angrily but Don Alfonso intervened sadly, saying: 'There is no need at all for discussion, my friends; my mind is quite made up and I shall leave the country to-night.' There was further discussion and it was decided that owing to difficulties of packing even necessities it was impossible for the whole family to leave. Count Romanones pledged his word to the Monarch that his wife and children would be safe. 'They are in the hands of Spaniards, Sire,' he said. In observance of the Republican ultimatum, shortly before dusk five or six powerful cars swung out of the private entrance to the palace grounds down near the wooded domaine called the Casa del Campo, and twelve hours later the King was sailing for Marseilles on the cruiser *Jaime I.*

Don Alfonso has been bitterly attacked for this sudden departure, leaving his family behind. He has been accused of cowardice. This is, I think, completely unjust and the accusation is undeserved. By staying longer the King would have endangered the lives not only of his family but of many others inside and outside the Palace. National animosity was directed solely against the King; by going he removed the pressure and assured safety for many hundreds of families who might have been in danger from mob violence if the situation had not been dealt with immediately. In some ways it seems rather strange that with some four hours to prepare the whole family could not have got ready. But the Prince of Asturias was in bed sick; and even if he had been taken in an ambulance or a comfortable car this could not have travelled at the high speed necessary in order that Cartagena might be reached before dawn, and it involved considerable personal danger to the King to travel with a small escort through provincial towns and villages where there might already be angry mobs in the streets. There was, as it turned out, a display of hissing and booing when the King was recognised at a stop for petrol at Murcia during the small hours. It was essential that Don Alfonso should be aboard the cruiser early in the morning. For the Queen to have left even one of the children behind would have been a hard decision to make.

Some quick thinking had to be done in the Palace at this moment and I think that events completely justified the course of action adopted. I cannot pretend to pontificate but I think from what I saw during those dramatic hours and from what I have heard and read on the matter since, that King Alfonso was completely justified in leaving at once and allowing his wife and family to follow; just as I feel that any attempt to defend the Crown by force would have resulted in much bloodshed and would have been useless.

Events were moving fast. Barcelona had already declared 'the Catalan Republic'. Beginning in the early hours with the small Basque town of Eibar, the Republic was being solemnly proclaimed in hundreds of towns and villages.

At noon I obtained entrance, with difficulty, to the solemn and somewhat patchy red and grey building of the Ministry of the Interior in the Puerta del Sol. There I found only the Under-Secretary, Don Mariano Marfil, and his Private Secretary, a plump young man named Francisco Casares who afterwards wrote a book saying that Gil Robles would govern Spain and which proved to be only partially true. Now in critical moments in Spain the Ministry of the Interior usually teems with life. The Minister sits surrounded by six telephones; messengers dash here and there; tape machines send out orders to civil governors; the control of Spain's assorted 40,000 police of one kind or another is centralised here and orders are flashed in quick succession. To-day it was dead. The bearded Under-Secretary seemed to be marooned on a desert island. He did not know when the Minister would come to the Ministry. There were few functionaries to be seen. There were plenty of telephones ringing but nobody seemed to be answering them. One could watch here the régime dropping like a juicy, over-ripe plum from the tree.

The Madrid General Post Office employees learning from Barcelona that the Catalans had beaten them in proclaiming the Republic, with much chagrin hastily hoisted the red, yellow and purple flag of Republicanism. An Army officer in uniform asked for the flag. He had no untoward designs. He merely took the flag and posing himself dramatically if somewhat uncertainly on the roof of a taxi-cab whose beaming driver was obviously not going to charge any fare, said the Spanish equivalent of: 'Drive on to the Puerta del Sol, cabby!' Hundreds gathered round and when I met the cortège on the Alcalá Street it was an imposing and very noisy affair. Afterwards the Republic punished the young officer for having performed this act while in uniform—that was the kind of naïve Republic which now came into existence.

By four o'clock in the afternoon there were so many people in the Puerta del Sol that the traffic problem became involved, especially for a slender reporter with not much weight to throw around. While Don Alfonso was sadly deciding which way to leave, Sr. Alcalá Zamora and his colleagues set out to the Ministry of the Interior. Their cars wedged their way through the delirious crowd at a speed which would make a snail's pace seem like the Grand Prix in comparison. The big wooden doors were shut and bolted. Bang, bang, bang, smote Sr. Alcalá Zamora and he called lustily on the guard within to: 'Open in the name of the Republic!' Civil Guards swung back the doors and Alcalá Zamora and his friends were swept up the stairs on a tidal wave of enthusiastic supporters. Ninety per cent of the danger was over. The key Ministry was in Republican hands without a drop of blood being shed.

For those who live in peaceful Britain where law and order rarely shows itself except under the guise of a bucolic police officer overflowing with satisfaction and highly unlikely to carry off some law-abiding citizen to the police station, there to club him with a baton because he belongs to the Socialist Party, will hardly realise what it meant to the Spanish Republicans to have obtained control of the Home Ministry. From this office the Civil Guard and ordinary police force receives its orders. The Civil Governor who rules each province with enormous local powers calls up daily to the Ministry to receive instructions. In elections, under the Monarchy, the 'machine' was worked from the Ministry and before election day lists were drawn up of friendly and opposition deputies who it was considered should win. The actual results varied strikingly little from the list drawn up beforehand.

There remained, however, the War Ministry, a thorn in the side of things democratic. Fortunately, stolid General Berenguer was a man of his word and little inclined to wild adventures. The only danger was that some wild young officer might try to seize control there. While Don Antonio Maura's son, Miguel, took possession of the Ministry of the Interior, another Republican, a pimply-faced Mr. Pickwick in appearance and by name Manuel Azaña, was sent to the War Ministry. And Don Damaso Berenguer solemnly handed control of this front-line trench of feudalism to the secretary of Madrid's Athæneum Club, a vociferous centre of Liberal literature and politics. Torquemada must have turned in his grave. The Republic now had the two main instruments of Spanish State control in its hands.

As night fell and when Don Alfonso was racing across La Mancha's plains, the police cordon was removed and at least sixty thousand inquisitive and noisy Madrileños gathered in front of the Royal Palace. A squadron of cavalry was lined up uneasily around the front entrance wondering what it should do about all this noise and turmoil. The crowd became noisier and seemed likely to get a little out of hand. Then up drove a motor-car. At the wheel was one Dr. Juan Negrin—you probably know the name. With him was one of Spain's most human artists, Luis Quintanilla. and Emilio Barral, a good little sculptor who died defending Madrid bravely in November 1936. On the running board stood two municipal policemen.

Something like the following dialogue took place:

DR. NEGRIN: There is a great deal of noise going on and might one know why? You know that the King has gone and the Republic has already been proclaimed from the Ministry of the Interior. The Palace is now the people's property and they must respect it.
MEMBER OF POPULACE: Indeed this may be true but there is no evidence of what you say and we dislike very much

those soldier-fellows with drawn sabres who sit so sullenly on their horses at the entrance.

DR. NEGRIN: That is soon settled. Hey, my good Major. . . .

MAJOR: At your orders, sir.

DR. NEGRIN: I speak for the new Republican Municipal Council of Madrid and in its name I order you to withdraw inside the courtyard out of sight of the crowd which is only irritated by your presence.

MAJOR: I am happy to obey your orders, sir, and the withdrawal shall be carried out at once.

DR. NEGRIN: What more do you wish, my friends?

MEMBER OF POPULACE: We think that there should be a Republican flag flying over the Palace.

DR. NEGRIN: That is rather more difficult for we have given the strictest orders that no Republicans, even those in authority, shall enter the Palace until the Queen and the Royal Family have left to-morrow evening. Quintanilla, a Republican flag. . . .

(Brief interlude while Quintanilla dashes into the crowd and emerges after a brief scuffle with a magnificent silk tri-colour flag.)

DR. NEGRIN: Now let us see if there are not any nimble young men who can scale the front of the Palace and place this flag on the balcony above the door.

In this manner the crowd was satisfied. Later on, about midnight, members of what was known as the Socialist Guard and who wore red armlets took up positions in front of the Palace entrance. But the crowd was merely noisy and demonstrative and no serious attempt to create trouble was made. Not that this could have been much consolation to those inside who merely saw a dense mass of yelling people and probably thought that they might get out of hand at any moment. Actually there was never any serious danger and even if this had materialised the armed Halberdiers, or royal guards, and the infantry and mounted troops on duty would doubtless have been able to deal swiftly with this.

Next morning Queen Ena, her two daughters and three sons, were safely put aboard the ordinary Irun Express at

47

El Escorial surrounded by many weeping friends and a few servants. The Duke of Saragossa, a strange little man whom I knew quite well and who alternated the hobby-task of driving locomotives—he was inspector of engine drivers on the Northern Railway and had driven 600,000 miles himself—with reading English poetry such as Byron and Shelley, was driving. We stood together on the track by the great steaming mountain-type locomotive and I asked him whether this would be his last trip or whether he would stay and drive the President of the Republic on official trips. He said he had no idea; but he came back and continued to drive his beloved engines. I believe he did drive Sr. Alcalá Zamora on one presidential trip although I am not quite certain.

So Queen Ena left in a train driven by a Duke and escorted by General Sanjurjo who had been confirmed in his post as chief of the Civil Guard under the Republic. Thus the Royal Family left Spain.

This day, April fifteenth, on which Queen Ena left, had been proclaimed a national holiday and jubilant Madrileños marched through the streets shouting: 'He did not leave of his own accord; we threw him out!' The merrier souls reverted to fancy dress and the most incredible felon figures shackled with chains were led through the streets to symbolise the departure. It was good carnival and not at all revolution. I only saw one spark of trouble. I was shoving my tired way through at least one hundred thousand citizens who seemed to have arranged to meet in the Puerta del Sol, when a procession came down Montera Street. It consisted of a tableau on a motor truck representing the virtues of Soviet Russia and it was escorted by about twenty young men and girls wearing red shirts who marched alongside singing the 'Internationale'. There was an awful row. People shook their fists at them and abused them. 'We want no Communism here!' 'This is a peaceful Republic!' 'No Russian nonsense here!' And suchlike shouts rang through the air. Police appeared from somewhere or other and half escorting, half protecting the Communists, wafted them away.

Everything seemed so pleasant and rosy this day. I myself was thrilled at the peace and order of the change. Poor

Spaniards. How they, and myself, were deceived in the ingenuous belief that feudal Spain had been dismissed in twenty-four hours. Feudalism had dropped King Alfonso overboard but its latent strength continued greater than any of us even guessed.

Down in Catalonia, the Catalans finally agreed to give up the Republic they had proclaimed and to revive an old autonomous body called the Generalitat which would have less powers and not have the same standing as a separate Republic in a federal Spain, which was what Colonel Maciá and his friends wanted. Looking back now it would have probably been far better for everybody if they had held on to their Republic. But the Republic was already in the clouds and seemed in a fair way towards shaping a state different in almost nothing from the Monarchy.

CHAPTER VI

THE KING'S RECORD

E VEN an intelligent and popular king cannot in the long run save an economy which is not adjusted to that which times and economic conditions require. Indifferent of kings, nations and empires come and go. The Tom Browns and Stalky and Co. build up empires and the Bertie Woosters and the Drones dissipate them with light-hearted indifference. 'Clogs to clogs in three generations,' is our Lancashire way of summing up nature's course with man and his creations.

So do not let us bestow on Don Alfonso all the responsibility for a state of affairs which in part was beyond his control. He reigned over a weak feudal nation which had lost in a few years, and with little resistance, the great Imperial possessions built up during centuries. Nevertheless, Don Alfonso wielded so much executive power in his position of active Head of the Spanish State that we cannot exonerate him entirely.

My conclusion is that he was on the whole a bad Monarch and had no small responsibility for the decomposition of Spanish politics which resulted in the Dictatorship of General Primo. I am not sure that the King could have enabled the change from feudalism to some kind of economy which could give new life to the nation without bloodshed, but at least I think he could have done much to have made this inevitable change less violent.

There is my opinion of Don Alfonso's reign summed up in a few lines. It cost me a great deal of trouble to arrive at this brief conclusion. I have read most of the books available in Spanish, English or French on the events of his reign from 1902 to 1931. I even took the trouble to read the files of Spanish newspapers day by day through these twenty-nine years and I suffered nearly as much in doing so as did the poor library attendants of Madrid's Athenæum Club who had to bring up the weighty bound newspaper volumes from a grimy basement. I do not pretend that my judgment is right. I find it opposed to almost everything written on Don Alfonso by other British writers and they may be right. I can only say that I took immense pains to form my opinion and if it is wrong at least I reached my conclusions in all good faith with the material available to me. In later years there will be much more material at hand, perhaps Don Alfonso will even publish himself, or allow to be published, much reliable information concerning his reign which would throw more light on the particular disadvantages and difficulties with which he was faced. The politicians in books and in newspaper interviews have been able to give their side of the picture more easily than has the King, although he also on occasion spoke quite freely with journalists.

It may perhaps be of interest if I describe in rather more detail how I arrived at my conclusions concerning the King. I find myself right away in disagreement with many writers concerning Alfonso's education. So much has been written about the careful upbringing of the King, who was born a sovereign owing to the death of his father, Alfonso XII, several months earlier. I do not doubt that his mother, the little Austrian, Maria Cristina, had good intentions. But I think that his education mainly in the hands of priests and army officers fitted him to be an excellent feudal Monarch. He was educated to think as a man of the fifteenth century and it must be said that this appears to have accorded well enough with his natural inclinations. Time after time throughout his reign we find Don Alfonso on the side of feudal Spain, against even the slightest effort of his Cabinet Ministers to introduce fundamental reforms. Alfonso's motoring skill and good polo gave him a modern man-of-the-world reputation which, in so far as his mentality was concerned, was entirely unjustified. To place him on the throne with practically unlimited executive power at the age of sixteen was criminal. If he had been sent to Oxford for a few years or allowed to travel until he was twenty-one, Spain might have been saved much bloodshed. His record as a king during the period from sixteen to twenty-one is disastrous; no political system could have stood up to the frivolous way in which he made and unmade Cabinets from 1902 until 1907.

Spanish politics were not in hopeless shape when Alfonso took the throne. From the death of his father in 1886 until the murder of Canovas in 1897, two politicians, Canovas and Sagasta, respectively heads of the Conservative and Liberal Parties, had alternated in office with lengthy and stable governments. Their united efforts, it is true, had lost Spain Cuba, the last remnant of her colonial empire, in addition to the Philippines and Porto Rico. But at home in Spain at least there had been stability based on a vote-manufacturing system which worked well enough.

Nevertheless, there did not seem to be any reason why the present fiction of universal suffrage could not be gradually converted into some more workable system to replace feudalism. Sagasta was an old man in his seventies, sick and unable to act or think efficiently, but his party contained Count Romanones, José Canalejas, Segismundo Moret and other Liberals of some capacity. The Conservatives, under the leadership of the very clever and rising Antonio Maura, seemed to have a future. Maura was a convert from Liberalism and seemed, therefore, likely to bring new ideas and new outlooks to the Conservative Party.

The hopes of political observers that with the coming to the throne of the young King on his sixteenth birthday a new era would begin for Spain were soon dashed.

Shortly before his birthday, Don Alfonso attended a Cabinet Meeting for the first time in order to familiarise himself with the workings of government. The Cabinet Ministers were dismayed to see him arrive in military uniform. That illustrated to some extent the outlook of the Palace; the constant glorification of things military and scant importance given to such things as the prestige of the civil institutions of the country.

But the first Cabinet Meeting, held as soon as the service raising Alfonso to the throne was ended, provided drama and tragedy. It had been assumed that this was a formal meeting at which the King made official contact with his ministers and nothing more. But this headstrong and highly precocious young man had other ideas. He wanted to know what General Weyler meant by ordering the closing of some military training colleges. The reason was clear. With the end of the war with America over Cuba and the loss of the remaining colonies, some ten thousand officers returned to the Peninsula and the Army was hopelessly over-officered. It was, therefore, only common sense to suspend the preparation of new officers for several years until the surplus had been absorbed in home service. In Army circles there was opposition, it being argued in the high-handed way in which Spanish military men argue most things that the State should care for the excess officers and still keep open its doors to new ones. The voice of the Army spoke through the lad of sixteen who had that day promised to serve the nation to the best of his ability. General Weyler defended his measure but Sagasta intervened on behalf of the King and insisted that his recommendation be accepted, that is to say the colleges were to remain open.

Alfonso had not finished. He recalled to his Ministers that the King held the privileges of conceding military honours according to the Constitution and that he meant to take advantage of this fact. A direct descendant of Christopher Columbus, the Duke of Veragua, thereupon, arose and respectfully recalled another article of the Constitution which said that no act of the King was valid unless approved and duly counter-signed by a Cabinet Minister. Again Sagasta intervened to cut short discussion and to support the King. Count Romanones, to whom we are indebted for a picture of this meeting in which he participated and an account of which is included in his book entitled *Mis Memorias*, reports that the Ministers were dumbfounded by Alfonso's behaviour and sighed with relief when the meeting ended.

This day of May 1902 was a tragic one for Spain. The situation was difficult enough already and now it was complicated by the direct intervention of an autocratic youngster of sixteen determined to play the part of the new broom.

There was worse behind the scenes. A Cabinet crisis before the accession—there is no coronation ceremony in modern Spain—was only avoided on the personal pledge of Sr. Sagasta that immediately the ceremonies ended Parliament should at once discuss measures calculated to restrict the activities of the religious orders. Don José Canalejas, a highly intelligent young Liberal, had insisted on this. The pledge was broken without so much as an apology, Parliament was closed at once and Canalejas was allowed to resign without the slightest attempt to keep him. But Alfonso who was so much perturbed about keeping military training colleges open and the concession of military honours to those of whom he personally approved, did not feel called upon to intervene on this occasion. The whole atmosphere was sordid and nothing but bad faith prevailed.

Canalejas achieved considerable popularity on his resignation and was received by great crowds in Valencia which sang the 'Marseillaise' to show their Republican feelings. As there seemed likelihood of a repetition of this reception when he arrived in Barcelona, Sagasta took steps to have large forces of police and Civil Guard in the streets to break up any attempt at demonstration in favour of his colleague of a few days before.

Meanwhile, Alfonso toured the north. His elder sister protested vigorously because the Minister accompanying the royal entourage, Sr. Gasset, was allowed to sign the Golden Book at the Cave of Covadonga; this book was not for commoners, she insisted. The tradition by which the Mayors of the towns should ride in the royal carriage when the formal entry was made was not observed; the Press was ostentatiously excluded from some semi-public functions. Alfonso was less to blame than the Palace clique which surrounded him but these things small in themselves were noted and did him much harm.

Soon the Liberal régime fell. The Conservatives came in. Maura, full of fire and enthusiasm, hoped to do great things in Spain. Yet within several months a bitter Maura was telling close friends: 'It is not true that I have resigned; I have been expelled from office by Don Alfonso.' He later denied these indiscreet words; nobody doubted their truth because they reflected the situation. This brilliant young Conservative was tripped up and forced to resign on the trifling issue of who should be Captain-General of Castile. He had named General Weyler for the post, expecting routine approval by the King. To his surprise the King was unwilling to accept the nomination and suggested another general who for some reason or other was thought by the King and a clique in the Army to have a prior claim. Maura, being new to power, promptly resigned. Later in his political career he would doubtless have raised his eyebrows and changed the name of the nominee. But he still had illusions about democracy under Don Alfonso.

In 1905 came another incident with the Army. Several hundred young officers in Barcelona raided the offices of a satirical weekly named *Cu-cut* which had attacked the Army on some unimportant issue. The officers wrecked the furniture and beat up the employees. The Captain-General of the region declined to punish the frivolous youths concerned; other Captain-Generals sent congratulatory telegrams to them. The Government ordered the arrest of the culprits. Monteros Rios, the Liberal Premier of the moment, was an old man. For several years he had not left home late at night for premiership was less exacting in those days. He was called to the Palace at midnight. He got up—but fell down and cut his head at the entrance to his home. He finally arrived at the Palace with his head bandaged to hear the behest of a young King aged nineteen who cared little indeed for the personal inconveniences caused to an old man. He wanted the Government's resignation and he received it. A new Cabinet was formed under the docile and ambitious Moret and not only were the officers not arrested but the Cabinet produced a Bill which placed under the jurisdiction of military tribunals attacks on the 'honour of the Army' or the 'unity of the nation', which might appear in the Press. For what was possibly Europe's worst Army the Spanish military officers worried a great deal about questions of honour.

It is, of course, possible to say that Don Alfonso could not have resisted Army pressure. But there is at least no evidence that he ever tried to. The system by which he displaced one leader of a political party and then persuaded another member of the same party to form a new government, was bound to end in splitting the parties into minute fractions. There was enough tendency to disintegrate already, but Don Alfonso did much to accentuate this. The system of relations between Don Alfonso and his Ministers was far from satisfactory. The

Prime Minister had to go every day to the Palace to discuss with the royal stripling the affairs of the moment. Then Don Alfonso received each Minister separately once or twice a week. This system enabled the King to intrigue behind the back of the Premier if he were so inclined, and this King certainly was so inclined. Feudalism had an efficient watch-dog which kept close vigil day by day over these very con-servative and far from progressive middle-class politicians who were tolerated by Army, Bishops and Crown but kept to cer-tain narrow frontiers which they were never allowed to cross. About this time Don Alfonso wrote a letter in which he warmly commended the zeal of the Bishop of Barcelona in arousing public opinion against a proposal by British Protestants resi-dent in Barcelona to build a chapel. Finally, after much negotiation by the British, the chapel was allowed to be built on condition that it did not resemble a church from the exterior.

It may be noted to Alfonso's credit that he recommended the Government to use clemency in the case of the shooting of Francisco Ferrer in 1909. This execution shocked Europe. Ferrer had preached Anarchy as a doctrine but there was no evidence that he planned the outbreak, due in fact to the call-ing up of reserves to send to Morocco which resulted in some days of serious rioting in Barcelona, nor that he took a leading part. But where in other cases Don Alfonso took care to impose his will, this time he merely made his suggestion and left it at that. He could have saved Ferrer's life—even a person so little suspect of Anarchist sympathies as the Pope telegraphed asking for mercy—but he made no move to put pressure on Maura who was a fanatic on the question of 'law and order' and was backed by a very cruel Home Secretary, Sr. La Cierva.

From 1907 onwards the pace of Cabinet changes slackened. It could hardly be otherwise, if not Spain would have had to have imported politicians. Maura, before his foolish and un-warranted decision to have Ferrer shot, had two years in office.

Although the Liberal Party, through the mouth of Moret, had agreed with Maura on the necessity for making an exam-ple of Ferrer, when this progressive body found that Europe was upset by the shooting of an Anarchist and that there was much political capital to be made out of the incident, its indignation at the shooting was promptly expressed and its leading members campaigned in the country against 'this monstrous injustice'. In due course Maura resigned and the Liberals came in and in 1911, with José Canalejas as Prime Minister, Parliament was still discussing the shooting of Ferrer. There was in fact much to discuss. There were considerable forces of police and troops in Barcelona but for two full days they scarcely intervened and those who argued that the authorities had withheld their forces in order to let the rioting achieve important proportions and then to step in with a terrible repression, had some grounds for this view. This discussion was, however, stopped by a message sent from the Army to Canalejas peremptorily ordering him to stop the debate, which seemed again to bring the honour of Spain's Army into question. The debate was stopped and José Canalejas stayed in office, which showed how much this one-time fiery Liberal had learned and how even a Parliament with a Liberal majority jumped through the hoop when feudalism cracked the whip.

José Canalejas was indeed a faded version of his former self. He toyed indifferently with religious reform and finally produced a useless measure called the Law of the Padlock which prohibited the establishment of new religious orders in Spain —many convents and monasteries had transferred from France owing to persecution there—and ordered all religious establishments to furnish full particulars as to the number of members and other details. At first the clergy refused point-blank but finally they filled up the required forms which were duly filed away in some Government office and forgotten and even the ban on new orders was emasculated by the provision that it should lapse in two years if not renewed by Parliament. Don Alfonso, as usual, appears to have worked hard to prevent any innovation which could place the slightest restriction on religious activities.

Even this limp and subdued Canalejas was watched with much suspicion in the Palace. The Queen-Mother's inelegant but graphic comment when she heard of his appointment was: 'My God . . . Canalejas!' An observer at the time records

57

that Canalejas was much fêted and banqueted by the aristocracy; it was believed that in this way he would be toned down and disarmed. It seemed hardly necessary. Later he was shot down by an Anarchist in Madrid's Puerta del Sol and yet despite this end, which seemed to entitle him to the respect of Parliament, this body did not even take the trouble to hold a session in his honour as is the custom when some distinguished politician dies.

For several years after the death of Canalejas, Don Alfonso enjoyed perhaps the greatest era of popularity he knew in his whole reign. He seemed to have taken a more Liberal stand. He received Gumersindo de Azcárate, Miguel de Unamuno and other leading figures of the 'intelligensia' in the Palace, despite the strong Left-Wing, and in some cases Republican, sentiments of the visitors.

But this brief flirtation with the moderate Left did not last long. Spanish Catholics held a Eucharistic Congress in 1915 and the final ceremony consisted of Benediction in front of the Royal Palace. The King requested the Cabinet to attend and it could hardly refuse but the Prime Minister, Count Romanones, has since recorded how embarrassed he and his fellow-politicians felt at being virtually forced to take a prominent part in what after all was a private congress of import only to Catholics and without national significance. The excuse that Spain was officially a Catholic nation may be proffered but anybody who knew the Spain of 1915 knew the strong anticlerical feeling among the working classes and among quite a sector of the middle class. Again when Spain was consecrated to the Sacred Heart of Jesus and to mark the event a monument was inaugurated in the geographical centre of the Peninsula, the Cerro de los Angeles, near Madrid, Don Alfonso not only attended but he pronounced the inaugural discourse. He seemed to forget that he was King of all Spaniards and not just King of the Spanish Catholics. There was no reason why he should not have been a most devout Catholic without necessity for exhibiting time and again his complete identification with militant clericalism, which can be a very different thing indeed from pure and simple catholicism.

The War brought Spain much money, and much trouble.

Mr. Winston Churchill, who includes Don Alfonso in his book *Great Contemporaries*, quotes the King as saying: 'Only I and the mob are for the Allies.' By 'mob' the Monarch denoted practically the whole working class, most of the intelligensia, all Socialist and Republican leaders, most of the petite bourgeoisie, and a considerable sector of the middle class including Count Romanones and other politicians of note. But feudalism was on the side of the strong, of tyranny. Army and Church through their Press organs extolled the virtues of the Central Powers and prophesied their speedy triumph. Don Alfonso may have been on the side of the Allies, but he who could be so indiscreet on occasion was discretion itself and no indication of this sympathy was ever made public while the War lasted.

Spain by merely adopting a sympathetic neutrality, that is to say by helping the Allies with supplies in return for capital and technical experts to reorganise her industry and agriculture, and without actually sending troops, could have transformed her economy. She would undoubtedly have done so if the forces of feudalism had not been too strong. They were able once again to suppress the desire of the great majority of the nation and to prevent Spain swimming boldly out to find the currents of the twentieth century. They thus made inevitable a bloody revolt in years to come.

But although money poured into the country and Madrid hotels had gala nights seven nights a week at which fortunes were spent on champagne and gaming, the shadow of unrest spread. The U-boats supplied with petrol and food by Spanish 'patriots' and thus able to patrol the Mediterranean, repaid this aid by sinking nearly eighty Spanish ships. Coal and other primary materials were short. Too much food was exported and there was shortage and high prices at home. The Army was highly discontented about a purely private matter. Skirmishing had gone on in Spanish Morocco since 1909 and considerable numbers of troops were kept out there. The officers in Morocco received double pay, were promoted quickly, and found many 'pickings' to add to their income. It was considered quite legitimate to falsify regimental returns in order to secure profits for the officers. The officers at home grew more and more angry at the prosperity of their colleagues in Africa, formed a species of trade union known as a Junta, and in 1917 proceeded to place a pistol at the head of the Government in office, demanding instant reforms.

The Army, of course, won. There is no need to go into the odorous details. The Government resigned. Said Count Romanones: 'We wished to defend the civil power and we found that we had no means with which to do so.' *Correspondencia Militar* told its readers, military readers as you may guess by the title, that Don Alfonso had sent a message to the rebels of the Junta in Barcelona—the seat of agitation—saying: 'Please do nothing rash. Have confidence in me and all will be arranged.' A denial was issued that the Monarch said this. But a new Government came and the Junta people were not punished and many of their demands were accepted and the officers simmered down again. And this gangster method of obtaining improvements adopted by this Army so meticulous in questions of honour, indicated that the authority of the civil power was even less than before. Don Antonio Maura summed up the situation neatly by saying: 'The only remedy now is to hand over power to those who will not allow anyone else to govern.' It was September 1923 before this happened and in the meantime there had been the first attempt at social revolution by the general strike of August 1917, an extra-official meeting of many members of Parliament to demand reform, and riot and bloodshed in turbulent Barcelona.

In the Riff territory in Morocco the dashing General Silvestre, formerly head of the King's Military Household, led ten thousand men into a death-trap. Several hundred only escaped from the followers of the redoubtable Abd-El-Krim. General Silvestre seemed to have been acting more or less as he pleased and several days before the disaster received a cable of encouragement from the King. The investigating commission was not allowed to examine the private belongings of the General, nor to cross-examine his son who was his aide-de-camp and who was one of the few survivors. The evidence available pointed to the existence of such a cable of which the gist was 'long live the men who possess great virility.' The existence of a cable was in fact not denied in royal circles but it was alleged that it was merely a cable of congratulation on the occasion of the feast day of the patron of the cavalry, to which arm of the service Silvestre belonged. Royal circles did not, however, produce the copy of the telegram in question which must have remained in the dispatching station. And two weeks before Parliament was to receive a full report of the disaster there ensued the *coup d'état*.

According to my notes, Don Alfonso had thirty cabinets and sixteen prime ministers between 1902 and 1923. He had nine ministries in the period 1902-1907.

That in synthesis reflects my investigations of the activities of Don Alfonso. It may be alleged that I have stressed all his mistakes and none of his triumphs. Frankly, I found no triumphs. I admit that Spanish politicians were difficult to deal with but I feel that Alfonso by making himself a master of political intrigue made matters much worse. If he had not tirelessly thrown himself again and again into the scale to prevent the slightest encroachment on feudal privileges, much might have been changed in Spain. And his responsibility for splitting up the political parties into small fractions seems to me only too clearly proven. An ex-Minister, Sr. Villanueva, tells us how one day he was with Don Alfonso and the latter said: 'Do you know that Alvaro came to see me yesterday and that he had prepared a very neat trick. I saw this right away and fooled him beautifully. . . .' 'Alvaro' was Count Romanones. A King who intrigued in this light-hearted way could hardly hope to win the respect of his politicians.

I will not go into his private life. I do not think that a public man can be judged by this standard. Suppose we were to base our opinion of Julius Cæsar on his morals? I do not think that the King showed himself as being sensuous or vicious while on the throne. The tragedy of disease weighed on his family life. His real love was motoring and he remained true to it. If he had been born in another sphere of life he would have made an excellent motor-racer and demonstrator of swift cars. If he had been highly intelligent one may doubt if he would have chosen this hobby which requires mental concentration over long periods and is thus not highly suitable for persons with weighty problems to resolve and whose mind is likely to wander from the road to these problems with disastrous results. I do not mean to say that no highly intelligent person can drive a car safely. But I do doubt very much if the average man in a post of very great responsibility and with innumerable problems constantly before him would choose high speed motoring in powerful sports model cars as a regular means of relaxation. However, I may be quite wrong in this for I believe that Mussolini frequently drives a sports car and whatever criticisms I might level against Il Duce I would never question his very powerful intelligence.

Don Alfonso was certainly clever and had a retentive memory which accumulated the piles of information which came to him by word of mouth or in official documents. One of his biographers has said that he never read a book from cover to cover after finishing his education. Certainly when he departed in 1931 the only books found in the royal study were a few military and sporting annuals. He had not been trained in a way likely to permit him to judge soundly the problems that came before him and although he was soon a 'well-informed person' in view of the stream of information which came his way, his only solid basis was that of feudalism and he clung blindly to this to the end. If his precocious and somewhat superficial cleverness had been turned into the proper channels we might have seen a very different Alfonso; as it was he wasted such talents as he possessed in cheap political intrigue which seemed to his youthful and untrained mind to be a great sport. Twenty years later, he lamented loudly in public that Parliament did not function. He had certainly done his share to make it a mockery and a dead-letter.

CHAPTER VII

TROUBLE IN THE REPUBLIC

M OB reactions vary a good deal according to nationality. An English mob will usually attack food shops, Germans look for some Jew to torture, the French usually look for political opponents with whom to exchange blows, but the Spanish mob for many decades has always made a bee-line for the churches. If you read the history of Spain for the last hundred years you will find very few cases of mob law ruling in the streets without the burning of churches.

So there was nothing highly surprising in the fact that the first real trouble under the Republic should take the form of the wholesale burning of churches.

The Republican honeymoon lasted less than one month. This time was occupied in no small part by much speech-making in praise of the bloodless way in which Spanish revolutions were carried out as opposed to the messy businesses of France and, more recently, Russia. The Monarchists had complete freedom. *A.B.C.*, the Monarchist organ, property of Don Ignacio Luca de Tena, son of the founder of the paper, a nouveau-riche whose money had been made in olive oil, gave great play to Don Alfonso's movements and splashed an extensive interview with him in black type on the main pages of the paper one day. It was all quite idyllic.

So idyllic in fact that the Monarchists agreed that what they ought to do now was to organise themselves politically, a thing that they had not managed to do in time to save the Monarchy. There was a meeting in Madrid and the Royal March was played on a gramophone. Somebody overheard it in the street and there was a fine uproar. A crowd gathered, cars of those attending the meeting were set on fire, people were beaten. The mob then decided to burn down the building of *A.B.C.*, where it was received by a volley of rifle shots which killed two and injured half a dozen. The peace of the Republic had disappeared.

Sooner or later trouble was bound to have developed. For the man in the street the Republic did not merely consist in seeing hundreds of middle-class Republicans take over civil governorships and other posts formerly held by hundreds of middle-class Monarchists. By Republic the man in the street meant the disappearance of feudalism; the disappearance of the hegemony of the Church, the landed proprietors, the Army, the Civil Guard, the Crown. The Republic in nearly two months of life had done nothing about these fundamental problems; the Crown was the only feudal artifice to disappear. The rest of the structure remained intact.

Hence the explosion of rage and violence among the Madrid crowds when they found that even the one limb of the octopus of feudalism which had been cut off was beginning to grow again. The forces of Monarchy were reorganising. The Anarchists who had been much upset by the peacefulness under the Republic now went around saying: 'We told you so. . . .' Mr. Man-in-the-Street discussed matters on the doorstep with Mrs. Man-in-the-Street and both agreed that it was all a pretty bad business and that unless something was done about it even Don Alfonso would be back pretty soon. The Government managed to save the *A.B.C.* building by massing police in front of it, who fired in the air. It was lucky that they did fire in the air because I was just in front of them and in my fright dived through a privet hedge which most unfortunately had strands of wire through it and I took a lovely tumble and ripped open a pair of perfectly good trousers.

But Madrid was simmering. Monday, May tenth, was a day of trouble. The Socialists worked hard to fight the general strike called by the Anarchists as a protest against the Monarchist meeting and the firing on the crowd from the *A.B.C.* building, which was done apparently either by caretakers or by two Civil Guards who were on duty. But the Anarchists were very active and the Madrileños very annoyed. Small boys and long-haired individuals trotted into churches armed with tins of petrol. Flames shot up. Crowds gathered. Firemen came and the police somehow disappeared. The crowds cut the hosepipes.

Afterwards it was said that Sr. Azaña, War Minister, had said: 'Rather all the churches of Spain shall burn than that the blood of a single Republican be shed.' I do not know whether he said that or not and I do not think it is really important in any case. Miguel Maura, who as Minister of the Interior had charge of the police, resigned but the Cabinet persuaded him to withdraw this resignation and took collective responsibility by remaining in session throughout the day. Martial-law was proclaimed; the troops were popular in so far as the people felt, I do not know with how much justification, that they would not open fire and all religious buildings were put under military guard; no mean task because Madrid alone has some four hundred churches and chapels. The Socialists got their people back to work and by nightfall Madrid had returned more or less to normal except for the churches which continued to blaze. People hired taxis to drive around to see the some ten buildings ablaze and ice-cream vendors did a good trade among the huge watching crowds. The principal buildings burned were the large Jesuit church in the Gran Via and the Jesuit church and school on Alberto Aguilera Street.

The provinces learned of the news and indulged in much church burning. Malaga was a nightmare. Violent Andalusia with its strong proportion of African blood, its poverty-stricken peasantry, wreaked, notably in Malaga, terrible damage on the churches. Almost every church in Malaga was burned.

In all I think about eighty churches, convents, monasteries in Spain were completely wrecked and several hundred damaged before the brief wave subsided.

There was a good deal of bloodshed because the police and troops in some towns opened fire on the mobs. I do not think any monks or nuns were killed. As so often happens in Spain no exact figures were available either at the time or afterwards. Statistics are not a strong feature of Spanish administration.

The sad feature of the May disturbances is, I think, that no lesson was learned by the Republicans. Despite the horrors, the bloodshed, and the loss of buildings in some cases of great historic value, the men leading the Republic did not realise from this outburst that they themselves must forestall mob violence by removing feudal control of the Spanish State. The Catholics learned more, they decided to work within the Republic for its reconquest. Not by proclaiming their conversion but by accepting the status quo, which showed a good deal of cleverness. What would have happened if the Government had followed the advice of Miguel Maura and had opened fire on the crowds around the churches in Madrid I do not know. The Republicans and Socialists in the Government would have become the object of intense criticism, if not of hatred, from the masses and one conflict would have followed another quickly.

For myself the events of May brought a difficult personal problem. I followed the whole course with the vivid interest natural not only to a reporter but to a Catholic. I was twenty-eight years old and since the age of six or seven had never missed Sunday Mass except through illness. For many years I belonged to a society known as The Knights of the Blessed Sacrament which implied the taking of Holy Communion at least once weekly. Religion and politics had never seemed to clash, although as I had no politics the issue was hardly likely to arise.

It was perhaps rather unnecessary but I felt after the May incidents that I must take a definite stand. The Catholics now attacked all that the Republic stood for, although they pretended to accept its outward form, and on the other hand on all sides the Church was the object of the bitterest hatred. All my sympathies were with the masses of the people. I had motored and travelled by train through various parts of the country. I had been shocked and horrified by the poverty of the peasants, the precarious way in which they lived, the brutality of the police and Civil Guards. I could not reconcile this with religion. I welcomed the Republic as meaning a step towards better social conditions and much as I disliked the mob violence and the burning of churches I felt that the people in Spain who professed most loudly their Catholic faith were the most to blame for the existence of illiterate masses

66

and a threadbare national economy. Perhaps my reactions were rather childish, but I felt that I could not even outwardly associate myself with Spanish Catholics by going to church. I had no desire to mix in any way in Spanish politics but I definitely felt that in Spain the Catholic religion was being used as a pretext for the committing of great social injustice and I did not wish in any way to be even physically identified with it.

It was a hard decision for me and I thought it over for several months before finally deciding to stop attending Mass.

People may think that I had been influenced by the agnostic atmosphere of the Republic. Possibly this is the case. But neither then nor since have I had any violent change in my outlook on religion. I have been to Mass often since, have taken the sacraments, and have been married in a Catholic Church. But I felt, and continue to feel, a strong dislike for this use of the Cross to cover up sordid material interests. And my feeling that I took a correct decision has since been strengthened by the attitude taken up by the Catholic Press of Great Britain towards the Civil War.

It is very hard indeed for the average British Catholic to realise conditions existing in Spain. The British Catholic enjoys many liberties, and clamours always for more. The Catholic Church in Spain offered no tolerance to minorities and it was not uncommon for Protestants to be stoned. I remember during my first months in Spain reading of the case of a Spanish vendor of the British and Foreign Bible Society's publications being surrounded by a mob and the house in which he took refuge set afire. The building of Protestant chapels for foreign residents was always the subject of endless opposition from the clergy.

Catholicism decayed in Spain when the decay of feudalism set in. The progressive Charles III expelled all Jesuits from the country. During the forties and fifties of the nineteenth century various Liberal generals sold the estates of the religious orders, mostly at low prices to their friends. A Concordat was made with Rome in 1851 by which it was established that three religious orders should be permitted in Spain. But only two were named; so any order in trouble could always claim to be the third. After the restoration of Alfonso XII in 1875, priests and monks and nuns increased greatly in number and this increase was augmented still further in the early part of the twentieth century when many religious orders moved from France to Spain as a result of anti-clerical feeling and legislation in the neighbouring Republic.

The fact that religious orders now lived more in the towns, no longer had large estates, took them even more out of touch with the people. Their funds were invested on the stock exchanges by expert third parties, who occasionally took advantage of their full powers to swindle their clients. And while a few orders lived with considerable wealth the village priest was often pitifully poor; completely dependent on any wealthy parishioners for his livelihood, for the Government salary might reach three or four pesetas daily. The priests had power to go to all schools and teach religion. Few of them took the trouble. There was no vibration in the soul of Catholic Spain. And eighty thousand nuns and monks, over thirty thousand regular priests and many thousands of buildings absorbed a considerable portion of the national income. If they had infused spiritual and mental vitality into Spain this would have been some recompense. But this was not the case. They educated half, or more than half, of the children of the middle classes. That is to say they educated those children who could afford to pay, leaving those who were a complete burden on the educators to the State. That is speaking in general terms; some orders did maintain schools for poor children. But, by and large, the children who went to the religious schools were the children of people who could afford to pay for this education. This situation also contributed to political division in Spain for the religious schools produced types with a completely different outlook on life from the product of the State school.

CHAPTER VIII

WORDS—NOT DEEDS

AFTER the World War, Europe had a spate of new Constitutions. There was the German, the Austrian, the Czechoslovak, the Polish and others. Most of them are now in shreds and such as their authors who have not been butchered are mostly political exiles or are tasting twentieth-century civilisation at Dachau or some similar organised centre of large-scale sadism.

But in 1931 the obvious thing for a new State was immediately to draw up an elaborate Constitution. This suited the Spanish temperament excellently. It meant that for months nothing would actually have to be done, just endless discussions of all kinds of sweeping reforms in the comfortable knowledge that these would only have to be carried out in some distant future.

Great Britain has survived for some centuries and has indeed made a niche for herself in the world without ever possessing a full-blown Constitution and managing to get along quite well with such ancient measures as the Magna Carta, the Bill of Rights and, of more modern vintage, the Dominions' Bill.

You may say, of course, that you can no more build a State without a Constitution than you can build a house without plans. But actually dramatic changes in the structure of a State rarely give time for elaborate planning. Revolution, even on such a mild scale as that of Spain, can better be compared to war. The politician who is caught up in it must strike swiftly and adjust his movements to those of the adversary. He must seize strategic positions and advance as far as possible. He can no more settle down comfortably to draw up elaborate plans for 'mañana' than a general can casually drop all military activity in the midst of war ignoring his

69

adversary while he dedicates long months to the elaboration of the most marvellous plans to make victory certain.

So Spain offered the forces of feudalism an excellent opportunity to regain strength and reorganise while Parliament in Madrid echoed day and night for three full months with wordy battles, wonderful oratory, skilful arguments, party quarrels, in order to produce an abstract piece of paper whose 121 Articles would later have to be put into effect—a much more serious and complicated business.

But the landed owners remained masters of their great estates. The Civil Guard still inspired terror through the four corners of Spain. No one of the four hundred generals had been dismissed. Cardinal Segura was the one priest of some 110,000 in Spain to suffer expulsion. Uniformed and secret police all continued in their posts. Fundamentally, nothing had changed in Spain except for the disappearance of the Crown which although it served as a point of union for the forces of feudalism was not indispensable to them. New servants would be found to defend Army and Bishops even though the Crown had gone.

There was no quick action by the men in command of the Republic. Four hundred and seventy-three members had been elected to Parliament. About 360 of them belonged to the Republican-Socialist coalition. For the first time since 1890 there was no 'electoral machine'. Instead of tiny electoral districts where feudalism could still have worked efficiently, the Provinces were used as constituencies. There was no reason why feudalism could not also control the Provinces too, but it had no system organised as yet. After the May riots the Government had suspended most Right-Wing newspapers and ordered the dissolution of the Monarchist parties, so the Right forces went to the elections with a certain amount of handicap. The Catholics hastily organised the Popular Action Party. It announced that it was 'neutral'. The defence of things that mattered in Spain should be its aim, said its propaganda, and such matters as Republic or Monarchy remained secondary issues. Feudalism, you see, soon found new servants.

Nevertheless the elections on the whole were fair enough

and shone with virginal purity as compared with any other elections ever held in the Peninsula. For the first time in Spain a man could vote as he pleased, more or less. For even with the Republic in the saddle there was many a business office where it was better not to mention that you had voted Republican, and many a peasant who voted Right because the 'Amo', the master of the lands, still sat in the big house and the sergeant of the Civil Guard still knew how to deal with people who were not friends of the 'Amo'. Imagination, this? Not at all. This is the reality of Spain about which the tourist folders said nothing. The Spanish family chest was full of skeletons despite its lovely exterior.

Theoretically there was no great need for endless palaver in the square and depressing grey Parliament building on Madrid's elegant Carrera de San Jeronimo. A Government with 360 Deputies behind it should have been able to dispatch business 'pronto'.

While elections were afoot the Government had already assigned to the bearded, Liberal lawyer Don Angel Ossorio y Gallardo the task of drafting a Constitution for the new-born régime. Sr. Ossorio described himself as being 'a Monarchist without King', and became quite famous just before the fall of the Monarchy by announcing in public that even his cat had turned Republican. Sr. Ossorio had dabbled in Christian-Socialism years before. I interviewed him and found him a solid, square figure with a King-Edward beard who would say nothing for publication. I had to sit before him and write down my question. Then he solemnly wrote down the answer. It would have been useful if he had had anything interesting to say but as far as I could see he had not. After the little school-boy business of writing question and answer was over he was pleasant enough and willing to chat amiably about the weather or Britain or any other non-political question.

He and a few lawyer cronies produced a stodgy draft Constitution which included a Senate, practically no restrictions on the Church, very limited autonomy for Catalonia, and indeed it resembled so much the Monarchist Constitution of 1876 that it seemed hardly worth while to have taken the trouble to change the régime at all. When Parliament met, its leaders looked at the draft in dismay and hastily appointed Luis Jimenez de Asúa, a clever young lawyer and member of the Socialist Party, with instructions to produce something that at least resembled twentieth-century ideas of what a Constitution should be. Parliament had to kill time until the end of August while Asúa and his friends toiled.

Meanwhile, Parliament frittered away valuable time in discussion as to whether or not Don Alfonso had incurred 'responsibilities' in connection with the *coup d'état* of General Primo and as to whether he had received commissions in connection with various State enterprises undertaken by foreign companies during the Dictatorship and many other points which all seemed rather unimportant considering that he had gone. The Crown property was confiscated but this meant an obligation for the State rather than otherwise for there were not large landed properties involved and the numerous palaces and residences cost a considerable amount in upkeep. If Spain had followed the gesture of Germany in returning to the Kaiser the enormously valuable Crown properties, it would have meant that Don Alfonso would have been obliged to send to Spain considerable sums of money annually for the upkeep.

Sr. Asúa and his assistants dipped into the Constitution of Weimar, thumbed the Soviet Russian Constitution of 1924, lifted little pieces from Mexico's national statute, considered Austria's contribution to Constitutional Law and at the beginning of September in this year of 1931 they were able to present to Parliament for discussion the draft plan to give battle to feudalism. That is to say, if the Republic wished to do this.

I forgot to mention that among other incidents discussed while Sr. Asúa was kneading the constitutional dough to bring to the parliamentary oven, there had been acrid comment concerning the conditions under which one José Maria Gil Robles, you will have heard of him, and José Calvo Sotelo, already mentioned, were elected. They seemed to have managed to have the old feudal machine function quite well in their benefit, Gil Robles in Salamanca Province and Calvo Sotelo in Galicia. The latter had been elected in his absence, but this fact did not make the election any cleaner. The financial manager of the Dictatorship felt Paris to be safer than Madrid. Parliament accepted the elections as valid.

For some months, indeed for some years, to come I was to spend endless hours sitting on the red plush benches of the Foreign Press gallery listening to Spaniards talk about Spain in the Republican Parliament. I learned a very great deal, and not only about Spain, in this process, but the Republic benefited relatively little. The Speaker was Don Julian Besteiro, a secondary-school teacher who had commenced life as a Republican and had graduated to Socialism. He also graduated to a university professorship in logic. He is a thin ascetic type with a fine head. He was condemned to death and reprieved in 1917 as one of the signatories of a manifesto justifying the general strike. Largo Caballero was another Socialist who suffered the same fate. Besteiro has always seemed to me to be at heart a good Liberal, influenced much more by Kant than by Marx, and who was in the Socialist Party rather because it was a 'decent' gathering and not an unreliable group such as Sr. Lerroux's Radical Party, to which he first belonged, was.

In the parliamentary chair he showed fine tolerance, quick to hurry to the support of the weak—in this case the representatives of feudalism who had ridden rough-shod over their opponents for many a century.

Well there was trouble about even the first Article. In fact it had to be shelved while platonic articles which guaranteed the workers the right to a living wage and the 'right to be able to work', went through in the easy way non-committal measures slide through debating bodies. Article One had as its mission that of describing what the Republic really stood for. Admittedly difficult this. A correct description would have been 'a feudal Monarchy without King'. But in the full blossom of Republican honeymoon, choicer and more succulent titles were sought. The Socialists wanted it described as a 'Republic of Workers'. The Catalans wanted the autonomy aspect stressed in the title.

Prime Minister Alcalá Zamora—the decision had been taken not to name a President until the Constitution was voted— objected strenuously to the title 'Republic of Workers' as did

73

many other Republicans. They averred that this would an-
tagonise Britain and France. The federal idea likewise had
many opponents. But a sour little man, José Ortega Gasset,
known as the 'Philosopher of the Republic', made a speech
in which he said that the Republic must decide between full-
blooded centralism or an equally rich dose of federalism. He
thought that the idea of inculcating an autonomous Catalonia
into a centralised Spain would result in a lop-sided State which
would not function efficiently. In the minds of many was undoubtedly the fear that without the Monarchist link, Spain
might disintegrate.

It was all settled in the end by describing Spain's new régime
as an 'integral Republic of workers of all classes'. I still do
not know what an 'integral Republic' may be, but everyone in
Parliament seemed quite satisfied, by the solution. It was
decided that such regions as desired autonomy should be entitled to have control of local affairs with a regional Parliament but the only active petitioners represented in Parliament
were the Catalans and it was they who fought tooth and nail
in the discussions and managed to obtain control of the police,
local taxation, ports, and—very important—education. Sr.
Alcalá Zamora seemed to have forgotten the violent attacks
he had made on autonomy projects in the years 1915 and 1916.
He showed great tolerance. Some said that this was due to
the really tremendous reception he was given when he went
to Barcelona a few days after the Republic was founded, in
order to persuade Colonel Maciá to give up the title of Catalán
Republic in favour of Generalitat of Catalonia. Alcalá
Zamora thought that this reception was for his person. In
reality it was a homage to the Republic. The Right-Wing
Press, now in full bloom after its suspension, attacked Parliament and Catalans viciously. Spain, said this Press, was being
hacked to pieces. But Catalonia had a strong middle class
and, despite divergencies on this issue, the middle class of
Spain held relatively firm. Because Parliament was not a
gathering of working people. There were, I think, less than a
dozen out of 473 members who described themselves as manual
labourers and some of these were trade union organisers who
had not actually performed such work for many years.

There were clashes about the Senate and about votes for women. Sr. Alcalá Zamora led opposition to the wish of Socialists and Left Republicans not to have a Senate. It was, he said, a necessary brake on the Chamber of Deputies. Considering the reputation of Spain's Chamber of Deputies of Monarchist days for doing less legislative work in longer time than almost any other similar body in Europe, and that is saying a good deal, Sr. Alcalá Zamora's argument seemed a little unnecessary. It was as if a purchaser of a fine new car with several kinds of brakes on all wheels, transmission brakes, etc., were to insist that a skid such as is used on the wheels of farm carts be fitted for added safety in descending hills. A second house probably has its uses in a well organised nation but when active executive work is needed the less people concerned the better and, it seemed so at least, Spain had a new State to build as rapidly as possible. Sr. Alcalá Zamora lost and 'he was not amused'.

The Socialists insisted on votes for women. The Republicans disliked this. They pointed to Germany and Britain and quoted authorities who insisted that women were naturally reactionary. They had something of a case, considering the attitude of the Spanish middle-class women on most social subjects. The Socialists would not yield—and they carried the day. Nationalisation caused shudders in many circles. But a smooth formula which merely said that if necessary properties could be expropriated or nationalised in the national interest and with due recompense to the owners brought sighs of relief. The Socialists said that this was not a betrayal of their revolutionary programme because it left the door open for a future socialisation of the State. Everything was left for 'mañana'. The polished British-public-school-educated son of a Spanish banker who sometimes joined a journalistic group in Chicote's Bar said to me: 'They leave everything to the future and that is just as we want it because the only future the Republicans and Socialists will have will be on the gallows or in gaol.' It would have interested some of the parliamentarians if they had visited Chicote's Bar on the Gran Via and heard young aristocrats and Army officers describing exactly what they meant to do with the Republic and the Republicans when they had had time to prepare a successful rising. But the parliamentarians were mostly hard-working, sober, middle-class people who never thought of spending five pesetas on a cocktail or six pesetas for a whisky and indeed the Republic had fallen into their laps so easily that even when one spoke to them of the dangers lurking around the corner they merely laughed with fine self-assurance.

Six weeks of day and night discussion in Parliament had been sufficient to reveal that Sr. Alcalá Zamora had little in common with the rest of his colleagues. Somewhat surprising this. Back in January and February when the Republican programme had been discussed by Socialists and Republicans who were sharing a wing of Madrid Prison after the failure of the Jaca rising, Sr. Alcalá Zamora had apparently favoured much wider schemes of nationalisation of property, of reorganisation of the position of the Church, than had been undertaken when they came to power.

The clash came on the Church issue. Parliament favoured dissolution of the Jesuit Order, nationalisation of the Church property, and said that the State salary to the clergy should cease. An iracund Sr. Alcalá Zamora left his seat on the Government bench and said: 'No, no and no. . . !' He had been fuming since the House had rejected his proposal for the establishing of a Senate; now he gave vent to pent-up feelings. It could, of course, be said that as a fervent Catholic he was justified in his anger. But why overthrow the Monarchy if everything feudal—and what so feudal as the Catholic Church in Spain—were to be left intangible? It looked very much indeed as if nothing whatever more than personal ambition loomed behind the Republican sentiments of Don Niceto Alcalá Zamora.

The situation was peculiar. There was no Head of the State to whom he could hand in his resignation. Those in power had pledged themselves to remain in office until the Constitution was voted and a President was chosen by Parliament. The Prime Minister had agreed to this, knowing quite well what was the intention of Republicans and Socialists with regard to the Church. It was decided that the Speaker should arrange the change of Government and the pimply-faced intellectual, Don Manuel Azaña, took over the premiership in addition to the War Ministry. The fact that he had only shortly before the Prime Minister resigned made a brief but energetic speech in favour of dissolution of the Jesuit Order helped his nomination.

In addition, Don Manuel had something practical to show for his six months in office. He had allowed some 8,000 Army officers to retire on full pay. This suited many officers excellently. They now took another position and lived very comfortably indeed on the double salary. Spain's Army had a tremendous surplus of officers but the surplus was not so much a danger to the Republic as the character of the officers themselves. And Sr. Azaña's measure did not remedy this. The diehards such as Sanjurjo, Goded, Cavalcanti, Franco, all remained at their posts and the type of man who retired was more frequently than otherwise a Republican sympathiser who felt out of place in the Army. However, as so few other Ministers had any practical effort to stem the tide of feudalism to show, Sr. Azaña stood out as a brilliant exception and the man-in-the-street felt that he was to be trusted.

There were minor riots in the streets about this religious issue raised by Article Twenty-six; twice thirteen and doubly unlucky, said the Spanish superstitious.

The crisis caught me, as most important events in Spain seemed to do, in a railway train. I had been holiday-making. In Valencia I made the acquaintance of a Canon of the Cathedral who was a fine fellow and who took me here and there and showed me everything worth seeing. He was the best type of Spanish churchman; but one in a thousand. We lunched with four great hulking peasant priests, masses of beef, in from their country parishes, and he tried to explain to them that the Republic had come to stay in Spain and that they would do well to accept this fact. But they roared with laughter; they knew better. The good Canon was a nice simple fellow but who did not know much about what was going on, so they said. Then I went to Palma de Mallorca and loved the interior of its cathedral and swam in the nude in creeks of Pollensa bay with a civil servant on leave from the Far East, and two American girls and, believe it or not, it was all very innocent.

And while Sr. Azaña was substituting Sr. Alcalá Zamora, I was on the way from Barcelona to Madrid, happy, broke and third-class. There is in Spain a tremendous difference between the atmosphere in first and third. First-class, in those days, was stiff, ultra-reactionary, the Spaniards apologised to you, the foreigner, for the Republic. In the third-class, people spoke well of the Republic. A square-shouldered sergeant of the Civil Guard held forth: 'People can say what they like about the monks and nuns but I tell you this that unless you burn down all their buildings and thus destroy their lairs Spain will never get anywhere.' This surprised me highly, coming from such a source. Like my cathedral Canon of Valencia, he was one in a thousand in his class. He was a good-looking man and was very gallant to a youthful actress on her way to join a theatrical company in Saragossa. Between whiles the company told stories which would have made an English horse blush and at which everyone, men and women alike, shrieked with laughter. I was introduced by the sergeant to another Civil Guard who had been chauffeur to a British diplomat for five or six years. He spoke English ungrammatically but with an upper-class accent. He obviously had a good ear and had simply copied the pronunciation of His Majesty's Ambassador who doubtless mutilated our poor language as only those can do who possess that vague but horrid affliction known as the Oxford accent. I asked him to have a whisky in the dining-car, but although he was on leave he was in uniform and it was against rules for a Civil Guard to be seen in uniform in a railway diner. On the whole I decided that in twelve hours in a third-class compartment I learned more about Spain than in twelve months in Madrid.

So the Jesuits were dissolved; not expelled as I have read since many a time in books and articles on Spain. They could not live in community. Although they opened a house at Brussels many of them remained in Spain, preaching retreats. The expropriation of their property meant the loss of some fine buildings but their reserves were not touched for, as I have already explained, they were long since safely invested in the name of third parties. The fact that Church property became Government property was no asset to the Republic. For it was

78

stipulated that it should remain in the service of the Church and there were no estates or property or liquid possessions to be seized—or at least none of any importance. The system of attributing any valuable possessions other than Church buildings to a third party was used generally and not only by the religious orders. So the Republic merely became the technical possessor of some thousands of Church buildings, mostly sadly in need of repair. It was decided that payment of the clergy should cease at the end of next year, that is to say in December 1932.

A more far-reaching provision was that the religious orders should cease to teach. But execution was left pending.

On the whole this seemed to me a very moderate programme but Spanish Catholics became quite hysterical and Sr. Gil Robles and his friends left Parliament during these mid-October days and did not return until the Constitution was voted. Yet, looked at coldly, the Church retained almost the whole of its old power. The miserable pittance of four or five pesetas daily given to thirty thousand secular priests, the orders did not receive State pay, could easily be made up by the faithful without any considerable sacrifice. The only really important blow was that of education, because the Church did manage to raise up a large middle-class sector to think in a way hostile to any progress or change. Even so it would be many years indeed before the effect of the State gaining complete control of education could make its mark on the country.

One evening at the end of November a group of Socialists and Republicans went to Sr. Alcalá Zamora's home and asked him to become President of the Republic. Despite his refusal to allow any tampering with the prerogatives of feudalism his friends and former colleagues had faith in his loyalty to the régime. There was no other suitable candidate in sight. Sr. Besteiro would have done well, but he was a Socialist and there was much fear as to what the attitude of Britain and France might be if a Socialist became President.

Sr. Alcalá Zamora accepted and was duly voted first President of the Republic by Parliament.

Despite the fine promises in the Constitution as to the future status of women in Spain, on the day when a crowded

Parliament heard the President take the oath of office—it was a simple promise to serve the Republic—sitting next to me in the Press gallery was the slender, white-haired Sra. Alcalá Zamora, who had no place in the ceremony. Yet the diplomats had brought their womenfolk. I could see Princess Bibesco, daughter of Lord Oxford and Asquith, and wife of the Rumanian Minister in Madrid, watching the ceremony keenly on the diplomatic dais. But the President's wife was hidden in a corner and indeed when we all hurried over to the Palace to see the arrival of Sr. Alcalá Zamora she was refused admission and an officer had to be found who knew her before the police would let her enter. It did not seem to me to be a very good augury for the future of women under the Republic.

The troops marched past and everybody cheered and the Civil Guard came along, stern, splendid, proud and cruel and three-quarters of the crowd hissed and booed and the other quarter cheered and applauded. I was sad and depressed; it seemed there could be no peace for Spain. The wind was cold and I stood among the crowd of poorly-dressed people who flocked around the Palace when all was over and I wondered why the Republic must use the Palace at all. I went home filled with gloom. But I think that Sr. Alcalá Zamora was a glad man that night: he had fulfilled himself; he occupied the Royal Palace as Head of the State.

CHAPTER IX

A MIDDLE-CLASS REPUBLIC

S PAIN'S middle class had now two sturdy representatives in command of the new Republic. Both Azaña and Alcalá Zamora are lawyers by profession and this also is in accordance with tradition for most middle-class youths in Spain take a law course if they have a university training, a fact which has given the nation many excellent orators and few men of science.

Neither man could be said to be a revolutionary in any accepted sense of the word. They represented those middle classes which had governed Spain, with the toleration of feudalism, under Don Alfonso and who had been excessively annoyed when this function was taken out of their hands by General Primo. Now they were back in office having momentarily joined forces with the workers' organisations to overthrow Don Alfonso and the question arose as to what their attitude would be towards the feudal powers.

Sr. Alcalá Zamora had indeed already defined his position. He would not fight feudalism. The Monarchy which had handed over to the Army the privilege of governing Spain had been overthrown but Sr. Alcalá Zamora had made himself very clear by his fight against Article Twenty-six; by endeavouring to preserve the privileges of the Church intact. Sr. Azaña's position was less clear. He had made a mild tilt against feudalism by reducing the number of officers in the Army and he had now led the decision to put through Article Twenty-six. He obviously disapproved aesthetically of Old Spain but it was not yet clear that he would definitely give battle to this force and try to destroy it. What was clear, however, was that feudalism would endeavour to destroy Sr. Azaña. Even if he had not the temperament to put on gloves and fight, at least there was nothing of the traitor in his make-up and under his control the Republic might wax still stronger and be infinitely harder to overthrow.

The problem facing Spain's middle class was indeed a difficult one. In Britain Cromwell, and in France the Revolution, removed feudal tutelage and established a bourgeoisie with sufficient economic power in its hands to rule their respective nations. But Spain's financiers, lawyers, men of business, did not derive from the rickety national economy sufficient power to sway the destinies of the country. This remained in the hands of landowners, churchmen and Army officers, with the two latter as far the most active existing forces. So the situation of the middle class was a bitter one indeed, for feudalism offered little hope as a twentieth-century programme for a backward, illiterate nation and yet the bourgeoisie was not strong enough to govern alone. Few of its members would be likely to take the only other alternative, namely, to have formed a permanent alliance with the workers' organisations and to have declared open war on feudalism.

Naturally the situation could have been settled if the landowners, Generals, Bishops had been prepared to make sacrifices; if they had come forward and admitted that after all their class had lived privileged lives for centuries and that now they would willingly sacrifice estates, reduce the clergy, lop off many expensive generals from a defence system which as such was merely a farce. They could have collaborated with the middle class for the reconstruction of Spain. Of course they did not, although this was obviously the path to follow if the nation were not to experience civil strife. But is there any reason why we should judge them harshly when we know that with sacrifice and reason Europe's troubles could be settled without war, yet we are heading towards a bloody strife which seems daily nearer and nearer. There is so much to be created, continents awaiting railways, irrigation, economic development; science offers us with both hands lavish gifts to solve our problems. Six hundred men of those who sway Europe's destinies could meet and in a few months so reorganise our economics that Germany and Italy could be geared into a giant effort to reconstruct our society. Yet we know quite certainly that they will not do so. We know that if they did, they would not be allowed to proceed with their plans. British producers would protest if our output were to be cut in order that Germany's might be bigger and Germany's manufacturers would raise their voices in terrible lamentation if their products were to lose markets to Britain. Not only the powerful proprietors; but also the man-in-the-street with a few shares, the worker who might lose his job, would join in the mighty outcry.

No. We prefer to go forward deliberately until the waters of discontent burst the dam and Europe is swamped in the most terrible war of ages and our cities are in ruins, the lungs of our children burned with gas, the flower of our manhood stinking in death on devastated landscapes. So why should we criticise Spain's stiff-spined feudalists who likewise preferred suicide to common sense?

Let us accept the fact that man is one of the most illogical creations of God and leave it at that.

Spain's President represented rather the country middle class than the city type. He came of earthy stock from Priego, not far from Cordoba, where he was born in 1870. His father owned some hundreds of acres of olive groves and wheat fields. A clever young man, he studied law and gained a coveted post in the Government corps of legal advisers. Count Romanones, ever on the lookout for promising young men, lifted him into politics and from 1907 onwards he was more or less regularly a Deputy. Andalusians speak almost as well as do the Irish. Young Sr. Alcalá Zamora made himself heard and by the time middle age came, ministerial rank likewise came his way and he held the public works' portfolio for some months in 1916. His differences with Romanones regarding the War and autonomy for Catalonia kept him in the background but surrounded by a group of ten or twelve followers he managed to keep his name in print. He was War Minister in 1923 but left office some months before the Dictatorship came. As a promising politician likely soon to be Premier, he naturally resented the Dictatorship more than some of the older men who had had their political day and were content to retire. His name was mentioned as participant in the proposed Midsummer Night's Plot to overthrow General Primo which cost Count Romanones so dearly. In all, a politician with few original ideas to handicap his career and sufficient ambition to take him further than his talents might normally have carried him. He was always a member of the Liberal Party.

I saw a good deal of him in the first days of the Republic. A man of middle-height, somewhat portly, lisping in the best Andalusian tradition, he was hard to report. His speeches were impossible to translate and rarely meant much when turned into English. They were torrents of oratory in which the green hills of Galicia, the snow-capped peaks of the Pyrenees and such-like geographical features romped around amidst social or international questions. Once I had the task of translating a ten-minute speech, which he broadcast for foreign lands, into English. It was made without preparation so that I had to listen and prepare a running translation to be broadcast immediately he finished speaking. It was utterly impossible and as I knew that this would be the case I had translated a previous speech. Nobody, as far as I know, noticed the difference. On another occasion he wrote some articles for a news agency with which I was connected. Some of the more moderate sentences ran to eighty words without even a comma. It was difficult indeed to imagine that any clear concept of a new State could emerge from such a poorly-organised brain. He was tremendously conceited and I feel sure that he completely identified the Republic with his own person. During the pre-Republican days he was endlessly patient and smoothed ruffled feelings with great tact and indeed he showed considerable personal charm as Prime Minister. But he behaved very much like a spoiled child and with great petulance when Parliament rejected his desire for a Senate and again when it decided to encroach on Church privileges. He speaks no English but his French is quite good.

A very different type indeed is Manuel Azaña with his grey-white face, obtruding pimples, huge square head, square shoulders, large paunch; he would make an excellent model for a sketch of Mr. Pickwick. His father both manufactured soap and owned a good deal of land at Alcalá de Henares, and Manuel was born in this town noted for two illustrious citizens, Miguel de Cervantes and Catherine of Aragon.

Manuel went the way of Spanish youth; first a religious college, then a degree in Law. At fifteen he told his priestly teacher that he had decided to give up practising catholicism and he tells in one of his books that he was somewhat hurt by the fact that the friar seemed neither greatly surprised nor upset by his decision. After the Law degree he went to Paris to study. His father had died in the meanwhile. Later came retrenchment. He took up farming and endeavoured to 'modernise' the family farms. But neither the friars, nor university professors, nor the studies in Paris had laid any foundations for agricultural success. The family fortunes suffered new disaster. Don Manuel had to seek employment.

Azaña entered the civil service. He passed examinations brilliantly and soon was chief clerk in charge of a department of the Registration Office; the equivalent of our Somerset House. Get up at ten, at the office by eleven, lunch at two, the siesta from three to four, then to the café, from there to the Athæneum Club to read or talk, late dinner at nine, then the theatre or to the café again and finally home at one or two in the morning. That was the life of the upper end of Madrid's civil service. A pleasant, cultured, unhurried existence, especially for a bachelor with some small means apart from his salary. Azaña became secretary of the Athæneum Club, El Ateneo, a strange turbulent literary-cum-political centre, different indeed from its sedate counterpart in London.

In 1927 Sr. Azaña, a close friend of his named Don José Giral, professor of pharmaceutical chemistry in Madrid University, and a few other intellectuals formed the party of Republican Action. They belonged to that sector of the middle class which was convinced that once the Dictatorship collapsed Spain must overthrow the Monarchy; in other words that Don Alfonso could not be trusted to return the government of the land to middle-class hands. In 1928, Azaña surprised his friends by marrying at the mature age of forty-eight. He wedded Dolores Rivas Cherif, a slender, handsome woman some twenty years his junior and sister of his life-long and intimate friend, Cipriano Rivas Cherif, a dramatic critic. He had written books in the meantime; a pamphlet on the organisation of the French Army; he translated Dickens; edited literary reviews; wrote a semi-autobiography entitled *The*

85

Garden of the Friars, a sombre picture of the physical and moral atmosphere of the school of the Augustinian Friars at El Escorial. Education killed rather than kindled in his soul, if one may judge by the book.

He conspired. He was a member of the provisional Government named by those who prepared the Jaca rising of 1930. The fact that he was little known enabled him to get away to France and after some weeks in Pau to return to Madrid unnoticed. There was much mirth in the salons of Madrid when he was named War Minister; the secretary of Madrid's literary club in charge of the Army seemed to be the Republic's chief joke. In La Granja café they smiled, but remembered the fierce way he would argue on occasion. In his office he was a martinet. The generals of Spain found no soft-mannered, bewildered dilettante but a crisp and rather crusty Minister who could both bark and bite; and did.

After retiring a number of officers he proceeded to the reorganisation of the Army and endeavoured to equip at least a few divisions properly. The first parade under his control caused much comment, the troops were better equipped and a much more martial tone was apparent.

Considerable·executive capacity and the fact that he was utterly devoid of any personal ambition gained him, as I said above, the full hatred of feudal Spain. Others might be tempted but not Azaña. I think he had almost separated himself from the ordinary currents of life. He was an observer with an almost super-human detachment, as if he lived on another planet. If he had wished to apply his cold, detached reasoning to fighting the feudal powers he might have routed them but I think that he feared just as much working-class domination as feudal supremacy. He painstakingly laboured to create a Spain ruled and administered by Liberal politicians and he was doomed to failure for there was no foundation for him and his middle-class friends to place their feet on.

Already a scurrilous weekly paper named *Gracia y Justicia* was selling enormously. It was filled with grotesque caricatures of Azaña and his fellow-ministers; holding them up as figures of fun. It made the insinuations which are apt to be made about a man who first marries at forty-eight. It played up the Anarchists, flattering them. It was packed with cheap vulgarity. I refused to believe that this paper was being published and printed by the Catholic publishing house which produced *El Debate* and other Catholic publications. But this fact was confirmed to be by one of the staff who told me moreover that it was bringing in a great deal of money. He had, I may say, the good grace to be thoroughly ashamed of the publication and I know that he personally did what he could to convince those in control that catholicism would suffer greatly from association with this disreputable type of political attack. But the order had gone out to discredit Azaña, and as his austerity and unimpeachable political record made it impossible to find legitimate handles for attacks, feudalism turned to other weapons.

It was not found necessary to attack all Republican leaders in this savage fashion. Don Alejandro Lerroux and his some ninety Deputies had left the Republican-Socialist coalition and had gone into opposition. The middle class was dividing even its puny forces.

CHAPTER X

AUGUST FIREWORKS

IN the very early hours of August 10, 1932, I was awakened by a crackling and rattling as if of fireworks. I mildly cursed the particular group or society which needed to celebrate so noisily and so late and went to sleep again. Nocturnal, open-air fêtes lasting until far into the night were common enough during the summer nights of Madrid. A few minutes later my telephone rang. The prophecies steadily uttered month in month out by smart-young-men-about-town concerning a military revolt, had at last materialised.

It proved to be a flash-in-the-pan. Apparently General José Sanjurjo's conscience reproached him for having aided the painless accouchement of the Republic. He was a hard-drinking, woman-loving officer with bravery and few brains. Apparently he and a mere handful of officers decided to prevent the Catalan Autonomy Statute and the Agrarian Reform Bill, then approaching conclusion in Parliament, from coming into force. Feudalism did not approve. The Church party believed that the Republic could be captured from inside. The Army did not feel excited enough either over the moderate autonomy now being given to Catalonia or over the Agrarian Bill which provided solid compensation for every acre of land seized, to launch into such an adventure as that proposed. The landowners for the most part would have preferred to have the money to their estates. The Monarchists did not feel very certain as to what was to follow the overthrow of the Republic, or indeed if this was to be overthrown or just to come under control of Sanjurjo and his friends.

The subsequent trial of the two leading figures, Sanjurjo and General the Marquess of Cavalcanti, did not throw much light on the organisation of the movement and indeed it looked much more like an improvised rising decided over a few dinner tables. In Madrid, only a few hundred cavalrymen from a remount depot revolted and they were speedily defeated by the police. General Sanjurjo reigned for a day in Seville where he announced that the Republic would be maintained, but in 'purified form'. It was a cruel revolt by the more thoughtless, and therefore least dangerous, sectors of feudalism. Sanjurjo himself after being head of the Civil Guard under the Republic had taken the well-paid and comfortable post of commander of the Carabineer Corps, some 14,000 strong, which guards the frontiers.

Sanjurjo fled from Seville and was arrested by one of his own carabineers when he got down from his car near the Portuguese frontier in order, apparently, to attend to a personal matter. He was sentenced to death and reprieved. He went into exile in Portugal and from there he appears to have prepared a great part of the successful revolt of July 1936, of which he would have been the leader if he had not been killed in a plane crash during the first days. Mobs rioted in various parts of Spain by way of answer to the revolt and monasteries and convents went up in flames, particularly in Granada and Seville.

The revolt was particularly cruel in view of the great tolerance the Republic had shown to the Army, which did little to hide its hostility to the régime. Only a few weeks before Sanjurjo endeavoured to replace democracy by the sword, there had been an incident after manoeuvres near Madrid. When the divisions which had taken part were reviewed by the Inspector-General of the Army, General Manuel Goded, he wound up by shouting: 'Long live the Army! Long live Spain!' After the parade there was a violent scene in the officers' mess in which one Colonel Mangada reproached Goded with not having included the regulation cheer of: 'Long live the Republic!' The General ordered the immediate arrest of Mangada for insolence to his superior officer and the War Minister, Azaña, took the side of Goded and imprisoned Mangada for some weeks, only releasing him after very strenuous representations from various Republican and Socialist groups. Even the very fact that Goded, well known as an intimate friend of Don Alfonso and as being of violently Right-Wing political views, should have been made Inspector-

General of the Army which was a nomination of the War Ministry and not a post reached by normal promotion, showed the efforts made by the Republic to co-operate with all Spaniards. In private conversation the officers for the most part expressed their opinion that the tolerance of the Republic was sheer weakness; although few were disposed to join in a wild and unprepared adventure such as that improvised by Sanjurjo. That was to say unless the Army, Bishops and other feudal elements could obtain control of the Republic. They were definitely finished with Don Alfonso and there was no other obvious candidate for the throne. Meanwhile the Republic lost valuable time with many fine words where much strong action was needed.

One timid reform made by the Republic gave fruitful results following the Sanjurjo revolt; that was the creation of a force of police named 'Guardias de Asalto', Shock Police. They were created by the first Republican police chief, named Don Angel Galarza. The Republic's programme was not positive enough to prevent a good deal of unrest and yet bloodshed in repression looked rather bad coming from the new leaders of what was felt to be a true democracy. So several thousand husky young men of solid physique were recruited and given rubber clubs. The first time they were employed in Seville, the Sevillan Anarchists whose backs took the drubbing went into hysterics. This was an affront on Spanish dignity. In Spain it is much more of an offence to slap somebody's face than to pull a gun on him. But even apart from the outcry against this outrage on Anarchist dignity, so many Anarchists or 'agents provocateurs' were using sub-machine-guns that the Shock Police had perforce to use similar weapons and they were soon weighed down with arms—they even had armoured cars with heavy machine-guns among their equipment.

However, as there was a great rush of applicants for admission into this corps and most of them obtained the post thanks to the recommendation of this or that Republican or Socialist Deputy, the result was that the new force was mainly composed of young men of Republican sympathies. The force was greatly increased and proved at least a slight defence for the State against its many enemies.

When the trial of those concerned in the Sanjurjo revolt took place there was mention of Sr. Lerroux, the Republican politician now leading the parliamentary opposition. He had, it seemed, seen General Sanjurjo on several recent occasions and a mutual friend had gone to and fro bearing messages. Some hours before the revolt Sr. Lerroux left hurriedly for his country home at San Rafael, in the Sierra Guadarrama. He had made several speeches in which he warned the Government that its policy might produce violent opposition. There was little that was concrete. But there was much comment and Sr. Lerroux found himself increasingly popular with the Right and correspondingly less welcome among the Left.

The Government felt moved to some action by this attempt to overthrow the régime and decreed the seizure of the estates of all the Grandees; in total some 1,200,000 acres. This did not include the town property of the some two hundred holders of the ancient title. It looked as if the Republic was actually going to come to grips with feudalism. But the initiative proved to be as much a flash-in-the-pan as Sanjurjo's revolt. Some months later a friend of mine bought a large stretch of land from a well-known Grandee without the slightest difficulty. A few estates were seized and divided up among peasant holders but by and large the land was left to the Grandees. There had been much outcry at home and abroad against this expropriation without payment. It was pointed out that Cavalcanti was the only Grandee charged with complicity in the revolt and nothing was proved against him. The Republic was always tremendously sensitive to the slightest charge of extremist tactics. And what seemed a really energetic measure, in practice meant nothing. No effort was made to put it speedily into action.

Several hundred officers and civilians including a Catholic priest, Canon Coll of Malaga, were dispatched without trial to Villa Cisneros, a parched coastal post on the West Coast of Africa as punishment for their part, or presumed part, in the plot. There were, however, no high officers among these exiles who stayed out there for nearly a year until some escaped in a large fishing smack and reached Portugal and the others were brought back to the Peninsula.

Both the Press of the extreme Right and extreme Left attacked the Government ferociously over this business of exiling without trial. Actually the Republic was rather helpless. It might have changed the legal code and have introduced new and speedier methods. But it retained both the men and the machinery of the old methods of justice which were slow in the extreme. It had to resort to arbitrary methods if it wished to punish effectively. How slow justice was in Spain is illustrated by the fact that in 1936 I reported the trial of six men who had set a church on fire in Lora del Rio, near Cordoba, in May of 1931.

The Sanjurjo rising stimulated Parliament, and the Autonomy Statute for Catalonia and the Agrarian Bill, amended to exclude Grandees from compensation, went through together in the month of September after a summer of intense parliamentary activity. The carrying out of the business of settling peasants on land which they would pay for over a period of thirty years, was in the hands of a bespectacled ex-schoolmaster, Don Marcelino Domingo. He died in Toulouse in February 1939.

So 1932 ended in dull fashion for the Republic with much hard work done but nothing spectacular to impress the Republicans. I went to Portugal and found it inexpressibly sad. Shabby students in tawdry frock coats; men with sheepskin coats and fierce black moustaches; tramwaymen who worked for a British company and who must perforce be shaved by the company hairdresser before stepping aboard their cars; Estoril's lovely coastline marred by grey-stone villas which would charm the eye in Wensleydale; men unloading coal boats by baskets which they carried on their heads—such slavery. Lisbon is beautiful—but steeped in sadness.

CHAPTER XI

BAD DAYS FOR THE REPUBLIC

S PANISH villages are as picturesque as any in the world. They 'belong' in the landscape; form part of it. Modern architecture does not break their line. They look much as they must have done two centuries or more ago.

But they are not nice places to live in. I am speaking here of the average Spanish village perched draughtily and water-less on some hill-top or merging into the rolling uplands of this or that region. On the coast roads, or at beauty spots which receive a stream of tourists, more comfort can be found.

I have stayed many a night in tiny God-forsaken villages. Not in the local inn but in some peasant's home. If it is winter you wake up in the morning with the back of your throat stinging from the cold and damp. The floors are earth. Glass is too expensive to use for bedrooms. There is just a wooden shutter as if it were a stable. In summer you are stifled or bitten by mosquitoes or other foes which inevitably accu-mulate despite the scrupulous cleanliness of the average home.

Breakfast for the family consists of a thin greasy soup made of a little flour and olive oil. Perhaps for you as a distinguished visitor there will be a piece of hard black bread and some goat's milk. On this thin fare peasant and family trudge off to what may be a very distant strip of land and toil until sundown. Few have their own holdings. They live in the villages and each year rent a piece of ground which varies in price accord-ing to its fertility and its distance from the village. The peasant may have a mule or maybe only a donkey. With a wooden plough which would have been considered modern in the days of Julius Caesar he scratches the surface of the land. Fertilisers are often beyond his reach and the water supply is usually very bad. Centuries of chopping down of trees and bushes for fuel without any policy of re-afforestation has aided erosion and lessened the rainfall. Large areas of Spain ought really

93

to be abandoned until re-afforestation and irrigation can bring effects, for farming cannot be profitable even under the most degrading labour conditions.   Large sections of the Spanish peasantry neither eat sufficient nor have a level of life which permits them to purchase products of the manufacturing centres.

You can argue if you like that people also live badly in Ancoats and in Whitechapel and I agree and I think that it is a disgrace to our nation, but the population of Ancoats, Whitechapel and their like in many of our towns do not form a substantial majority of our total census.   In Spain the poverty-stricken peasants still form the majority of the nation's population.

The landowner, even the small landowner, put no money back in the soil.   Anything he could get from it in the way of rents he used in order to live in Madrid or some provincial town.   That is speaking generally.   There are, of course, fertile parts of Spain especially in the North and near the coast where farming showed substantial returns.   On the whole to put money back into the land meant losing it unless there were a complete and thorough change in Spain's agricultural economy.   Meanwhile it was an impossible situation.   The landlords drained the land steadily of its capital and often invested it in companies which could not in the long run have any economic stability because the poverty of the mass of the people prevented a modernised production, even of products in the first line of necessity, from being acquired in large quantities.   It was a hopeless circle and nothing could be done unless it was broken, but this meant breaking feudalism with its component Grandees, Bishops and Generals and also—lest we forget—having some workable system to put in its place.

However, forgive my meanderings on the subject of Spain's economy and if you have patience look on your map of the Peninsula until you find Casas Viejas.   If you have not the patience you can take it from me that it is a tiny white-washed village like thousands of its ilk up in the hills about forty miles from Cadiz and with Medina Sidonia some fifteen miles away. A lonely isolated small village of peasants and shepherds, it became an unhappy centre of trouble for the Republic.

Cases Viejas gives a striking example of the disastrous results to the Republic of the lack of any active and positive social and agrarian reform to replace feudalism.

The first time I heard of it was on a freezing night of February 1933 when I clambered out of bed to answer an awkwardly-placed telephone which would not be quiet. My 'tipster', a Spanish journalist who kept his eye on news while I slept, told me that in a place called Casas Viejas eighteen people had been killed in a clash with the police. 'And how many wounded?' I asked automatically. 'None,' was the reply. That seemed strange to me. It is very difficult in a straight fight to kill eighteen and to have no injured whatever; virtually impossible in fact. However, I decided that there was probably a mistake somewhere and that it would be cleared up next day so I tapped out a routine story and phoned it hurriedly, for it was after midnight, and went back to bed. If I really had the makings of a great journalist in me I suppose I would have hastily jumped into a car and left for Casas Viejas.

The Anarchists had called a revolutionary general strike throughout Spain but there had been very little trouble. Theoretically, the Anarchists had some show of reason, the Republic obviously needed stronger methods. But practically their ultra-revolutionary methods played into the hands of the Right. They had no programme to offer; nothing but death and destruction and thus, mainly unwittingly I think but undoubtedly with 'agents provocateurs' of the Right using money and influence among them, they upset the Republic and yet brought no solution.

Apparently, word of the Anarchist rising reached the little village of Casas Viejas and the local peasants decided that this was the time to revolt against the old order of things. So they staged a one-village revolution; Casas Viejas against the Spanish State. They surrounded the Civil Guards barracks and shot one of the Guards dead. The Guards in return shot several of the peasants dead. The Government evidently feared that the revolt might spread and sent to Casas Viejas from Madrid a company of Guardias de Asalto under one Captain Rojas. In all some sixty men and about three officers. They joined with local Civil Guards at Medina Sidonia and hurried up to Casas Viejas to relieve the marooned Civil Guard post. This they did with practically no resistance, but a group of peasants held out in one house. The police set fire to it and several peasants perished and others escaped. That was bad enough. But what came next was of unparalleled barbarity considering that the revolt had not spread in any other part of Spain nor was Casas Viejas near centres with considerable populations to which revolt could have spread with serious consequences. The Guardias under Captain Rojas went from home to home and dragged out men whom they thought might have some connection with the affair; took them down to the yard behind the burned cottage, which belonged to a peasant called Seis Dedos (Six Fingers), and there bundled them together and immediately and without the slightest inquiry, fired into them with rifles and sub-machine-guns until they were all dead. Captain Rojas is reported to have finished off several who still showed signs of life with his revolver.

I think the Government acted in good faith when it, at first, denied the terrible affair. I think the police reported that the men had been killed in fighting. But the incident was much too horrible to be kept quiet for long. The Anarchists, whose 'revolutionary general strike' never got under way except in Casas Viejas, pounced on the case as an example of the brutal anti-proletarian attitude of the Republic. The Right-Wing politicians and Press waxed red-hot with fervent indignation. The thing became a major scandal; the Government had to admit that its servants had sinned. At once and without hesitation the Cabinet proposed the naming of a Parliamentary Commission to investigate the happenings. A decided contrast this to the behaviour of the Lerroux-Robles Government in 1934 which resolutely refused to allow a Parliamentary Commission to investigate the slaughter in Oviedo and other towns by Moors and Legionaries when the revolt in the mining district was suppressed.

The Government fumbled the whole affair shockingly. The Home Minister, Casares Quiroga, a Galician politician with means of his own but neither with great initiative nor with good health, he was sick at the time, did not take the ruthless steps to make an example of the police who could behave with such bestial barbarity. Most of the actual administration of the police was in the hands of a superlatively inefficient and muddle-headed Republican, the Under-Secretary for the Home Ministry, Carlos Esplá, and the ambitious and equally inefficient chief of the police forces in all Spain, Arturo Menendez. Both of them were politicians of Azaña's Republican Action Party.

To show you the kind of man Esplá was I will relate what happened when I went to him to try to get him to do something about four American tourists in gaol in Palma (Majorca). One of the Americans had had rather too much to drink. But he was hurting no one. A Civil Guard tried to arrest him. The American was not violent but the Civil Guard punched him in the face, although the man was wearing glasses. The Guard smashed the glasses and cut his hand. The woman of the party, angry at seeing the Guard treat a harmless drunk in this way, slapped the Guard fair and square on the cheek. All four were thrown into gaol as if common prisoners. The woman, a cultured American, was locked into a cell with a half-mad beggar woman. This might have been overlooked for one night. But at the end of six weeks they were still locked in common-criminal cells awaiting a court-martial for the terrible offence of 'assault on a Civil Guard'.

I saw Esplá and suggested that this punishment was out of all proportion to the crime and that at least they could be released on bail or, at the worst, given decent quarters and treatment. He was quite angry with me. 'Do you know that the woman struck a Civil Guard?' he asked me in tones as full of horror as if he were describing an exploit of Jack the Ripper. He pushed me off quite indignantly and refused to even consider milder treatment for them. It horrified me to find a high Republican authority who thought it just punishment for a cultured woman who had only given way to very legitimate indignation to be shut up day and night, week after week, with a half-mad beggar. The case had an interesting sequel. Namely, an American friend of mine was able to see Azaña who reacted with a rather more humane and modern idea of justice and obtained their release on bail. This infuriated the military officer in command of Majorca and when a court-martial acquitted the prisoners he cancelled the sentence on some vague grounds and ordered both a re-trial and that the Americans should return to gaol. So anyone who likes can figure just who ruled in Spain. The case ended with another acquittal and in good time for American public opinion was beginning to seethe with indignation.

The Republic sent down some of its best agrarian experts, gave the peasants of Casas Viejas lands and credits, and in February 1936 the small but thriving agricultural district of Casas Viejas voted almost to a man for the Popular Front.

Another incident of a similar kind caused a lesser but still considerable uproar. In Castilblanco, in Estremadura, Civil Guards arrested hungry peasants who had been gathering acorns to eat. But the acorn in Estremadura is a sacred crop; reserved for the pig. The peasants broke loose and attacked the Civil Guard, killing four. Mob passions ran wild and they more or less tore the bodies to pieces. Fortunately, an officer who kept his head arrived on the scene and prevented any massacre of the peasants. About sixty or seventy, including women, were arrested and kept in gaol for a year before receiving heavy sentences.

There was an air of gloom and depression in this sad year of 1933. The Republicans continued their line of action completely indifferent to the events going on about them. It was as if a ship's captain having charted his course across an ocean kept to it relentlessly despite ice-bergs, storms, fogs and other obstacles which counselled variation of the route.

Elections for the Tribunal of Constitutional Guarantees went against them and the Opposition Press played this up as a 'defeat of the Government in the country'. This Tribunal was appended to the Constitution at the last minute in order to make up for the lack of a Senate and thus to appease somewhat President Alcalá Zamora's fear that there were not sufficient brakes on any kind of executive action. It consisted of twenty-five members elected variously, some by the municipalities of the eleven regions of Spain, some by bodies such as universities, colleges of lawyers, and such entities. Finally two representatives and the president were elected by Parliament.

Such bodies as the lawyers' colleges and the university faculties were in great proportion Right-Wing in politics and it was to be expected that they would return anti-Government candidates. This might also be expected from many peasant regions of Spain. Thus Don Juan March, the noted financier, was returned by his political feud in the Balearic Isles where he still reigned supreme. Government supporters were in a decided minority in this body, which had power to declare laws to be unconstitutional and which could investigate any charges of corruption made against Ministers or the President. Here was a fine handle for feudalism, for any law to which it objected could be brought before the Tribunal for examination. It had not occurred to the Republicans (or their Socialist allies whom one is apt to forget) to think out beforehand what their chances were of having control of a body to which they proposed to give such full powers. Parliament elected a man of Azaña's Party, Don Alvaro de Albornoz, to the ticklish task of presiding over a body in which he and his supporters were in a minority.

The Bill dealing with the cessation of teaching by the religious orders was terminated in the early summer. And what a mess that was. Because although the orders as such were forbidden to teach there was nothing to prevent the members of the orders doing so in their private capacity; if they can be said to have a private capacity. The Republic did not take away their school buildings so the State found itself faced with the necessity of taking over the education of some 400,000 children and providing the necessary teachers and buildings. Most of these schools were secondary schools so that it meant that teachers of a high grade were needed and that the purchase of laboratory and other equipment for the schools would be most expensive. The only schools the Republic could seize were those of the Jesuit Order and even all these could not be taken for private owners came along and proved that the property belonged to them. The Jesuits were not easy people to beat. I remember that when the State in taking over the belongings of the Jesuit Order came to the very valuable site of the Iglesia de la Flor, an aristocratic church on the Gran Via in Madrid which was burned down in May 1931, an American citizen resident in New York promptly claimed it as belonging to him. He had the full legal documents of ownership and there was nothing to be done about it.

Nor was it much easier to deal with the other religious orders. They neatly fooled the Republic by forming commercial companies to operate schools as private enterprises. Gil Robles, Martinez de Velasco and other Right-Wing politicians figured prominently on the directorate of one of the biggest of these concerns which prepared to operate scores of establishments. A lay headmaster or headmistress was installed. The monks or nuns remained as teachers and appeared at their posts in civilian clothes. As these companies took over schools which were already equipped and as the monks and nuns were content with a mere pittance, they were even quite a good commercial investment, for the majority of the children educated in these establishments were middle-class and their parents could afford to pay fees. The Republic decreed that the Bill should come into force at the end of this year, that is to say of 1933.

The State, therefore, saw most of its prospective pupils snatched away before its eyes. In any case it could not have found the some 10,000 teachers and three or four thousand schools in the six months left before the measure came into force. Actually, the measure was never enforced for elections were held before the end of the year and those who came into power suspended application indefinitely.

The Catholic Church took good care to retain control of education of the middle class.

To add to the embarrassment of the Government, President Alcalá Zamora kept the measure in his possession for two weeks before signing. If he had kept it one day more this would, according to Spanish constitutional law, have been tantamount to refusing to sign the measure. He hesitated to do this, but as day by day went by and speculation grew in the Press as to whether or not he would sign, the position of Sr. Azaña and his Ministers was decidedly unpleasant.

Azaña reshuffled his Cabinet in June 1933, but he would have been wiser to have refused to continue in office. In September it was decided to hold municipal elections. Immediately the parliamentary opposition protested noisily in the

Press, of which it had now obtained almost complete control, and in the House. 'Was this a fit Government to hold elections?' asked Sr. Lerroux after relating the failures, which according to this veteran Republican, it had to its credit. President Alcalá Zamora called Sr. Azaña to the Palace and asked him whether he felt that he had 'sufficient authority' in the country to preside over municipal elections. It is worth noting the old concept of elections framed by the Government, which both Lerroux and Alcalá Zamora seemed to hold. Azaña promptly threw up the sponge and resigned.

President Alcalá Zamora decided to dissolve Parliament and named Lerroux's youthful, right-hand man, Don Diego Martinez Barrio, to be Prime Minister. The Left breathed a deep sigh of relief; Martinez Barrio had quite a good political reputation; a thing possessed by few Radicals.

If I was sure that on reaching this point all my readers had at hand their favourite brand of whisky or a box of succulent chocolates, according to their particular taste, I would explain in detail the Spanish electoral law. In the doubt and in the security that this chapter is just as likely to catch you in a crowded compartment on the 8.15 to town as cosily installed in an armchair by a big fire with refreshment at hand, I will skim over its details.

Briefly, the underlying idea of the new electoral law produced by the Republic is to guarantee a united and cohesive majority and a strong minority. To do this it abolished the individual polling area and made the province, or the large town, the electoral district. Each 50,000 residents have one representative in Parliament—that is to say, in the Chamber of Deputies, for there is no senate. Madrid, for instance, has seventeen members elected at one swoop. A small province may only have five or six representatives. Coalitions or large parties thus have a premium for few men could afford the expense of canvassing a whole province or even support the physical strain of trying to cover the large areas involved for the purposes of propaganda. The minority receives protection because each voter may only ballot for four out of every five representatives. Suppose, for instance, the Province of Granada is entitled to fifteen Members of Parliament. Then each man or woman of twenty-one years of age or over may vote for twelve candidates only. If you think this over you will see that this prevents a complete landslide. The party, or group of parties, which predominates will likely get twelve men returned because the supporters will all cast their votes for these twelve. The minority are sure of three seats.

Of course, this system would be an awful muddle if you had scores of candidates representing different parties, or views. But this situation has not so far arisen in Spain.

Another factor which is intended to encourage the formation of strong parties is that unless one candidate receives forty per cent of the total votes then the election is null and void and must be held again. In the second round this clause is not operative. So that if a town has 200,000 voters one of the candidates must have 80,000 votes if the election is to be sustained on the first polling.

On paper this all sounds complicated. Actually the system seems to have worked well enough in the three elections I have witnessed in Spain. Mind you I think almost any system works well provided that there is fair play and the electorate is interested; two factors which are not consistently present even in the best of democratic States. Definitely, however, the small electorates were disastrous in Spain where the peasant could never venture to oppose the will of the 'Amo', or landowner, of the district. This electoral system was one of the few positive blows struck at feudalism by the Republic. I do not know who it was who thought out this system for on general terms it was applied in the elections for the first Parliament of the Republic in June of 1931, two years before the measure embodying these ideas was passed by Parliament.

By October 1933 the situation had changed very greatly indeed. The Republican-Socialist coalition—the term 'Popular Front' had not then been coined—had collapsed. The Republicans thought that they would do better alone at elections and thus went blithely to their doom; that is to say all except Sr. Lerroux and his Radicals who had already wriggled out of the coalition in December 1931 and who were now in active flirtation with what one might call the Left-Wing of feudalism. For feudalism was to a certain extent divided. The more intelligent sector, namely, that composed of the Jesuits and other elements of the Church believed in the possibility of capturing the Republic, using Sr. Lerroux as a stepping stone. They had organised tremendously, had large sums of money at their disposal, and believed earnestly in their success. The stubborn, die-hard feudalists would have none of this. They would scrap the Republic lock, stock and barrel and stamp it out. But as they had not sufficient strength to do this at the moment they bided their time and presented their own candidates partially in co-operation with the more intelligent feudalists but always making very clear that for them there would be no nonsense about a democratic Republic. They would either put in a King or a 'strong man' to run their dream State; possibly both.

Even the workers were divided. The Anarchists trumpeted loudly throughout the land that all good proletarians should abstain from voting. They recalled Casas Viejas and denounced the Socialists as terrible reactionaries. The result of these tactics was to rob candidates of the Left of some hundreds of thousands of much-needed votes. It is surprising the things that are done in the name of progress.

The feature of election day was the procession of monks and nuns who went to the polling booths. Women now had the vote and special permission was given by the Bishops, or by Rome itself where this was necessary, for nuns to leave their houses and vote. In Madrid they were roundly hissed and booed but the streets were full of police and even machine-guns were mounted in order to prevent any rioting which might have influenced the nuns and induced them to stay in their cloisters. This was done all over the country.

When the results commenced to come home to roost the outstanding feature was the complete collapse of all Republicans, except of Sr. Lerroux and his friends. Of the Radical-Socialists led by Marcelino Domingo and Alvaro de Albornoz, only four or five survived out of sixty in the former Parliament. They brought this up to eleven in the second round. Azaña's Republican Action had a couple of survivors in the first round and managed in the second bout to pull this up to eight. That was all that was left of Azaña's minority of forty in the first Assembly of the Republic. Azaña himself, after attempting the impossible by seeking election in the ultra-feudal district of Leon, in Castile, was saved, thanks to Socialist charity. Sr. Prieto ordered Julian Zuzagagoitia, editor of Madrid's *El Socialista*, who had a safe seat in Bilbao, to retire in the second round and give up his place to Sr. Azaña and in this way the outstanding figure of the Republic was able to sit in its second Parliament.

The Left Republicans had not realised that unless they hitched their wagon to some force with money and organisation they had no possibility of success. It was very nice of them to have been extremely impartial and to have struggled with might and main to prevent the Republic from taking any turn towards extremism, but they were much mistaken when they thought that this was sufficient. They had no money, virtually no Press, and were very small parties whose members were of the poorer end of the middle class. They had attempted to copy the French Radical-Socialist type of politics without any of the conditions existing in Spain which existed in France. In Spain the small middle class must run in double harness either with the Socialists or with feudalism. And the majority of the middle class having succeeded in turning out Alfonso XIII now preferred to come to terms with the feudal powers.

It was a remarkable sight indeed to see the veteran anticlerical Don Alejandro Lerroux running in joint candidature with the Catholic groups. The collaboration between Lerroux and the forces of Gil Robles was tentative in the first round but in the second round it was open and sweeping. In some provinces, Cordoba for instance, the Catholics after fighting the first round with the Monarchists dropped them overboard and fought the second round in joint candidature with Lerroux's followers. The Monarchist daily *A.B.C.* wrote a stinging editorial denouncing the Catholics as traitors but the result of the elections was that Robles had about 115 followers in Parliament and Lerroux had ninety-five while a group sympathetic to both, the Agrarians, had another forty. The Socialists with between sixty and seventy were the strongest opposition minority. The Catalan middle class alone showed some fidelity to the Republic and mistrust of feudalism and the Esquerra, or Left Republican, party won a majority of the seats in Catalonia, thus sending some thirty Deputies to defend the Republic. Monarchists, divided between those supporting Alfonso or one of his sons, and the Traditionalists who still had faith in the other Bourbon line represented by an eighty-year-old Archduke resident in Vienna, totalled some sixty. In a house of 473 it was clear that the power lay in the hands of the middle-class-cum-feudal group represented by Robles, Lerroux and the Agrarians who could control a solid mass of 250 Deputies.

So the thin end of the wedge of feudalism was now thrust into the Republican log. I think it is worth while staying the story awhile in order to tell you something about Robles and the men around him who represented the advance guard of this attempt to reconquer control of the State for feudalism and about Lerroux who was the obliging hall porter willing and ready to open the doors of the Republic to its enemies.

CHAPTER XII

VATICAN POLICY IN SPAIN

A BOUT the year 1915 there was a small and struggling newspaper named *El Debate* published in Madrid. It was in the hands of a priest named Father Basilio Alvarez, a lusty red-faced cleric with a loud voice and a limp, who in addition to his priestly duties had a solicitor's practice and also was a battling political figure in Sr. Lerroux's Radical Party. Despite his militant activity in an anti-clerical party, he appeared to have no open conflict with his Bishop and attended his office and political meetings in priestly garb.

But *El Debate* made no money. One day in 1915 it was sold. The purchaser was a mild-voiced young man under thirty named Don Angel Herrera, a functionary in the legal department of the State and with a brother in the Jesuit Order, Father Enrique Herrera, S.J. The capital for the purchase was supplied by a group composed of various Bilbao financiers, the Bishop of Madrid and several people close to the Jesuits. The time was propitious for an enterprising daily. People read eagerly of the World War and Allies and Central Powers vied with each other to secure favourable presentation of their cause. *El Debate* took the German cause with fervour and furnished excellent information. The paper gained ground under the business managership of Don Francisco Herrera, another brother of the managing editor, and was one of Spain's most important dailies when the World War ended. *El Debate* was published with ecclesiastical sanction and was thus an authorised voice of the Church, although on some issues it did not necessarily see eye to eye with the hierarchy in Spain.

Under close guidance from the Vatican, *El Debate* had shown little sympathy for Don Alfonso in the last years of his reign. The King on his one visit to Rome annoyed the Pope considerably by referring to the fact that no Spanish-speaking cardinals were named for South America, a sore point with the Catholics of those lands but after all not precisely a matter for the King of Spain to raise during a formal visit. Cardinal Pacelli, the Vatican Secretary for Foreign Affairs, now Pope Pius XII, backed ably by the tall handsome Mgr. Tedeschini, who had been a follower of Dom Sturtzo, the Italian Catholic leader, and who was persona non grata to the Fascists, from his post as Papal Nuncio in Spain, appeared to think that the Republic was coming and I think that they had hopes that it could be kept in moderate channels, and thus extremism avoided. Hence to the amazement and displeasure of many Spanish Catholics there appeared shortly after the Jaca rising a series of editorials written by Don Angel Herrera, in which *El Debate* laid down the duty of Catholics to accept the established form of State even if they did not directly approve of it. This was a roundabout way of saying that Catholicism would not fight to save the throne of Don Alfonso. It was an extremely nasty blow for Don Alfonso who had always gone out of his way to emphasise that he was before anything a 'Catholic King'. This was precisely what the Vatican objected to; it would have preferred a more subtle way of doing things and, in my opinion, the Pope and most of those around him definitely feared that Don Alfonso's way of ruling would bring about a very violent and bloody revolution in Spain. Hence these editorials entitled: 'Submission to the Constituted Powers'.

It must be said that probably the majority of Spanish Catholics neither liked nor trusted this policy. Loudest in his opposition was the Primate of All Spain, Cardinal Pedro Segura, who indirectly, through the columns of the Traditionalist daily paper *El Siglo Futuro* (The Future Century; a more appropriate title would have been The Sixteenth Century), denounced *El Debate* as being 'a Liberal sheet' and on more than one occasion demanded that the Vatican cease to grant the 'Nihil Obstat', daily conceded to the paper by the religious censor.

Cardinal Segura was certainly the wrong man in the wrong place. He was a man who suffered, I think, from serious liver trouble. He had an unbearable temper and was a vivid ascetic and fanatic. Don Alfonso met him when he was bishop of a diocese in Estremadura and was so impressed by his violent sanctity that he promptly made him Archbishop of Burgos and within six years he was Archbishop of Toledo, Cardinal and Primate of Spain; a record in swift ascent from a lowly bishopric. To a brightly superficial person like Don Alfonso, Cardinal Segura doubtless appeared a shining light of Christian purity, but to have a rabid fanatic as Primate in these troubled times was to seek trouble with open arms. So much did the Vatican disapprove of him that it even accepted his resignation from the Primacy after he had been expelled by the Republic, an almost unheard of act of censure by the Church.

The Vatican policy was sound enough in its way. The Monarchist political parties had collapsed with the fall of the régime, indeed they had virtually reached exhaustion by 1917 thanks to many factors of which Don Alfonso's love of intrigue was not the least, and the Dictator puffed them aside as if they were feathers. So the middle class had only the Republican parties as practical instruments of Government. Now the Vatican did not believe that unadulterated feudalism could do anything for Spain, so it took the path, logical enough, of trying to ally part of the Old Spain with the middle class again under the Republic. It wished for a return to former conditions by which the middle class would rule under feudal tutelage and it was willing to do all it could to induce the feudalists to make concessions. To encourage the generals, grandees and even the majority of the clergy and the partisans of the Church to accept even the very name of Republic constituted no small effort.

But when the exact situation was analysed with care it could be seen that the eventual hopes of successful alliance between feudalism and the Republic were not bright. There was little hope of galvanising the corpse of Spain into life without drastic changes which must include the taking of the land from the owners and giving it to the peasants, the pruning of the Army, the drastic reduction in the size of church establishments and the removal of religion from politics. These were things that had to be done for a start; unless the peasants had the land they would never make the heartbreaking effort necessary to reform Spanish agriculture and make it a going concern. Therefore the Catholic political forces depending for their strength on the support of the clergy and the funds supplied by wealthy aristocrats were not likely to get far. As soon as the Catholics tried to discipline feudalism their own people would turn. Many of their own people were, as I have already pointed out, hostile from the start.

However, the Spanish Clericals and their Vatican friends thought the attempt worth while. *El Debate* shed few tears over the passing of Don Alfonso. Immediately, the forces associated with it were mobilised into National Action, a party which excluded the form of régime from its programme. This weakened it from the start, but the strength of feudalism was so great that if it had declared itself Republican it would have been cold-shouldered by many wealthy Monarchists whose subscriptions were needed. It had to adopt an ambiguous stand which left it equally open to impose Monarchy or Republic once control of the State was obtained. National Action gave way to Popular Action, because of a pettyfogging Decree of the Republic which forbade political parties to use the term 'national' in their titles, and finally merged into the CEDA (Confederación Espanola Derechas Autonomas; Spanish Right-Autonomist Confederation).

Herrera himself was well adapted to the role of Eminence Grise but his timid manner, weak physique and lack of talent as a speaker made him quite unfit to lead a youthful battling political party. Unlike most people with political talent he realised his deficiencies quite clearly and set himself to find a leader. He picked José Maria Gil Robles, born in 1899 in Salamanca and consequently thirty-two years old when the Republic came. It was a brilliant choice. Truculent, forceful, an excellent executive and with considerable judgment in men and politics, Gil Robles, backed by the shrewd brains of Herrera, was the most formidable opponent which the Republic could meet. I have often heard Robles described as arrogant and stupid but this is not my opinion. I think that his natural talents for leadership were such that if he had had a different upbringing in a different environment so that he had resulted a man of the Left he could have made himself the leading figure in Spain. But it is so often overlooked that it is the situation which makes the man. Robles had all the qualities necessary to lead masses; but he had no masses.

I first met Robles in 1933, although before this I had often listened to him in the House. Slightly over middle height, inclined to show a paunch, plump faced, pasty-white in colour with a pear-shaped head going bald on top, he was full of bounce and vigour. In the two years since Herrera gave him carte blanche, and one presumes very substantial funds, to organise a powerful Catholic political force, I do not think he had rested for one whole day. Out of the tiny handful who formed National Action in April 1931 had grown the vast political organisation, the CEDA, which included powerful groups such as Popular Action, Valencian Right Regionalists, Navarre Right Party, La Mancha Regional Party. He had literally scoured the land. As a youth in 1923 Robles had taken part in the attempt to form a Christian-Socialist Party in Spain in company with Herrera and Ossorio y Gallardo. This had failed because the Monarchists would have nothing to do with it but he had continued in contact with a group of young Catholics who formed a group known as 'Friends of El Debate', and which included many energetic people whom Robles was able to use now in his new organisations. The 'Friends of El Debate' originally devoted their efforts to aiding the paper financially and increasing its circulation and as the paper waxed more powerful and prosperous many became members of its staff.

Robles himself was a police court magistrate in Madrid and, in addition, had a private legal practice and wrote editorials for El Debate; it not being considered incompatible in Spain to be a magistrate of a city police court and at the same time a practising lawyer. However, he had left all this now.

I tried many times to obtain even an approximate idea of the numerical strength of the CEDA but was never able to do so. I was told by someone who was in a position to know that Popular Action, the component of the CEDA which dominated politically in Castile, Andalusia and some other parts, had in Madrid about 12,000 members; not very much in a city of 1,000,000 inhabitants. But nevertheless the power of the CEDA at the 1933 elections was enormous. Many even of the aristocrats who disliked Robles's ideas and would not tolerate any idea of even remote political connection with the Republic, gave generously both to Robles and to the Monarchists. Afterwards I heard of one aristocrat who gave half a million pesetas (£10,000) for election propaganda, others dived deeply into their pockets. Count Romanones and Don Juan March are reported to have contributed heavily to the CEDA.

El Debate, established in a fine new building with a printing press which had cost £20,000 and was the fastest of its kind in all Europe, was running *A.B.C.* neck and neck for prior position as Spain's most important daily. It had staff correspondents in Rome, Paris, Berlin. It bought the exclusive Associated Press of America service for all Spain thus giving its readers an excellent service of news from all over the world. An evening newspaper, *Ya*, printed on very good paper, sold enormously and was undoubtedly the best produced evening paper in Spain. In Badajoz and Granada, daily papers were produced. The Logos news agency, also run by *El Debate*, with a battery of teletype machines sent its home and foreign news to forty provincial dailies.

I thought over all this one day as I sat in Robles's ante-room waiting to get news of the campaign. Money was being spent on propaganda on a scale unknown in Spain. I was shown one poster alone which cost sixpence per copy and of which half a million were being printed; large printing shops worked night and day for weeks on work for the CEDA alone. The massive six-story building of *El Debate*, which was also headquarters of the CEDA, literally teemed with people. Youths at the door, wearing armlets with a sheaf of arrows as the insignia, had to turn away scores in order to make any kind of movement possible on the stairways. There were people of every social class. In the next room to me Robles was sitting with a commission of Monarchists led by an elderly dandy, Don Antonio Goicoechea. An ex-Minister of the Monarchy, he at first joined the ranks of National Action but when he found that it would not guarantee the restoration of the Monarchy he left and started the Spanish Renovation Party. He, along with the suave Count Rodezno, leader of the Traditionalists, was now sitting with Robles elaborating electoral co-operation. In some places they would go in coalition, in other parts one or the other would abstain. Meanwhile an endless crowd filed by me. Women predominated. There were noisy young men smartly dressed, with small and cultivated moustaches. Yet there seemed to be something missing.

Earlier in the evening I had waited outside the office of a Socialist organiser in the Casa del Pueblo, trade union headquarters, and there crowds likewise teemed through drab crowded passageways. Yet somehow the atmosphere there was alive. Here in the *El Debate* building one had the feeling that they were all phantoms; in the flush of triumphant action they all seemed somehow uneasy, insecure. However, for the present the phantoms were winning.

Now let us take a brief glance at the career of Robles's new political ally, Don Alejandro Lerroux García, the son of a veterinary surgeon and born in La Rambla, Cordoba, in 1868. About 1900 Lerroux was working in Madrid as a journalist. Several years later we find him in Barcelona founding his Radical Party, a Republican organisation which had as its aim the grouping into a solid body of opinion of the some hundreds of thousands of non-Catalans who had poured into Barcelona, mainly from the poverty-stricken areas of Murcia and of Aragon, in order to find work in the factories which had sprung up in the latter part of the nineteenth century.

For six or seven years Lerroux was one of the outstanding figures of Barcelona. He had a strong sense of the picturesque and had earned the title of 'Emperor of the Paralelo', for he had established his feud around the night life quarter situated on the Paralelo Avenue. He was to be seen parading the streets wearing 'alpargatas', or rope-soled canvas shoes as worn by labourers. His vogue was considerable. The immigrants from Murcia with the oppression of the political and landowning bosses and of a life of stark misery engraved deep in their souls, tended to forsake the Anarchist ranks in the hopes of finding in Lerroux a man who would represent their bitterness and desires. But success for him brought disillusionment for the workers. When he triumphed in the municipal elections in Barcelona defeating the Catalan middle-class parties organised always with a programme of autonomy for the Catalans, the administration of his followers became a classical example of corruption. They still talk in Barcelona of the building industry racket built up by the Radicals and of which the basis was that members of the municipality collected so much per ton on all cement used in Barcelona. It was a 'racket' on the best Chicago lines. Moreover it became an open secret that Lerroux, the Republican, was being helped by the Monarchist Governments because his triumphs over the Catalan Autonomists pleased Madrid. The masses drifted away from him and he himself had to escape from the country in 1907 after the famous elections Don Antonio Maura carried out in that year. They became famous because Maura announced that they should be 'brutally sincere', which meant that he applied through his Minister of Interior, Don Juan La Cierva, the full force of the electoral machine to secure the election of his own party members but he did not follow the accepted custom of providing for his political opponents. This was one of the rules of the parliamentary game in Spain; it was essential to see that the principal opposition figures were returned. Many politicians never forgave Maura for this lapse. Don Alfonso said dryly of these elections: 'They secured the return to Parliament of a great many friends of the Government and enemies of the régime.'

For instance in Catalonia, Maura instead of doing as his predecessors and helping Lerroux to secure election refrained from interference with the result that the Catalan Autonomists swept the board, including among their triumphant candidates a fiery young Army officer named Francisco Maciá, later to become President of the Generalitat. Lerroux lost his parliamentary seat and promptly found the Public Prosecutor camped on his trail on a charge of having published subversive articles in a political weekly. Actually he had not written the articles but merely signed them. It was quite frequent in Spain in those days for Deputies to accept responsibility for all kinds of things done by other people, using their parliamentary immunity as a shield. Now, as he was no longer able to plead that he was immune from prosecution for political propaganda labelled as subversive, he left hurriedly for France.

Several years later we find the Socialists and many Republicans disassociating themselves from Lerroux and his party in Parliament because the latter declined to adopt a strong attitude against the Government on issues which most Left-Wing people believed to be vital.

Throughout the length and breadth of France, posters were pasted in the first days after the outbreak of war in 1914 bearing the translation into French of declarations by Sr. Lerroux saying that Spain should join the Allies. When he returned to Spain he was pelted with stones at San Sebastian. After that we hear very little of Lerroux and his men until the ferment commenced which ended in the downfall of the Monarchy.

CHAPTER XIII

LERROUX IN CHARGE

THE 1933 elections left a strange state of affairs. The strongest minority in the new Parliament was not Republican. It was neither fish nor flesh. Here were over one hundred Deputies of the CEDA, well-drilled pupils who inevitably gave the reply: 'We accept the Republic. . . .' Nothing more; they would not say that they were Monarchists or Republicans. Their programme was equally vague. They propounded a 'corporate state', which would naturally be under their control, that was to say they openly promised to impose an authoritarian régime of Fascist or semi-Fascist character. The CEDA Party had a youth movement, Juventud Accion Popular, and generally known as the JAP, which went further and announced as one of its basic points of action that 'degenerate democracy' must be swept away. In private, leaders of the CEDA said that the question of Republic or Monarchy would be decided once they had obtained control of the State.

Now what was President Alcalá Zamora to do? According to parliamentary practice he must call Gil Robles to the Palace and offer him the post of Prime Minister as leader of the strongest minority in the House. Yet Sr. Gil Robles declined to say that he was a Republican and made no move to compromise, so the parliamentary crisis was settled without the strongest party in the House being consulted by the Head of the State or having any direct contact with him. Robles and his men were in the Republic, but not of it.

Behind the scenes there was much turmoil and the shapers of Catholic policy had to do some quick thinking. The Monarchists, despite being bitter and resentful at the change in partners made by the CEDA in the second round, when it excluded some Monarchists and incorporated Radicals in the lists of candidates, demanded that the Right-Wing of

Parliament unite forming an opposition block of over 200 Deputies who by obstruction could obtain their will on almost every issue. Some Monarchists went further and described the result as a sweeping victory which should be interpreted as a plebiscite and that it was now up to politicians and generals of the Right to seize control of the nation. The Catholics refused to be stampeded; they maintained through thick and thin that the only policy to be followed for the moment was to allow Lerroux and his Party to take office and to support them in the House with votes. Lerroux would be completely dependent on these votes for if he became difficult to handle and sought support from the Left then CEDA, Monarchists and other Rightists in the House could always unite to form a crushing opposition force. Finally, the Monarchists, against their judgment, accepted the Catholic thesis and Lerroux was informed that he could rely on the CEDA votes in Parliament if he were called upon to form a Government; which was what happened.

The Anarchists staged one of their pseudo-revolutions, which misfired except in a number of villages in Navarre and Aragon where the local revolutionaries worked up sufficient energy to seize the municipal records containing notes as to their debts or supposed misdeeds, burned the church and then sat around in puzzled fashion until the Civil Guard arrived to arrest them. This pretence at revolt would have offered a magnificent opportunity for a drastic repression of the whole Left if, as I have already related, the Catholics had not decided to pursue a pacific policy and to avoid any violence against the Republic for the time being.

Thus the Republic survived a critical moment, for with the Left in confusion and disunited and the Right pulsing with the exhilaration of victory, a *coup d'état* by the Army might have overthrown the régime. The Catholics believed that this must be done with caution and rather by modification than by a definite overthrow; they thought that there was plenty of time. The instinct of the Monarchists turned out in the end to be better justified for the Left thrown out into the wilderness commenced to knit together and to reorganise and the ideal moment for a violent coup passed.

CHAPTER XIV

SEMANA SANTA

I N the spring of 1934 Seville's Holy Week was held again for the first time since the Republic was proclaimed. It was my first Semana Santa.

Day and night the processions wound their way through the narrow streets to the 'Thump! Thump! Thump!' of the drums and the quavering of the 'saetas', or verses sung in Moorish, trembling cadence by professional and amateur singers. Each time some quaverer felt the spirit move him and burst into song, the bearers would set down the towering dais on the top of which swathed in silk and bright with gold and jewels would stand the doll-like figure of a Virgin.

The procession of the Virgin de la Macarena came down narrow winding streets where the bearers had to perform miracles. This procession is preceded by men dressed as Roman soldiers. I and a colleague drank Anisette at ten centimos a glass with several 'soldiers' who had slipped out. We ate, drank and were merry with the Sevillaños. It was coarse, uproarious, brutal; sheer animal spirits. It reminded me of Cologne Carnival and little of things religious.

The night wore on and somehow faces seemed grey and I was tired of everything. I stood before the Town Hall as the Macarena came along. Niña de la Puebla, one of the best of these singers of 'saetas', and who is plain to look on and blind but who drives the Andalusians almost to a frenzy with the plaintive anguished wail which contains the whole heart-break of Andalusia, quavered verse after verse. And almost next to me stood a lovely Andalusian girl with her father and mother and there was ecstasy in her face. Olive-skinned, dark-eyed with fine breasts showing even under her light overcoat, and with all that dignity that Spanish girls have in their bearing; I wondered what life would have for her in ten years time. Would she learn, as a few Spanish girls were learning, to care for her body; to go in for physical exercises and sports; shower-baths? Or would she sit at home and grow fat, like her mother, and let her brain rust, and have children in quick annual succession, becoming an incident in the life of her husband who would seek mental and physical recreation with others? I thought almost with awe of what a race the women of Spain would breed if they could learn to care for their bodies and their minds and obtain the proper food for both. Perhaps the day would come, but only after much bloodshed. There is no intelligent progress in this world except by war or revolution which break forcibly the iron frame of custom which we have neither the intelligence nor the good will to take off freely with mutual sacrifice.

Then all at once I was weary of the flowers and the candles and the incense, and the Anglo-Saxon blood in my veins revolted, and I wished I were in a cold, austere English Minster with a crowd of English around me singing: 'Oh God, Our Help in Ages Past . . .' Up on the dais in front of the Town Hall stood pudgy, little Rafael Salazar Alonso, Minister of the Interior and a great harrier of the peasants of Andalusia and Estremadura. His father too had been a peasant and Rafael had started life as a Republican and now he was a henchman of Lerroux and a great friend of the Clericals.

I wandered alone down the still streets of the old Barrio de Santa Cruz, with its barred windows, white walls, masses of flowers. Once it was a ghetto; how lovely a ghetto indeed. A little peace came back to my soul.

I went back to my hotel and found the crew of a German aeroplane drinking cognac in the lounge. And they didn't give a damn for Semana Santa but were full of how they had flown from Berlin to Seville in one day and had Berlin's morning newspapers in their pockets. Next morning they would be winging their way down Africa's coast in their great silver Heinkel and still another day and they would be in South America having crossed the Southern Atlantic. Here was the twentieth century bumping up against the sixteenth with a vengeance. I felt that the Heinkels and shower-baths and physical training would win. They must win.

CHAPTER XV

JUAN MARCH

I HAVE related how the middle class after assisting in the expulsion of Don Alfonso either by inhibition or direct collaboration, later turned in part back to a policy of friendship towards the feudal forces of Spain. Juan March, of Majorca, one of Spain's wealthiest men, and reputedly worth £6,000,000, was a typical example of this new hostility towards the Republic. It is true that this régime had gaoled him from June 1932 until October 1933, so there was some reason why he should have hard feelings.

Before, however, I go into the details of the career of this remarkable man I should like to raise one point. Namely, that those of my readers well acquainted with Spanish affairs may think that the brevity of the chapter hardly does credit to the interest of the subject. That is, in fact, my own opinion on the matter. But this is no easy subject to handle. In the ten years during which I spent most of my time in Spain I heard sufficient stories about Sr. March to fill a book, let alone a chapter. Naturally, I cannot set down statements which it is not possible to prove. If I were not in leafy Kent at the moment of writing but were in sunburned Castile, then I would go to the library of the Congreso de los Diputados (Parliament Building) and cull from the records for transcription here some extracts from the numerous debates around the person of Sr. March which have taken place in the last thirty years. Perhaps some day I will have the time and opportunity to write something further about Sr. March, although I think that most interesting of all would be an autobiography by Don Juan March himself. That would, I am sure, be a best-seller.

One June night in 1932, I listened from the Press gallery of Madrid's Parliament while an elderly, hook-nosed, pale-faced individual shrieked at the House with a rasping, metallic voice defending himself against the imputation that the monopoly concession to sell tobacco within the city limits of the Spanish towns in North Africa, Melilla, Ceuta and Tetuan, which are incrusted in, but do not form part, of the Spanish Protectorate in Morocco, was illegal. He received this concession from the Dictatorship in 1926. I watched him in the lobbies: a shambling creature of middle height, badly dressed, aged fifty-three—this was Don Juan March.

His hard scream found support in the House. Not much, it is true. So many good friends were absent. Where, for instance, was Don Alejandro Lerroux to-night? But there was a young man with booming voice to defend March and to denounce the Government of the Republic in scathing terms; the voice of Don José Maria Gil Robles. Somewhat of a step it is true from the high ideals of Christian-Socialism; from the fiery speeches to the Catholic young men of Spain calling on them to abolish 'degenerate democracy' and to build a pure and clean new Catholic Spain. The House did not accept the arguments of the youthful leader of Catholic Spain, it raised March's parliamentary immunity and next day he went to prison awaiting the pleasure of the Commission of Responsibilities—what a fine-sounding name for as slow and muddle-headed a committee as ever a Parliament named. In November, Parliament had as a purely platonic gesture declared with but one opposing vote, its 'moral incompatibility' with March and also with one of Lerroux's henchmen named Don Emiliano Iglesias. The action of the House was based on an allegation that an attempt had been made by March through Sr. Iglesias to obtain information concerning the investigation being made by the Commission of Responsibilities into Sr. March's activities. A Traditionalist Deputy and member of the Commission, Sr. Bau, reported to the Commission an attempt to suborn him. Sr. Iglesias claimed that Sr. Bau had misunderstood a conversation which took place between them. This Commission, I may point out, was formed early in the Republic to investigate all kinds of alleged political irregularities and not only those alleged against Sr. March. The Finance Minister of the Republic, Don José Garner, said sententiously: 'Either the Republic makes Sr. March submit to its power or he will sooner or later dominate the Republic.'

March was born in Santa Margarita (on the Island of Majorca) in 1879. His father sold cattle to Barcelona and garlic to Porto Rico, but all in a small way.

Juan March became partner in a tobacco factory in Oran, in Northern Africa, and he also became the prosperous owner of a fleet of ships in the Mediterranean.

The Treaty of Algeciras brought new grist to the March mills. Among other of the clauses which removed authority from the Sultan to the Spanish and French States was one establishing a tobacco monopoly in the respective zones and Don Juan March became the holder of this privilege in the Protectorate under Spanish control.

He had many interests on the Spanish mainland also.

He found peasants with money and landowners who were needy. He bought land at low prices and sold it to peasants on the instalment system. Electricity concerns, paper mills, foreign investments, newspapers, all attracted him. Typically, he had two newspapers in Madrid; *La Libertad,* Republican, and *Informaciones,* Monarchist. His tentacles spread. Virtually all the Spanish steamer routes between the mainland, the Balearics and Northern Africa came under a March monopoly and received so many pesetas subsidy for every mile steamed. When I went to Palma in 1931 I went on a steamer owned by March, as I entered Palma harbour I saw a petrol refinery, it belonged to March; I saw a fertiliser factory, it belonged to March; I changed my money at a March bank and even when I paid a visit to the local Casa del Pueblo, trade union headquarters, I was told that it 'was given us by Sr. March'. The World War had business opportunities for a man with a huge organisation spread out over the Mediterranean.

General Primo had used very harsh words about Sr. March in the days before he came to power. Sr. March did not waste a moment in disappearing across the frontier to France when General Primo clattered into office. The Dictator with much strong language had his home searched and spoke of prosecution and trial, but somehow it all faded to naught. General Primo's police found no incriminating papers in their search. Doubtless Sr. March's numerous friends put in a good word here and there for the hue and cry died down and Sr. March was back again in a few months.

The Republic attacked March on the ground of a new tobacco monopoly he acquired from the Dictator in 1926. Primo, having decided to reconcile himself with his former enemy, apparently was inclined to admire March's financial aptitude. He proposed to separate Melilla, Tetuan and Ceuta from the mainland monopoly and hand them over to March in order that the State should at least make some money from these places; for bootlegging from the surrounding zone was so effective that practically nothing was sold by the State in the three towns. The Republic had cancelled this privilege and was vainly trying to sell cigarettes in these towns while smugglers ran their merchandise into the towns accompanied by armed men ready for any affray. In July 1931, before the Republic cancelled the March privilege, tobacco to a value of 132.000 pesetas was sold in the shops authorised for such sale in Melilla. In April 1932, six months after he lost the monopoly, these shops sold tobacco worth 10,000 pesetas. In six months the sale of tobacco in the shops licensed for this purpose decreased by 800,000 pesetas as compared with the corresponding six months of the previous year when they were selling the tobacco supplied by March.

The Republic sent him to prison in June of 1932 and there he stayed until September 1933. The charge which the Commission of Responsibilities asked, and obtained, permission to imprison him on, was that in accepting the monopoly for the North Africa towns in 1926 he participated in an infraction of the Law of Accountancy, a measure destined to ensure that all monopolies and suchlike State sallies into business affairs be governed by certain rules of the Finance Ministry.

The prisoners who were in Madrid's Model Prison with March still speak with reverence of that period. He distributed cigars to all and sundry and the boredom of prison life was relieved by the spectacle of this super-prisoner worth £6,000,000 who had two large cells, one as a bedroom and the other as a sitting-room. Two prisoner-orderlies were in attendance on him throughout the day. His meals were hurried from the Palace Hotel in big steaming receptacles.

The Republic felt proud of itself. It had placed an alleged offender against the laws of the nation in gaol despite the fact that he was one of the wealthiest and most influential citizens of the land. So pleased was this young Republic that it forgot to do any more about the matter, and while Don Juan languished in a durance not too vile its Commission of Responsibilities talked and talked and talked; but produced no evidence nor any disposition to take the case to court. Manuel Cordero, a fine upstanding ex-baker and a figure of the Socialist Party, presided over this Commission. He may have been an excellent baker in his day and he had an imposing paunch and a fine crop of whiskers which seemed to indicate infallibly that if the Republic lasted long enough he would one day be made the Mayor of Madrid, but he and his fellow-commissioners were as impractical a group as ever got together. They had, of course, many difficulties to face. The best lawyers of the land watched over the March interests; his spies were everywhere.

The publicity which, at least within the prison walls, accompanied Don Juan March, had its inconveniences. An attempt at escape, for instance, was made much more difficult. So Don Juan's legal advisers found the ear of the Minister of Justice and told a sad tale of the prisoner's health and secured his transfer to a pavilion which he had all to himself in the garden of a reformatory near completion in Alcalá de Henares. Few prisoners can have enjoyed such tranquillity, for his gaoler did not disturb him before eleven o'clock in the morning. One morning in the early autumn of 1933, the gaoler knocked in vain. There was much fuss in Madrid. Don Diego Martinez Barrio, the Radical Premier who had replaced Sr. Azaña, and his Minister of Justice, a melancholy Republican from Asturias, Sr. Rico Avello, took immediate steps to have the frontiers watched. Half an hour before the order reached the frontier post of La Linea, Don Juan March crossed to Gibraltar. With him went the prison official who arranged the escape and his friend and medical counsellor, Dr. Ruiz, better known as a writer and radio commentator under the pseudonym 'El Tibi-Arrumi'. Many of those who listen in to the Franco radio stations will hear him singing the glories of Fascist Spain.

CHAPTER XVI

THE STORM-CLOUDS GATHER

F EW women in public life are so outspoken as Margot Asquith, but her daughter Elizabeth who married the Rumanian Prince Antoine Bibesco is less pungent in written and spoken word. Her interests are more purely literary and if you take the *New Statesman* you will have read book reviews by her. But she has the same warm ideas of hospitality as her mother and the open house in Bedford Square of the Asquith family had its counterpart in Madrid in 1934, where even stray newspapermen like myself were welcome and could meet a stream of interesting people.

Elizabeth Bibesco lived in Madrid from 1929 until the summer of 1934 during the period that her husband was Rumanian Minister to Spain. They occupied the beautiful home of Prince Alfonso of Orleans, who left Spain when the Republic came and who is a cousin of King Alfonso. They took over the staff with the house and it took all the tact of an Asquith to reconcile the servants who had grown old in royal service to seeing Don Manuel Azaña drop in to tea. They were quite as horrified as if the devil himself had descended on the house complete with horns and trident. Even after they had been installed for several years, the look on the butler's face when asked to send out for some Left-Wing newspaper, such as *Heraldo de Madrid* or *El Socialista*, was worth seeing.

I found little to say to Prince Antoine, a distinguished, polished figure. But his wife was very much wrapped up in Spanish politics. She had an admiration for Azaña, which I could not feel, and a liking for José Antonio Primo de Rivera, elder son of the dead general, which I fully shared.

In no year in the present century perhaps has Spain's middle class been so tormented by doubts and pulled in so many directions at once as in this year 1934 and nowhere could this state of affairs be studied better than in the shuttle-cock conversation at a Bibesco luncheon, almost invariably brightened by friendly or even sharp argument between representatives of this or that group.

It seemed impossible that such a small and relatively weak body as Spain's middle class should be split into so many tendencies. Azaña and his friends were out in the political wilderness because they thought that the Republic was being falsified and destroyed by Lerroux. The latter was anxious to instal a régime more or less exactly like the Monarchy, without a King. Gil Robles and the Catholics wanted to set up a kind of corporate state on Austrian lines; a sort of 'clerical Fascism'. Young Primo de Rivera had founded Falange Española, Spanish Phalanx, on orthodox Fascist lines with even a trace of anti-clericalism. Another small group founded the J.O.N.S. (National-Syndicalist Workers' Youth). Then there were the Alfonso supporters under Don Antonio Goicoechea and Traditionalists led by the tall, distinguished Count Rodezno who still supported a restoration of the Carlist-Bourbon line. The Army stood more or less aloof from all these movements and many officers felt that they alone could overturn the Republic when the time came.

Spain in 1934 would undoubtedly have seen a Fascist coup carried out if there had been any strong middle-class force capable of doing so. The reason that this was possible in 1936 and not in 1934 was that the international situation had changed. Neither Britain nor France liked the Spanish Republic but they were not prepared to interfere actively to overthrow it. Italy might have done so, but Il Duce was far too wise to launch on such an adventure alone and Germany in 1934 was still too preoccupied with internal affairs for Hitler to divert attention to the promising fields which Spain offered for international manœuvres.

The two men who set out to organise Fascist shock troops during the turbulent months of 1934 were two people whom I personally always found both charming and courteous, namely, Don Ramon Serrano Suñer, brother-in-law of General Francisco Franco, and José Antonio Primo de Rivera. Serrano Suñer, small, active, slender with a constant smile and a black moustache, organised the Catholic Youth known as the J.A.P.,

Juventud Accion Popular, with only relative success. Gil Robles, undoubtedly following closely the line of action apparently planned by Mgr. Tedeschini, the Nuncio, and Sr. Herrera and approved by Cardinal Pacelli, would not come out into the open on a Fascist programme. He wished to keep one foot in parliamentary Democracy and the other foot in anti-democratic Fascism with 'direct action'. Robles was perhaps the one man in Spain with the talents to have led a really strong Fascist movement. I have pointed out earlier his great personal capacity for leadership. But he and his advisers saw that there was no possibility of incorporating the Spanish masses in any such movement and they quite wisely relied mainly on parliamentary activity which yielded them considerable fruit.

I was tremendously interested in this Catholic effort because although I had disapproved so intensely of the use to which the Cross was being put in the Peninsula as to have ceased attending Mass regularly while in Spain, I nevertheless always had faint hopes of a revival of what I call 'real catholicism', that is to say of people really trying to imitate Christ and loving and helping the poor. But I had seen enough in Germany to make me a little doubtful. There I had many friends in the Windhorst Bund, the Catholic Youth movement in the days of the Republic there, and I had seen how little they counted for and how little they had to offer, intellectually or in action, to the German nation. I told them my opinion pretty sharply one day when they commenced to hustle a young woman Communist who was distributing leaflets as we came out of Church one spring morning in Elberfeld. This treatment of a girl all alone by a group of muscular young males, seemed to be typical of the impotence of the whole movement. Perhaps, however, the fact that she was pretty and courageous moved me to action rather than any deep thinking!

We all knew that Serrano Suñer had failed when the first big mass demonstration of the J.A.P., held amid a blinding rainstorm, proved to be a fiasco. Despite the large sums of money spent, the special trains organised, the tremendous publicity given, only about 20,000 arrived at the courtyard of the lovely old Escorial to hear a field Mass and listen to Gil

Robles. No Republican flag was in evidence. Many young men wore khaki breeches and leggings. The new salute was the right arm held horizontally across the chest, just as a British soldier salutes when holding a rifle in his left hand. It was a singularly colourless salute and as ill-adapted to crowded gatherings as the Anarchist salute of shaking hands with one-self above one's head in the best style of a boxer saluting his followers on entering the ring. There were too many peasants at El Escorial who told reporters quite cheerfully that they had been sent by the local 'political boss' with fare and expenses paid. The actual number of young men who might form part of 'shock troops' was not more than eight or ten thousand according to competent judges and if this was the best that Madrid with 1,000,000 inhabitants, not to mention the special trains from all over Spain, could do then there was no reason for the Republicans to lose any sleep.

José Antonio Primo de Rivera had even less success. The J.A.P. at least had plenty of money behind it and young Primo did not even have this. Tall, thirty, soft-voiced, courteous, José Antonio was one of the nicest people in Madrid. I often chatted with him in the lobbies of Parliament and several times I interviewed him in his offices just off the Castellana Avenue. I remember going to see him one day to borrow a review which contained the only fairly complete record of his father's life that exists. The Spaniards are really an amazing people. General Primo de Rivera governed Spain for over six years, yet no single book was published with details of who he was or of his career. At least that was what Don José Antonio said and I myself in my long researches in the Ateneo Library never found anything.

On this day in question he led me through an ante-chamber in which a dozen elegant young men were lounging and arguing politics in loud voices and as he shut the door he nodded behind him and said: 'You see, Mr. Buckley, there are a group of typical Spaniards talking, talking eternally. It is very difficult indeed to organise our race for constructive work.'

José Antonio Primo de Rivera, in addition to being Member of Parliament, had what was, I believe, quite a prosperous legal business. I never met his two brothers, one of whom, Fernando, was in the Army and the other, Miguel, was, I think, farming at Jerez de la Frontera. José Antonio was so tall and elegant that he could have had an enormous success in feminine society, but he took life very seriously and I think was so fond of literature, and especially of poetry, that the average society señorita had not a great deal of attraction for him. He spoke English with a very charming accent.

He looked very unreal in his role of a Fascist leader. For some months I happened to vary my journalistic work by taking temporary charge of the Commercial Counsellor's office of H.M. Embassy during the dual absence of the Counsellor and the chief clerk, and this office was just across the street from that of Primo. From my window, as I prepared to leave at lunch time, I would see Primo stride out and take the wheel of his Chevrolet limousine. He would be preceded by his 'bodyguard', which was composed of half a dozen weedy looking toughs. They all had their hands ostentatiously in jacket pockets in the best Hollywood detective tradition, and after glowering ferociously up and down a street which was almost invariably empty at this hour they would pile, still glowering, into an open Ford car and race noisily down the street behind the 'Jefe' (Chief). José Antonio lived in a nice villa out at Chamartin. He was unmarried.

I only remember one attempt to hold manœuvres by Primo's forces and this was some time during 1934 when three or four hundred men under him drove out in trucks and cars to a place called Cuatro Vientos and commenced to carry out military exercises. The Civil Guard came to see what it was all about and arrested everybody. He was at once released when he explained that he was a Member of Parliament and finally everybody was set free without there being any court case. I do not think that his personal followers in Madrid could ever have exceeded 1,000; that is to say of people actively engaged in the Falange; he had a great many sympathisers. But José Antonio's ideas could not get him the financial support the movement had to have to be a success. He only waxed really enthusiastic and became convincing when he denounced in fervent tones the sad lot of Spain's peasants. I once heard him make a brilliant speech in Parliament in which he scathingly attacked the landowners. He quoted cases of women working ten hours a day in Andalusia under a scorching sun for one peseta. Spain, he said, must be completely reformed. Many large areas should be evacuated completely and others given increased fertility by irrigation and re-afforestation. The very young and very elegant Marquess de Eliseda who was reported one of the chief financial supporters of Falange, left the movement ostentatiously because of what he described as its 'anti-clerical tendencies'.

Another day in Parliament after the podgy Socialist leader, Indalecio Prieto, had rendered a tribute to certain aspects of General Primo's work while Dictator, José Antonio left his seat and walked across to shake hands with Prieto. That was very nice, but Fascist leaders are not built that way. Gil Robles and Calvo Sotelo had all the Fascist tricks; they would sit glaring at their political opponents always ready to jump up and launch into a furious and bellicose tirade against Bolshevism in general. Out in the lobbies they would on the other hand be much more jovial and cheerful with their opponents of a minute ago than would Primo.

It would, of course, be a mistake to let oneself be led away too much by the personal charm of José Antonio and to overlook the fact that apart from the handful of young people of his own class who supported him, his organisation also had a number of paid followers who were not choice in their methods. Not to put too fine a point on it, they were simply hired gunmen. If in theory they were only supposed to protect party headquarters and to accompany José Antonio and act as guards at meetings and rallies, in actual practice they were apt to get mixed up in strike-breaking and such-like activities and to shoot with little provocation. I happened to know one of them, the brother of the concierge of the flats I lived in. He was a mechanic who had been out of work for two years and he had been engaged by Falange and given a regular salary and a gun. The shooting was not always one-sided. In April of 1934 a bomb was thrown at Primo's car and several shots fired as he left the Model Prison where he had been giving evidence against several Anarchists accused of shooting a news vendor who sold *A.B.C.* during a strike of newspaper workers. He was not hurt.

Primo was in contact with other Fascist movements and about this time he went to Rome where he was received by Il Duce. A report in the Spanish Press had it that Mussolini told him that he did not see any immediate hope for Fascism in Spain and that he thought Largo Caballero the most outstanding leader of masses. Primo also went to Berlin and was received by Hitler. But in 1934 the time was not ripe and in any case José Antonio's attitude of wishing to unseat rural feudalism and to put the Church in its place robbed him of all hope of the interior financial help he must have had to have built up a militant organisation of any importance.

It is not easy now in retrospect, after having passed through so much uncertainty both nationally and internationally in the last few years, to do justice to the nervous tension in which Madrid lived during 1934. There were three general strikes, newspaper strikes, taxi strikes, with the streets strewn with tacks. In my home we had large stocks of beans to eat on strike days when the shops were closed. The underground struggle for possession of the Republic was unceasing.

There were new splits in the middle-class ranks. Don Diego Martinez Barrio, tall, plump, energetic, a former linotype operator who had become owner of a printing plant and pushed his way up to an important position in Republican politics, seceded from Lerroux's Party taking with him two Cabinet Ministers and about twenty Deputies. I was in Seville to hear him make his secession speech, for Don Diego was a native of Andalusia. 'Manos limpias . . . las mias!' (My hands at least are clean!), he told the great crowd, holding forth the hands in question with a delightful gesture. Barrio, aged about forty, was the best man in the Radical Party, both from the point of view of morality and that of capacity, so the loss to Don Alejandro Lerroux was considerable.

My life was hectic indeed because I was doing the work of several newspaper colleagues who were away during the summer months and also deputising, as I noted earlier, for Mr. A. A. Adams, Commercial Counsellor to the British Embassy in Madrid, which meant that I signed papers prepared for me efficiently by a staff which knew the work and dictated an occasional report in my 'prentice fashion. But I was very interested, and in no small measure dismayed, to have an inside glimpse of how the commercial side of our diplomatic service functions. Its members are mostly university men, often with literary honours, who take the consular examination with a few variations. They then do one or two years' work in the Department for Overseas Trade and after that go abroad to this or that diplomatic mission and begin to work their way up the scale. Now compare this with my *Herr Kollegue*, the German Commercial Attaché in Madrid, Herr Enge, whom I knew quite well as I had met him ski-ing in the Sierra Guadarrama. He was ski-ing while I was generally engaged in active ju-jitsu encounters with my skis— and who for fifteen years had managed a German Bank in Barcelona before his appointment as Commercial Attaché.

It seems to me that diplomats in the commercial branch should have a commercial training, both university and in practical business. In reality, and this becomes more so every day as trade becomes totalised and mass barter replaces private deals, they are the salesmen of the nation. No matter how clever they are I do not see how they can gain sufficient commercial experience by a year in the Department of Overseas Trade. Maybe I am wrong. Maybe this is just the new broom wanting to sweep well. But if any Member of Parliament should happen to read this paragraph and wants to give the British Empire a helping hand then he could do no better than to delve into this question and see if he could not get some bright young Bachelors of Science in Commerce into the service and perhaps eventually have the whole method of entry into the service changed. Maybe my ignorance lets me down, but for the life of me I cannot see why the commercial men should take the consular examination at all for one job has virtually nothing to do with the other.

All this is getting us a long way from the dour year of 1934 with events drifting fast towards the explosion of October in Asturias, but more than one reader will probably have noticed by now that my inability to keep to the point is chronic.

One hot August afternoon I interviewed Francisco Largo

Caballero who as president of the General Union of Workers (U.G.T.) and secretary of the Socialist Party, was the man who mattered at the moment. Stubby, aggressive but restrained in his manner, he was quite willing to make sensational statements. He told me: 'Believe me, we shall fight if the President of the Republic admits members of Gil Robles's Clerical Party into the Cabinet. That would be the thin edge of Fascism. They are not Republicans. They themselves refuse to call themselves Republicans. Why then should they be admitted to the Government of the Republic?'

The Socialist Press said the same thing as openly as it could. Lerroux was not censoring the Press. He had a new scheme. Every newspaper had to send the first copy off the machines at once to the Home Office, or the Civil Governor's office if in the Provinces. If there was anything to which the Government objected in the paper, a motor-cyclist at once raced down to the printing plant and served an order expropriating the whole issue of the paper. Between the beginning of January and the end of August of 1934 over ninety numbers of *El Socialista* were seized in this way.

The argument of the Socialists was, of course, open to the objection that the Clericals had been elected and were, therefore, entitled to a place in the Government. Still, I imagine that supposing in general elections in Britain a party had over 100 members elected which refused to accept the Monarchist régime, which at meetings and parades ostentatiously avoided ever showing a Union Jack or permitting the playing of the National Anthem, there would be some little outcry here against any of these elected members taking cabinet office without their exact status being explained.

I could not, however, refrain from asking Largo Caballero exactly what they would do to fight the tremendous forces at the disposal of the Lerroux Cabinet which had 120,000 soldiers, including the tough Tercio, Foreign Legion, and Moors, in addition to 30,000 hard-boiled Civil Guards, 15,000 Shock Police—recently supplied with large numbers of machine-guns and armoured cars—10,000 ordinary police and about 12,000 Carabineros or armed customs' police. 'Ah,' he replied, 'the masses will go into the streets and there is nothing that can withstand the mass of the people when they are aroused and resolved to defend their rights.' All that sounded high-flown to me. In the days of the French Revolution maybe that kind of thing was possible, but to-day when angry women and men who protest can be mowed down by the score by one single policeman safely installed behind a machine-gun in the turret of an armoured car, it is just a shade ironical to speak of 'the force of the masses'.

Actually, of course, Caballero knew this just as well as I did. What he was anxious to do, and rightly so, was to convince President Alcalá Zamora that to admit the Clericals to power would mean violence and bloodshed. When a revolutionary leader shouts to the four winds: 'Look out! I and the people behind me are about to break out into bloody revolt!' then it is fairly logical to deduce that the last thing he wants to do is to stage a revolution which would only stand at least some faint chance if it were unexpected and a surprise stroke.

There was nothing revolutionary about Largo Caballero despite the fact that he was being described in the world Press as 'The Lenin of Spain'. Caballero was just a good, stolid trade union leader who topped with a bowler hat, pipe in mouth, black suit and black lace-up boots, fitted exactly into the picture at a trade union congress of the Fédération Syndicale Internationale. If you had seen him there you would indeed have been hard put to it to say if he represented British railwaymen, or Swedish miners, or French steelworkers.

Caballero in 1934 was aged sixty-five. He began life as a stucco worker, alternating this with road-building in winter. He was born in Madrid in 1869, had no schooling and learned to read and write when in the twenties. He became interested in trade union work and began as secretary of his local section and slowly climbed the ladder until, I think when he was about forty, he finally became a whole-time union organiser, municipal councillor and in 1918 a Member of Parliament. This latter election brought him back from a penal settlement in Africa where he was serving a life sentence as one of the signatories of the general strike manifesto of 1917. From 1918 onwards he became the leader of the trade union movement in Spain and one of the chief figures of Spanish Socialism.

Behind Caballero was an Eminence Grise—the squat Luis Araquistain, publicist, publisher, fervent propagandist for the cause of Britain and the Allies in general in Spain during the World War, and also a very moderate person with as great a dislike of Bolshevism as Caballero. It used to amuse me to hear diplomats and others speaking in hushed tones in Madrid of the terrible 'red revolution' threatened by Caballero and Araquistain. They were as revolutionary as Sir Walter Citrine or 'Jimmy' Thomas. But they argued, I think quite rightly, that the Spanish Right-Wing was seeking positions for a 'come-back' and looked upon the Clerical entry into the Cabinet as a critical test. They had, therefore, to make a fight even if it were a hopeless one because not to do so meant leaving it until too late, just as the Austrian workers had done. Spain had, of course, been much moved by the pathetic dying kick of the Austrian Socialists before they were finally squashed by Herr Dollfuss early in 1934 and the Spanish Socialists felt that the lesson for them was to fight before it was altogether too late.

Then one afternoon in July I was sitting having coffee with the chief reporter of *El Debate*, the clerical organ, when one of his assistants brought the news that Dollfuss had been murdered by the Nazis, so the Spanish Catholics had something to think about also.

Actually there was a good deal in common between Socialist and Catholic interests in Spain now as the summer of 1934 wore on and the fierce Nazi efforts to smash the Catholic corporative movement in Austria became evident. Gil Robles married a society woman in June and chose this time to go honeymooning for six weeks. His honeymoon took him to Germany and from there on a German cruise in northern waters and it looked, of course, as if he was in contact with interesting people while in the Reich. I think he was, but, as I have said before, Germany was still not turning full attention to Spain and Robles was much influenced by Rome. It was Cardinal Pacelli, Secretary of State, who was reputed to sway Spanish clerical policy. Now I do not think that the clever Pacelli wanted to smash the Spanish Republic, he just wanted to get it under clerical control in order to avoid the Socialists obtaining the upper hand, but I think that, especially after the death of Dollfuss, he was just as much opposed to the extreme Spanish Right-Wing getting back into the saddle.

When the Socialists said that the Clericals were the thin end of the Spanish wedge this was a partial truth. If it had been possible Robles would probably not have forced the issue and brought down Lerroux's substitute, Sr. Samper, who had taken the premiership because it was thought that if Lerroux stood down for a while this would have a pacifying effect on the Left. But Pacelli, Tedeschini and Herrera had to reckon with the mass of Right-Wing opinion in Spain. The Clericals had obtained a certain amount of support, and a great deal of money, frankly because the people who gave it thought that the Robles policy of edging into the Republic and even into the Government was just a very clever ruse and that once inside he would throw off the mask and kick out the Republicans and set up a Dictatorship. They did not approve, at least the majority of the Right-Wing aristocrats and wealthy people who were supporting the CEDA so lavishly would not have done so, of merely obtaining office in order to consolidate a rather Right-Wing, Conservative Republic with relative freedom for the Left. As the summer of 1934 wore on the Radicals bungled things so much and were so slow in putting the clock back to complete reaction that Calvo Sotelo, amnestied by Lerroux in February and now back from exile full of fire, was speaking openly against Robles and accusing him of having betrayed the Conservative cause. Robles had no alternative but to go ahead and demand Cabinet posts and when he returned from honeymooning at the end of August he commenced to prepare the ground for this.

The Home Minister was that Rafael Salazar Alonso about whom I wrote in connection with the Seville Semana Santa. He spent July writing a book in which he glorified suicide as the escape for the man who had not achieved success. He was a strange mass of complexes and queer company for the Catholics. In addition to writing this book he had to deal with a timid effort of the Socialists to obtain some arms. They attempted to obtain some 300,000 rounds of rifle ammunition, 400 rifles and 24 machine-guns along with 750 tear-gas bombs.

These arms had apparently been earmarked for the use of Portuguese revolutionaries who staged an abortive attempt against Dictator Salazar in 1932, but they had never come into possession of the Portuguese and had been stowed away in Seville. Now by a little juggling with signatures they were taken out of the store-place and loaded aboard a steamer named the *Turquesa* in Cadiz and from there proceeded to near Gijon (Asturias). There about half the cargo was landed before the local Civil Guard swooped down, seizing part. The steamer went off to Bordeaux. A very wealthy Bilbao industrialist, Don Horacio Echevarria, was put in gaol in this connection, apparently he was thought to have had something to do with chartering the ship.

The Basques as a whole, and Sr. Echevarria was a stalwart Basque Nationalist, were up in arms against the Lerroux Cabinet. In an effort to raise more money, Lerroux brought out a measure putting the Basque region on an equal footing in taxation matters to other parts of Spain. Now they had hitherto enjoyed some autonomy in this question. The local Basque functionaries collected taxes and then paid a lump sum to Madrid. The Basques protested violently. They decided to hold municipal elections, as a means of ventilating their grievances. The elections were overdue, but the Lerroux Cabinet forbade them. Thereupon the elections were held despite Government efforts to suppress them, and refusal to recognise the councillors, nearly all Basque Nationalists, who were returned. This happened in August 1934.

The Catalans too were up in arms. They had, under the local autonomy they enjoyed, drawn up an Agricultural Bill which reformed local conditions and gave possibility to the 'Rabassaires' (share-croppers, or people who give the landlord part of the crop instead of money, a favourite form of land tenancy in Catalonia), to obtain possession of their land by small payments over a series of years. The Catalan land-owning classes objected vehemently. Madrid mixed in the local quarrel and annulled the law. Then Don Luis Companys, who was Prime Minister, President of Catalonia and Representative of the Central Government in Catalonia, all at once, got into a further quarrel with Madrid by dismissing some magistrates who made trouble about a lawyer who insisted on addressing a Court in the Catalan language.

But behind both Catalan and Basque agitation was the fear that Lerroux was opening the door to let in once again feudal Spain and take Spain back to intolerant Dictatorship in which local autonomies would be ruthlessly suppressed. Indeed it was this fear that kept the whole of Spain on edge. Lerroux and his Ministers to justify their policy gave out the most astounding statements. Salazar Alonso told a foreign journalist gloomily: 'There are now 1,000,000 Socialists ready with arms to establish Communism at the first opportunity.' The Socialists had, with difficulty, obtained only a few of the 400 rifles aboard the *Turquesa*. They also had a few hundred more rifles and several dozen light machine-guns, smuggled from Germany. The police and soldiers stationed in any small provincial town had more effective arms among them than the Socialists in all Spain. They had, of course, a fair number of revolvers because Spain manufactures large quantities of very good small arms and most Spanish young men think that it is the thing to do to carry a small pistol, or revolver. But a revolver is not a very convincing answer to a rifle.

The Socialists also had several tons of dynamite and there was some kind of plan to mine I think it was the Home Ministry with the idea of threatening to blow it up if the Minister did not surrender. It seemed a pretty crazy scheme altogether. The first sign I got that things were coming to a head was when on the day after a shooting affray on the outskirts of the town I was at the cinema with Luis Quintanilla, a fine rugged artist and a keen taster of life, and I asked him if he had heard anything about it. I knew that he was a Socialist. To my surprise he said: 'Yes, I was there. Republican sympathisers in the police force tipped us off that they had received orders to raid the home of Sr. Moron, a Socialist Deputy, and we had therefore to take away the dynamite hidden there. I drove half a ton through the centre of Madrid in a taxi and had to spend half an hour in the main street waiting for someone to come with instructions as to what I should do with it. The police came on the scene just as we were hiding it out in the grounds of the University City.' This was the first time I had ever come into contact with revolution as such. I was very upset because Quintanilla, Araquistain, Dr. Negrin and other intelligent and cultured people I knew in Madrid were not in any way extremists. If they were preparing to fight, the situation was indeed tragic. I remember going home and writing a passionate dispatch saying that Spain was heading towards bloodshed and destruction and that someone ought to mediate to prevent a disaster. But, of course, no one did. The world was on holiday. Only in Germany and Italy there was no holiday respite, there the changing of Europe's face was being plotted and planned. And Spain, a pawn in the great schemes being prepared, shuddered in anguish.

I remember as well as if it were yesterday the film Quintanilla and I saw on that afternoon when I first realised how close death and the other accompaniments to revolution stood around the corner. The picture was *Ecstasy* with Hedy Lamarr playing the lead; a Czech film with a bitter-sweet melancholy which seemed to foretell tragedy even if at that time Czechoslovakia was not directly involved in any trouble. *Ecstasy* had been banned in several countries and the Catholic Press in Spain had protested vehemently against the showing. In this film Hedy Lamarr played the part of a girl of good family who was married to an impotent and elderly man. This unhappy wedding, however, awakened sleeping emotions and while her elderly husband in desperation committed suicide, she captured the affections of the stalwart and finely-built young foreman of a gang building a railway near her home. Having gratified, however, the emotions awakened, she had no mind to marry a foreman ganger and slipped off to lead her own life with the baby which was born in due course. The moral of the film, as I saw it at any rate, was that youth can on occasion feel the necessity for physical intercourse without that necessarily being tied up with any lasting sentimental feeling. The idea was put across by much galloping of stallions across grassy spaces and on the whole the film seemed to de-bunk to a certain extent the over-lush and sickly sentimentality which has grown too thick in our Anglo-Saxon civilisation. The main objection to the film was based on a scene in the small hut where the virile ganger lived and which showed the face and one hand of Hedy during the minutes when her aroused emotions were appeased. The scene was unreal from every point of view, added nothing to the genuine artistic value of the film and was obviously rather dangerously exciting for young people to witness. Madrid's smartest cinema, El Callao, was packed to suffocation, despite Catholic disapproval, and a young woman seated near me went into shrieks of hysterical laughter during the moment when the scene so much debated was being shown.

Quintanilla and myself walked over to Los Italianos Bar after the show, but I excused myself from going in when I saw two obvious detectives standing on the pavement watching the entrance.

CHAPTER XVII

TO SAVE THE REPUBLIC

THIS revolution of 1934 certainly ran according to time-table. On October 1, Parliament opened and Gil Robles got up without much enthusiasm and turned out the Cabinet on a no-confidence issue. Late at night on October 3, a new Government was formed with three Clericals included as Cabinet Ministers. Robles himself stayed out. This was to be the thinnest part of the thin end of the feudal wedge. It was made known that President Alcalá Zamora had insisted that the Clericals should not hold 'key positions' in the Cabinet; a fine distinction which most British people would not appreciate. To argue that a man is sufficiently loyal to be Minister of Justice but not sufficiently trustworthy to hold the War Ministry seems to us to be contradictory and unsatisfactory, but to the tortuous legal mind of President Alcalá Zamora, who with clumsy, unaccustomed feet was trying to walk the tight-rope without falling either on the side of real democracy or into the feudal pit on the other side, this was, apparently, a satisfactory solution.

The Clericals had presented their most moderate figures and notably Sr. Jimenez Fernandez, the new Minister of Agriculture. Sr. Jimenez Fernandez, professor of Seville University, was the outstanding figure of the Christian-Socialist element among the Clericals. He was really a first-rate man, with the interests of the working class at heart and a genuine democrat. If he were a typical figure of the Spanish Right, then Spain would be the most peaceful country in Europe and I should be writing a book about Greece or Mexico.

The Big Bad Wolf of Spanish feudalism tried, in fact, to look its most grandmotherly.

The Socialists merely said that they had for months in their newspapers, on platforms, in interviews, promised that they would not accept a Government which contained Ministers whose party had not pledged its loyalty to the Republic, and they would, therefore, call a general strike in the whole of Spain. They announced this for midnight of the night October 4-5, thus giving Prime Minister Lerroux a chance to call a truce or make a peace offer—and also twenty-four hours in which to arrest all agitators and take all precautions against infidelity in Army or police circles.

The Republicans issued a manifesto signed by all the parties except, of course, Sr. Lerroux's Radicals, in which they announced that they could not recognize as legal a Government which included members of a non-Republican party. Already Miguel Maura and Martinez Barrio, two Republicans who certainly could not be styled as extremist, had been to see President Alcalá Zamora and to plead with him not to do this thing. After all, he could always have held elections and asked the Clericals to state their position to the country. Or he could simply have called Gil Robles to the Palace and asked him straight out for a pledge that his party would always respect and defend the Republic.

It was not my affair, but the stupidity and wickedness of the whole conflict filled me with fury.

Over a whisky in Chicote's Bar where I and an Australian journalist who was on a short visit to Spain, Elliot I think his name was, sat waiting for the storm to break, I said bitterly that I wished that I had been born a donkey. The reply was, I know, obvious. But we were not in frivolous mood that night. I pointed out that a donkey works hard, goes out to grass, sleeps, but never sets out with the fixed idea of killing fellow donkeys. I concluded that the donkey had reached a higher stage of civilisation than had mankind. Someone else told a story which he attributed to the Prince of Wales, now the Duke of Windsor. When asked by a gushing young thing what he thought of European civilisation, His Highness was said to have replied: 'European civilisation? I think the idea is excellent and that it should be tried out at once.'

Chicote's Bar was strangely silent that night. The officers and smart-young-men-about-town who for three years had been promising to show us Socialists and Republicans chopped into mincemeat, were nowhere to be seen. A sinister sign that.

A young supporter of Primo de Rivera looked in for a moment. 'We have 1,500 armed men on the streets and many thousands ready to act as strike-breakers,' he said. Little French Susie and Greta, a big blonde German girl, habitués of the bar, sat glumly and nervously in a corner. I called up the Liberal *El Sol*. 'Trouble in Barcelona,' I was told briefly and dourly. I called up *El Debate*. 'The trouble will start any minute in Madrid. Barcelona is already proclaiming a separate Republic,' they said.

I got into an argument with an American employee of the Telephone Company. He hoped that Lerroux would 'sock the Reds good and hard and stop all this revolution nonsense once and for all.' I asked him if he knew that there were workers in Madrid, married men with families earning five pesetas daily which then was half a crown or, in American money sixty cents. The father of the maid of a friend of mine earned that for eight hours' work in the open air in all weathers as shunter in the Atocha goods station in Madrid and the maid, aged sixteen, was the eldest of six. They used to think it quite a treat to get meat once a week. Could people like that be blamed for wanting changed conditions? Well, said the American, life was cheaper, much cheaper, in Spain. 'I thought,' said I maliciously, 'that you employees got substantially extra money when working in Spain as compared with pay in your mother company in the United States.' Well, that was so. But that was different. I admitted that my argument was childish, but still life wasn't so cheap in Spain that a man could keep six children on five pesetas. He guessed maybe there was something to that. We drank up and left.

We went over to the Ivory Bar which has big windows that give you a fine view up and down the Calle Alcalá. What was quite important too there was the excellent iced Lager which went down wonderfully accompanied by hot, toasted sandwiches filled with Dutch cheese. Over there we found Dr. Negrin, del Vayo and Araquistain sitting at a table reading the evening papers and looking pretty down in the mouth. 'Is the strike fixed for midnight?' I asked Araquistain more for the sake of saying something than anything else, for it was common knowledge that strike orders had been sent out. He nodded gloomily. 'Why on earth cannot something be done to stop this madness?' I asked. He shrugged his shoulders and said: 'You should ask your friends the Clericals that!' For he knew that I was a Catholic and had good contacts with the Clerical paper, *El Debate*. And what would be the use of my saying that the Clericals didn't want the scrap either but were forced into it by the extreme Right, which was true. I did not feel proud of catholicism that night.

I wandered alone around the town until a shot rang out near the Puerta del Sol. Shutters began to go down with a bang. Tramwaymen fixed 'Depot Only' signs on their cars. The taxi drivers drove off the ranks. Cinemas emptied and people rushed for the Underground stations. Truck-loads of Shock Police, each man superbly armed with rifle, bayonet and sub-machine-gun, with large quantities of ammunition, raced through the now deserted streets with sirens screaming.

I picked up the telephone when I got home and commenced to dictate a story to the Paris office of my paper. I would have liked to begin: 'Another crime was written in the debit account of humanity to-night. . . .' But I remembered that I was a reporter and not a philosopher and led off: 'A revolutionary general strike began to-night in all Spain as a protest against the Clerical-Radical Cabinet. . . .'

After that for the next three weeks it was a question of hardly eating or sleeping with the telephone bell jingling day and night.

It is a horrible business to have to compress all the events of October 1934 into one brief chapter. They merit a whole and lengthy book. So far as I know, not even in Spanish has any complete record of the revolt been put down and this is a pity because the events had great historical importance both nationally and internationally. Nationally, we saw how a weak, unintelligent and corrupt section of the Republican middle class was turning against the rest of this class and the working class to side with feudalism, which in turn kept well in the background pushing forward the Catholics to do its unpleasant work. It meant that Spanish feudalism would not compromise. There could be no give-and-take. Internationally, the hand of Germany could be seen very clearly. Gil

Robles's summer trip to the Reich had not been without interest and there had been other comings-and-goings. But Robles was not a very pliable instrument, he was too much controlled by the Vatican. The ground had not been well prepared by Germany and only tentative encouragement could be given. Yet I think that Nazi statesmen had already taken the decision that a friendly Spain was an absolute necessity for any decisive action against Britain and France. So long as the two latter nations had free communication with their Empires and with North and South America it would always be difficult for Germany to crush them, even with Italian help. But with a Spain friendly to Germany and from which, either under pretended neutrality or open hostility, submarines and aeroplanes could be used to harass our Empire communications, then the Reich could indeed prepare a coup with much greater confidence. Actually it took five years before Germany finally smashed the Spanish Republic and thus the whole cycle of international events was changed. If in 1934 the Spanish Republicans and Socialists had taken this challenge inertly it would only have been a question of months before an iron Army Dictatorship would have been in the saddle and which would naturally have provided the situation needed by Germany for her own plans. I write this with no rancour against the Germans. They wish to be the greatest nation in the world. To do so, they need to encircle France and be able to menace her, and our, Empire routes. In 1934, Germany was frustrated, not by vigilance on the part of the statesmen who are supposed to watch with care over the safety of our Empire, but by the dogged resistance of Spanish Socialists and Republicans.

Our Barcelona correspondent called me up late on this night of October 4. This was Larry Fernsworth, the only foreign journalist I know who really understands Catalan politics. If he ever writes a book on Catalonia it will be well worth reading. But we were cut off before he could tell me much.

I tuned in the radio and picked up Radio Association of Barcelona, which was intelligible despite jamming from Madrid. The Catalan sender was calling piteously for help. The speaker was in the lovely old Gothic Palace of the Generalit which was being shelled steadily but not with much insistence by General Batet, a soldier whom the Catalans had wrongly believed to be on their side. Between appeals for aid, Catalan music was played; 'Els Segadors,' the fierce sad cry of a people used to fighting for their freedom against an oppressor, sent shivers down my back as it wailed out in the small hours of the morning. Even the 'Sardana' dance called 'La Santa Espina' (The Sacred Thorn) and the words of which are in themselves joyful ('God passed through Catalonia in spring-time; everything smiled as He passed by') sounded incredibly sad. Poor Catalonia! After two centuries and a quarter of oppression since Philip V abolished the regional autonomy at the beginning of the eighteenth century, Catalonia had been free once again for only three short years since the Republic was proclaimed in 1931 and now Feudal Spain was again out to smash her independence.

The Catalans led in the October revolt, just as they did when the Republic was proclaimed in April 1931. But this time it was a short affair. Curiously enough almost the entire resistance was made by the middle class, that is to say by the Esquerra Catalana, the Liberal Party led by Luis Companys, and the Estat Català, the separatist movement which was working in co-operation with the former group. The workers hardly helped at all. This was due to trouble between Companys and the Anarchists for which Companys was not so much responsible as his Home Secretary in the Catalan Cabinet, named Dencas. This man had organised a movement of youths who wore green shirts and were known as Escamots and the organisation seemed to be run on completely Fascist lines. On several occasions the 'green shirts' were used to break strikes. Dencas was also the outstanding figure of Estat Català. This was rather a muddling situation, for Companys and the Esquerra stood for all that was Liberal and Left-Wing in Catalan and national politics and here they were co-operating with a group which was Fascist in tendency. As far as I could figure it out, Estat Català represented a sector of Catalan middle-class opinion which was essentially very Right-Wing but at the same time anxious for Catalan independence.

At any rate, the peculiar situation arose in October 1934 that while the Catalan middle class offered resistance to the new Lerroux Cabinet, the workers did virtually nothing. Barcelona was controlled by the Anarchists, who swayed the easily-aroused passions of the peasants from Murcia and Aragon newly incorporated into the industrial life of Catalonia, and when the Generalitat asked for a general strike and withdrew from the streets the ordinary police replacing them by 'Mozos de Escuadra', Catalan regional police, whose loyalty was certain, the Anarchists remembered their recent squabbles with Dencas and not only refused at first to strike but sent gunmen to snipe at the 'Mozos de Escuadra'.

Sr. Dencas seems to have done very little to prepare any adequate resistance. When President Companys read from the balcony of the Generalitat Palace a proclamation saying that the 'Federal Spanish Republic' had been set up with its centre in Barcelona to fight against the new Madrid Government, thousands of people in the square below shouted for arms. If you have to fight there is nothing like having some kind of weapon. But Sr. Dencas, also on the balcony, did nothing. Later on in the evening, President Companys sent a message to General Batet, the Military Commander of the Catalan region, asking him to place his forces at the disposal of the Catalan Government. General Batet replied that he required an hour in which to think this over. After telegraphic communication with Madrid he proclaimed martial law and a military patrol which he sent towards the Palace of the Generalitat exchanged shots with the Mozos de Escuadra. The leisurely fashion in which the Socialists in Madrid moved, allowing twenty-four hours to go by before they put a general strike into operation, naturally disconcerted many who would have been prepared to give discreet or open help to the movement.

The Barcelona episode was soon over. Sr. Dencas, who as Home Minister should have organised resistance, did nothing at all, limiting his efforts to barricading himself in the Home Office and escaping down a sewer when he heard that the remaining Catalan Ministers had surrendered in the Generalitat Palace. Untold ridicule was heaped afterwards on Dencas because he escaped down a sewer. I do not know why. It seems as good a way as any to leave by when one is in danger and

146

surrounded. But the fact remains that he never again, as far as I know, played any part in Catalan public life. When he escaped he went eventually to Italy where he had, apparently, close contacts with Italian Fascism, a fact which confirmed the worst suspicions of the Anarchists. Major Perez Farras defended the Palace of the Generalitat as well as he could against the troops sent against it, but by six o'clock in the morning Companys, realising that nothing could be done and that the fine old Palace would merely be wrecked by the artillery fire directed on it, gave the signal for surrender.

There was also resistance in the headquarters of the Shop Assistants' Union which, for some reason which I find difficult to account for, was a stronghold of Catalan nationalists. General Batet wrecked the old building with shell fire, killing twelve persons including Jaime Compte, a veteran fighter for Catalan freedom.

The Anarchists belatedly decided to strike and seized several buildings near the port and in the Exhibition Grounds on Montjuich, but they had no heart in this particular fight and on October 6 when the fiercest revolutionary movement ever seen in Spain was raging throughout the country, I heard Anarchist spokesmen from Barcelona radio station calling on all the local workers to return at once to work. This enabled Lerroux to bring troops and police from Barcelona to help in other parts. The Anarchist in politics is an incalculable factor and most liable to do the unexpected.

The Madrid episode was less sensational but lasted much longer and was more noisy. The first few days, the ceaseless rifle fire resembled my impression of what the Battle of Waterloo must have been like. In all, over three weeks of rioting, about ninety-eight people were killed of whom I think eleven were police or soldiers. I am not able to check these figures at the moment as I have lost the notes containing them but I remember very well collecting them and checking them at the time.

The plan of the Socialists, as far as they had any, was to continue resistance in Madrid over a length of several weeks in order to weaken the Government. They had organised groups of young people whose mission was to keep up constant unrest by firing odd shots either in the streets or from house-roofs. The police struck a smart blow at this organisation from the first for on the night of October 4, before the general strike had begun, they raided the headquarters where the young men were assembling in Buenavista and after some desultory firing took fifty youths prisoner and captured most of the arms.

This initial success heartened the authorities. Sunday morning, October 5, saw a parade of Primo de Rivera and four or five hundred of his men up Alcalá Street and it was indeed an interesting spectacle to see the Fascists gathered in front of the Ministry of the Interior saluting and cheering that one-time rebel, Alejandro Lerroux. But if Lerroux welcomed the Falangistas, Madrid certainly did not. No crowds joined the marchers and they were hissed despite their escort of several truck-loads of heavily-armed policemen. Several cafés thought to defy the strike in the pleasant sunshine of Sunday morning. The Café Colon at the head of Alcalá, much frequented by bull-fighters and prostitutes and a place where a good beef-steak could be had quite late at night, was serving drinks as usual with a skeleton staff of non-union waiters, when two shots rang out and two waiters serving the outside tables on the streets dropped dead in their tracks. A car roared away down the street. The cafés closed up for the day.

Army officers in uniform with rifles and revolvers began to appear along with the police. Many of them were officers who had retired under the Azaña scheme. Socialist sharpshooters banged away from roofs all over the city. Jittery police fired constantly and in all directions and for three days and three nights that city was kept in constant pandemonium by a hand-ful of kids. Finally someone explained to the police that in-stead of firing at the sky for half an hour every time a stray shot was heard, the thing to do was to keep quiet and try to locate the point from which it was fired. After about a week one could sleep again in Madrid and a poor, hard-working reporter could get about town in a straight line and not by a series of hops from doorway to doorway.

The Basques in the North put up a tough resistance. They barricaded the main roads and made progress almost impossible along the main routes. Twenty were killed in fighting in San Sebastian alone. The mining area around Bilbao was entirely in revolt. Down in Estremadura, the peasants revolted under the leadership of Margarita Nelken, a woman Socialist Deputy, but this business did not get far because no shot-gun or sickle invented yet can make any showing against solid Mauser rifles backed up by machine-guns and sub-machine-guns. The rather strong peasant union under Ricardo Zabalza actually did not pull much weight during the strike, nor did the railwaymen under the beefy and good-looking Trifon Gomez. They had to answer a lot of questions from their fellow-Socialists about this lack of activity in later months. Despite the large quantities of dynamite which had caused so much worry to my friend Luis Quintanilla, no one tried to blow up any railway bridges and troop trains got about easily enough.

Yet the heart of the movement proved to be in out-of-the-way Asturias where 30,000 miners suddenly flared out of their cottage homes, took Oviedo with all its 90,000 inhabitants, took Gijon, Mieres, Trubia, with its arms factory, snipped the main railway line at the Puerto de Pajares and thus isolated themselves from attack save through Galicia or from the sea. Inside three days there stood a small Communist State, or Communist-cum-Anarchist might be a more accurate description.

Why this surprising fury and revolutionary feeling? Frankly, I still do not know. Possibly a combination of many circumstances. Asturian miners were among the best paid workers in Spain and despite much unemployment were not in any state of desperate misery or anything like that. But if pay was high, mining conditions were bad. An English mines expert who had great experience told me: 'I have visited mines in every part of Europe, including Russia, and I have never seen such terrible working conditions as in Asturias.' Decades of working under bad conditions must leave its mark on the men, the iron must eat in. The Republic did what it could for them, it pulled hours down and pushed wages up, subsidised production, and I can imagine that they felt very strongly at seeing the Republic near shipwreck.

149

I think the personal element also played a part. A very passionate Socialist named Javier Bueno had gone up to Oviedo some months earlier and had taken charge of the daily paper of the Socialist miners union, *Avance*, the newspaper was called. I knew Bueno slightly for he was a brilliant young journalist, spoke four or five languages and rose from reporter to editor-in-chief, while still under thirty, of the Madrid evening newspaper *La Voz*. To me he seemed too intense to last. He was one of those rabid supporters of a cause who take things with such zeal and fervour that you feel that sooner or later they will wear out, and probably end up holding the opposite views.

What he did to the miners in those months was just tremendous. *Avance*, under his expert direction, it was all child's play to him after running a big Madrid daily, was a flaming torch which each day crossed the Asturian mountains from end to end.

Nevertheless, I do not think that Bueno's propaganda was more than a secondary cause. Men do not go out and die because of an article which they have read in a daily newspaper. There had been a good deal of Communist propaganda in Asturias despite the relative unimportance of the Communists in Spain, and I think this also was secondary. But I think that when it came to actually facing the bullets of the well-armed forces of law and order in the region, the most important reason was the desire that the Republic should live; that Spain should not turn back her political and economic clock to feudal conditions again. These men had suffered, most of their bodies were scarred, there were few families in which sickness or an accident had not disabled at least one member. They wanted better things for their children, they wanted to see Spain go forward; not backward.

One thing which contributed to the unanimity of the movement was the formation some time earlier of a Workers' Alliance. Socialists, Communists and Anarchists had in this way formed a 'united front' of all workers.

As communications were cut with Asturias it took us several days to realise that what was going on in Oviedo was something tremendous and not merely a rather noisy general strike.

Then we all rushed to find a way of getting to Asturias as fast as wheels could turn. Then we dropped all that. From Marseilles came urgent cables every few minutes telling the story of the death on the usually gay and care-free Canebière, one of the streets of Europe with most character in my opinion, of the French Foreign Minister, Louis Barthou, and of King Alexander of the Jugoslavs, who had landed only a few minutes earlier on an important visit to France. And all that uproar simply pushed the dramatic gesture of the miners of Asturias right back-stage. Quite rightly so. Because the death of M. Barthou ended the policy which he was pushing vigorously and which might have saved Europe from much trouble. M. Barthou felt very strongly that Herr Hitler, now at the helm in Germany, boded trouble for Europe. This idea of M. Barthou's ran counter to the opinions of most British and French statesmen and of the influential people who stay back-stage but do quite a lot to shape governmental policies. There seems little doubt that the reason for the early armistice and the decision of the Allies not to follow up and smash the German army machine to pieces was that they believed that the Prussian Army might still be needed as a bulwark to defend Western Europe against any spread of Bolshevism. Later, we see how Fascist Italy and Nazi Germany were able to borrow money for their rearmament plans from both Britain and France. It was felt, apparently, that these two Powers were good guardians of law and order in Europe. Now M. Barthou was virtually tearing this policy to pieces. He was saying in so many words that Hitler was not an armed watchman against Communism but a dreamer who wished to smash the British and French Empires and lead Germany to world domination. He wanted to do something about it and had proposed to Britain in June of 1934 a pact of mutual assistance which would cover Eastern Europe, the Balkans and the Mediterranean. Britain would have none of it. As one diplomatic correspondent neatly said: 'Britain killed the proposal by giving it her platonic approval.'

M. Barthou was also meeting heavy opposition at home, where the wise men of the Empire, like their colleagues in London, laughed heartily at the idea of a solid fellow like

Hitler ever doing anything to upset Western Europe and in their more confidential moments hinted that 'poor old Barthou was going a shade ga-ga, getting touched by pink propaganda in his old age.' Nevertheless, he went ahead with his plans, even without British help, and invited King Alexander to come to France to talk mutual defence proposals. And so the bullets of an assassin met two marks. The French Sûreté, with its long reputation for unerring vigilance, had that day only a minimum service of protection for two men who had so many enemies at home and abroad.

In Madrid, special correspondents such as Edmond Taylor of *The Chicago Tribune*, Leland Stowe of the *New York Herald Tribune*, Sefton Delmer of the *Daily Express*, rushed for the Sud-Express, which was functioning quite normally thanks to Trifon Gomez and his railwaymen, and hurried away for France. The local correspondents, such as myself, got cables saying 'hold down!' World attention was focussed on Marseilles, but the Asturian miners went on fighting.

Meanwhile, Lerroux and his fellow-ministers had recovered from their first elation at the smashing of Barcelona's revolt and the keeping under control of Madrid, and were working furiously to deal with the situation in Asturias. They rushed up troops from Leon but as the railway had been cut by the miners they had to proceed on foot and as they went up a narrow valley, without the precaution of occupying the heights on either side, they were caught and held by a few miners with machine-guns and a couple of pieces of artillery. Actually the troops and their officers showed little energy in this situation for a few well armed military patrols could certainly have detoured and have caught the few hundred relatively disorganised miners by surprise. But none of the conscript soldiers and not all of the officers felt much enthusiasm about shooting fellow-Spaniards at the behest of Alejandro Lerroux.

It must be said that Lerroux acted decisively. He promptly installed in the War Ministry as 'advisers', two of Spain's best, youngest and most energetic Generals, namely Franco and Goded. The fact that they were both known to hold very strong Right-Wing political views did not hinder Lerroux.

From that time onwards the tired-looking Notary, Hidalgo, who was nominally War Minister, practically disappeared from the scene. The telephone communications with foreign countries were cut off. An iron censorship was installed, controlled by General Franco, and it was he who received applications from journalists such as myself for permits to go to Asturias, which were promptly turned down. He and Goded quite realised that the ordinary troops were in no mood to fight the miners and they hurried over from Morocco, first the Tercio, comprised of a few foreign and many Spanish troops, and who numbered about 10,000, and then, as these were not sufficient, they also called on native Moorish regiments with which to crush the movement. They gave command to General Lopez Ochoa, a strangely erratic personality who had quarrelled with Primo de Rivera during the Dictatorship but who also was looked upon as rather reactionary by the Republicans. Moors and Foreign Legion were landed in Galicia and on the shores of Asturias while the battleship *Libertad* shelled Gijon and aviators bombed both Gijon and Oviedo.

Asturias was not easy to get at because the Bilbao and Santander districts to the north were restless and there was much rioting. The few mountain passes leading in from the Leon Province were held by the miners. Troops, therefore, had to be sent through Galicia.

It was very hard to piece together afterwards the exact story of the two weeks during which this small chunk of Spain remained a communistic island in the Spanish Republic. The Madrid newspapers at first did not appear, because of the strike, and when they did come out they were heavily censored and only published information approved by the Government. The Foreign Press carried little, for its attention was turned elsewhere. The main protagonists could not be interviewed because they were in gaol or in hiding.

This terrible explosion of human passions began under the form of an ordinary general strike on the night of October 4-5, as in the rest of Spain, except Barcelona. Oviedo at first was peaceful. But in Gijon, Mieres, Laviana, Campomanes, armed groups attacked the police and forced them to withdraw to their barracks. In some of the smaller towns and villages the Civil Guards were surrounded and shot. In Mieres there was a battle lasting for several days in which sixty Shock Police held out with the help of Civil Guards. Finally, they were overcome everywhere except in Gijon. The first intimation of grave trouble near the Asturian capital of Oviedo was when two truckloads of Shock Police being rushed to Mieres ran into an ambush just outside the town and many were killed. Soon, thousands of miners, armed mainly with dynamite, began to converge on the town. The officer in charge of the small arms factory, where there were 15,000 new Mauser rifles, feared that he had not sufficient soldiers to guard the place and he withdrew to join the permanent garrison in the Pelayo Barracks. So the miners now had arms, although little ammunition. They had taken over the cannon factory at Trubia likewise and thus got fifteen pieces of artillery, but here again the munition trouble arose because the director had hidden all the fuses and the few shells available were, therefore, virtually useless.

The miners advanced through the streets of Oviedo, preceded by dynamite squads. These men had small packages of dynamite, brown demerara sugar is what it looks like, to which they attached a small piece of fuse-cord. They then lit this from a cigarette and hurled it through the air. It was not a very efficient weapon against rifles and machine-guns and there were about 1,500 soldiers and policemen in Oviedo. I do not know exactly how many miners took part in the attack. But I doubt if the number ever exceeded 5,000, for a great many of the miners from the zone were in their own particular towns and villages and some hundreds, possibly several thousand altogether, were watching the various mountain passes through which troops might be rushed from Madrid. The centre of the town was held sturdily by the police, who should have made a better showing than they did considering the excellent arms they had. The some eight or nine hundred soldiers remained shut up in their barracks, more or less isolated and not very active.

The chief figure of the miners' union, Amador Fernandez, was in Madrid when the trouble broke. Javier Bueno, the man who wrote words of fire, had been taken prisoner from the first moment and was in the cellars of the barracks in Oviedo. So the chairman of the union, Ramón Gonzalez Peña, a rather pompous, mild-mannered man, considerably less Leftist in his politics than say Mr. Arthur Horner, found himself at the head of a small 'Communist State'. I imagine he felt about as happy as an amateur from a gliding club would feel if suddenly called upon to land a big Frobisher four-motor air liner in a thick fog at Croydon. He was probably as surprised as anybody at this sudden explosion of human passions and the collapse of the armed forces in the district.

He did his best to hold in the men. This did not prevent about twelve priests being shot, most of whom were from a seminary in Oviedo. It was less easy to hold the miners in when the Army planes began to come over and bomb and machine-gun them in Oviedo and Gijon and on the roads. As the miners had no anti-aircraft guns they were, of course, completely at the mercy of these pilots, who could come low and take their time in aiming without running the slightest risk. In Mieres, the miners took out and shot about fifteen mining engineers and others whom they accused of having ill-treated members of their organisations at one time or another. There were some blood-curdling stories of priests burned alive and of the body of a priest which was supposed to have been placed in the window of a butcher's shop labelled: 'Pork!' This latter story was disproved by the investigation of several people, including Sta. Clara Campoamor, a Radical Deputy and Director-General of Social Welfare under Sr. Lerroux. Her testimony to the falsehood of this story, incidentally, caused her to be at once removed from her post by Premier Lerroux. The story of the burning was half true. The body of one of the seminarists who was shot lay for some time on an open piece of ground and one day a group of miners poured petrol over the corpse and burned it. An unpleasant business, it is true, but not quite the same as burning a man alive. In the reports published in various Madrid papers details of the burning alive of a parish priest in Oviedo and his obituary were given. Several weeks later he wrote a letter to the papers concerned explaining that he was well and alive and had not been molested in any way by the miners. The fact that nearly thirty civilians not bearing arms were executed showed, of course, that the revolutionaries were liable to use rough methods.

The Bank of Spain branch in Oviedo fell to the miners and made them about £1,000,000 richer. Curiously enough, the Anarchist elements in some villages had already 'abolished money', made bonfires of bank-notes and announced that in the 'Libertarian-Communist State' no money would be needed. Shopkeepers were forbidden to charge money. Goods could be given only against chits ('vales') issued by the local revolutionary committee. This was not, however, done in villages where Socialists or Communists had more influence. On the whole, the various political groups worked well together; they devised a platonic name of Union Hispanica Proletaria (U.H.P.).

Soon the fight in Oviedo became a deadlock. The Shock Police held the Cathedral tower, known as the Torre Vieja, where they had installed a machine-gun. The revolutionaries in an attempt to get at the tower, after burning down the Bishop's Palace, dynamited one of the walls of the Treasury Chamber, the 'Camara Santa', a place of much historical interest and containing valuable treasures. The local high school, the 'Instituto', was blown up to clear the path of the strikers. The police in turn burned down the local theatre because it obstructed their firing and enabled the strikers to get too close. There was brutality, kindness, cowardice, heroism. The driver of an armoured car, armoured in a primitive fashion with a few iron plates, was shot dead while an attempt was being made to storm a police stronghold. Another chauffeur, a friend of his and in bed with a severe wound, got up and went out to bring the car back. Tempers ran high, as time ran on and the failure of the movement in the rest of Spain became clear. Ramón Gonzalez Peña, with a Socialist Deputy named Teodomiro Menendez, who in private life was traveller for a firm of flour merchants and true to his class could tell the raciest stories of any Deputy in the lobbies of Parliament, was working all the time for moderation and saved the lives of scores of people. They were pushed aside and replaced by a group of Anarchists and Communists. Disputes broke out as to whether to continue to struggle against the police strongholds or whether to leave a guard to watch them and to use the available men to guard the mountain approaches to Oviedo from Galicia. Sergeant Vazquez, a deserter from the local garrison, was the 'military expert'.

The port of Gijon fell on October 17 after being shelled by naval units and bombed. It was taken by the Tercio, or Foreign Legion, which was landed from an Army transport. These forces advanced towards Oviedo from one side while General Lopez Ochoa at the head of 10,000 men was advancing rapidly from Galicia. By October 18, and without opposition of any importance, he was near Oviedo and, advancing during the night at the head of a detachment of Foreign Legion, he broke through to the Pelayo Barracks while the main part of his forces, which included Moorish troops, began to encircle the town. Once inside, General Lopez Ochoa crisply offered the miners good treatment and no reprisals if they would lay down arms in the various towns and villages. The local garrison could hardly have felt proud at being relieved by a handful of troops less than their own numbers.

The activity of the Tercio and the Moors in taking the town of Oviedo gave rise to much scandal afterwards. Both behaved, although resistance scarcely existed, as if they were taking a village of rebellious tribesmen in Morocco. Anyone found with arms in his hands was shot; and many who had no arms. Sr. Gordon Ordas, a Republican Deputy, drew up a list of forty-six persons, including two women and two children, giving names and addresses and specifying their cases, and who had been shot summarily without any trial. All of them were non-combatants and had taken no part in the fight. Some of them were of Right-Wing politics. That the actual list was much longer is highly probable because it was very unhealthy to make inquiries in Oviedo. The names on that list were obtained by two Madrid journalists, Luis de Sirval and Andres Barbeito. The Foreign Legion heard that such inquiries were being made and sent out men to find these journalists. A detective of the ordinary police force warned Barbeito in time and got him out of town but Sirval was taken to gaol, where he was shot dead in the courtyard by a Bulgarian officer of the Legion with a Spanish Army officer watching.

It was reported in the Madrid Press that 'one thousand bodies had been burned in Oviedo by the Red Cross in order to avoid infectious diseases breaking out'. Whether there were actually so many dead seems a little doubtful. The burning was done undoubtedly as much in order to hide the fact that many of the bodies were of people shot down during the taking as in order to prevent disease. One of Madrid's best newspaper photographers got pictures of the bodies being loaded pell-mell into the incinerators used for burning the city garbage. He told me later how he found out where the bodies were being burned. He went to a brothel frequented by the Foreign Legion officers and there soon had one of the girls excitedly telling him about her new and rich officer friend of the Foreign Legion 'who spent his nights burning bodies at the Municipal Incinerator'. What news and picture reporters have to do to get news. . . .

Arms were laid down in most parts of Asturias, except by groups which took to the mountains and were still being pursued weeks afterwards, but the pledge to respect the lives of those who surrendered was not honoured. In Mieres, the occupying troops were reliably reported to have shot sixty miners, some of whom were alleged to have been buried before they were dead. At Campomanes, 120 miners were reported shot. So the civilians, less than thirty, who were killed by the miners were avenged in lavish fashion by the troops of General Ochoa. How many were shot in Oviedo itself will never be known.

A member of the Tercio described how a girl named Fernandez held out with a group of strikers near the Oviedo railway station and when they refused to surrender he and others shot them dead. As neither he nor his companions were injured it hardly sounded as if the resistance they were meeting was very serious. She was known by some picturesque name which now escapes my memory and afterwards became a local heroine.

The Government placed police duties in the charge of Major

Lisardo Doval and prisoners—between two and three thousand in Oviedo alone—trembled when they heard that he had arrived. Tall, handsome, a magnificent Spanish 'caballero' in his uniform of a Major in the Civil Guard, Doval had earned a reputation for severity in the fierce days of Barcelona unrest during the years 1921 and 1922 when at one period a murder a day was occurring.

Sr. Gordon Ordas, in a report he sent to the President of the Republic, told terrible details of the treatment of prisoners. He reported men immersed in cold water for hours, and of men jerked off the ground by a cord attached to their wrists which were already tied together behind their back, and of deformation of the private organs. The authorities, it seemed, were anxious to know where the money stolen from the Bank of Spain in Oviedo was hidden and what had become of the rifles taken from the small arms' factory, of which seven thousand were still missing. They also wanted to know where Ramón Gonzalez Peña was hidden, who had given orders, who had prepared this or that plan. There were indeed many things which the authorities wanted to know and men shrieked in horror and some went to asylums, not many perhaps but a few. And some would soon be coughing up their lungs from consumption after the water treatment.

In the past century such happenings would have caused demonstrations in Britain and trade unions and Liberal societies would have protested and organised meetings. To-day, things are not the same in Britain. But there are still champions of the cause of humanity in our land and out from London came energetic little Ellen Wilkinson along with the Earl of Listowel. Premier Lerroux was at his most gracious: 'Go to Oviedo? Of course you can go there. The Spanish Government has nothing to hide; nothing at all. My secretary will give you a letter to Commandante Doval.' Next morning, after a night ride up to Oviedo, the British group were greeted with booing and hissing when they entered a local café for some hot coffee. What Sr. Lerroux said in his letter to Major Doval is not known, but that worthy called on the delegates and said that they must prepare for another journey, to the frontier. He personally escorted them at once to the French frontier and watched them cross it. Journalists in Madrid asked Sr. Lerroux if Miss Wilkinson and Lord Listowel had been expelled. 'Expelled? Oh dear me, no, but Major Doval thought it better for reasons of public order to escort them to the frontier,' said Don Alejandro Lerroux. Opinion in Spain and abroad could hardly be blamed for deducing that the Government had something to hide in Oviedo. Several weeks after the British visit, Major Doval was removed from his post and his successor, Don Angel Velarde, released 1,000 persons from prison within a week following Doval's departure on December 9. Strangely enough as I was writing this chapter, a friend in touch with Spain came in and told me of a reliable report from Madrid that Major Doval had arrived there during the month of April of this year, 1939, following its fall to the forces of General Franco, and that he had been shot dead shortly after his arrival there. I have not so far been able to confirm the report.

CHAPTER XVIII

NO DICTATORSHIP

THE Sud-Express from Paris to Madrid—two coaches off at Miranda del Ebro for Lisbon, s'il vous plait—is one of Europe's glamour trains. We have none of those marvellous transcontinental expresses which run for days on end across endless America but we like to build up our own little European-scale romances about trains such as the Flying Scotsman or the Train Bleu, which clatters rapidly and expensively from Berlin to Paris, or the Simplon Orient, which will whisk you from Paris to Athens without change of car. There used to be a train which left Paris every night, it probably still runs, which wandered for several days across Europe to end up at the Russo-Polish frontier, and it used to give me a thrill to watch it pull out of the Gare du Nord on its long run. Twice I rode to Cologne on it. But this was a humble train with wooden-seated, third-class coaches in addition to sleeping-cars and nobody had ever given it a name.

Glamour trains never take third-class passengers, or only near the end of their runs in distant Balkan countries where coarser railway officials may hook on a third-class coach discreetly at the rear and which the Wagons-Lit conductors, who have ridden from Paris and are superior persons, pretend not to notice. The Sud-Express, the Simplon Orient and suchlike, mostly carry diplomats whose fares are paid by taxpayers in this or that country, arms or motor-car salesmen with expenses and commission, an odd reporter whose paper is paying, and maybe one or two genuinely rich people paying their own fare. As a matter of fact the glamour trains to-day are less snooty and less exclusive. Aeroplane competition is serious and although the well-nourished stomachs of Sud-Express or Train Bleu category do not always take kindly to the ups and downs of air travel, such sudden ups and downs I find them, nevertheless time presses and many important travellers, especially arms salesmen, I imagine, have to take the swifter means of travel.

The Sud-Express enjoys privileged position among our European trains, largely, I think, because it runs to Spain and Spain, before it spelt war and revolution, used to spell romance to us. But actually the Sud-Express as such has nothing to boast about, for the train which leaves the Gare d'Orsay each morning only has a twelve-hour run to the Franco-Spanish frontier and there the passengers have to hop out and change into a Spanish version of the same train. Spanish railway engineers built large-gauge roads because they wanted the fare-paying public to ride easily and also because someone or other thought that if Spain had a railway gauge of a different size from that of the rest of Europe then it would be very hard for the rest of Europe to invade Spain. Or at least their soldiers would have to walk in. For that was, of course, in the days when soldiers went as far as possible by train and did the rest by foot-slogging and Europe in that day did not have to cater for small armies which by racing swiftly here and there along smooth autobahns can upset all the Queensbury rules of international warfare.

One night in October 1934, about the twentieth, I think, a very hot and bothered Henry Buckley shuffled up and down the corridors of the Sud-Express, Spanish version, just about to pull out from Madrid for Hendaye. It seemed to me ridiculous that 200 tons of steel should be mobilised in order to take five people across Spain, for there were only five passengers in the train. There seemed to be at least fifty secret policemen on the platform, all of whom I felt were watching me. I have explained how General Franco cut off all telephone communications with the rest of the world and that an iron military censorship slashed the most innocent cables to pieces. Now it looked as if the Republic was going to be finally washed overboard by a military dictatorship. President Alcalá Zamora, in repentant mood now that it looked as if he might lose his position, was having a big fight with the Army over death sentences. The Army said briefly, and with soldierly logic, that rebels who were caught and condemned to death by court-martial should at once be shot. President Alcalá Zamora, apparently, said that he was still President of the Republic and as such had to confirm all death sentences no matter what kind of court they were passed by and that he intended to inquire into each case and he would give his signature in due course if he approved and refuse it if he did not approve. The President, I think, although I have no proof, also had something strong to say about the considerable number of people shot out of hand in Oviedo and elsewhere without the benefit of the most primitive inquiry. The Army officers stormed and fumed. For nearly three weeks they had been running Spain. It was quite like the old days when what the Army said was done and any politician who objected was given short notice to leave office. Those happy days had ended in 1931 and it had been so nice to find them back again. So in Madrid people in the know whispered mysteriously: 'Have you heard about Franco?' 'Do you know what Goded said last night?' 'Is it true that Alcalá Zamora has sent his presidential archives to Paris?'

I was trying to get the story of the threatened coup out of Spain. I was trying in fact to get two stories out, one for myself and one for Jay Allen, of the *Chicago Daily News*, whom God made a man and nature a reporter. Jay had got the story and shared it with me and after writing a couple of pieces we stormed down to the Norte Station, not forgetting to bring with us Dollfy, Jay's little Dachshund called at first 'Dollfuss' because he was so extra-small and stumpy and modified to 'Dollfy' after Austria's Dictator was murdered and it seemed bad taste to use the original name. The sentry at the gate—everything was still under military control—said we must show passports in order to go on to the platform at the Norte Station. Jay had no passport with him so I had to go alone on to the train and try to find someone, either train employee or traveller, who would take our stories to the frontier and give them to an hotel porter in Hendaye who worked for Jay and who would telegraph them at once to Paris. This little job would have been child's play to Allen who for ten years had been tearing around Europe as a special correspondent and to whom a little set-to with the police meant nothing at all. But I was just a local correspondent in Madrid with a nervous, middle-class conscience which danced a rumba at the thought of any trouble

163

with the police or authorities. I climbed the steps of a sleeping-car nervously. An attendant hustled up: 'Your berth
number, please, sir. . . .' I stuttered: 'Well you see I am not
really travelling on the train but . . .' Then up behind him
stepped a green-clad Civil Guard complete with rifle. He was
only one of the couple on regular duty on the train and already
looking for a place to take a quiet snooze once the express got
on the move, but my mouth went dry and mumbling something or other, I have no idea what I said, I dived down the
steps on to the platform again. Whistles were already being
blown. Thoroughly jittery, I climbed into the next car.
'Conductor!' I called. 'Here,' came a distant reply. The train
was already beginning to move. I hurried down to where the
voice came from. The conductor was arranging the bed of a
General in full uniform who stood by asking the man some
question or other. I turned and fled from the train and the
station, watched, it seemed to me, by dozens of eyes. Jay was
sitting in the taxi, playing happily with Dollfy. 'All okay?' he
asked. I handed him back his story. A silence. 'Let's go and
eat,' said Jay and we went back to his flat where Margaret
Palmer, a charming American who has lived in Madrid for
more years than she cares to recall, had dropped in and was
cooking some lovely bully-beef stew. But I was so sick of
everything that I left and walked slowly back through deserted
streets to my home.

Yet as things turned out, the fact that our stories never went
was unimportant. Help came to the Republic from a surprising quarter. José Maria Gil Robles gathered the Press around
him and announced firmly: 'There shall be no Dictatorship in
Spain! We Clericals will not permit the overthrowing of the
parliamentary régime!' Premier Lerroux who had gone to
earth like a good rabbit and pretended that the reported dispute between President and Army officers had nothing at all
to do with him, now, apparently, came out too on the side of
democracy and that kind of thing. For a few hours the situation hung in the balance. But apparently the Army officers
decided that the spirit of the mass of the soldiers, and even some
of the officers, which had made it necessary to bring in the
Tercio and Moors to crush the miners, was hardly the right

frame of mind for the staging now of an Army *coup d'état*. Moreover, the united opposition of all Republicans and of the Clericals and the necessity for overthrowing President, Prime Minister and Parliament without any legitimate pretext, made the cooler heads decide that 'Der Tag' had not yet come.

The moment was in some respects favourable. The Left was down and out. Its principal figures were in gaol or in flight. The revolt had been defeated. General Ochoa had taken Oviedo. But in Madrid the strike had lasted a full eight days and longer in some trades. Despite mass dismissals of strikers and threats again and again that 'men who do not present themselves to-morrow will be dismissed', Madrid strikers and those elsewhere only returned to work when they received orders from their trade union delegates. Spain was full of resentment. This would probably crystallise into hard opposition, said the Right-Wing. But the Republicans such as Alcalá Zamora and Lerroux had, of course, no mind to see themselves ousted by a military Dictatorship. Robles, one imagines, had received inspiration from the Vatican which since the death of Dollfuss had as little wish to see a Fascist Spain as a Communist Spain. Maybe there are other reasons why Spain was saved from a military coup at that critical moment. I can only give those which I know.

CHAPTER XIX

THE REPUBLIC MARKS TIME

THE year of 1935 was a period of convalescence for Spain. Of 60,000 political prisoners cramming the gaols, about 50,000 were released during the year. None of the leading figures were shot, but half a dozen lesser lights faced the firing squad of whom the best known was that Sergeant Vazquez who deserted from the Oviedo garrison and tried to drill some military sense into the miners. The Army was adamant about his being shot.

Ramón Gonzalez Peña went to gaol for thirty years, after a death sentence had been commuted, as did Luis Companys and the other members of the Catalan Generalitat. Francisco Largo Caballero was exonerated 'for want of proof', which said a good deal for the discreet way in which the rising had been organised. It was amazing that despite the 60,000 prisoners who had all been interrogated and the various documents seized, not a single proof could be found to show that he had had any part in the rising.

This extraordinary lack of evidence was probably due to the fact that nothing was ever put into writing. Caballero would give instructions, say to Araquistain, and the latter would repeat them by word of mouth to someone else. Caballero was arrested on October 14, in his home in Madrid. As far as I could find out he had, however, been in contact with other Socialists during the revolution and had left his home and returned several times, deceiving the police guard by wearing the clothes of his chauffeur. Actually, the movement did not appear to have had any very elaborate organisation and had been more or less abandoned to its own devices. If by any chance it had succeeded then, of course, Caballero would have become Premier of a Government which would I think have included some Republicans and such Socialists as del Vayo and Araquistain. Dr. Negrin, who wrote the 'revolutionary news bulletin' which was circulated during the rising, was not, I think, down for any Cabinet post.

I was never able to find out what exactly was the arrangement between Socialists and Republicans. I think the latter gave approval to the revolt against Lerroux but they were, of course, shocked and a little frightened by Asturias. I know that in August of 1934 the intelligent and wealthy young Lluhi Vallesca, one of Companys's right-hand men, had come to see Caballero in Madrid to talk of preparations for resistance to any move to put the Clericals in office and for collaboration between Catalan Autonomists and Socialists in such an event. But, as I have pointed out earlier, there was no co-ordination of timing between Barcelona and Madrid when it came to the revolt in October. Manuel Azaña's visit to Barcelona was quite by chance. He had attended the funeral there of honest José Carner, that former Finance Minister who told Parliament what fate the Republic might expect if it did not subdue Juan March. Azaña took no part in the Catalan revolt and was arrested in the home of a lawyer friend. Considering that he was an ex-Premier he was not well treated by Lerroux's Government and was kept under arrest for several months without it being possible to make any charge against him. Sr. Azaña wrote quite a long book following his release, in which those who hoped to find reflected the terrible sufferings of Spain and the Spanish people in this upheaval of October were sadly disappointed. The whole of the lengthy book dealt minutely with the sufferings of Don Manuel Azaña.

Much scorn was poured by the Press of the Right on Don Indalecio Prieto, a leading figure of Socialism. It was alleged with much gusto that he had escaped from Spain to France in a case such as is used for fighting-bulls and with all the appropriate labels to show that this 'bull' was consigned for a bull-fight to be held in Southern France. Actually, he stayed for some weeks in the house of wealthy friends who were above suspicion and then was driven to the frontier by Ignacio Hidalgo de Cisneros who was, or had been until recently, Air Attaché in Rome. He was well known to the frontier guards and his car marked C.D. (Corps Diplomatique) passed through from Spain to France without any inquisitive officer opening the dickey-seat, in which case he would have found a very perspiring and uncomfortable Sr. Prieto. The latter had many friends in the Army and he had had strong hopes that some corps, and possibly part of the Civil Guard, would come over to the side of the Republican-Socialist revolutionaries. But the leisurely way in which the strike was called, with twenty-four hours for Lerroux to take precautions, had made it virtually impossible for any Army man to move.

Prieto was quite famous for his escapes to France. In 1917 he was the only outstanding figure of Socialism to get away from Spain after the August strike. In 1930, after the Jaca rising, he escaped to France disguised as a friar and nearly betrayed himself when a Customs' Guard at Irun stepped on his bare, sandalled foot causing the outspoken Don Indalecio to let loose an explosive string of epithets which amazed the guard when he saw the clerical garb. Fortunately for Sr. Prieto, there was nothing quick-witted about this particular limb of authority.

Prieto is a solid—both physically and politically—figure of the Right-Wing of the Socialist Party. He has both feet on the ground, however, unlike Besteiro who is a charming old man but who credits his political opponents with the same ideas of Liberalism and fair play which he himself possesses in considerable quantities. Prieto is, rara avis in Spain, a self-made man who in the best American tradition has risen to own *El Liberal* of Bilbao, a newspaper he used to sell on the streets as a boy. His newspaper was not Socialist in tendency, although liberal and sympathetic towards the Socialist Party. Actually Prieto had quite good contacts with many of the Bilbao ironmasters such as Echevarria and others who through their sympathy for the Basque Nationalist movement took a more tolerant view of politics than did the wealthy folk of Madrid. Many observers consider both Prieto and Besteiro as standing nearer to Liberalism than to Socialism. But there was no Liberalism which carried much conviction under the Monarchy, or not since Canalejas died, at any rate, and the only Republican movement of importance, up to 1930, was that of Sr. Lerroux's Radical Party which enjoyed a very poor reputation from the ethical standpoint. So Prieto, a prosperous newspaper proprietor, was one of the pillars of the Socialist Party.

Usually his voice was raised against all violence but in October 1934 he had believed this necessary and he had even, so I was told from an informant who was usually reliable, had much to do with the organisation of the Socialist Militia, wearing red shirts, which had been formed during the summer of 1934 and whose members had done most of the sporadic shooting from house-tops during the revolt which kept Madrid without sleep for a week, and which went on sporadically on the outskirts of the town for well over two weeks, despite the fact that the police were liable to shoot out of hand anyone they caught. 'Shot while trying to escape' was the formula of the authorities.

Prieto had been greatly attacked as Minister of Public Works in 1931 and 1932 because of a tunnel he built under Madrid, which ran from the Atocha Station—where the trains leave for the South of Spain—out to the suburb of Chamartin, where a new station was to be built as the terminus of the new direct line from Burgos to Madrid, sixty miles shorter than the line which wanders around by Avila or the other one via Segovia, and which was nearly completed as one of the valuable works of General Primo de Rivera. Prieto set out to finish the direct line from Burgos. With the direct line finished and the new tunnel, trains would have been able to run from Irun to Algeciras, instead of passengers having to transfer from the Norte Station to Atocha by motor-car. This would have cut the journey from London or Paris to Tangiers by some hours.

But there was violent opposition. This appeared to emanate from the German Embassy which saw British and French imperialist designs behind this apparently completely non-combatant tunnel. 'Spain will be dragged into the next world war because Sr. Prieto under orders from abroad is building a tunnel so that French colonial troops can be rushed from Africa to France if war should break out. . . .' Thus ran the arguments splashed across the columns of newspapers such as *Informaciones*, edited by Juan Pujol who was a stout defender of the German cause in the last war, *A.B.C.*, *El Debate* and in fact by all the Press of the Right.

The tunnel was always referred to as the 'Tubo de la Risa', the 'Tunnel of Laughter' of fairgrounds which is so difficult to walk through, and, in short, no effort was spared to discredit and ridicule both Sr. Prieto and the scheme. I have no proof that there was no French influence behind the scheme, but I believe that there was not. In the event of an international conflict, if Spain were to decide to allow the passage of French native troops then the delay of a few hours occupied by their crossing from one station to another in Madrid would hardly prove an important obstacle.

In fact I should have been much happier at the time if I had felt that British and French politicians were worrying about Empire communications. Mr. Winston Churchill is really our only full-blooded Imperialist left. M. Barthou was the only one left in France who really lost sleep about the safety of the French Empire and he has disappeared from the scene.

There were a few French interests which were interested in the Trans-Sahara railway and who advocated that its head should be brought to Tangiers and there, with a tunnel running under the Straits of Gibraltar, connected through Spain to Paris. I wrote at the time suggesting what a fine thing it would be if the Channel Tunnel, the Gibraltar Tunnel and the Trans-Sahara Railway could be built and trains could run from London into the heart of Africa and eventually to the Cape and how vast areas of Africa would be opened for development and how hundreds of thousands of people would find work. I remember reading a suggestion that many negroes from the United States, accustomed to the tempo of modern life, might care to come over and take part in the development which would follow this throwing of a railway line across Africa, and also that the construction of tunnels and railways should be an international work in which Britain, France, Germany and Italy should work together. I still think how much better it would be if the great Powers instead of squabbling about their differences were to get together on schemes to change the face of the world and which would bring work and wealth to all, instead of misery and destruction. I am a dreamer? Maybe, and perhaps at that it would do no harm if there were more dreamers of a constructive character.

However, Sr. Prieto's plan was more modest. He merely thought that it would be an excellent scheme to have fast, through trains running from Irun to Algeciras thus benefiting Spanish tourist traffic and encouraging through passengers and merchandise from other parts of Europe to Morocco. However, the opposition was successful and the tunnel was left unfinished. By the way, I forgot to mention that part of Sr. Prieto's scheme was to use the tunnel also for fast electric trains which would thus leave the heart of Madrid and go out to the Sierra Guadarrama Mountains, so that Madrid people would have quick and easy contact with the health-giving, pine-clad slopes of those lovely peaks.

I was very sorry myself in 1934 and 1935 that there was not a faster train service to the South of Spain because Jay Allen had left active reporting and taken a charming little cottage in Torremolinos, which looks across the bay to Malaga, and I went down there a good deal, especially in 1935 because it was a year without much news and I liked Jay's company, and there was a girl named Lisa down there who attracted me quite a lot. But, believe it or not, the Madrid-Algeciras Express, a train bringing international passengers bound for Africa, at one part of its trip stopped nine times within thirty miles. I asked why there was so much stopping at insignificant stations and was told that it was because the local 'political boss', usually either the local landowner or his representative, would have political pressure put on the railway company to have the main trains stopped at his little town because it gave the town more importance.

I wish there were more people in the world like Jay and I wish I were a good enough writer to describe him adequately. But for me his company is always a wonderful tonic. Conversation with him is like drinking at a cool, refreshing wayside fountain. Jay, like myself, has as far as I know never belonged to any political party. His father is a prosperous lawyer in Portland, Oregon, and Jay has been sailor, Harvard graduate and, finally, foreign correspondent. He has an X-ray mind which goes to the heart of the most intricate questions. And

he can, and does, explain them clearly. I am morally lazy.
I know that it is all wrong that a Spanish peasant should toil
endlessly and remain half-starved and that factory workers
should sicken and die of consumption because hygienic conditions are not looked after, and I know all the sordid beastli-
ness of poverty, but I am very apt to just forget about it and
to feel that after all I am not to blame and that instead of pointing out the dark spots of our civilisation in my writing as a
reporter it is so much simpler to gloss over this and pat the
man in power on the back and thus sit pretty with the people
who count. But Jay does not have my faculty for putting my
conscience into a twilight sleep. His alert and vigorous mind
sweeps the cobwebs from the problems of the day.

I loved to awaken in the morning with Madrid far behind
me and the train clattering easily down beyond Cordoba and
there would always be a small boy in a large hat swaying along
on a donkey near the railway track and singing: 'Ay . . .' in
that endless nasal warble which is so near to the genuine
African chant of the Moors that it is hard to tell the difference
at first. But at wayside stations, small and very dirty and
hungry-looking children came to ask for food and coppers. At
Boadilla, where the train was divided in leisurely fashion, one
part for Malaga and the other for Algeciras, an endless collection of dogs hunted about for food and kept me jittery because
they were always wandering in and out across the tracks while
the shunting to divide the two trains went on. No, all was not
well in Andalusia. There was hunger where there should have
been plenty. We rattled down to Malaga at tremendous speed
past the deep chasms where General Primo had built big dams
for irrigation of the dry plains lower down. Malaga was so
nice and friendly and the first thing I always did was to go
and buy some Eno's, or toothpaste, or any old thing, at the
chemist's shop on Larios Street because there was such a pretty
little fair-haired girl, a genuine blonde, behind the counter
that it was a pleasure to look at her and hear her Andalusian
accent.

Then just near the bus terminus there was a wine cellar
where they had rows and rows of huge barrels of the sweet old
Muscatel wine of the region. For one penny you got a glass in

which the shirt-sleeved boy who served mixed you three or four different wines and threw the halfpenny tip you gave him into a bucket kept for the purpose. Then out by bus to Torremolinos or maybe with Ruth Allen and Jay and Dollfy the dog and myself crowded into Mme Vandervelde's Ford roadster which she drove with a ferocious bull-terrier, which was no friend of Dollfy's, seated on her knees. She is short-sighted, very short-sighted, and drives fast and furiously so the trip was never dull. She is the divorced wife of the late M. Émile Vandervelde, the Belgian politician, and a nice person. Then she was living in one of Europe's nicest hotels, a white dot on the cliffs at Torremolinos with lovely gardens and nice swimming.

At night I would wander through the beautiful, scented gardens with the sound of the waves breaking on the shore, with my Austrian friend Lisa, a charming girl with an intelligent face and ripe, heavy breasts. She worked as housekeeper to an incredible German married couple who would have a free fight every few weeks and hit each other hard and then make it up with kisses.

One day, Jay and I motored to Gibraltar and what a strange feeling it is to come out of the heart of Andalusia and find yourself at the gates of Gibraltar with an 'English policeman' and a sentry of the Gordon Highlanders to receive you. The day Jay and I were there was quite animated because two battalions of the Gordon Highlanders, which had not met for 120 years in coming and going about Empire duties, had at last come together. And very temporarily, because one battalion was hurrying from Palestine to the West Indies—you know how our War Office leaves troops in some God-forsaken place for years and then suddenly rushes them at top-speed to some other equally remote point there to leave them once more in oblivion—and two hours ashore at Gibraltar was the maximum that could be allowed. So the two battalions paraded and it was a very moving sight and so dignified because the Highlanders move with such a quiet easy swing completely unlike the little-wooden-doll stiffness which the Guards and some other regiments affect.

Gibraltar is a strange place, and so English. Tea rooms

everywhere. Steak-and-kidney pudding, with the temperature at ninety in the shade. Jay and I laughed at a sign on one brick building which said: 'Married quarters. Trespassers will be prosecuted.' There is nothing Spanish about Gibraltar; it is just a small transplanted bit of England. Jay wanted to know how the soldiers amused themselves and whether there were any licensed houses on the Rock where they could go. But we were told that for that purpose leave was given to go to the small Spanish town of La Linea. Was there any kind of clinical control when they came back, asked the ever-inquisitive Jay. It seemed that there was not. Jay thought that was bad and that in America they would soon change such a sad state of affairs. On the way back our driver knocked down and killed three dogs, which was pretty un-English.

Hand-in-hand with Lisa, I watched the processions of Malaga's 'Semana Santa' and found it a very dull affair compared with that of Seville. In the poorer districts the people showed little enthusiasm, nobody knelt when an image swayed by on the shoulders of the hidden bearers. Groups of police and Civil Guards with rifles and sub-machine-guns stood all along the route. In the centre of the town the atmosphere changed and people cheered and shouted.

We had a mild touch of excitement in the realm of news in April, that is to say April of 1935, when President Alcalá Zamora had some kind of friction with Gil Robles and the Head of the State was reported to have said that he 'would not tolerate a Vatican Republic in Spain'. The Clericals left the Cabinet, but everything was patched up after a month of negotiations and the Clericals returned, this time five strong and with Don José Maria Gil Robles now occupying the War Ministry. Among those dropped overboard was the Clerical Minister, Sr. Jimenez Fernandez, whose strong Christian-Socialist leanings led him to land reform schemes in Estremadura and elsewhere which were not to the liking of the landowners. In fact he was rotundly denounced as a 'Red' by Monarchists in Parliament not long before the Clericals replaced him.

On August 21, Robles created a mild sensation both nationally and internationally by suddenly rushing troops to the

Straits of Gibraltar. This was on the eve of a meeting of the British Cabinet to decide on the attitude we were to take up regarding sanctions against Italy as a result of the Italo-Ethiopian conflict. It had been reported in some international circles that Britain might close the Straits of Gibraltar in order to prevent Italy from receiving supplies of raw material. Without any warning, Gil Robles sent three infantry battalions from Malaga to Algeciras and a regiment of cavalry from Seville to Algeciras which, of course, lies opposite Gibraltar. Other troops were moved to Ibiza, in the Balearic Islands, and, I believe, some were sent also to Cadiz. Sr. Gil Robles was anxious to give the British a rap across the knuckles and newspapers which followed the Government politics stressed the fact that 'it must not be forgotten that no decision can be taken regarding the Straits of Gibraltar without consulting Spain'.

Robles himself gave no logical explanation of this demonstration of armed forces against a friendly nation such as Great Britain. He told the reporters who went to question him, he was staying in San Sebastian at the time: 'I am simply putting into effect plans for the military reorganisation of the nation.' When asked whether it were usual for normal reorganisation to be carried out at several hours' notice and without giving men or officers time to prepare their belongings or to arrange for the transfer of heavy luggage and of families, he shrugged his shoulders and changed the conversation.

If British prestige were to be maintained it was necessary that Britain should at once have demanded an explanation of this sudden massing of forces in Algeciras, but so far as I could find out at the time nothing of the kind was done. I gathered that in British diplomatic circles the tendency was to regard it as a foolish and indiscreet act by a political novice but without further importance. In my opinion the incident was of considerable importance because Robles after all belonged to the moderate sector of the Spanish Right and yet on the flimsy grounds of a piece of international gossip he was quick to show an anti-British attitude. It is possible that pressure had been put on him through the Vatican to act thus in the interests of Italy. But it is possible also that the pressure came from Germany for Robles was much under the influence of Army officers such as Generals Franco and Goded who belonged to an Army clique which made no secret of its warm sympathies for Nazi Germany.

I never kept very close contact with the British Embassy in Madrid but when I did talk to any of our diplomatic officers I found them very complaisantly disposed towards the Spanish Right. They looked upon them as a guarantee against Bolshevism, much preferable to have in power than either Socialists or Republicans for this reason, and they would gently pooh-pooh any suggestion that the Spanish Right might one day side with Germany and Italy and we might suddenly find our Empire routes in danger. When I made any such suggestion I would receive a paternal pat on the shoulder and be told: 'No, young man. Spain will always be on the side of Britain because we buy her goods and she knows which side her bread is buttered on!' And that was that. I hasten to add that I did on occasion meet very intelligent British diplomatic officials who took a broader view of things, but they were definitely in the minority.

Robles took another opportunity, early in September 1935 I think it was, to show his dislike for the British policy towards Italy. This was on the occasion of a visit to Madrid by Dr. Montheiro, Portuguese Minister of Foreign Affairs. International gossip said that Mr. Eden had asked Dr. Montheiro to come to Madrid, he was on his way back from Geneva to Lisbon, in order to press the Spanish Government to lend support to British policy with regard to sanctions against Italy. There had also appeared in the Portuguese Press some feelers regarding a closer co-operation in foreign affairs between Portugal and Spain. On the day Dr. Montheiro arrived in Madrid the Catholic *El Debate* made a sharp attack on the Portuguese Press which had put out these feelers and said that this was just an indirect attempt to hitch Spain to the British wagon and that no such attempt could be tolerated. To back up this attack, at an official banquet offered that night by the Spanish Cabinet to the distinguished visitor, there were five empty chairs. Only the Republican Ministers attended. All five Clericals ostentatiously stayed away. When interrogated by newspapermen next day in the War Ministry as to the reason for his absence from the banquet, Sr. Gil Robles answered: 'The banquet? Oh yes, last night I had a fearful lot of work here in the Ministry and was kept at my desk until after midnight. That was the only reason why I was not there.' All the other Clericals had been similarly detained, it seemed.

In the earlier part of the year when the Model Prison in Madrid was jammed with prisoners I went several times to have a look at things. I had not been there since August 1932 when I went to see Don Ramiro de Maeztu who had been locked up for no particular offence, as far as I could find out, after the Sanjurjo revolt of that same month. Sr. de Maeztu, a Basque with English blood and married to an Englishwoman, was a charming, elderly man rather of the same type as Javier Bueno. He took his causes with rather too passionate a gusto. And he had various causes for he had begun life as a most fervent Anarchist and was now an ultra-Conservative. In those days there was no difficulty in obtaining a permit to speak to prisoners. Now it was different and I was told emphatically that no journalist could be given permission. However, as relatives were allowed in, I conceded myself the honorary rank of brother-in-law to one of the prisoners whom I knew and went in with his wife without any trouble.

I hate prisons myself. In fact I suppose most people do so. I can never visit one without thinking of the moral and physical scars left on the bodies of those inside by these terms of isolation from the world. And a prison filled with political offenders upsets me even more. It is unpleasant to think of a robber or a pickpocket leaving gaol as an addict to some unpleasant vice or with consumption eating his lungs, but it is much more unpleasant to think of someone suffering this fate just because he held this or that political view.

Inside the gaol I found a whole mob of people crowded into an oblong room with prisoners talking to them through iron bars on three sides. I saw Sr. Largo Caballero looking grave and pontifical. I called to him through the bars: 'How are you being treated in gaol, Sr. Caballero?' He looked at me with very cold blue eyes and without the slightest change of expression on his face and said: 'I have nothing whatever to say to the Press.' What a fine interview that was. . . . But others were more cordial. There was that jolly artist, Luis Quintanilla, busy stuffing into his leather wind-jacket a brandy bottle which he had whisked through the bars without the warder on duty noticing anything. Quintanilla had even wheedled the Governor of the gaol into allowing him to use a large cell as studio and to have an easel and drawing materials sent in and he was busy at work sketching his fellow-prisoners. The Governor, in a burst of good humour, had even given Quintanilla Madrid's smartest pickpocket to serve as his orderly and sharpen pencils and sweep the floor. Luis Quintanilla had ended up in gaol because a revolutionary committee of some kind or other led by a young Socialist Deputy named Hernandez Zancajo, a former taxi-driver, had been found sheltering in his studio. Standing near Quintanilla was a nice and quite young man, despite his grey hairs, Ogier Preteceille, foreign editor of *El Socialista* and correspondent for a London newspaper.

Preteceille told me that he had been beaten up with rubber clubs by ten Shock Policemen after his arrest. They said: 'That will teach you dirty foreign Reds to come and meddle in Spain.' He was of French origin and a naturalised Spaniard, I think. The charge against him was eventually withdrawn. The correspondents had not escaped altogether unscathed in the trouble. Ilse Wolff, a German woman journalist, had been expelled as had also Simone Tery, daughter of the founder of *L'Œuvre* of Paris. Mr. Reginald Calvert, of Reuters, was arrested but released within a few hours after the intervention of Sir George Grahame, the British Ambassador, and Mr. M. B. T. Paske-Smith, the British Consul.

In one corner of the prison visiting-room a fine tall young man leant against the bars and held the hand of a very beautiful girl. They never spoke and indeed seemed oblivious to the din around them; maybe it was the first time she had seen him since the police took him to gaol. The studious Ramos Oliveira was also there behind the bars. He afterwards became an admirable Press Attaché to the Spanish Embassy in London.

I often thought what a theme the Model Prison in those days offered for a great novelist or dramatist with its strange cargo of about 3,000 souls, ranging from Francisco Largo

Caballero and Luis Companys and including idealists, agitators, bread-and-butter politicians, murderers awaiting trial, pickpockets, swindlers, down to a score of young men stowed away in the basement and forgotten in the political upheaval and who had all been arrested in a raid on a café in the Calle Jardines which had been catering too exclusively for a male clientele.

Caballero was in gaol for twelve months before being acquitted, but some weeks prior to his release he was allowed out for one day to attend the funeral of his wife. The funeral inevitably turned out to be a demonstration of sympathy for Caballero and 20,000 people followed the hearse. It was the first time I saw the clenched fist salute used. I believe it was invented by Edgar André, a German Social Democrat, who was beheaded by the Nazis. It may have been used earlier in Spain, but I never saw it until this afternoon of September 1935. Then it was used more as a menace because the route of the funeral procession lay past the private house of President Alcalá Zamora and as the procession went by those in the files raised clenched fists in silence. Among the mourners was one of Alcalá Zamora's sons, Luis. He had been court-martialled and acquitted for some strong remarks he had made while a corporal in the Army during the October revolt and only recently on receiving £1 5s. od. as his share of the monetary reward distributed to all soldiers on duty during the repression of the revolt, he had returned the money ostentatiously to the War Minister.

That funeral procession was an interesting symptom of political feeling and showed how strongly the tide of sympathy ran in favour of those who had taken part in the October rising. Those in power were not helped by the publicity attached to several scandals involving the Radicals which had recently come to light and notably the 'Affaire Daniel Strauss', known as the 'Straperlo Scandal'.

Mr. Daniel Strauss, variously said to be of Dutch and Mexican nationality, had written to the President of the Republic complaining that sums of money he had laid out for 'expenses' in connection with an unsuccessful attempt to obtain a monopoly in Spain for the use of a gambling machine of his invention, had not been returned at his request. Apparently, the 'Straperlo' machine resembled a roulette table but with twelve numbers instead of thirty-six, besides the zero. The ball and the cylinder carrying the number were said to operate mechanically. Mr. Strauss claimed that it was a game of dexterity and not a gamble. It may have been, and it may be that the fact that the table which functioned for a week at the lovely and secluded Formentor Hotel, which lies beyond Pollensa Bay on Majorca Island, won £20,000 for its operators only goes to show that Spaniards are not expert mathematicians. Mr. Strauss, however, made no mention of any such gains in his complaint to the Head of the Spanish Republic in which he emphasised that he had spent £14,000 for 'expenses' and had received a promise that he would be allowed to instal twelve tables at various resorts. He had actually opened a table at the Casino of San Sebastian on September 12, 1934, but after three hours' play the Casino was closed by Government order and again at Formentor, Majorca, several months later, after one week's play the table was closed by the police.

Spanish interest centred on the way in which Mr. Strauss had incurred expenses. According to this enterprising, and now much annoyed, personage he had made various presents of money to Don Aurelio Lerroux, the adopted son of the former Prime Minister, and to other persons. Among gifts he claimed to have made was one to Don Rafael Salazar Alonso to whom he said that he gave a silver watch when he was Minister of the Interior. A parliamentary commission of twenty-one found eight persons involved and recommended a judicial inquiry. As far as I know this was never carried out. Among those mentioned in the commission's report was the adopted son of Sr. Lerroux, so the latter resigned from Cabinet office on October 29. He was at that moment Minister of Education for he left the premiership on September 21 after having presided over the eighth Cabinet in two years. He left the premiership because of the rumours already current about the gaming scandal, giving way to an economic expert named Don Joaquin Chapaprieta who was a post-Republic recruit to the Radical Party. Just after Lerroux left the Ministry of Education there was an inquiry into an irregular payment of £40,000 made to one Sr. Paya, a shipowner, and it was only after an all-night session that Parliament finally decided to exonerate Sr. Lerroux—the incident took place while he was Premier—and to place the responsibility on his former Under-Secretary, Sr. Moreno Calvo.

Stark tragedy began to loom very close again because here was a party which represented an appreciable sector of Spain's middle class revealed as engaged in petty corruption and immorality at a time when it should have been working night and day to help to create a new democratic Spain. Once again Spain's middle class was revealed as weak, incapable and frivolous. The Radicals had taken advantage of the fact that the Clericals, who managed to keep their hands clean amid so much dishonesty, kept them in power because they would not respond to the wooing of the feudal sectors who wished to put Spain under an iron Dictator and smash the Left once and for all as had been done in Germany and Italy. Nevertheless, the Clericals could hardly escape some of the public condemnation showered on their allies-in-office and they began to lose ground also to the extremists of the Right.

CHAPTER XX

AZAÑA HAS NO ANSWER

So great was the faith of the Spanish people in the Democratic Republic that the greatest crowd ever seen in Spain at one point gathered on a stretch of waste land known as the 'Campo de Comillas', at Carabanchel, on the southern outskirts of Madrid one grey Sunday morning in November of this year of 1935 to hear the voice of a Republican speaker, Don Manuel Azaña.

To few statesmen in world history has been given such an audience as Azaña spoke to on that Sunday morning. At least 200,000, and probably many more, filled a terrain so unfitted for this kind of use that more than half the spectators could not even see the stand from which the former Prime Minister addressed them. The loudspeakers functioned only partially and therefore tens of thousands not only saw nothing but they heard nothing either. This meeting had not been widely advertised. It was frowned on by the authorities and in some cases the Civil Guard turned back convoys of trucks carrying spectators. All vehicles bringing people from afar were stopped some miles outside Madrid, thus causing endless confusion and forcing weary men and women to trudge a long distance after a tiring ride. Admission was by payment. The front seats cost twelve shillings and sixpence and the cheaper ones ten shillings and half a crown. Standing room at the back cost sixpence. No one was forced to go to that meeting. Presence there, in fact, was much more likely to bring the displeasure of employer or landlord. How many of the great figures of Europe to-day could bring together spontaneously, without the slightest party organisation or preparation, a mass of 200,000 people in order to hear a speech lasting less than two hours and not accompanied by the most simple form of parade or demonstration which could appeal to the spectator fond of pomp and show?

From the farthest points of Spain there were groups who had travelled in some cases six hundred miles in rainy, cold weather in open motor lorries. When the speech was over they got back into the trucks for the same cold, bumpy journey back. I sat with my friend Emilio, whom I mentioned in connection with the elections of 1931, and who was the village jeweller of Egea de los Caballeros and brother of a friend of mine in Madrid. Since then I have received a letter which tells me that 'Emilio died on September 6, 1936, as a result of an illness caused by his visits to Madrid'. The letter was written to pass the Franco censorship and the 'illness' caused by a firing squad which punished trips to Madrid such as this one of November 1935. A prosperous, industrious citizen who had been a strong supporter of General Primo de Rivera, Emilio was to pay dearly for his sympathy for the under-dog and his hopes of a new, regenerated Spain. Forty peasants, including a number of women, had come in motor-trucks from his small town of Egea de los Caballeros.

Those 200,000 who stood patiently in Carabanchel as Azaña began his speech represented 20,000,000 Spaniards; they represented the Spain which wanted to hear the real voice of Democracy. They had seen Azaña fail once, yet they were here to-day hoping against hope that a miracle would happen; that they would hear a decisive voice announce that Democracy was not dead, that it would act decisively. They wanted to hear a forceful declaration that the Spanish Republicans of Good Faith meant to act! That they would announce a programme in strong, clear-cut tones. Land for the peasants, industrial reorganisation with the State taking over where private enterprise was too weak, ejection of the Church from politics, cleansing of the Army of the shoals of high officers who never even took the trouble to hide their wish to smash the Republic at the first opportunity, disbanding of the Civil Guard and its replacement by a Republican force, education once and for all under State control, and short shrift for anyone who dared to stand in the way of these essential minimum reforms.

That was what Spain wanted to hear from Sr. Azaña. Nothing has been so terrible, so tragic, in Spain in these years I have watched it as the pathetic, the pitiful earnestness with which the mass of the people again and again, despite every disappointment and every failure of the Democrats, have asked them for inspiration, for leadership. And, alas, asked in vain.

As I sat on my narrow bench and watched the crowd, I hoped against hope. It seemed to me that even a man with printer's ink in his veins instead of blood could not fail to respond to the passion and desire of that crowd. But it was like watching a ham-handed bungler at the wheel of a super-tuned Bentley just waiting to feel sensitive hands on the wheel and the gear-shift, to see Manuel Azaña handling that crowd.

He talked to these workers and peasants about international relations, about gold reserves and monetary complications, and all in an uninspiring, matter-of-fact voice. It would have been an excellent address for a Rotary Club luncheon. I think he was terrified of the crowd, afraid of what it might do if he warmed its passions. He was afraid that he was not big enough to dominate this crowd. And he was right. He had nothing to offer it. His life diet had been nineteenth-century Liberalism. According to this, one fostered civil liberties and then sat back to watch the nation flourish in the bracing airs of freedom. But here was a nation still with a feudal economy and with no strong merchant bourgeois class to seize control and reform and reshape the economic machine to fit twentieth-century needs. In a speech several months before, I heard Azaña say rather pathetically: 'When I was in power I pulled levers and the machinery did not answer. . . .' If Azaña had been a bigger man he might have set to work to form a party, to build up a machine which would work and which would have answered the heart-breaking plea of the people of Spain. But he was a cultured, intelligent product of his environment. With his intelligence and ideas he could have attained the rank of statesman with no difficulty in either contemporary Britain or France. But it was not enough. He was not big enough to adjust himself. And even if he had' been big enough, he would have had to have ploughed a lonely furrow at first for few of his class would have understood him or have followed him down the virgin trail of a new, progressive, battling concept of Democracy.

So these people went back home. They had no answer. There was no hope that new things would come, that their children might go to secondary schools or universities, that hygienic houses might replace their hovels. One knew how it would soon be again, as it was in 1931. With the lack of hope would come violence. Shots at the Civil Guard. Churches in flames. Well-dressed, well-fed people would hold up their hands in horror. Army officers in their mess rooms would fume and ask if 'decency and civilisation were to be stamped out by uncontrolled hordes led by self-seeking agitators?'

But, my God, how awful to be a Sr. Azaña and to have had the answer, or at least some answer, some attempt at an answer, so near at hand and not to have given it. Indeed not to have been able to give it; that must have been awful, I felt, as I wandered home on foot, dejected and without hope.

CHAPTER XXI

VICTORY

THERE were three Cabinets in the last three months of 1935, which was good going even for Spain.

In fact, when the white-haired and dignified Don Manuel Portela Valladares took office on December 9 and formed a Republican Government without Clericals, with which he eventually carried out the elections of February 1936, this was the eleventh Cabinet since December 1933. Lerroux had presided over five Governments, his henchman Ricardo Samper over one and his other right-hand man until he deserted, Martinez Barrio, had led one also. Then there were two under Sr. Chapaprieta. This was the way in which Spain's middle class irresponsibly wrecked the Republic. Of course, there was much grist to the political mill as a result of so many changes. Spain has a pleasant law which enacts that any Minister who has taken possession of his office, even if the Government he be in only lasts half an hour, thereupon receives a life pension of ten thousand pesetas, that is to say, £250 per annum, on leaving office. I once took the trouble to go through the list of Cabinet Ministers belonging to the Radical Party during this two years of Radical-Clerical domination and found, I think it was thirty-eight, who had held a portfolio and therefore qualified for a life pension. There were less than 100 Deputies in the Radical Party, so the proportion is noteworthy. Even these eleven Cabinets in two years and several months did not cover all changes. I remember how Sr. Gil Robles by neat manœuvring managed to eject first Sr. Samper, then War Minister Hidalgo, and later Don Filiberto Villalobos from the Cabinet without there being a crisis in any of these cases. They were just substituted by persons of more 'confidence' in the opinion of the Clericals.

The Clericals, I may say, did not follow the Radicals in this game of hunt-the-pension. And a most noteworthy example of political honesty is that of the Socialist Party which from April 1931 until the fall of Sr. Azaña in September 1933 kept the same three Ministers, Sres. Prieto, Caballero and de los Rios, in office without once making a change, despite the fact that there were four reshuffles of the Cabinet when the Party could quite legitimately have changed its representatives in order to assure others of its members pensions for life at the State expense.

As a 'finale' to the disastrous and inglorious reign of Don Alejandro Lerroux came the economic expert, Don Joaquin Chapaprieta, who presided over two Cabinets but finally was ejected from power by Clericals and Monarchists, who flatly refused to accept his tax reform scheme which was probably the most moderate in Europe as far as the middle and upper classes were concerned. It is hard to write calmly of the utter lack of responsibility which these classes showed at such a critical period of Spain. Consider the fact that until Sr. Chapaprieta proposed some mild tax reforms, income tax for the wealthy in Spain was only three per cent and it began at 100,000 pesetas per annum (£2,500). And nobody ever paid anyway. There was no country in Europe at this period where a wealthy person could get such value for money and pay so few taxes as in Spain and the proof could be seen on Madrid's Gran Via any afternoon in the number of super-elegant, modern limousines outside the clubs and fashionable tea salons. Spain, as somebody once wrote about Greece, was a poor country with many rich people.

When Chapaprieta had been thrown out by those who would not make even the slightest pecuniary sacrifice to contribute towards economic reform, by which alone political stability could be restored, in came Don Manuel Portela Valladares, known familiarly in political circles as 'El Consorte' (The Consort) because he is married to a woman who is countess in her own right.

Portela, who had been active in local politics in Barcelona where he was Civil Governor for some time in 1909, was a veteran in his seventies, with many financial interests, much wealth, and a completely nineteenth-century concept of politics. He convinced President Alcalá Zamora that the thing to do was to create a small Centre Party, led by Portela himself, and go to elections. Apparently he believed that he could produce sufficient Deputies out of the political hat to keep a balance between Left and Right in the next Parliament. Portela, although theoretically in the Radical Party, behaved with complete independence. He could not have governed for two days with the House open, for the Clericals were not included in his Cabinet and were furious at his proposal to go to the country at a moment bad for them and also at his intention to manufacture a new party which would, if it had any success, probably take votes from Robles's Party. Portela could legally close Parliament for thirty days but when those days were up he still did not open the Chamber, on the pretext that he was going to elections. Most political experts agreed that this was quite irregular and that with the thirty days terminated he must perforce face Parliament or resign. Robles in a furious public speech threatened to impeach Portela and several months later President Alcalá Zamora was censured by the new Parliament and dismissed from office because he signed the Decree dissolving the old Chamber when Portela was alleged to be behaving irregularly and infringing the Constitution of the Republic.

Spain hummed with political activity as the elections of February 1936 drew near. On December 30, 1935, the United Front composed of all Republican parties, except the Radicals, together with both Communists and Socialists was formed. Among the parties of the Right there was violent discussion. Some wished to ostracise Robles's Clericals for their lack of success when in power and indeed many suggested abstention. So furious was the squabbling that not until February 6, just ten days before election day, did Clericals and Monarchists form a Right Front. This meant that the Right forces were behind-hand in their propaganda. Nevertheless, they had apparently large sums of money at their disposal for they engaged a considerable number of paid employees for propaganda work, a thing which no other Spanish group could afford to do, and their issue of posters and pamphlets was in quite as extravagant style as in 1933. Yet how they stood with the country was partially brought home to me one day on the Calle

Alcalá when I was given a pamphlet with a hammer-and-sickle on the cover and on opening it idly to see what the Communists had to say for themselves, was amazed to find that it contained Clerical propaganda. It looked very much as if the organisers of the Right had found out that people were refusing even to accept their literature unless it were disguised. At least that was the only explanation which occurred to me at the time. I heard of many gifts to the Right for propaganda from wealthy persons, one of whom, I was told from a usually reliable source, had given £12,500.

Portela, who although he had lived most of his life in Barcelona had important interests in his native Galicia, relied principally on that region to produce his Centre Party for which not many candidates were forthcoming.

We none of us guessed how much hung on these elections, nor how they would come to be discussed and debated the world over. On election eve I took a walk with several other correspondents through the working class districts of Cuatro Caminos. In almost the whole of that area there was not a single poster of the Right parties to be seen. It was not that they had been torn down. It was just that popular feeling was boiling over to such an extent that not even the toughest gunman or the most fervent idealist had ventured to stick bills favouring any but Left parties out in that quarter.

I had dinner one evening with Luis Quintanilla, the artist, and he told me: 'Our United Front will sweep the country.' Quintanilla had quite recovered from his stay in gaol, which had ended after eight months with the charge against him being withdrawn. He had, however, had a slight contretemps since then as a result of a fervent Fascist propagandist having thrust a leaflet at him rather rudely—so Luis said—in the Café Negresco whereupon Quintanilla in his wrath seized one of the very solid glass water bottles of the establishment and broke it on the head of the unfortunate youth, who needed some stitches before he could go home again. So whenever I happened to take a morning constitutional walk in the lovely Parque del Oeste and dropped in to see how Quintanilla was getting on with his monument to the pioneer of Spanish Socialism, Pablo Iglesias, I would see a revolver butt sticking out from among the brushes Luis used in painting his frescoes. He kept the gun handy in case any Fascist might consider vengeance.

Quintanilla was right in his forecast and I was wrong in mine. I estimated that the United Front could count on the support of at least seventy-five per cent of the voters, in theory, but that in practice the obstacles in their way were so great that they would be lucky if they secured half the seats in Parliament and probably they would have rather less. Because despite their quarrels I believed that Portela would help Robles's candidates where he could and I knew, for instance, that a special telephone connection had been installed between Robles's office and the private office of the Director-General of Police Forces of all Spain. Reports of intimidation which came to Robles would at once be reported by him to the police chief so that there would be not the slightest delay in action by the authorities. Moreover, the Right forces were straining every nerve in Madrid. In the offices of one insurance company a large portrait of Don Alfonso was hung, obviously as an indication to the employees as to which way they should vote. In another important office, employees known to be of Right opinions and who had a vote outside Madrid had their fares paid in order that they could vote and were given leave of absence for this. The manager of this office and several employees who belonged to Left parties and who had intended to act as interventors (party representatives who preside over the various and numerous ballot boxes in order to watch the interests of their respective parties and to prevent faking) on election day, had to give up the idea as the managing-director dropped a hint that trouble might follow if they did this. I knew of one landlord owning seven houses who warned the concierges of the houses that he would call for them with a car in order to take them and such of their families as had votes to the polling station. This meant, of course, that at the door of the booth he would hand them a voting paper for the Right and watch from the door-way to make sure that they dropped it into the box. And various women of the Right whom I knew had made arrangements to take their servants to the polling booth with them, just as they had done last time.

You may think this all sounds petty. But these were individual cases which I could vouch for. There were thousands of which one never heard. The Clericals, and the Right in general, paid many of their interventors twelve shillings and sixpence for the day, in addition to sending them hot meals, plus coffee and cigar. . . . To be an interventor for a Left party meant that you could be pretty sure of finding yourself on the black list of your employer if he found out, and he generally did. I mention all this because one hears so little in general about what it meant to the man-in-the-street to support the United Front. And as for money for propaganda, the only party of the Left with any considerable funds was the Socialist Party, which in turn relied on subscriptions from the individual trade unions. I dare say, although I have no proof, that the Communist Party had help from the Comintern but totalling together the money spent by the Left it obviously could not be compared with that of the Right because the latter simply overwhelmed towns and villages with posters, which numerically in most places—with the exception of a few districts such as that of Cuatro Caminos which I mentioned earlier—far exceeded the modest efforts of the United Front. A gigantic picture of the head of Gil Robles which obscured the side of a seven-story building, dominated the Puerta del Sol. Another enormous poster of the Right in the Calle Alcalá after being stoned by some youths received a permanent guard of two mounted policemen.

You may say that many workers too voted out of fear that they would be maltreated if they did not vote Left. But, at least in the towns, it was hard to control the vote of a worker unless you did as some employers did and that was to escort them to the door and then hand them the voting paper which made it hard for them to avoid placing it in the ballot box, which is on an open table in Spain, unless they were proficient at sleight-of-hand. I never heard of any cases of workers' organisations using such tactics on their members.

What the workers could do was to organise minor street riots which would keep the womenfolk, on whose votes the Right pinned their hopes, and also monks and nuns, from voting. And this was done in some cases. But on the whole there was little intimidation for the entire police force of Spain, with machine-guns in the streets in the large towns, stood ready to repress the slightest incident. In all, as far as I could learn, there were three dead and seventeen injured, which in England would mean a good deal but for Spain with passions running at fever-heat it constituted what could be considered a pretty normal election. I did a round of Madrid polling booths and found things quiet. Police cars with rifles peeping out scurried here and there as a warning to any mischief-maker. What was amazing was the way in which at some polling booths where voting was slow, for in Spain it is necessary to prove one's personality before being allowed to vote and cantankerous interventors of this or that party will sometimes raise objections and slow voting to a snail's pace, both men and women stood patiently in queues for hours to register their votes. Presiding over one of the voting tables was the Duke of Alba, one of the few Spanish aristocrats who have consistently endeavoured to fulfil their civic duties.

The Left secured an easy majority in the first round and improved this greatly in the second round because such a ferment followed the elections that it was virtually impossible for the Right to take any active part in the second elections held in those districts, Granada, for instance, where the first voting was not decisive. The Clericals held their own well but the Radicals were wrecked as a Party. The Left Republicans, with seventy-five candidates triumphant in the first round alone, must have proved a pleasant surprise for Don Manuel Azaña but I fear me that many of these seats were a gift from Socialists and Communists. Afterwards the results, which I append to this chapter in order that those who like figures may consider them, showed that Right and Left more or less divided the 9,000,000 votes but that the Left got more advantage from their votes because they were solidly united and the Right lacked cohesion. The Right would have secured more votes if conditions had been normal at the time of the second round but against this must be set off the fact that as the Left supporters in these districts saw that the result was a foregone conclusion, they also in part did not vote. Reporters should not, I know, have views. But I do stick to my opinion here that if these elections had been held under such conditions as prevail at a general election in England, then the United Front would have had a far greater victory because the pressure of the Right was so tremendous everywhere that people could not, or feared to, vote freely, and gave their votes to the Right to make sure of their bread and butter.

One factor which played a great part in the triumph of the United Front was the complete breakdown of Anarchist discipline, which was always used to prevent voting by the trade union masses under Anarchist leadership. The Anarchist argument that 'Monarchists, Clericals, Socialists, Communists are all tarred with the same political brush and are enemies of the working classes', was not accepted by a Spain which knew that the Republic was in grave danger. Still another thing which influenced results—I am sorry that I harp so much on this election but we all know how important it was—was the sweeping dismissal of literally tens of thousands of people from their jobs after the movement of 1934. The way it was done was quite ruthless. One bank in Madrid simply dismissed forty clerks from their posts because they struck in October 1934. Now in Spain's rickety economic world to lose a job like that may mean years of unemployment. It is not like Paris or London where there is a chance that you may find something else to do. In passing, I may say that the manager who fired the men was shot during the first troubles of July 1936 so he paid dearly enough for his act, which in Madrid virtually meant sending forty men, nearly all with wives and families, to starvation or to living on the charity of friends and relatives. I knew one man who held a post in the Norte Railway, a quiet office employee but apt to speak a little freely when he had taken a few drinks and who one night in a bar made some comment about his sympathies for the Asturian revolutionaries, this while the resistance was still going on. He was arrested and released a few days later as he obviously had done nothing to further the movement, but he was dismissed his job, which he had looked on naturally enough as a post for life. He had a wife and child. The newspaper *A.B.C.* alone had dismissed 300 men. So it is not difficult to imagine the way in which all these people and their friends and their fellow-trade-unionists worked desperately to win that election. It also says little for the political common-sense of the Right that they did not soften their attitude a little and at least take men back who were not obvious extremists before they faced elections.

The election returns were: Moderate Republicans (followers of Azaña and Martinez Barrio), 162; Socialists, 94; Communists, 19; Right Coalition (Monarchists, Clericals, Agrarians, Traditionalists), 144; Centre Parties (Portela and Lerroux supporters), 58.

CHAPTER XXII

ADRIFT AFTER VICTORY

THE Republic won a striking victory, but it ran the risk of losing everything within a few hours. Since then, Sr. Portela has revealed how, when the first results of the elections became known, General Franco went to him and proposed that he, Sr. Portela, should stay in power and refuse to hand over office to the victors of the election. The Army, said General Franco, would intervene to support Sr. Portela and maintain him in power. In other words, a military coup was proposed to prevent by force the taking over of governing powers by the victorious United Front.

It was not only Sr. Portela who courageously refused to abet the overthrow of the electoral results but also Don José Maria Gil Robles, who alternated between moves which were disastrous for the régime and good turns to it. He saved the Republic after the October revolt of 1934 by definitely opposing the menacing attitude adopted by officers belonging to the clique to which Generals Mola, Sanjurjo, Franco, Goded and many other senior and junior officers belonged. Now he once again set his face against a dictatorship. My impression is that the hand of Cardinal Pacelli, now Pope Pius XII, was behind this opposition to a military dictatorship in the fear that this would lead to a fascist régime in Spain which might be as anti-Catholic as the movements in Germany or Italy.

I obtained full proof of Robles's part, it has never been made public up to now as far as I know, quite by chance. I had rushed to Robles's home on the day following elections to obtain an interview. His secretary showed me into a salon and then went back into an inner room, where he had some visitors whom I could not see and to whom he spoke in quite a loud voice. He said: 'Yes, last night the Monarchists tried to persuade Our Chief (he meant Robles) to join in a *coup d'état* to forestall the results of the elections and to prevent the Left from reaching power, as it was clear that they would do judging even by the early voting returns. Our Chief was furious. He refused point blank. He told them that they were irresponsible and quite mad to suggest such a thing and that neither he nor his Party would consider participation in such a wild adventure. . . .' At this point, the secretary suddenly realised that he had forgotten to close the door and he hurried across the room and slammed it shut. The rest of the conversation was lost to me. I was sorry that I could not have listened a little longer as I would have liked to have known who had made the proposal on behalf of the Monarchists. Presumably it was Calvo Sotelo or Don Antonio Goicoechea, or possibly both. It would have been interesting to know whether they were identified also with Franco's plan to keep Portela in power. My own guess, as I have no proof, is that Franco was in contact with Calvo Sotelo and went to Portela after Robles had rotundly refused to co-operate.

Robles was in a peculiar situation. He was so much hated by the people in general, because he was accused of provoking the revolt of October 1934, and he was so unpopular with the Right and the Army because people in those circles alleged that he had twice refused to co-operate in a military *coup d'état*, that it was hardly safe for him to appear in public. He announced that he had deputised party leadership in Don Enrique Jimenez Fernandez, the champion of Christian Socialism, and that he was going to rest. He took a nice villa in France, Rayon Vert, near Biarritz Lighthouse, and spent a good deal of time with his family there although he never actually gave up his leadership. In order to make things quite clear, however, Robles made a formal statement committing the Clerical Party to 'submit to the verdict of the country'.

This statement was countered by Sr. Calvo Sotelo with a public announcement in which he said: 'If there is a moment of great danger for the country from Communist agitation I believe that the Army will step in and save the situation, if there are no politicians capable of doing this. The Army will not let Spain fall into Red Revolution.' That was pretty plain speaking.

I have dealt with the threats at a *coup d'état* very fully here

because so much has been written since then about the preparation of the movement which finally shook the peace of Spain
on July 18. As far as I can learn the general lines of the July
revolt were drawn up some time towards the end of 1935. A
foreigner holding an important position in Spain and with
exceptionally good sources of information, received news in
December 1935 of a plan for a movement to be executed at
some future date and which tallied almost exactly with the
way in which the *coup d'état* of July 18, 1936, was eventually
carried out, both as far as the generals and the garrisons involved were concerned. If both Sr. Gil Robles and Sr. Portela
had been agreeable it seems likely that the coup would have
been put through following the elections of February 16.

Looked at, of course, from a cold and calculating point of
view one doubts to some extent whether Robles and Portela
did really help the Republic. I think that both very genuinely
meant to do so. But to any really intelligent political observer
it was obvious that for Franco or any other general to have carried out a *coup d'état* at that moment would have almost certainly meant disaster for those attempting it. In those first
hours, when they were prepared to strike, there was absolutely
no pretext or justification such as arose later after months of
disorder, strikes, church-burning, and the final episode of the
shooting of Calvo Sotelo. I know that justification is not necessary if one has the force, but that is what they would have
almost certainly lacked. Outside this small clique of officers
who for long had made no concealment of their dislike of the
Republic and their sympathy for Fascist methods, a great many
military officers would have hesitated to take part in a movement which crudely and without the least pretext set out to
smash the results of elections held a few hours before and of
which the final results were not even available. To have asked
the police who had been guaranteeing the impartiality and fair-
ness of the elections to turn round at once and herd into gaol
and perhaps shoot down those who had triumphed as a result
of this impartiality, would not have been easy.

Whereas by waiting and watching there was almost certain
to be ripe fruit to be gathered.

Don Manuel Azaña had already made it clear in his speech

in November that he had no remedy for Spain's troubles. Instead of grabbing power when Portela said that he was going, he had to be persuaded and fussed over by the leaders of the United Front to become Prime Minister. The Socialists were for the moment arm-in-arm with the Communists and, despite the efforts of Sr. Prieto, they declined to enter the Government. So a weak Cabinet was formed of third-rate men from the Left Republican and Republican Union, Sr. Barrio's party. Martinez Barrio, the only man with any energy, was side-tracked into the Speaker's post, which annulled him politically.

A group of as weak teamsters as well could be found faced a nation boiling over with resentment and demanding that the Republic should become a living entity. Weakness and stupidity hampered every move. First, Azaña promised an Amnesty Law. But the prisoners were already bursting out of the gaols, so he had to rush through an emergency measure legalising what was already done. Employers were ordered to take back all men discharged after the strike of October 1934 and to pay them back wages and also to keep on or indemnify the men taken on in their place. This was impossible. For instance, the newspaper *A.B.C.* had discharged 300 men and taken on other employees in their places. It now found itself double-staffed and owing £75,000 to the men who had returned. There was no strong attempt to cut through these problems, which every day became worse. Every employer who could do so cut down staffs and unemployment was at 700,000 officially and probably 1,000,000 in reality.

A British personage of note in the financial world who was passing through Madrid called on Sr. Azaña. 'As I understand it,' he was reported to have said, 'the situation is, Sr. Azaña, that it is a race between you and the Socialists as to who shall lay the foundations of a new Spain?' Sr. Azaña assented, agreeing that this was more or less how things stood. 'Then, Sr. Azaña, what is your programme?' asked the logical British man of affairs. Sr. Azaña could not tell him anything beyond vague generalities.

For myself the whole situation degenerated into a nightmare which lasted, except for several visits to London which were no rest at all, until August of 1937 when quite by chance and

on the slender recommendation of the hall porter of the Hotel
de Russie, at Geneva, I found myself at peace up in Caux-sur-
Montreux, looking down on the lovely eastern end of Lake
Geneva. There for three weeks I found rest. Strangely
enough in reading *Insanity Fair* and *Disgrace Abounding*, in
which Douglas Reed punches heartily some things which need
punching and hits other things which might perhaps be let
down a little more lightly, I have since found that he too loves
this corner of Europe very dearly. I only wish that I had
Mr. Reed's power of description in addition to sharing a liking
for the Montreux district with him, for I think that he is one
of the great contemporary writers of our day and that his
writing improves by giant strides.

I wish that I could tell you in his vigorous style the tale of
this nightmare Spain which began in February 1936. I would
not care if this were just the tale of Spain I were to tell, but in
this Spanish tragedy is wrapped the whole collapse of our
Western Democracy and, I am afraid, it marks the opening
scene to a major tragedy in which our British Empire will be
involved.

The people of Spain called to Democracy and received no
answer. They had urgent problems and there was no one to
resolve them.

Night and day my telephone rang. The Fascist Party which
had not secured the return of a single one of its thirty candidates at the elections, revenged itself by setting its gunmen
hard at work. A group of them opened fire on March 12 on
Luis Jimenez de Asua, the active Socialist lawyer who by his
efforts had secured the release of thousands from prison after
1934. They missed him but killed a policeman. The murderers were said to have been flown out of Spain by various
of the Ansaldo brothers, five of whom were aviators. Enrique
Ansaldo was arrested. Left-Wing rioters countered this outrage by burning down the offices of the Fascist newspaper, *La
Nacion*, and setting fire to three Madrid churches. There was
rioting in Cadiz because of some local incident and the police
killed eleven before restoring order. Many churches were
burned there. In Granada, Fascists fired on workers, injuring
fifteen, and promptly came a general strike and more shooting

and the Carmelite Convent and the Nazarene Church were set ablaze.

Always belated in their actions, the Government finally suspended the Fascist Party and arrested Primo de Rivera, but it did not finally get around to dissolving it until April 17 nor to trying Primo de Rivera until May 28, when he was sentenced to five months in prison for illegal possession of firearms. He behaved very badly in court, jumping on top of a desk and throwing a pot of ink over the clerk of the court.

In the meantime, trouble was fast and furious. President Alcalá Zamora, disliked equally by Left and Right, was dismissed from office on April 7 because he overlooked the fact that Sr. Portela kept Parliament closed for more than thirty days without appearing before it to ask for an extension of the closure, as the Constitution required. The manœuvre undoubtedly had the warm approval of Manuel Azaña, who obviously hated his job. He welcomed the promotion offered him to the Presidency. The Right refused to take part in his election. He was replaced by the well-meaning Santiago Casares Quiroga who, like Azaña, had no solution for the situation nor any policy except to survive from day to day as best he could.

The Fascist gunmen continued to shoot straight. As Don Manuel Pedregal, a Madrid judge, left his club on April 13, he was shot dead. Two days before he had sentenced a Fascist gunman to thirty years in gaol for the murder of a vendor of Socialist newspapers. Socialist gunmen shot a man dead during a parade on April 14, sad anniversary of a régime born with so much hope and slowly strangled by this lack of courage and lack of vision which is strangling all Democracy in Europe. The fact that the man held some position of importance in the counter-revolutionary movement of the Right, he was a lieutenant of the Civil Guard wearing plain clothes and with a loaded revolver in his pocket, was shown by the fact that his funeral was attended not only by all available members of the Fascist Party—he had a membership card in his possession—but by a great many figures of the Right such as Sr. Goicoechea and Sr. Calvo Sotelo.

And what a funeral that man had! I have forgotten his name but he certainly had one of the wildest funerals anyone ever had. All the Fascist gunmen in town were on the job just to show their weight and numbers, and the Socialist Youth organisation had turned out snipers in force, so that soon there was a running battle all along the Castellana Avenue with black-coated politicians lying down for shelter and the numerous officers of the Civil Guard who had attended the funeral taking an active part in the fray. The Fascists would not follow the original route. They decided to parade the corpse down towards the centre of town. They shot their way to the Plaza Cibeles before more responsible persons managed to head them back towards the cemetery. Socialist snipers were in the Retiro Park and what a battle there was along there! I happened to get rather close just here and rarely have I dived for shelter with such swiftness, for the 'mourners' by now were in such a state of excitement that short of blazing at their own shadows there was little else they did not fire at. I think there were in all ten or fifteen killed, of whom one was Don Andres Artela, cousin of Primo de Rivera, and all that I could not understand was how so few were killed with so much shooting.

This shooting did have the wholesome effect that the Government began to investigate the politics of the officers in the police force and the Civil Guard. Twenty-five Civil Guard officers including a lieutenant-colonel, a major and three captains, were arrested. They were, apparently, members of the Fascist Party. A great many officers of the Shock Police were removed and replaced by officers known to be Republicans, or at least not to be actively anti-Republican, which was about as much as this régime asked by way of recommendation for a post of trust.

But it was not only the actual shooting which caused unrest; the whole atmosphere was uneasy. Never had Madrid seen anything like the long parades to celebrate the electoral victory and then to celebrate the Amnesty and then there was another parade on May Day. Sometimes great masses streamed along the streets at night demanding this or that and cafés would close and everybody would be nervous. The parades too were different. Endless thousands went by as before but now they were better organised. They chanted slogans. Smart young men and girls stalked along with military stride and wearing red (Socialists) or blue (Communists) shirts. Moscow had come to town. Communism had appeared overnight, thanks in no small part to the efforts of the International Red Aid organisation, which had done wonders since 1934 not only in Asturias but all over Spain in distributing money to the dependents of those in gaol, sixty thousand, and mostly wage earners, by arranging for legal defence for the prisoners, and by helping those who were in hiding to escape abroad with false passports. Much of this work was done, of course, by the trade unions but nevertheless the Socorro Rojo Internacional had managed to do a great deal of work and had made many friends for the Communists.

Even more than any help, of course, was the fact that the Communists always came along with a definite policy and the people of Spain were getting more and more tired of these worthy Liberals such as Azaña, who would never take steps to settle drastic problems. Even the Socialists were apt to fumble a good deal. The Communists won because they could provide a policy and even if it was not the right one at least the people felt that they were actually working towards an end and not just sitting as helpless prey ready to be gobbled up by the first energetic Fascist with the courage to overthrow the Republic. The young people of the Youth Organisations looked very pretty in their coloured shirts but they had few weapons and could not do any harm unless some Government handed out arms to them.

Somehow, with the revolutionary spirit abroad in the air went hand-in-hand a back-to-nature movement and the Spaniards from looking at fresh air as a thing to be enjoyed only on a café terrace and fresh water as a thing to admire in the lake at the Retiro Park in Madrid, suddenly developed a veritable craze for rambling, picnic-ing, swimming. In a few months five or six huge open-air swimming pools opened. Every Sunday tens of thousands flocked from Madrid and Barcelona to the country, and the Youth Organisations in nice white overalls would stride off to the most un-martial strains of guitarists. Sometimes political opponents would clash. One Sunday in a shooting affray between Socialists and Fascists in the Pardo Park, a great rolling expanse of countryside, a Fascist youth was badly injured. I do not know whether he died or not.

Thereupon a group of Fascists cruised around Madrid in a car until they saw some young people returning from an excursion and promptly fired a volley into them killing a girl named Juanita Rico and two other persons. It was a barbarous, cold-blooded, senseless piece of work for Juanita and her friends had no connection with the people who had shot the Fascist, except in so far as they all belonged to workers' organisations. About this time General Federico Berenguer, brother of the former Prime Minister, was murdered at San Sebastian by Left-Wing gunmen.

German influence was now very much in evidence. General José Sanjurjo, who was looked upon as likely to be a principal figure in any effort to establish Fascism in Spain, spent six weeks in Germany during the spring on the pretext of visiting the winter sports' section of the Olympic Games of 1936. He visited Krupps and other armament factories, it was creditably reported, and also that he had seen Herr Hitler. I believe he went back to Germany in June accompanied by Colonel Beigbeder, who later became High Commissioner for Morocco under General Franco and, still later, Foreign Minister in the summer of 1939. Colonel Beigbeder had a very intimate knowledge of German military circles for he had previously been Spanish military attaché in Berlin and he was, therefore, competent to act as liaison officer in this affair. A new daily air service was opened from Stuttgart to Madrid. A tourist office of the German State Railways was opened on the Calle Alcalá. The German official news service, Deutsches Nachrichten Bureau, which had previously been content with a few odd cables from Madrid now opened premises in a fashionable part of town and had two staff men at work. Under cover of an association of Germans living in Spain, arms were brought to Spain, mostly side-arms, I think, and distributed. The Italians were active, although less so. It was afterwards stated that an agreement promising help from Italy had been signed in Rome between Goicoechea and Il Duce and photostatic copies were circulated, but I do not know exactly how much

truth there was to this. I think that the events which followed showed that the ground had been well prepared.

Unrest continued. Madrid waiters struck. The bull-
fighters under Marcial Lalanda, who shortly afterwards was
demonstrating his enthusiasm for the cause of General Franco,
upset the season of bullfights by a conflict with fighters hailing
from Mexico. A cavalry regiment at Alcalá de Henares, of
which some members had fired on townspeople during some
kind of dispute and killed one civilian and wounded nine,
mutinied when the War Minister wished to transfer them to
Valladolid. The lifts did not function in Madrid and even
the grave-diggers had left their jobs. The Anarchists were
busy in Malaga where they shot a Communist. The latter's
friends retaliated. On June 10, a battalion of the Foreign
Legion in Morocco burned down a trade union headquarters
with their officers looking on with approval.

Fascist gunmen also shot and killed Sr. Malumbres, editor of
La Region of Santander, and Sr. Andres Casaus, editor of *La
Prensa* of San Sebastian.

There was a horrible story from a village in Almeria, I forget the name now, where the peasants ambushed a Civil Guard
and killed him following some trouble about timber rights.
Thereupon the Civil Guards of the district got together and
hunted down the villagers, shooting, I believe, sixteen of them
dead. The story was ghastly because, apparently, the Civil
Guards ran amok and pursued men who took refuge in a drain
under the road, killing them in the drain itself.

Behind the scenes the U.M. (Union Militar) was functioning, a secret military organisation which was violently Fascist
in character, and to which apparently a considerable number
of officers belonged. Republican officers countered this with
U.M.R., Union Militar Republicano, a secret organisation to
watch over the interests of the Republic. The Union Militar
circulated a list with some twenty names on of men they intended to murder because they were regarded as 'dangerous
elements'. The first man on the list, Captain Faraudo,
they shot one Saturday afternoon as he was walking home
along the Calle Alcantara with his wife on his arm. They
were obviously professional killers for they neatly put six

bullets into him from a motor-car without touching his wife. This captain had been drilling the Socialist Militias.

Recently, Socialist and Communist Youth organisations had fused as a result of negotiations carried out by Julio Alvarez del Vayo, who had not long before returned from a trip to Moscow. Caballero and his 'Eminence Grise', Araquistain, had not liked this fusion. They were already much worried about the Communist increase in strength and Araquistain told a friend of mine that he and Caballero disliked this linking of the juvenile organisations and were 'much disturbed' by it.

I do not know how many they numbered but as I have said before, they had not at present arms. So far as I could find out, both Socialists and Communists were on the defensive. They may have been plotting a *coup d'état*, as was afterwards alleged, but I certainly never saw any sign of it. Most of them were worried as to their chances of surviving a Fascist coup. The Youth groups used to keep watch at night on all ministries, especially the War Ministry, waiting for any signs of unusual activity. They knew something was coming and were doing their best not to be caught unawares. Some said that the new unified organisation, Unified Socialist Youth it was called, numbered 100,000. This seemed unlikely to me.

The second man on the military black list, Lieutenant Castillo of the Shock Police, was shot on Sunday night, July 12. He had married only three weeks before, and his fiancée received a letter on the eve of the wedding saying: 'Why marry a man who will soon be a corpse?' As he left his home on this Sunday night he was shot dead by men who escaped. There was, as far as I know, nothing 'extremist or subversive' about Lieutenant Castillo. He was just a good Republican who said so if questioned on the subject.

I heard of the murder after having seen Dickens's *Christmas Carol*, as done by Hollywood, and having enjoyed it immensely. I remember that when I heard the news I was standing with Jan Yindrich, of the United Press, in a billiard room on the Gran Via watching Colonel Fuqua, American military attaché, and Eddie Knoblaugh, of Associated Press, playing snooker.

The Shock Police in Castillo's squad along with some of his friends, gathered around the body of the dead man and took a silent oath. Shortly afterwards, a group of men wearing police uniform went to Calvo Sotelo's home. They knocked him up. 'You are wanted at police headquarters,' they told him. He tried to telephone the police station to find out what it was all about, but his phone was out of order—a policeman in the entrance hall had cut the line. So he decided to go along. Shortly afterwards he was handed in at the city mortuary, shot dead.

The gloves were off now. The Republic was to pay dearly for this stupid murder. Now the Right had every pretext for drastic action. It was true that there had been a terrible amount of trouble during the last months but no important person had been killed. Eighty churches had been set afire, but not all had been gutted or even seriously damaged. There had been lacking some big dramatic act on which to hinge the *coup d'état* which had been constantly postponed since February. Now, here it was.

Of course, those who did the murder were not in my opinion as much to blame as were Premier Casares Quiroga, who was also War Minister, and his Cabinet. They had been far too easy-going. They had done nothing about Union Militar or the Black List. For weeks the report had been going around that General Mola was engaged in some kind of subversive activities at Pamplona, where he was military commander of the region. The Madrid Press had even discussed the matter. With the writing in huge letters on the wall of trouble brewing, the Government attitude still appeared to be that comfortable one adopted by Sr. Azaña in March when he told a journalist: 'Fascism is of no importance in Spain. . . .' The police knew better than most people just who was behind Union Militar. They saw their officers threatened and even murdered while no effort was made whatever to take measures against those whom they considered responsible. So they just went out and committed a terrible crime. It was true that they removed the cleverest brain from the extreme Right, Sotelo in my opinion came second to Robles in capacity if we regard the Right as a whole. But of the ultra-Right sector there was nobody who could match him as a political leader and debater.

CHAPTER XXIII

PERSONAL REACTIONS

THERE have been, so far, two brief periods in my life when I have been completely, blindly, drunk with passion, quite as effectively as if my veins were throbbing from the stimulation of too much potent, Valdepeñas red wine. The first of these was when the Spanish Generals revolted following the murder of Calvo Sotelo. The second was when I watched that pitiful river of 400,000 refugees flowing into France from Catalonia early in 1939.

For days in the fierce heat of those July days in Madrid I was in a state of complete, mental inebriation. I banged the keys of my typewriter with furious conviction. I wrote: 'The humble men and women of Spain facing death to save their cherished civil liberties. . . .' 'Just as Cromwell fought to establish the reign of democracy and to suppress the last effort of feudalism to preserve its privileges, so in Spain to-day. . . .' 'We may well live to see the taking of Montaña Barracks from the military rebels in Madrid stand out as being as important a landmark in Spanish history as is the Fall of the Bastille in the annals of France. . . .' Such phrases and many more, I turned out at white heat, ablaze with indignation and hope.

In my fury I could not understand how anyone to whom Democracy meant anything at all and no matter in what part of the world he lived, could not be thrilled to see the way in which civilians with little experience and few arms had partially checked a well-prepared military revolt, the organisation of which was good and which on paper should have achieved immediate success. Later came shootings of civilians and all kinds of complications but in the first few days the issue seemed clear enough to me. Moreover, although I could not go into this in my passionate dispatches because space would not allow it, for me the whole future of our British Empire rested on Spain. I had seen growing German intervention with a network of spy organisations cleverly camouflaged as this or that tourist or social activity sweep over Spain in the last months. Even in our Foreign Press Association, the German correspondents tried to secure the expulsion of a Jewish woman journalist of their own nationality, because they already felt so much at home. Their relations with the Right were of the closest. They wanted Spain as a strategic point for the menacing of our Empire routes.

After a week or ten days I came out of my dazed state. I was physically exhausted anyway. Moreover, innocent that I was, I felt that the battle was over. I remember writing: 'A military coup which does not succeed within twenty-four hours has inevitably failed. . . .' On paper, mind you, I was right. The Generals were rebels with no international status, no money at all, with only a very precarious hold on most parts of the half Spain they held, and they had no air force of importance. The Republican Government had the sixth largest gold reserves in the world at its disposal, was a legal régime which presumably could purchase at once unlimited arms. The people in its area were on the whole full of enthusiasm to fight and only short of training and arms. The only really large towns in Spain, Madrid and Barcelona, were in Government hands. At the most, according to my calculations, it would take the Government two to three months to restore order in Spain and in Spanish Morocco and at that I allowed for the rebels obtaining in clandestine fashion a few aeroplanes and arms which would be paid for by some of the wealthier supporters of the movement, who would certainly have money deposited abroad.

I knew that the Germans were in no position to go to war for they had had no time to build up cadres of officials, nor to equip their Army in the relatively short time since conscription had been re-introduced. The Germans could not face the French Army as yet. Or at least, if they had done the result was a foregone conclusion and could only have been an easy walk-over for the French Army. Therefore, although they had been working desperately to provoke a rising in Spain, the chances of their carrying this to the extent of fighting were virtually non-existent. I imagined, therefore, that Britain and France being thoroughly interested—to the point of it being a life-or-death question for them in fact—in keeping Germany from obtaining a friend in power south of the Pyrenees, would smartly check any outside intervention.

Well, I am a wiser and sadder man now.

I was very amused to meet not long ago, in 1939, a very clever German woman journalist who had lived long in Spain before the civil war and, as she had married a Spaniard, she had a Spanish passport. She was in Germany when the Spanish War broke out and she told me that as she was very eager to find out what attitude the British were taking up she decided to come to England. She had already changed her Spanish passport for one issued by the Insurgent Agent in Berlin, a document which, theoretically, had no value in Britain as we had not recognised the Burgos Junta. She told me how she went with some trepidation to the British Consulate General in Berlin, expecting that they would immediately refuse to recognise her passport. To her surprise the consular officer was very charming and courteous and assured her that she would not have any difficulty in travelling to Britain with such a document. This, she said, proved to be the case. She had not the slightest trouble with immigration officials; they accepted this document issued by the Insurgents without question. 'So now,' said my clever friend, 'I had settled one point, namely that British officialdom was recognising the Insurgents on an equal level with the Republicans, but I still had to find out what the City was thinking. So I went to see some old friends'—she had been educated in England—'who had some influence in financial circles and both they and the people I met at their home assured me that there was no doubt that General Franco would triumph and that they hoped that he would have a speedy victory. I asked some questions about what the financial world thought in the matter of giving credit to Franco, as he had no gold, and I was informed that there should be no difficulty about his obtaining reasonable credits. So I went back to Berlin and wrote some articles explaining why the victory of Franco was certain, and you see how right I was.' And how right she was. . . .

Strangely, about the same time I met another old friend, a clever international journalist who had been in Madrid during the first days of the war and before it became advisable for a journalist of his nationality to move to another climate. He used to read my dispatches with curiosity and amusement, for he was a good Fascist, and my fervid orations on behalf of Democracy surprised him. 'But do English people really feel that way about things?' he asked with, I think, some respect for he had obviously been well fed on the usual Fascist propaganda that Britons to-day are a degenerate race with no interests beyond golf and cocktails. I assured him, God forgive me, that they did. I really believed it in fact. Then he disappeared and I never saw him again until I ran into him in Perpignan just after Barcelona had fallen. He was going in; I had just come out. He had been two and a half years with the Insurgents; I with the Republicans. We dived into the Duchesse de Berry Restaurant and for a couple of hours the conversation was fast and furious. He laughed about my dispatches of the first days. He said: 'You see I was right and you were wrong because the English people did not feel as you said they did about Spain and Democracy and such things.' And I could only say: 'My friend, you were absolutely correct.'

CHAPTER XXIV

THE EXPLOSION

THERE were several hours in the evening of Saturday, July 19, 1936, when a decision of tremendous importance, not only for Spain but for the whole of Europe, had to be taken by the Government led by that small, bird-like Galician, Santiago Casares Quiroga. They had to decide as to whether they should give arms to the people. If they had not done so, the rebellious Generals would almost certainly have triumphed within a few days and thus, abruptly, the whole situation in international politics would have been changed. The friends of Germany and Italy would have been in power in the Peninsula. Sr. Casares Quiroga and his Ministers delayed that date by two years and eight months. They were all men of the Left Republican Party or the Democratic Union; they were all quiet, middle-class Liberals. Not one of them personally stood as far to the Left in general politics as does, say, Mr. Lloyd George. I think one can say with complete conviction that there was not a single Minister from the Premier down who did not hate the idea of arming the masses and know the dangers involved. But not to do so involved the handing over of the Republic lock, stock and barrel to an iron military Dictatorship. They gave an order. Minutes later, police wagons loaded with heavy boxes were racing through the streets to the trade union and political headquarters where anxious crowds stood wondering whether they were to survive or to be crushed. Delirious cheering went up everywhere as the trucks sped on their way. At least Madrid would go down fighting.

It was impossible either in Madrid, or Barcelona where the Generalitat took a similar decision, though whether or not after consultation with Madrid I cannot say, to be sure of Army, Civil Guard and Police forces. In Morocco the revolt had started on the night of July 17-18 and had succeeded completely, Ceuta, Melilla and Tetuan falling within a few hours.

General Franco had been flown from Las Palmas in the Canary Islands to Tetuan by Mr. C. W. H. Bebb, a British pilot, in an aeroplane hired in London. In order to give an air of innocence to the trip, Major Hugh B. C. Pollard, a British subject, his daughter Diana and her friend, Miss Dorothy Watson, accompanied the aeroplane as 'tourists'. Later, Mr. Bebb was given the Grand Cross of the Imperial Order of Red Arrows, by General Franco. Major Pollard was made a Gentleman of the same order and his daughter and her friend were given medals of the order. Apparently, General Franco did not feel sure of the garrison he commanded in the Canary Islands. There was, as a matter of fact, some bitter fighting before the loyal police and military were subdued by the Nationalists.

General Sanjurjo, who would have been the figure-head of the movement, crashed and was killed at the Lisbon Aerodrome as he was taking off in a plane, piloted by one of the inevitable Ansaldo brothers, bound for Spain. General Mola, another of the Army clique which had been in mutinous mood for the past two years, had risen in Pamplona, and down in Seville, General Queipo de Llano, who held the trusted post of commander-in-chief of 14,000 Carabineros, Customs' Guards—incidentally, Sanjurjo held the same post when he revolted in 1932—had risen but was hard pressed despite the thousands of armed men at his disposal and he did not overcome the furious resistance of the unarmed Sevillanos until help came by air from Morocco in German troop-carrying aeroplanes.

In Saragossa the white-bearded General Cabanellas, intimate friend of Sr. Lerroux—who had fled to Portugal—had revolted, thus cutting the direct communication between Madrid and Barcelona. The railway line to Valencia was also cut for there had been a mutiny in Albacete. So Madrid was almost isolated, for much of Castile had gone. Bilbao and the Basque Coast district were resisting and so was Asturias.

In Madrid, the officers concerned simply could not make up their minds to take the plunge. A man whom I knew and who was doing his military service in a Madrid barracks described to me afterwards how the officers in their quarters argued furiously hour after hour as to whether they should rebel or not. General Fanjul, who had been Under-Secretary of War to Sr. Gil Robles, waited until Monday morning, July 21, before he showed signs of rebellion. By then Madrid Republicans and trade unionists were already heartened by the Republican triumph in Barcelona, where General Goded had surrendered after some very picturesque fighting in which taxidrivers drove their cars into the muzzles of artillery pieces and which was decided by the Civil Guard which, under Colonel Aranguren, remained loyal. Strange to remember this, when only the other day I saw a newspaper report that Colonel Aranguren, now General, had been shot by the Nationalists. He stayed behind when the war ended and was tried and condemned to death for that piece of loyalty to his oath in Barcelona. In Madrid, the police were in barracks and the Youth Organisation had taken over the streets.

The Government stepped out of office after arming the people. Casares Quiroga felt unhappy and responsible. He had had information time and again as to the preparations being made for a coup. But he had hesitated to act. He always argued that he did not believe that any responsible General would rebel against the Republic.

President Azaña now took a strange step. With half Spain already in revolt and the masses armed in Madrid and Barcelona, he tried to halt the avalanche. Casares Quiroga resigned about ten o'clock on Saturday night, July 21, and at four o'clock on the Sunday morning we got the list of the new Cabinet formed under Martinez Barrio with moderate Republicans, including Spain's best-known lawyer, Felipe Sanchez Roman, who had refused to accept the United Front programme in February last because he said it was too advanced. It was said that Generals Mola and Cabanellas were asked to join, and refused. But I was never able to check on exactly how they were asked, in view of the general cutting of telephone lines, and what precise answer they gave if they really were asked. They are both dead now.

Trade union circles in Madrid bubbled over with anger. Here was Madrid in the utmost danger, isolated, and a Cabinet which looked as if designed for pacting had taken office. Left circles insisted that they meant to fight and wanted no hesitation from above. Azaña changed the Cabinet again, putting into office most of the Ministers of the Casares Quiroga Cabinet with his close friend Don José Giral, a mild, bespectacled professor of pharmaceutical chemistry as Prime Minister.

So by Sunday noon, the now much-shrunken Republic had its third Cabinet within fourteen hours, which seemed to indicate a nervous and uncertain hand at the helm. It was open to the Republic to surrender, but to talk of mediation, which was merely to encourage the authors of the plot against the régime to redouble their efforts, was a policy of suicide.

Monday morning, July 22, I awoke after a few hours' sleep to hear the boom of cannon. It was the first time that I had heard artillery fired in anger and I felt a strange sensation way down in the depths where we keep both food and feelings.

Out on the streets I saw a new Madrid. Overnight, the youths, girls and more mature citizens of the trades unions and political organisations had apparently adopted a more or less general uniform of a blue overall. Cars had been requisitioned. Groups of workers drove fast and furiously around town, having the time of their lives. They had revolvers, shotguns and a few rifles. The Fascists had adopted the same tactics as those which gave such modest results to the Left in October 1934, they sniped industriously from roof-tops and windows.

The district in which I was in was so full of minor battles that my progress was slow when I set out from home. I approached a church which was ablaze. A worker came running down the street after a boy who had stolen a chair. He took the chair off him and smashed it to pieces. 'This,' he announced solemnly, 'is revolution, not robbery.' It still seemed to me a pity to smash the chair; people would have to sit somewhere even under the most revolutionary system. I ventured to ask this severe and, it seemed to me somewhat impulsive, citizen just how it came about that the church was on fire. He looked over my more or less presentable suit, collar, tie and so on, somewhat suspiciously before answering: 'Comrade, the priests fired on us from inside the church, so we had to teach them a lesson.' Whether priests, or some other persons, actually did fire from this church, the Covadonga Church, I cannot say. I know that in a college run

1. British newspaper correspondent Henry Buckley with his driver during the first months of the Spanish Civil War.

Battle of Teruel

2. Civilians fleeing the city of Teruel, where fighting between rebels and the Republicans caused hundreds of casualties on both sides.

3. Prisoners taken by the Republican army, probably during the Battle of Teruel.

4. The car that took the international correspondents daily from Valencia to Teruel. Henry Buckley, Ernest Hemingway, Herbert Matthews and Robert Capa are pictured here in the car.

5. Ernest Hemingway, photographed by Henry Buckley giving the raised fist salute.

**Girona enthusiastically receives the 43rd Republican Division—
18 June 1938**

6. Soldiers of the 43rd Republican Division marching to the Plaza de la Independencia in Girona, to great popular acclaim.

7. The military orchestra played *El Himno de Riego*, the anthem of the Second Republic, in homage to the soldiers of the 43rd Republican Division.

8. Side view of the stage that held the civil and military Republican authorities who presided over the event.

L'Espluga de Francoli—farewell ceremony of the International Brigades—25 October 1938

9. The unarmed international volunteers entering the courtyard of the Hotel Villa Engracia in L'Espluga de Francolí (Conca de Barbera).

10. Another contingent of volunteers cross the courtyard area of the hotel. The women present are nurses working at the hospital into which the hotel had been converted. At the end of the farewell ceremony, the nurses danced with the volunteers.

11. A general view of the square where the volunteers gathered.

12. A group of volunteers—behind them hang the Catalan and the Republican flags.

13. Colonel Juan Modesto Guilloto addressing the International Brigades. In the background is the famous photographer David 'Chim' Seymour and the head in the foreground is Robert Capa.

14. In the centre of the image is the Prime Minister of the Republic, Juan Negrín. To his right, General Vicente Rojo, and to his left, Colonel Enrique Líster. Also pictured are Republican commanders André Marty, Bibiano Fernández Osorio, Juan Modesto Guilloto, Antonio Cordón, Hans Ludwig Renn, Luigi Longo and John Cates. Robert Capa is on the far left.

Barcelona—farewell parade of the International Brigades—28 October 1938

15. The Plaça de Francesc Macia (as it is now known) at the crossing with Avinguda Diagonal was the venue for the start of the parade of the International Brigades (p. 52).

16. President of the Republic Manuel Azaña arriving at the Plaça de Francesc Macia on 28 October 1938 (p. 53).

17. President of the Republic Manuel Azaña and Prime Minister Juan Negrín walking onto the platform to address the volunteers (p. 53).

18. Troops from the International Brigades carry the distinctive three-pointed star, marching towards Avinguda Diagonal in Barcelona (p. 54).

19. The Abraham Lincoln Brigade of North American volunteers, with their flag at the corner of Avinguda Diagonal and Carrer d'Enric Granados (p. 54).

20. The people of Barcelona in traditional costume offering bouquets, garlands of flowers and laurel wreathes to the international volunteers.

21. The women of Barcelona offering flowers to the volunteers (p. 56).

22. Volunteers from the British Battalion, commanded by Malcolm Dunbar (seen on the right) (p. 57).

23. Travelling towards the Ebro Front on 5 November 1938, Buckley photographed the group of international correspondents that accompanied
him. Clockwise from left—Ernest Hemingway, Robert Capa, Vincent 'Jimmy'
Sheean, Herbert Matthews and Hans Kuhle. Capa fills the cups of his colleagues
with champagne. Afterwards, they crossed the River Ebro in a rented boat to
see the effects of Franco's bombing of Móra d'Ebre. Buckley was travelling from
Sitges, the rest from Barcelona.

24. Ernest Hemingway with Colonel Hans Kahle, 5 November 1938.

25. View of the town of Móra d'Ebre from the left bank, with the ruins of the medieval castle on the hill and other ruined buildings. The bridge had been bombed by Franco's air force.

26. By the jetty on the left bank of Móra d'Ebre. Left to right, Colonel Kahle, watching with binoculars and a map under his arm; Ernest Hemingway; Herbert Matthews, with a Rolleiflex camera; and Vincent 'Jimmy' Sheean, lighting a cigarette. A few moments later the group persuaded a boatman to take them to the opposite shore.

27. The boatman and the boat used by Buckley, Hemingway, Matthews, Sheean, Kahle and Capa to cross the Ebro on 5 November 1938.

28. This cable car was installed across the Ebro River in early November 1938 in order to enable access to Móra d'Ebre. The bridges had been bombed and destroyed by Franco's troops and the ingenious contraption hanging from a steel cable was one of two ways available for Republicans to go from one side to another. The camouflage of tree branches disguised the occupant.

29. Remains of a destroyed bridge on the right bank of the Ebro.

30. Colonel Hans Kahle of the International Brigades observing the damage to the town of Móra d'Ebre from the left bank of the Ebro River.

31. Crewman of a T-26B tank near Móra d'Ebre.

32. A Soviet-manufactured T-26B tank on the road near Móra d'Ebre.

33. Half-ruined house in a bombing inside Móra. When Hemingway (who was travelling with Buckley and Capa that day) noticed that the table and two chairs in the dining room on the second floor had survived the bombing, he exclaimed in a tone of sarcasm: 'This shows clearly what to do when you start bombing: sit quietly at the dining table.'

The road from Tarragona to Barcelona—the withdrawal and evacuation of civilian and military Republicans—15 January 1939

34. A group of Republican refugees watching the approach of Franco's air force.

35. Refugee family travelling to Barcelona. To avoid being discovered and attacked by the Fascists, they have covered their truck with branches.

The border at Le Perthus—the civilian and military refugees flee into exile—30 January 1939

36. A truckload of military and civilian Republicans just metres from the border.

37. The border at Le Perthus—the pile of weapons on the left was confiscated.

38. Republican troops on horseback going into exile. These could be the remains of the 2nd Division commanded by Enrique Líster, which crossed the border at Le Perthus on 9 February 1939. The troops are unarmed.

39. A large contingent of international volunteers crossing the border unarmed and in formation at Le Perthus. Brigadier André Marty stands in front of the group wearing a coat and beret.

40. A Republican soldier is searched by the French Border Guards.

41. British Brigadier Molesworth watching the flood of refugees.

42. Two British volunteers identifying themselves at the border at Le Perthus. They had decided to remain in Spain despite the decision of the Republican government that foreign fighters should leave the country in October 1938.

43. Civilian Republicans entering French territory.

44. The flag of the International Brigades with the emblem of the three-pointed star.

45. The main street of Le Perthus, full of military and civilian refugees who have just crossed the border. In the centre of the image, a policeman requisitions a camera from an unidentified correspondent.

Argelès-sur-Mer and Sant Cebrià—internment camps for refugees—early February 1939

46. A group of refugees on the beach at Argelès surrounded by huts built from canes, bags and blankets.

47. One of the shelters built by the exiles on the sandy beach at Argelès.

48. View of the camp at Argelès during the construction of a wooden pavilion.

49. The bodies of three Republican refugees in the internment camps at Argelès, wrapped in blankets, ready to be buried in the sand on the beach in the area used as a cemetery.

50. A group of refugees cook food around a campfire in the fields surrounding Argelès.

51. A refugee observes the beach at Argelès. Behind his back is a French newspaper which includes reports on the recent events in Spain.

52. Henry Buckley, on the left of the photograph, interviewing an observer from the League of Nations visiting the camp at Argelés.

by monks in the Calle Ayala people inside, I cannot say who, fired shots. A friend of mine lived near there and Shock Police occupied his flat in order to answer the fairly heavy fire from the college. In all, about five churches were gutted and half a dozen others more or less damaged.

The main battle fought in Madrid, the taking of the Montaña Barracks which stand above the Norte Station, had been over for some time when I reached the scene. General Joaquin Fanjul, a rather pompous little man who had been Under-Secretary to Gil Robles, had shut himself up in the barracks on Saturday along with some 300 Fascists. Including the garrison there were some 800 men, armed with rifles. Apparently, they sat around waiting for someone else to do something, though why is not quite clear for 800 well-armed men could have done a great deal in Madrid. A picturesque but determined motley of police, soldiers, workers, lookers-on, assaulted the barracks furiously with the aid of some ancient artillery from the nineteenth-century wars and light bombs dropped from aeroplanes. In four or five hours the battle was over. The mob rushed the gate. The soldiers surrendered but the Fascists tried to escape and ran into a machine-gun planted on the west side, which mowed them down by the score. About 160 Fascists who were caught were shot in the courtyard.

I found Luis Quintanilla in charge. 'Dear, dear,' I said: 'You are a soldier?' 'Yes,' he said, 'I am commander of this barracks for the time being and it is to be a reserve centre where militias will gather ready to be rushed to any point they may be needed.' He showed me the blood in the yard where the executions had taken place. He showed me bullet marks which furrowed the door to the officers' quarters. The officers had run in there with the attackers firing furiously at them. He said that only with the greatest difficulty had they got Fanjul out alive, for the people were boiling over with fury. They had had to bring an armoured car into the barracks and put him inside. Even then people had tried to overturn the car. Poor Fanjul. His story at the court-martial was pathetic. He said that he had been at the flat of a French woman friend and someone had asked him to go to the barracks to lend a hand in view of the general upset. He was sentenced to death and executed. Out at Carabanchel an artillery regiment mutinied under General García de la Herranz and he was shot and the whole business quelled pretty quickly. This also took place on the Monday. By nightfall, Madrid looked safe from inside. But the outskirts looked bad for Toledo to the south, and Alcalá de Henares and Guadalajara to the north were all in Insurgent hands.

How the motley crowds which streamed out to these towns with primitive weapons, no discipline, no plan, just took them in their stride is beyond me. There are two explanations, I think. The first and most important is that those taking part did not know the danger; they just charged ahead despite the bullets. The second factor was that the rank and file of the rebellious troops did not fight very hard. At Guadalajara, according to the figures I received, there were no less than eleven girls from the Socialist Youth killed. In that town, General Barrera, one of the more active of the ultra-right clique, was caught and shot. I do not think he had any trial, but I am not sure. In Toledo, the troops retreated into the Alcazar so that the town was in the hands of the Republicans. Yet, by the end of the week, not only had these towns been taken, but also Albacete which was captured by a column from Valencia and thus the railway to the coast and via Valencia to Barcelona was re-opened. Nor was this all. Military columns had come down from Burgos along the main roads and occupied the Somosierra Pass on the main Burgos-Madrid road and the Alto de Leon Pass, just above the village of Guadarrama, on the Avila-Madrid road, so further nondescript crowds had been rushed up to these places pell-mell to stem the advance. It was a week of miracles, during which God certainly seemed to be on the side of the little men.

The members of the British and American colonies were greatly perturbed by the situation. With bundles in their hands those who lived near hurried for shelter to the Embassies of their respective countries. A motor-car service quickly organised brought in others. After a few days there were few British or American women or children who were not safely on diplomatic territory. As a matter of fact they were better there because it facilitated the work of protecting members of the colonies in the midst of so much trouble. The only two persons whom I heard of who were actually molested were a man and his wife, I forget their names but he was manager of an insurance company, who were standing on the balcony of their hotel in the Gran Via. A party of armed militia passing along the street waved them to go inside but they misunderstood and waved back cheerfully, whereupon the silly young fools in the car below had no more sense than to blaze away at the pair, wounding them both fairly seriously.

Unfortunately, the Government of Great Britain did not at first give due attention to the plight of the some 300 persons crowded into the Madrid Embassy. The officers of the Embassy were all in San Sebastian where temporary offices, far from the seat of government, were opened during the hot months in Madrid. The Consul was on holiday. The whole tremendous business of looking after 300 refugees, and of keeping His Majesty's Government informed as to the dramatic events now afoot in Madrid, was left to the Vice-Consul, Mr. Milanes, and the assistant to the Commercial Attaché, Mr. Keith Unwin. These two men and their wives worked like heroes almost without rest for several weeks on end, aided by responsible members of the Colony. It was not until August 13, that finally the Counsellor of the Embassy, Mr. G. A. D. Ogilvie-Forbes, now Sir George Ogilvie-Forbes, who was on leave in England, finally received instructions to return to Madrid. Before he arrived in Madrid, a whole month had elapsed since the dramatic events began their course without there being any diplomatic official in Madrid to look after the colony or to inform the British Government as to exactly what was going on out there. It looked very much indeed as if our Government had been waiting; that they thought that General Franco would win and that they would avoid having any diplomatic representative at the seat of Sr. Giral's Government.

Yet mark you, in that period the most dramatic decisions which must perforce affect vitally the future of Europe and of the British Empire had been taken. We were already launched on Non-Intervention. One would have imagined that with the first hint of trouble Mr. Baldwin would have hastily instructed Mr. Eden to see that such an intelligent man as Mr. Ogilvie-Forbes was at once rushed to his post to begin the task of informing precisely and in detail the exact position in Madrid, in all its social, political and martial phases. One imagines that this information would have been supplemented by the simultaneous dispatch of unofficial observers of insight and experience to hurry to the spot and to return with reports on conditions. With all this fresh and accurate material at hand, Mr. Baldwin and his Ministers might still have plumped for a ban on arms for Spain, but they would at least have done so with sound information at their disposal as to the dramatic fight which ill-armed civilians led by a very moderate Government were putting up against overwhelming odds, and they would also have been able to receive and study interesting copies of documents found on German premises, which showed the active intervention of Berlin in affairs in Spain. No British statesman can rise to office without knowing that our Empire safety must always depend on the existence of a friendly Spain. At the bottom, the question for them to decide was not as to whether Sr. Giral was a 'nice person' or a 'red hooligan', or whether the Duke of This had been murdered and the Countess of That tortured and imprisoned. No, the sacred duty of Mr. Baldwin and of Mr. Eden was to decide which Spain better served the needs of our Empire, that of Sr. Giral or that of the Junta of Generals.

I am afraid that this incident illustrates how the policy of our Empire to-day is shaped too much by prejudice, by facile decisions about So-and-so being a 'decent chap'. Disraeli, Palmerston, 'Joe' Chamberlain—they did not work that way. In those days, mistakes might be made. But there was vitality, great capacity, quick penetrating decision. Well, I suppose all empires grow old. But it is not much fun to be a young man in an old empire.

CHAPTER XXV

OFF TO THE FRONT

WHY is it that war films and books like *All Quiet on the Western Front* cannot kill that thrill which comes at the phrase 'off to the front'. I am naturally a nervous person, given to anticipating danger long before any could possibly arise, yet I do not think I have ever got such a tremendous kick out of anything in this life as I did when I finally got a pass and a car to visit the fronts of the Sierra Guadarrama. I danced into the restaurant of the Gran Via Hotel with most undignified glee, could hardly eat any lunch, and was ready half an hour before the appointed time.

I was going in the company of two veteran and famous war correspondents, Karl von Wiegandt, of Hearst's Universal Service, and Edgar Ansel Mowrer, of the *Chicago Daily News,* and already famous as author of *Germany Puts the Clock Back.* Von Wiegandt, low-voiced, plump, about sixty, the acme of courtesy, very German-looking although he is an American citizen, had been with the German Army in France as correspondent in the World War and Mowrer had been with the Allied forces, so the sum of their knowledge of war is formidable. Mowrer is tense, with a shock of dark hair and the face of a Christ on the Cross; no journalist in the world to-day reflects so accurately, I think, the tragedy of Europe to-day as does Mowrer. He virtually lives its sufferings, and writes of them with truth, poignance and passion.

The journalist and Socialist politician, Julio Alvarez del Vayo, had arranged the visit and we were to trail along behind himself and Largo Caballero, who were making a tour of the mountain front, which had stabilised in a few days although there was still fighting going on. We found Caballero in blue overalls and with a revolver strapped around his waist, with a blue forage cap to complete the ensemble. But he still looked as stolid as ever. He held no post at the time but the General

219

Union of Workers and the Socialist Party were playing such a decisive role in the struggle that naturally anything he said had much influence. I wondered idly whether he could use the revolver. I chatted with him while we waited to start off. 'What chances of your people winning the war?' I asked him. He came back quickly: 'There is nothing that can withstand the tremendous force of the mass of the people which is aroused and ready to die for its liberty. . . .' It sounded very much like what he had told me in the summer of 1934. Anyway, it was not the kind of answer which helped me much. I wanted something positive which I could use as news.

We speeded along the Burgos road. My education as a war correspondent in Spain began at once. I learned that the chances of death from a shell or a bomb were much less than those that I would die in a car smash. Later, members of the International Brigade summed up the situation in a song of which the chorus ran: 'If the shells don't get you the chauffeurs will. . . .' On this particular occasion, our little chauffeur meant well. But he was a Madrid taxi-driver who for the first time was at the wheel of a big car, an eight-cylinder Packard, and it was always surprising him—and us—to find out the kind of things a Packard will do when one flies hard around a sharp corner at forty or fifty miles an hour. We spent quite a good deal of time on the grass verges alongside the road but St. Christopher, or maybe some other providential interventor, watched over us and somehow we always avoided disaster and reached the safety of the tarmac again, still upright on four wheels.

At last the front line? Not quite. On some low hills behind Buitrago, about fifty-five miles from Madrid, we saw troops. That is to say a mixed crowd of soldiers in uniform, volunteers in blue overalls, a few Shock Policemen, civilians, girls, of whom many wore overalls. There was a General there, however, General Bernal, an artillery officer, a quiet, modest little man in civilian clothes. For some reason or other which I cannot remember, he did not want the Insurgents to hear of his presence in the Government ranks. He made a good impression on me. He had I think it was two batteries of seventy-fives with which to hold the road to Madrid. The men with him were artillerymen and reserves. A film operator who had come along wished to take some pictures of Caballero with the troops and everybody gathered on the crest of the hill while these were taken, a perfect target for the rebel batteries standing some eight miles away. We went down into Buitrago, which had been shelled that morning, and saw Captain Francisco Galan, an officer of the Carabineros, brother of Fermin Galan shot at Jaca, and now leader of a group of very youthful-looking Communist militia. Apparently he was getting the front into order. During the first days the Insurgents had sent a column of regular troops with several batteries who had occupied the Pass of Somosierra. An improvised 'mobile column' from Madrid, composed of the usual medley of soldiers, bank clerks, good girls, bad girls, police, had gone dashing up to take back the Pass. Apparently, it was awful. They went on and on while the trained troops on the Pass just mowed them down, but they were so crazy that not until more than half were wiped out did they give up and withdraw. Then they said that the Colonel in command of the column had tricked them. So they shot him. Everybody had been crazy, those first few days. Which was one reason why Madrid survived, I think.

Then we turned west along the valley of the Lozoya River, which supplies what I think is the best water I have ever tasted. It comes cold, sparkling and invigorating from the tap in Madrid.

We passed under a tall new viaduct built to take the Burgos-Madrid direct railway line across the River Lozoya and I thought of how General Primo de Rivera had planned this to bring prosperity to his land and yet here was the railway still unfinished and Spain wasting money and men in civil strife. And all because those who have something will not cede, will not make sacrifices. What is this blind passion of possession which grips and holds men once they own something, even though it be but a mite? What is there in us which makes us prefer to die in war rather than to yield a grain to the man who has less? Will a time come when in times of crisis the men of the nation will gather and propose sacrifice for peace instead of for war; when the rich man will say that he will take his child from the university, get rid of his car and the more modest folks will give up tennis or a summer holiday, in order to join in a great national effort to make life more bearable for all?

My philosophical efforts were interrupted by the cars stopping, in order that we could investigate four corpses which lay by a lovely, small spring. Four men clad in blue overalls lay crumpled, but very easily, as if death were something not hard to bear. A shepherd near by said that they were spies who had come over the mountains from Segovia to find out details of movements on this side for the Insurgents. 'Well, thank God we have four more dead Fascists,' commented our chauffeur who seemed to be as good a hater as he was bad at driving. Apparently, the men had been executed after some kind of rough investigation. I thought of wives, children, parents, somewhere over in Segovia, waiting for these men who would never come back. How hateful it all seemed.

I took advantage of the halt to change to Vayo's car, thus basely deserting my friends. But we were going to climb up a dizzy, winding road to the Lozoya Pass, where there had been a battle the day before, and Vayo had managed to requisition not only a beautiful saloon car but he also had a really first-rate driver. The only drawback was that in Vayo's car was sitting a German Social-Democrat, a former journalist and politician, and then in exile. He was a charming, kindly man, but the German episode had broken his faith. He was completely defeatist. Republican Spain could not resist long, the outlook was hopeless, etc. I began to feel some sympathy for Herr Hitler. . . . It was not quite logical of me to be annoyed with him when I had just been critical of Caballero's easy optimism. But I hated to hear anyone so gloomy in the midst of such a passionate resistance as we were witnessing. The Spanish people might in some cases be committing outrages, murdering and robbing, but by and large the individual man and woman was showing a fierce, vital courage. These people vibrated with life and blood. They were human beings who fought and battled, not worn-out robots. Suddenly I hated defeatists, and smug, thin-blooded individuals breathing soot in London and Paris, who thought that they were important and could dictate to the whole world.

Nearly 6,000 feet high among the pine woods, our car lurched to a standstill and a crowd of blue-overalled boys with rifles in their hands gathered around us. They took us to see the rough graves in which had been buried the Fascists killed in yesterday's attempt to capture the Pass of Lozoya from the Republicans. Carlists had made the attempt. The graves were shallow. A foot protruded from one. The foot of a priest, I was told. A priest had, apparently, led the Carlists in an attempt to catch the Republican guard napping. They had failed and a score had been killed before the rest fled through the woods down the other side again.

On again through this lovely scenery, over Navacerrada Pass, where Madrid used to ski and toboggan, and down to Cercedilla which lay unpleasantly near the enemy lines. Here we met Quintanilla, the artist, who said that they had had a fierce attack during the morning by some hundreds of well-armed Civil Guards and that they had only saved Cercedilla by quick thinking. The commander of the district had telephoned to him at Montaña Barracks for reserves and artillery. He had managed to get together a few men and some new trench mortars which had been stored in the basement of the building. They loaded the mortars into taxis and set off for Cercedilla. The Guards were attacking fiercely over a wide front. There is a network of roads in this district. used by the winter sports enthusiasts and summer holiday visitors, and an artillery officer conceived the idea of rushing the mortars from one spot to another in the taxis, firing a few rounds and then moving on again. In this way they might convey the idea that they really had a great many mortars. For several hours the 'mortar brigade' rushed here and there. As the Fascists were attacking in very broken and densely wooded country, they could not follow very closely the movements of the militiamen. Finally they abandoned the attack and retreated. Quintanilla felt sure that his mortars had done the trick.

It was dusk as our powerful cars raced along the road from Cercedilla to Guadarrama village and Insurgent and Republican batteries were engaged in counter-battery fire, over our heads. It was most unpleasant to hear the shells coming and going overhead. I thought of sitting on the floor of the car but then I realised how silly the idea was. Our driver drove like a demon. We stopped at the crossroads, with shells still dropping only a few hundred yards away. The sentry reported the village street to be under machine-gun fire sporadically. It was decided that Caballero should not go up, as his life was important, so he sat down on the chair used by the sentry at the crossroads. I could have imagined nicer places to sit than a crossroads with shelling going on near by, but apparently this was a very serious counter-battery duel and neither side allowed themselves to divert valuable shells to crossroads or other strategic points.

How wonderful it had felt at lunch-time to be 'off to the front'. Now I wished heartily that I was back in the Gran Via Hotel. First the whine of the shells had been most upsetting. Shells on the screen never hit the hero. At the most they get the man who has nothing left to live for and is glad to die for his friend or his country. But these shells all sounded as if they were meant for me. Now we were spinning up a grimly deserted village street which was supposed to be 'under machine-gun fire', and that meant very close range shell-fire if the Fascist artillerymen should get tired of their personal argument with their colleagues of the Republican artillery. Actually we found out that only spent bullets from a machine-gun nest somewhere up in the hills reached the street. One could hear it occasionally go rat-a-tat-tat-tat-tat. . . . Then one laid low and would hear a cheep-cheep-cheep-cheep as a few spent bullets went by, well overhead.

In a charming, rose-covered cottage we found General Riquelme, in charge of the sector. He seemed excited and there was a good deal of arguing going on. A shell had fallen in the garden of the cottage that afternoon, it looked as if the Insurgents had it marked. I felt that it would be a good place to leave very quickly. Mowrer and von Wiegandt were in their element and already were busy arguing over maps. They were both as full of zest as war-horses which hear a trumpet. On the way there had been many polite arguments. Mowrer would say: 'I think that is a battery of seventy-fives which we can hear firing.' And von Wiegandt would answer solemnly: 'I beg to differ, Edgar, that is definitely the sound of six-inch guns.' In the meantime, I learned much from their experience.

The strategy of Guadarrama needed little explaining, it seemed to me. The Insurgents had very swiftly rushed many troops and volunteers to Alto de Leon Pass where the main road running from Madrid to Avila and Segovia crosses the Sierra Guadarrama, a business-like mountain range not to be confused with the small village of the same name where we were consulting with General Riquelme. The top of the Pass is about four miles from Guadarrama village, as a plane flies, but the road winds a great deal and is possibly six miles in length. The Insurgents had received help from Madrid itself in this sector. The colonel in charge of an infantry regiment in El Pardo, just outside Madrid, was anxious to revolt but apparently he was not sure of his men or he had decided that the atmosphere of Madrid was not suited to heroic ventures. At any rate, he did some active telephoning and then harangued his men, calling on them to be ready to save the Republic against rebels who threatened its existence. The men were enthusiastic. Caballero's son was one of the soldiers. The colonel loaded them into trucks and drove off at full speed with the soldiers cheering for the Republic and shaking clenched fists. He drove them through Guadarrama and up to the Alto de Leon Pass where they met the Nationalist forces already arriving. I do not know the story of what happened there or what the soldiers said when they found out. Caballero's son was imprisoned, I know. I dare say some of the soldiers who had been a little too enthusiastic in showing the clenched fist on the way, soon regretted this.

The Insurgents had quite a lot of men on the top of these hills. At least I had read a dispatch from a British correspondent on the other side published in a London newspaper and which spoke of eight hundred motor vehicles comprising the column which seized the Pass. The residents of Guadarrama were all set to receive the Rebels with honours. The Rights of the village met and constituted a small committee. They saluted each other awkwardly with the Fascist salute, which they had never used before. They sent out the town crier to tell all good citizens to stay inside their homes for 'the military forces from Avila are about to occupy our village'. The Leftists departed speedily, the more worried for Madrid, and those slightly less anxious to neighbouring fields and woods in order to await developments. But nothing happened. Then truck loads of militias and police roared out from Madrid and swarmed into the village. The committee of Fascists tried to disappear. They were mostly shot. The baker was shot. They shot the tobacconist and his wife. In all about fifteen people were killed. Such at least is the story I got from a person who was in the village. Something similar was going on in scores of villages in disputed areas. Sometimes the Right shot the Left; other times the Left shot the Right.

The arriving militiamen with the impetus typical of these first days, stormed straight ahead up to the top of the Pass. And the story was much the same as at Somosierra. The well-officered troops at the top just sat pretty and waited until the militias were within range—then they let them have it. A few did get nearly on top and Madrid announced the recapture of Alto de Leon. But they were driven down. The Insurgents came down the hill and took a number of strategic points including the big white sanatorium on the hillside.

This evening, we motored a short distance up the road above the village. Fighting was going on in the woods. General Riquelme, who was with us, was wearing a khaki overall with a General's badge pinned on it; he wasn't taking any chances in a country full of surprises—and snipers. He was a little man, about five feet two or three, and he had none of the snap and bounce of some small-statured persons. The pine woods were on fire from incendiary shells, smoke drifted down. We stood uneasily in the road. Militiamen came and argued with the General about this, that or the other, mostly very trivial things. Girls in overalls staggered wearily up the hill with buckets of water for the men who were fighting, for the heat was terrible in full summer and with the woods burning. It was just hell. I talked to some of the volunteers. One was a man of forty-five, a metal-worker with a wife and two small children. Another was aged sixteen, an apprentice. They knew nothing of war and practically nothing about handling a rifle and yet all seemed very cool and sure of themselves. All of them said they were fighting to save the Republic from becoming a military Dictatorship. There was a German girl, a Communist refugee, very slender but efficient-looking in grey overalls. That morning she had taken part in a reconnaissance which had gone nearly to the enemy lines.

There was a good deal of criticism already of the women in the militia. Obviously some of them were prostitutes of the lowest scale who had just been caught up in the whirl of excitement and had gone off with friends to the front. I say prostitutes of the lowest scale because all the others, as far as I ever saw or heard, were all pro-Insurgent. But the majority of the girls had come along to cook and care for the men. It must be remembered that these hastily-flung-together units had no cooks or kitchens or first aid men or anything like that. The maid in the next flat to that in which I lived in Madrid went off to the Somosierra front to look after her two brothers. Several weeks later she returned, giving the matter no importance, putting away her overalls and serving lunch as efficiently as ever. Her brothers needed looking after—and one had to help the Republic. That was her explanation. As soon as regular units were formed and cooks found, she left and came back to her work.

Amid the heat, confusion, and complete disorder which prevailed, one wondered why on earth the Rebels with their efficient units and skilled officers up there on the hillside were unable to break through. The patient heroism of these simple folks, who up to some days before had nearly all been working in factories, driving trams, clerking, and now found themselves front-line-soldiers with few officers and less equipment, was astounding. I had always been a little doubtful as to whether the average man in the street felt sufficiently strongly about the Republic to die for it. Now I saw that he did, and was actually dying for this cause.

General Riquelme pointed out that there was one aspect of the war in which the Insurgents were having a bad time. This was in the air, for the Republic had kept the principal air bases and had four or five planes to each one held by the Rebels. Each day, and most of the day, they bombed, with light and somewhat primitive bombs, the road running up to the Alto de Leon from Avila and thus hindered Insurgent movements. Nevertheless, the latter at night were free to move as many transport columns as they wished.

We raced back towards Madrid in the darkness, picking up Sr. Largo Caballero, who was sitting composedly in his seat at the crossroads despite the fact that the shelling was still going on in desultory fashion. At Villalba Railway Junction he stopped to review several hundred volunteers of the newly-formed Largo Caballero battalion and it seemed strange indeed to see this reserved and most unmilitary trade unionist walking along the ranks of these militiamen.

Vayo's car had a powerful radio. We picked up Stuttgart as we drove fast through the night. Stuttgart was speaking on Spain and was in great form, taking towns and villages for the Rebels with aplomb, and comparing the cowardice and barbarism of 'Die Bolshevisten!' with the nobility and heroism of the Insurgents. It was obvious how Germany hung on the result, hoping that quickly General Franco and his friends would be in power and in alliance with the Reich and Italy. He might some day open the gate to Africa and help to smash the British and French hegemony in that continent. I turned over to a B.B.C. station. It was relaying dance music from New York, from Radio City I believe.

I am fond of dancing. I can work much better with jazz music playing softly near by. But on this night the rather too-emasculated voice wailing: 'The love bug'll get yer if yer don't look out,' made me furious. I preferred the brutality of the German speaker. He was arousing the hopes of his fellow-Germans for a great and new triumph of the cause of Fascism and which would place the Germans and their allies in control of Europe's most strategic link with Africa.

We were democrats, or said we were, and so were the Americans but we left the heroic Madrid civilians to die unsung in the pine woods of the Guadarrama. Later on in the evening the B.B.C. would broadcast a sober news bulletin carefully designed not to give the slightest offence to any other nation, especially to Germany or Italy. Then the listeners would be given more of the 'Love Bug Biting . . .' before they went contentedly to bed, blithely indifferent to the fate of their Empire being fought out near Madrid.

Half asleep in a corner of the car, I wondered idly whether I should be fired from the American daily I worked for if I led my dispatch this night with: 'A little love bug gently bit the great British Empire to-night. . . .'

Back in Madrid, war did not seem so bad after all. Over dinner at the Gran Via Hotel one spoke with some authority of 'things out at the front'. People asked: 'Is it very dangerous?' And one answered casually: 'No, not at all. Just have to watch your step in Guadarrama, but there's no real danger of course.' One felt a very heroic and superior person. One forgot all about the men, and women, who were dying on the Guadarrama Mountains with rifles in their hands which they did not even know how to fire.

CHAPTER XXVI

MOORS IN CASTILE

Out on the rugged countryside lying north-west of Navalperal de los Pinares we found the dead bodies of two
Moors. 'We' comprised Jan Yindrich of the United Press, a
group of Red Cross workers, and myself.

In Madrid, reports had arrived of the 'first attack by Moors'.
Jan and I had immediately set out to find how much truth
there was in the story, just in the normal way of work, for,
although some people criticise the accuracy of newspapers
without knowing much about the operation of a British or
American daily, the fact remains that reporters and correspondents take endless pains and travel considerable distances
in order to verify facts of greater or lesser importance. There
are, of course, newspapermen who write long and vivid
dispatches dealing with facts which they are not in a position to verify at all, but these are a minority and they do not
usually keep an outstanding position in the Press world for
long.

We drove along precipitous, winding roads to find Colonel
Mangada's column. which was reported to be at Navalperal by
the Government and to be in full flight by the Insurgent radio
stations, which last night had captured Navalperal with great
gusto and much slaughter—purely radio slaughter, fortunately. This kind of thing was not, in any case, confined to the
Rebel radios; the Government wireless transmitters were just
as prone to fantasy as their opponents.

Jan is a tempestuous driver, always eager to reach his destination, and the fact that our car had no brakes and no horn
added to the excitement as we tore along winding mountain
roads at full speed through a pitch-black night. Fortunately,
there was excellent and ice-cold beer to be had at Cerbreros,
a quaint little village with a great massive church built like
a fortress, as are most Spanish village churches. We sat under

its shadow in the cool of the August night drinking beer and afterwards found a place to sleep in, picking our way carefully through the streets, for it seemed that sewage ran down open channels. We got our passes duly stamped by the local commander, who turned out to be an adventurous soul named Enrique Lumen, who by profession was a journalist and had travelled a good deal.

We did not find Mangada, a wizened wisp of a man, nearly sixty years of age and a loyal Republican and Regular Army officer all his life. He was the officer who quarrelled with General Goded in 1932 and was imprisoned. But we found his second-in-command. He told us how Navalperal had been taken about a week or ten days earlier. He said that they found the local priest and several women in the church tower with guns and had shot them, but that most of the defenders had escaped. Since then there had been two attacks of which the most recent, two days earlier, had been carried out by Moorish troops commanded by Spanish officers. They had no prisoners, for the attackers after being routed had fled back to Villacastin taking their wounded with them but there were still a few dead bodies lying on the hillside which had not been buried and which a detachment of the Red Cross was now going out to find and burn. We could go along if we liked. We heard several weeks later that this second-in-command had been shot for treason, he certainly looked a rather unreliable person but then many people were shot by mistake in those days.

The Mangada Column comprised some five or six hundred police, militiamen or volunteers—whatever one likes to call them—and a few companies of regular soldiers. They had three or four machine-guns and two or three pieces of light artillery but I am not sure that the latter functioned. The sidearms ranged from Mausers of a more or less modern vintage to ancient and decrepit shot-guns. Yet this nondescript column had had considerable success and reached within twelve miles of Avila. The question of attacking Avila had been raised but dropped for it was one thing to take small villages but to attack such a town as Avila with no artillery worth the name and few arms of any kind would have been a hopeless adventure if the Insurgents could have managed to place half a dozen good machine-guns in position, and presumably they could easily have done this.

We drove up the road towards Villacastin in an ambulance which bore the sign 'Burgos Municipality', for it had been left behind by the attackers. We left the front line—and it did not feel very nice to think that we were out in no man's land even though the general impression was that the attackers had retreated at least three or four miles. A guide led us to the Moors. Somehow I had always pictured Moors as small wiry beings, but these were hulking great fellows, at least six feet tall and powerfully built. Both had been stripped at least half naked and one showed signs of having had a bad sexual illness.

Jan and I wandered away as the ambulance men poured petrol over the corpses and applied a match. But the Spaniards are a strange race. The doctors who had come with us, hastened after us and insisted on bringing us back to watch this ghastly roasting, taking delight in explaining the more unpleasant incidents connected with the burning of a human body. We did manage to escape having to witness any further cremations by alleging the necessity of returning to Madrid in order to write our dispatches. In Navalperal, I saw an old acquaintance, Santiago Delgado, an Aragonese who had worked for some years for a British firm of chartered accountants. He was a very sick man, but he was an old Republican and had insisted on taking an active part in operations. He was in charge of the intendancy, a post he held but a short time for the strenuous life made his illness more acute and he collapsed and died not long afterwards. Delgado was one of thousands; no extremist, a middle-class man of Liberal leanings, who was willing to sacrifice everything for the defence of the Republic and who did so. When we last saw Delgado he was issuing blue overalls to two hundred Civil Guards who had just been sent up. They were throwing away their green uniforms and one could see how many of the older ones were sad and depressed at saying good-bye to the old uniform which they had worn ever since they joined the service. Two hours later we were eating a fine lunch of roast chicken in El Escorial, which only goes to show how hardened even a sensitive person becomes to conditions of war within a few days, for if I had been told a few weeks before that I could watch the bodies of two Moors burned and then go and eat a hearty lunch, I should certainly not have believed it.

Jan and I had proved to our satisfaction that there really were Moors in Castile. What a tragic reversal of the whole Catholic history of Spain to find the rebellious Generals—it is worth noting that Gil Robles as leader of the Clerical Party had announced from his residence in France, where he was staying when the storm broke, that he had no part in the movement—bringing the Moors back to Spain. The whole of Spanish feudal history is permeated with this dramatic struggle of seven hundred years to free Spain from the Moorish conquerors of the eighth century and now the small remnant of feudal Spain, impotent to win on its own basis and with popular support, was bringing Moors to subdue the proud men and women of Castile.

The Moors had been flown to Spain from Morocco first by a few hired aeroplanes, one a British plane with a British pilot, and afterwards by a regular service established by seventeen big three-motor Junkers troop-carriers from the German Army and flown, of course, by Army pilots wearing civilian clothes. In one month they flew 14,000 troops from Ceuta to Jerez, of whom 10,000 were Moors and 4,000 Foreign Legionaries.

The man in charge of the German troop-carrying aeroplanes sent to save the situation for General Franco was Colonel von Scheele, an officer holding a high position in the German Air Force. The Press reported General Franco afterwards as saying: 'Ah, my dear Scheele, if it had not been for you. . . .' Colonel von Scheele took an important part in German intervention throughout the war. He was killed in an aeroplane crash near Barcelona on August 7, 1939, while holding the post of Air Attaché to the German Embassy in Spain.

These troops, according to reliable reports, were magnificently equipped, one man in six having new automatic rifles. The men had to be flown over because the units of the Republican Navy had command of the Straits of Gibraltar until sufficient German and Italian aircraft were available to drive them away. One of the big troop-carrying Junkers on the way from Germany and piloted by an uncertain young man, first landed in Madrid but took off after a German on the aerodrome had informed him of his mistake, and then landed again in Government territory in Estremadura. Yet with evidence of this kind available, Non-Intervention was proceeded with at full speed. Italy had been caught just as flagrantly. Two Savoia-Marchetti bombers, forming part of a flight of twenty-one planes, had landed in French Morocco owing to lack of petrol while flying from Sardinia to Spanish Morocco. They had been too heavily laden with machine-guns and ammunition. They came down on July 30. The machines were Italian military planes, some of the pilots were military pilots and several of them admitted that they had been asked to take part in this service three days before the revolt broke out in Spain. A Spanish plane flew over the spot where the Italian planes had landed and dropped a note and a bundle of uniforms of Spanish Legionaries with a message in Italian saying: 'Put on these uniforms and tell the French authorities you belong to the Legion stationed at Nador. We will send you two barrels of petrol and mechanics to help you start again. Don't walk into the lions' den!' Fancy referring to non-interventionist France under Léon Blum as 'the lions' den'! A shocking exaggeration indeed. Both the Insurgents and the Government had indeed bought planes from Britain and France, until non-intervention on their part became effective, and a nondescript collection of civil and military planes had been received by both sides. But they were not, of course, Army planes with regular pilots and ready equipped for immediate action. The Government fleet went to bombard Ceuta, where bombs and other war material from Germany was being landed, on August 4 and found the *Deutschland*, the German pocket battleship, patrolling off the entrance to the harbour, thus making bombardment impossible.

Why go into this and a hundred other incidents to show that Germany and Italy meant to see the Generals win? The hard fact for the Republicans was that there were considerable forces of Moors in the Guadarrama, for on August 14 Badajoz had fallen and the last Government stronghold in Estremadura had gone, for General Franco, who had progressed from Morocco to Seville and then to Caceres, had made liaison with General Emilio Mola in the latter town. So the Moors could now be entrained from Jerez to Avila. Presumably the same force, apparently comprising about 1,500 Moors, attacked again a day or two later and this time swept down and captured Peguerinos, a small village which lies in a valley about twenty miles west of El Escorial in very rough mountain country. I had been there the day before and found everything quiet. But then the Moors had swept down and taken the village, sending the some seven or eight hundred men there into swift retreat.

Quintanilla told me of the fight because he went out with reinforcements of Socialist Militia. I think Dr. Negrin was there also. Colonel Asensio, a clever if somewhat erratic officer who had done much to save Malaga from falling, was now at Guadarrama village where he had cleaned things up snappily and had ejected the obnoxious machine-gun which commanded the village street, and he came along with his reserves. The militia still had some of their first impetus and the fight went with a swing and after three hours the Moors fled. Quintanilla saved the life of one Moorish prisoner but the militia shot at least a dozen Moors who were caught. After that they went through the houses and found a girl of fourteen in a state of collapse after having been assaulted by a number of Moors. Two old people, a man and his wife, who were sick in bed, had been shot as they lay there. They looked very peaceful now on their death-bed and Quintanilla made a sketch of the bodies which he showed in New York later.

CHAPTER XXVII

FRANCO ADVANCES FROM THE SOUTH

DARK days came for Madrid. The balance of the war was being changed. French help, which had been hoped for, was now not forthcoming and door after door closed until finally twenty-six nations met in London on September 9 for the first meeting of the International Supervisory Committee on Non-Intervention in Spain, forming an ill-fated body which sealed the fate of the Spanish Republic definitely.

In the north, Irun had fallen. So few guns and so little shot and shell would have saved this town yet it was not sent by France and indeed trucks sent with munitions through France from Barcelona were held up when about to re-cross the frontier. Even this slight concession was regretted and finally withdrawn by the Government of the 'Front Populaire' in France, whose trade union supporters were engaged in a riotous series of strikes to secure and ensure the forty-hour week and a number of other social and financial advantages. That they should care little indeed about the fate of the French Empire might possibly be understood but that they should turn France upside down financially by demanding these tremendous reforms at a time when they might have devoted their energies to helping their working-class friends in Spain is hard to comprehend. In fact, trade union movements in Britain and France seemed to care as little for the fate of Democracy in Spain as did the other so-called Democrats of Europe.

The British trade unionists passed many resolutions in favour of their friends in Spain. But at Plymouth on September 11, the Trade Union Council on a card vote, after a speech by Sir Walter Citrine, voted 3,029,000 votes against intervention and only 51,000 in favour and again at the Socialist Party Conference in Edinburgh at Usher Hall on October 5, the principle of non-intervention was approved, despite a moving speech by small, dynamic Isabel de Palencia, writer and a

Socialist, and half Spanish, half Scotch. She had had some difficulty in getting to the Conference because despite the fact that
she was travelling from Madrid to Stockholm as the accredited
Minister to the Court of King Gustav, she was detained while
inquiries were made by the Immigration Officers at Croydon.

The Catalan front held up but the extravagances of the
extremists and the Anarchist hegemony in Barcelona made
Catalonia almost more of a hindrance than a help for the time
being. In Andalusia, somehow or other, the straggling militia
columns managed to prevent any very striking advance by the
well-armed Franco columns. But Estremadura had proved a
calamity. After an initial and lucky success when Government bombers managed to catch a fine mobile column near
Medellin—the incident is graphically described in André
Malraux's *Man's Hope*—practically destroying it with many
lucky hits; it was impossible for the Government to stop the
advance of General Yague and his men. The latter had a
force of some fifty or sixty thousand well-disciplined Tercio
and Moors along with a good supply of artillery, armoured
cars and tanks. Apparently, some of these were German.

This force was backed by fine new aviation of German and
Italian origin. As early as August 13, that energetic reporter
of the *New York Times*, Frank L. Kluckhohn, had visited
Seville and got out through Gibraltar the story of twenty heavy
Junkers bombers and five chaser planes piloted by German
army pilots in plain clothes having landed for service in Seville.

There was nothing that the Republic could do to halt this
force. It swept irresistibly up the Valley of the Tagus, taking
the key town of Talavera de la Reina on September 5. Night
and day, the Government would organise further columns
each of four or five hundred trade unionists. These could
have fought other small columns but they could do nothing
against a well-organised force which was composed in great
part of trained troops led by their regular officers. The Government had no army, properly speaking, down there at all. It
sent General Riquelme for a time but he muddled things just
as wonderfully as in Guadarrama and indeed not Napoleon
himself could have whipped this conglomeration into a unified
force with a tremendously superior enemy always pressing.

After the loss of Talavera, General Asensio was sent to bring some kind of order out of chaos; albeit an inevitable chaos.

Fortunately for the Government it is over 300 miles from Badajoz to Madrid. If General Franco, now directing operations in the whole of Spain, had launched this force suddenly from the Guadarrama I do not know what would have happened.

In Madrid the Government had been changed on September 4 in an effort to turn the tide of affairs.

The stolid Caballero was now Premier to replace the mild Don José Giral. Del Vayo, a restless wanderer who earned journalistic fame in Berlin and Geneva before returning to his native Spain to take up politics, had gone to Foreign Affairs to replace the highly incompetent Don Augusto Barcia. A Socialist named Angel Galarza had taken the Home Office. Finance went to Doctor Juan Negrin. Highest hopes of Leftists were pinned on Indalecio Prieto who it was hoped as Minister of Aviation and Navy would provide fireworks. Caballero had taken the War Office as well as the premiership.

A novelty was provided by the introduction of two Communists to Cabinet rank. Education was given into the hands of the very witty and alert Jesus Hernández while the Party theoretician, Luis Uribe, became Minister of Agriculture. In all there were six Socialists, three Republicans, two Communists, one Basque Nationalist, one Catalan Autonomist. This did not prevent many commentators from abroad from continuing to label it a 'Red Cabinet'. The same people had always labelled Sr. Giral's very moderate team also as a 'Red Cabinet'.

Mind you, I can see that the fact that sometimes several hundred people were being shot in one week in Madrid alone without having had a proper trial, prejudiced people abroad. People were being arrested by Socialist, Communist or Anarchist groups of self-constituted police and were being tried summarily in secret tribunals. ' There was one in the new but terribly ugly Fine Arts Club on the Calle Alcalá with a bearded old man presiding. I could never find out his name. A sentence of guilty meant immediate death, but the trials were not entirely formal and I know of people who were exonerated and set at liberty. The difficulty was that so many tough characters took this opportunity to settle off old scores and thus connived at the shooting of some innocent person. The bodies would be found in the mornings on the Prado de San Isidro, where the May fair used to be held, and later the shootings began to take place in the huge grounds of the University City. What also happened sometimes was when these self-appointed police arrested someone whom they thought a danger to the régime they shot him because they thought that a regular court would absolve him. Both the Giral and the Caballero Government did everything they could to organise these self-appointed police of the political parties into a new and politically-reliable although naturally not very efficient force but this took months and no great progress could be made until the Government received arms from Russia at the end of October and was able to commence to assert itself.

Nor was the situation helped by exaggerated reports of atrocities from the other side. Unfortunately these reports were not without foundation. Right from the first moment of the revolt in Tetuan and Ceuta, the Insurgents shot down Leftists ruthlessly and in great numbers. The Badajoz massacre is well substantiated by the reports of Senhor Neves, a Portuguese journalist, Jacques Derthet of *Le Temps*, and Marcel Dany of the Agence Havas. All these journalists visited Badajoz and returned to Portugal from where they sent their dispatches. M. Derthet said that 1,200 militiamen were shot. Even if the number were only a quarter of this it would still be greater than any massacre in Madrid.

There was a bad shooting affair in Madrid Prison on August 9, apparently after some noisy protest by political prisoners. It is said that they set a cell on fire and fired on the warders who came to put it out, but I was not able to confirm this. Anyway, a large number of prisoners were taken out and shot following this incident. They included Dr. Albinaña, a weird little man who had begun his political career as a most violent Republican and had ended up with a blue-shirt Fascist movement all of his own, but which had never prospered because he was mixed up in a divorce case which caused the Right to frown on him; Don Melquiades Alvarez, former 'political boss' of all Asturias, and Sr. Martinez de Velasco, who was leader of the small Agrarian Party and an intimate friend of Sr. Alcalá Zamora. This shooting did the Government a great deal of harm as Melquiades Alvarez was quite well-known abroad and, to a lesser extent, Sr. Martinez de Velasco also.

One of the difficulties of the situation was that the militiamen were always coming and going from the front in cars and what happened on some occasions was that a group of survivors after some terrible grilling by the enemy would come back anxious to avenge this on some victim, or victims. Without in any way condoning this it is only fair to say that much of the fighting at the front was very near being murder, for the militiamen who did not know one end of a rifle from another and had no officers to lead them would wander right into the line of fire of the skilled machine-gunners of the Moorish units or the Foreign Legion and literally be mown down by the score. And time and again the militiamen were manœuvred into traps by their own officers who had feigned loyalty.

Even writing to-day in August 1939, four months after the end of the war, I have been unable to obtain any exact figures of the number of people murdered. I am told by people in close contact with the Franco authorities that they estimate the number murdered in and around Madrid, and including small towns in the neighbourhood such as Chinchon and Alcalá de Henares, at about 100,000. Independent estimates by people in Madrid put the figure at sixty or seventy thousand for the capital.

I am, however, inclined to wait for concrete proofs before accepting such large figures. If we reflect that before the war the number of male adults over the age of twenty-one in Madrid was about 220,000 and that most of those who were murdered were full-grown men, it can be seen that the figure of 100,000, even allowing a liberal addition for the male population of the surrounding villages and towns, would mean that well over one-third of the men of Madrid were murdered.

The Spanish Civil War lasted 986 days; so that if we accept

the figure of 100,000 it would mean that 100 people were murdered every single day in Madrid from the beginning to the end of the war. Now in the first, and worst, days of the war the average number of murdered people brought into the Madrid Morgue did not usually number much over thirty. I believe there were over 120 on one single day. I do not think that many people were shot without trial after the end of January 1937. Even if we accepted that fifty people a day were murdered in Madrid from July 18, 1936, to January 31, 1937, then the total would be about 10,000. That seems to me bad enough as a figure and I should rather doubt if so many as 10,000 were murdered.

During the whole of the worst period in Madrid I was working there and most nights at very advanced hours I walked back from the Press Censorship Office in the Telephone Building to my home, about two miles. Yet I never saw any corpse on the street. Nor in my almost daily trips from Madrid to various fronts, often leaving early in the morning, did I, except on one occasion, see the dead bodies of murdered persons by the roadside. Many bodies could, of course, be seen in the early morning on the grounds of the University City or down on the Prado de San Isidro. It seems to me that if it is true, as alleged, that many tens of thousands were being murdered at this time, one would have seen the interior and surroundings of Madrid literally strewn with corpses.

Of the number killed in Franco territory it is impossible to give even any remote estimate. Books such as *Burgos Justice*, by Sr. Vilaplanas, give a sad picture which indicates that the number of murders was very high. Whether or not it be coincidence the fact remains that about forty Members of Parliament were shot on each side. Whether it is fair from this to deduce that about an equal number of victims were shot on each side I do not know. The testimony of various witnesses shows that the number of those murdered in Andalusia, under General Queipo de Llano, was particularly high. One of the victims was the talented Federico García Lorca, author of *Yerma* and *Bodas de Sangre*, two excellent plays, and of many poems. He was murdered in Granada and his friends said that the murder was carried out by the Civil Guard in revenge for a poem he wrote about that corps in which he said that the patent-leather helmets they wore were matched by 'their patent-leather souls'. (Con sus almas de charol!) One particularly sad murder seemed to be that of the wife of a Spanish journalistic colleague of mine. He worked for a foreign news agency and although a Republican I do not think he ever mixed in politics. He was in Madrid when the revolt occurred but his wife, a woman of fifty, was holiday-making in territory seized by Franco forces and she was taken to Burgos and murdered. I think his name was Barrado.

People would ask me frequently: 'Why does not the Government stop this killing?' The situation was that arms had been handed out to the masses in the first place and it was not now easy to get them back. Such loyal police, Army or Civil Guard units as could be fully counted on were relatively few and they were at the front facing the Insurgent thrusts in the Guadarrama and in Estremadura and there were not the forces with full confidence available for the control of Madrid where at the most modest estimate there were ten per cent of the population of nearly 1,000,000 in full sympathy with the Insurgents and many more either tepidly so or sitting on the fence. Indeed the Insurgents' radio stations with a foolish disregard for the consequences did not hesitate to boast of the large numbers of sympathisers they had in Madrid and whom they said would soon give a good account of themselves. The only humane and just solution would have been to have rounded up some fifty or sixty thousand people most likely to take active part in hostility to the Republic and to have interned them in huge concentration camps. But how could a Government which sat until dawn many a night figuring out how to rake together enough rifles to send volunteers to this, that or the other point where the Generals threatened to break through, or were already breaking through, suddenly improvise gigantic concentration camps, make lists of suspects, arrest them, convey them to the camps, provide guards and food supplies? It just was not possible.

Foreign diplomats had sheltered some 20,000 refugees in buildings under diplomatic protection. There were suggestions that foreign nations should provide a refugee camp to which people could go who feared reprisals for their political beliefs, but nothing was done. Hundreds, possibly thousands, of lives could have been saved if the Government had been able to purchase rifles and machine-guns with which to hold the attackers and then to have turned its attention to internal conditions in Madrid and other towns and villages. But no. Already on July 25, France was proposing Non-Intervention to Britain and early in August the two nations which as neighbouring Democracies and as the centres of far-flung Empires whose routes ran by Spain should have assured the stability of a friendly power, had pledged themselves to send no arms. A legitimate Government was refused the right to buy arms to maintain order in its own country. International law and pledges were thrown overboard in a shameful 'sauve-qui-peut' of the Democracies while the Germans and Italians smiled with glee, prepared more shipments for Spain with natural indifference to their own pledges, and hoped that 'Der Tag' was nearer than they could ever have believed. First Spain, then Austria, Czechoslovakia, and so force a way, or prepare a certain way, to Rumanian petrol and oil. The plan was excellent. That many excellent Fascists were being murdered in Madrid? That was too bad, but sacrifices must be made. Once France was encircled, one could begin to think of big moves. Perhaps they would not even need to fight. A France with three hostile frontiers! Yes, life was good in Rome and Berlin. Little to eat, but great things to come. And for the time being one must jolly the Democratic Powers along, play the anti-Communist record every day; it really was all too easy to fool these comatose giant Empires who knowingly and willingly handed over vital strategic points and were glad to do it.

CHAPTER XXVIII

TOLEDO IN PEACE AND WAR

I LOVE Toledo above all Spanish towns; its whole is a perfect harmony, a grey symphony nestling on a small hill looped almost completely around by the Tagus. And Toledo is of such exquisite taste because its builders who put up these houses with such grey roofs were short of ground and huddled them together and so there was never room to lay down tram lines or to modernise. Then again, Toledo is an ex-capital, a modest market town to-day. Some people prefer Seville. But Seville is more sensual, more spacious, with white walls and much beauty, something very much of the flesh. Toledo is more spiritual, it speaks to the soul. Even its women, neat-ankled, dark-haired, black-eyed maids, seem somehow second-ary to life in Toledo and contrast sharply with the heavily-built, all-absorbing Sevillañas.

And I wonder if any painter has ever reflected the soul of a town the way El Greco, otherwise Kyriakos (Dominic, if you prefer it that way) Theotokopoulous, mirrors Toledo in his work? That lovely grey, those pale but sharp colours at sun-down, you find it all in the sometimes eccentric work of El Greco. It could not have been hard for El Greco to accustom himself to Toledo because they have a hard light like that of Toledo in many parts of Greece, and they have strong red wine and good roast mutton also in Greece, just as in Toledo. And Greece is not sensual either and youthful British aris-tocrats doing the 'Grand Tour' find Athens very restful after Bucharest. I was very fond of spending much time in Madrid in the Prado Museum gazing at Greco's 'Christ Carrying a Cross', because it is so rarely that so much beauty has been put into the face of Jesus Christ. The last I heard of this pic-ture, an ex-priest of Toledo Cathedral was trying to sell it in Perpignan during the refugee exodus from Catalonia this year. But I still hope that maybe this was only a copy. If not, I hope that it has not been seriously damaged and that some day I will be able to go to Madrid again and gaze at this Christ. But there are other pictures of his which I do not care for. I have looked at the Burial of Count Orgaz for hours and could never make much sense of it.

I have been so often to Toledo and have spent so many happy days there that I like to sit back and pick them again out of my mind. There was Toledo on Good Friday of 1930 with its Procession of Semana Santa, a lovely piece of colour in such a setting with its robed priests, its penitents, the swaying statue of a Virgin, the brave uniforms of the officers of the Military Academy and of the Civil Guard. Then there was the day in 1932 when Cardinal Gomas took possession of the Primacy of Spain, I think he was still only Archbishop then, in succession to that saintly but irritable fanatic, Cardinal Pedro Segura. I walked behind him through the Cathedral and met a priest I knew who told me that it was a pity that the Primate was a Catalan. They didn't like Catalans much in ultra-Castilian Toledo. In the crowd at the door I met a Toledo girl who spoke good German which she had learned, she said, from a Czech lady who lived in Toledo. She was a nice girl and intelligent and I said I would go back next Sunday to see her again, but of course I did not because something or other turned up and that is the way a reporter's life is.

Or there was a lovely day I spent there one January, a day of bitter cold such as is rare even in Toledo, with a Newcastle girl, and we ate stuffed partridge at the Posada del Viento and roamed hand-in-hand through the narrow streets and near sunset, although it was so cold, we went into the Cathedral Tower and up near the bells we looked over Toledo's loveliness as the sun set and everything was such an even winter grey that it seemed hard ever to find again such a harmony of town, sky and landscape. And we drank lots of Anis—Anisette they call it in France—to keep us warm on the bus going back.

Then, suddenly, the easy Spain had gone. And I went many times to Toledo in a few weeks to look at stark tragedy both within and without the walls of the Alcazar, which if the truth be told was an unbeautiful building, and I cannot regret that it has been burned so often. The original building was on the site of a Roman castle and it was burned down in 1710. The French burned it down before leaving in 1810 during the Napoleonic wars and then it was burned again in 1887. The architect who re-built it decided to make a real job of it and he used plenty of concrete and steel girders so that 9,000 shells, 500 aerial bombs and half a dozen mines still did not completely wreck it when the Republicans tried to subdue the brave defenders.

I went there early in August when the Rebels inside still dominated the road entering town with a machine-gun and one had to make a detour by the Plaza de Toros and how jittery the town was and quite crazy with militiamen with big straw Sancho Panza hats—they were peasants—and Anarchist red and black scarves and at least twenty committees and practically nothing to eat. Every hour or so there was a false alarm that the Rebels were coming out and a minor panic, and quite rightly because there were 1,100 well-armed men inside, many of them Civil Guards, and they ought to have been able to take the town back right away. But they never tried. Sitting up in an attic beside a machine-gun in a house on the Plaza Zocodover it was fantastic to look across at the hulking building towering just a couple of hundred yards away and to think of 1,600 people shut inside, completely surrounded by their enemies.

Later a tremendous romance developed of the long defence of the Alcazar by the cadets, but actually there were less than a score of cadets inside because the Military Academy contained within its walls was on holiday. The chief force comprised the Civil Guards of the whole Province of Toledo who were called in by the Civil Governor to the capital because, he said, they were required to defend the Republic against an attempt to overthrow it. Which was one way of putting the case. Soldiers and local sympathisers with the military *coup d'état*, including the Civil Governor himself, completed the total of 1,100 fighting men. They made little attempt to hold the town and on withdrawal took in many women belonging to the families of Left-Wing persons as hostages. There were

570 women and children inside. Before withdrawing they shot a number of people, including a Socialist councillor whose name I have forgotten. I was told that he lived near the Alcazar and as he left his home with his daughter some Civil Guards saw him and pushing his daughter aside they shot him dead. Peculiarly enough, when you see what a dead little town Toledo is normally and with only clergy and officers and a few peasants in its streets, it seems strange to think that it has a tradition of Liberalism. Yet this is the case. Colonel Moscardo, the commanding officer, therefore, found it difficult to hold a town latently hostile, and quickly went within the Alcazar. On July 22 I think it was that the withdrawal was complete.

In 1938, I saw a story sent from Nationalist Spain to a British newspaper reporting that Sir Arnold Wilson, M.P., had offered to place a memorial stone on the ruins of the Alcazar, engraved with the following quotation from Byron's *Childe Harold's Pilgrimage*:

> 'True Glory's stainless victories,
> Won by unambitious heart and hand
> Of a proud, brotherly and civic band,
> All unbought champions.'

That seemed to be rather fulsome praise, for despite the great heroism showed by those within, a great many of them certainly did not in the first place take up arms with any intention of installing Fascism in Spain.

I found the Civil Governor very proud of the fact that all the art treasures were safe and sound and under guard. Some Right-Wing people had been shot, I learned, but I could not find out how many; they had been shot on the open space just behind the El Greco House. The militiamen were in their element banging away their rifles from behind sand-bags at the walls of the Alcazar.

I went again and again to Toledo and I always hated it; just the thought of those people inside with the shells crashing into the building every few minutes was terrible. One day a Government plane bombed it. We saw the plane coming and I hurriedly left the Plaza de Zocodover because most of the time the Government pilots had no bombing sights and accuracy was not always outstanding. Jan Yindrich stayed up there and the first bomb fell short and killed two militiamen and blew Jan down two flights of stairs. From a safer point I watched the bombs gliding down for they were of aluminium and glistened in the sunlight. It is a horrid sensation to watch them come down and I would just as soon not see them. Every bomb seemed to be heading right at you even if it fell five hundred yards away.

Another day I had just come from the front behind Talavera where things were not going well for the Republic. Out in that rolling country with little cover the Franco forces could make fast progress. We had found Colonel Asensio, tall, suave, smartly dressed as ever; he was not one of those officers who wore an overall; busy planning on a map. He was quite frank, describing how he had men out on both sides of the main road from Talavera to Madrid and that he hoped to encircle the enemy's advanced forces. He puzzled me. For there he was planning, and carrying out, operations which would have been normal if he had had a force roughly equivalent in strength to the attackers. But he had not. In front was a compact, disciplined force under professional officers; whereas the Republican forces were mainly composed of amateur fighters under improvised officers and quite incapable of carrying out any co-ordinated movements. They had only just one chance and that was that if put in a fortified position they could hold it. This was almost impossible because there were not the forces to hold any long line and therefore the Insurgents could always have outflanked any defensive position. I used to think that Asensio in the small room full of maps in Santa Olalla was just cynical and took the line that as a fight had to be fought and they were sure to lose it did not much matter what he did. But maybe I misjudged him; perhaps he really believed that planned out-flanking movements could be carried out by incoherent amateur fighters, poorly equipped, and lacking food and supplies almost continuously.

He lent us his car to go to the front. On the way we met tired troops drifting back. 'Where are you going?' we would ask. 'We have lost the other companies who were with us and we are going to see if they have moved back to the next village,' they answered. They were lying and they knew we knew it. But they were very young and very hungry. We found the actual front held by tough Shock Policemen. Planes were scrapping overhead. Two fighters went down in flames on the brown stubble some miles away. Back at headquarters we found that an Italian pilot had been in one of the planes and had come out of the smash almost unscathed and immediately sent in a car to Madrid. He was Vincenzo Patriarca a handsome lad, an Italian, but who had lived many years in New York. He had been a volunteer aviator in Abyssinia and had now moved on with Italian officers who were in Africa with him over to Spain. He was the first Italian pilot to be caught and the Government, naturally, made a big song and dance about it but it made no difference abroad because the important people who could have changed things already had full information as to the number of Italian and German pilots in Franco's forces.

Jay Allen, who was in Gibraltar in July and August, told me one day how he went down to the port to see some Italian aviators land on their way to Seville. As he watched them coming ashore from the tender from the big Italian liner off which they had come, a policeman came up to him and asked him to go away. Jay protested and the policeman only desisted when he was shown an American passport and told that there would be trouble from the American consul if he interfered, for this was a non-military area and open to the public. So you see that the authorities in Gibraltar had only to count the pilots as they drove from the port to La Linea. Nobody can say that the playing fields of Eton to-day do not produce a courtesy of a superlative character. Here were Italian pilots coming to Spain to help a friend of their nation to defeat the legitimate Government in order that Germany and Italy with the aid of the new-found friend could encircle France and prepare a death blow at the French and British Empires. Yet we courteously allow these men to pass through a stronghold of our Empire, Gibraltar, and our policemen give hectoring lectures to a representative of a British newspaper who might give offence to these honoured guests by staring at them or even asking them questions.

The Italian pilot, Patriarca, had been brought down by Corporal Urturbi, a Spanish pilot who was in Franco territory when the revolt broke out but after pretending to accept the revolt he took the occasion, with a friendly mechanic, to seize the bomber in which they were making a raid on Malaga. They killed the other three occupants and flew the plane to Madrid. Now Urturbi was dead because he had brought Patriarca down by the simple but dangerous process of ramming the Italian machine, a new Fiat fighter, with the old plane he was flying. This showed great heroism but the Government could ill afford to lose planes and pilots in this manner.

However, to return to Toledo. On this particular day, Sunday, September 16, after watching these dramatic events near the front we drove over to Toledo where we found the Chilian Ambassador to Madrid, Don Aurelio Morgado, shouting through a loudspeaker at the Alcazar asking for a truce in order that the women could be evacuated. Morgado was speaking, I think, as Dean of the Diplomatic Corps. There was no reply. It seemed strange amid the confusion of Toledo to see the thin, suave Morgado with a car driven by a smartly-liveried chauffeur. Colonel Vicente Rojo, a professor of the Military Academy, and a man without politics but loyal to his oath, had entered the Alcazar blindfolded. But Moscardo refused to consider evacuating the women and only asked that a priest be sent to give Holy Communion, which was done.

Then one morning a mine was blown up under the western wall and a great gap rent. But Captain Barcelo in charge did not organise things well. All troops and civilians had been ordered out of the town while the mine was blown up; it took the militias twenty minutes to get back and launch the assault into the breach. Barcelo was wounded in the foot in the attack and his second-in-command was also hurt, so command devolved on Quintanilla, the artist, who had come out with some reserves from his depot in the Montaña Barracks. But although the western side of the Alcazar was seized, somebody raised the cry of alarm: 'Be careful, our artillery is getting ready to shoot again!' And the hundreds of militiamen panicked out again. Before anything could be done the defenders had their machine-guns back in position. I arrived soon afterwards and found every window in the town broken. The militiamen used for the assault were very young, some of them aged sixteen or seventeen. They belonged to the 'La Pasionaria' Battalion. Why the fairly tough Shock Policemen of whom there were about three hundred in the town were not used instead of these beardless, inexperienced lads, was beyond me. The Shock Police had their headquarters in the Castilla Hotel, where one could get very good food and the owner was a charming man who loved travelling and whenever he could save up enough money he would take a holiday and patronise the hotels of other lands. What I did not like much about the Hotel Castilla was the fact that it was the place to which many Madrid society couples came on their wedding night. It was 'the place' to come to before starting on a trip to Paris or London, in order to avoid spending this supposedly happy first night in a sleeping-car. It seemed to me that the walls of this hotel must surely have stored much knowledge of pain, disillusion and unhappiness. Maybe I was too pessimistic, but at any rate I never liked that hotel.

In the whole war, I have never felt quite so depressed about anything as about Toledo. I could never get over the feeling of horror that came over me as I sat in the Plaza de Zocodover as shell after shell howled by like a shrieking demon. The horror of 1,600 people cooped up inside a building against which thousands of shells were fired and on which hundreds of bombs were dropped was fearful. It must have been terrible to be inside waiting for the next shell. Of course, it could all have been ended in a few hours if the Government had cared to use tear-gas. I remember how in a building strike in 1934, workmen staged a stay-in strike down in the deep cellars of the new part of the Bank of Spain in Madrid and the Shock Police soon moved them out with the aid of half a dozen tear-gas bombs. But as far as I could find out, the Government would not permit this in Toledo because they feared reprisals and also that it would be said abroad that they were using poison-gas.

The last time I went to Toledo was on Saturday, September 26. The Rebels had taken Maqueda, which is the point where the Toledo road joins the main road from Talavera to Madrid. There were no defences at all along this road and General Varela pushed ahead at record speed. Near Torrijos, half-way to Toledo from Maqueda, one of the officers commanding the Government forces suddenly raced down the road towards the enemy forcing his chauffeur to drive at revolver-point. But he did not get out of range before his own men realised what was happening and turned a machine-gun on the car, killing officer and chauffeur. It was one of the main difficulties of the Government that few of the higher officers could be relied on; they would pretend to be loyal and then would try to desert or else would by omission or commission upset the march of operations.

It was a lost town as I walked through its streets that Saturday morning. There was an aerial battle overhead with the last few existing Government aeroplanes fighting very bravely; they brought down a big bombing plane which I heard at first was manned by Italians, but they afterwards proved to be Spaniards. Around the Alcazar, the Shock Police were there just as usual exchanging shots with the defenders, who must have felt pretty good. Out on the hills to the West there was heavy fighting. The Government forces had counter-attacked and taken a small column of men and a dozen motor-lorries, but the odds were too great.

Next day, Sunday, September 28, it was all over. The Insurgents broke through at twenty points and it was a 'sauve-qui-peut' in which very many of the braver died because they waited for orders to withdraw which never came. Not, mind you, that Toledo could have been saved at that stage. But just sufficient military knowledge to have realised that it was a lost town on the Saturday and the giving of the necessary orders for evacuation would have saved hundreds of lives.

There is a horrible story current of the Tercio entering the largest military hospital in Toledo and throwing bombs into the wards, and then setting fire to the building. I hope it is not true but I have never seen any firm denial from responsible persons on the matter. There are believed to have been three hundred wounded in addition to doctors and nurses there.

Even a big consignment of pictures of El Greco, ready packed, were left behind. The committee in charge escaped death by rowing across the Tagus in a small rowing boat when the Moors were already at the Puerto de Visagra. These pictures had been ready for removal for ten days but the trucks which were to have been sent never came. Later, so one of the committee men who escaped from Toledo told me, the order for the removal and for the sending of trucks which had been signed by the Minister of Education several weeks earlier, was found hidden in a file in the Ministry. Sabotage or incompetence? Who could say in such hectic moments.

The defenders of the Alcazar were thus relieved. They had lost 140 killed, a low number considering the terrible ordeal they had gone through and I, for one, always felt they earned the tremendous praise they received after the relief.

CHAPTER XXIX

THE TELEPHONE BUILDING

I AM very fond of modern buildings. Not, of course, of freaks or exaggerations. But of clean-limbed buildings which run easily up to meet God's sky. In Madrid I grew to be really fond of the thirteen-story Telephone Building which stands nobly on the Gran Via and which houses the machinery for nearly all of Madrid's 50,000 automatic telephones. It is a massive building with dignity and the architect after worshipping at the shrine of American architecture for thirteen stories suddenly decided to render homage to Castile and he placed thereon a rather ornate tower so that at a far distance you might think that this was a castle in Spain.

We spent much of our time in this building during the first months of the war, for our stories were censored there and afterwards we telephoned them to London from the fifth floor of the building, still with the watchful censorial eye, and ear, keeping guard. But we spent even more hours each day there as the tide of battle drew near, and finally early in November we could sit and watch the front line through field glasses on the twelfth story. This was armchair-reporting of a war.

In this building I found how well the alert blood of the new Spain blends with the industrious temperament of the Americans, for Spain's new telephone system was installed by Americans in the days of Primo de Rivera and although the company is called the National Telephone Company of Spain it is affiliated to the International Telephone and Telegraph Corporation of America. In a way Spain gives a spiritual life to the rather exaggerated materialism of American ideas. Americans tend to worship at the God of Efficiency's altar just because they like to see wheels go around with complete smoothness. The Spaniards say: 'With the creations of the God of Efficiency we will build a new world, a new civilisation.'

I like the Spanish viewpoint. I love efficiency. I hate dirt and disorder. I like to see life run smoothly like an intricate machine. I love such things as stream-lined trains, when they are properly stream-lined and not an amateurish job like the Royal Scot; swift flying-boats; antiseptic, service-giving hotels; powerful American cars which eat distances effortlessly; white overalls; polished floors. I am a child of my age; or at least I am of my age, shall we say. But, like the Spaniards, I want to see something come of all this. I want a 'brave, new world' in reality and not the horror reflected in Mr. Huxley's satire in which under the pretext of opening up new horizons he regales us with a caricature of the one we see every day.

But I am drifting away from Madrid's Telephone Building. There I loved to glide swiftly and noiselessly from floor to floor in very fast lifts, to watch the great halls full of automatic machinery which clicked away efficiently almost without human attention, to see the neat, smart offices filled with very beautiful 'Madrileñas' clad in uniform black dresses with white collars who made hundreds of office machines clatter vivaciously.

And the people there were such real people. The service was never idle day or night. You could get London at five o'clock in the morning if you wished, for the telephone girls always kept watch. The concern was, as so many other places, under the control of a committee of the workers. There were some of the American engineers there at first, but they were finally withdrawn to Valencia and Barcelona. Yet the services ran faultlessly. You might have thought that the telephone girls would have said: 'Now let's strike for higher wages and shorter hours; we only have a committee of our own people to deal with. The big boss and the bosslets have departed!' But they never did. I shall not easily forget the November afternoon of 1936 when Franco had closed in on Madrid and he opened fire for the first time with his batteries on the Gran Via in general and the Telephone Building in particular. The first shell hit the building. I and some other correspondents thought at once of the basement. The fact that the first shell had hit an outside wall on the fourth floor did not seem to us any guarantee that the next shell would not come in through a window into our room on the fifth floor which faced the direction in which the guns were lying. We hurried to the lift and the usual lift girl swished us down to the second basement. That was the first thing that seemed wrong to me; to be going down when this lift girl was staying at her job. After all, if one of the numerous shells flying around the town were to hit the lift machinery, the elevator might easily crash to the bottom. Down in the deep second basement we found a number of people.

After a few minutes I decided to go up and see what was happening. When I got back to the fifth floor and into our phone room I passed through one of the more unpleasant moments of my life for a black-overalled, little telephone girl with headphones was calling out my name, and when I answered she said rather angrily: 'Well, where have you been? London is waiting for you.' The censor, who had likewise stayed at his post, sat down beside me and allowed me to dictate without first writing it, a story of what was going on. Another shell hit the front entrance to the building while I was talking to London. I was so ashamed of my little exhibition of 'nerves' that I never again took refuge in the basement, not even during bad air raids; or at least until the censorship was moved downstairs. The courage and discipline of the telephone employees was really first rate.

It was this courage of the mass of the people which prevented General Franco from taking Madrid as he did Toledo. At least I can offer no other single reason. I have read, and I have heard men who know Spain well, expound many explanations. The one I have heard most is that it was saved by the International Brigades. I do not agree. As far as I could learn 1,500 men of the XVth International Brigade arrived about November 8, and an equal number composed of three battalions of the XIth Brigade about eight or ten days later. But Madrid's fate was really decided, in my opinion, between November 7 and 11. The Government had some 80,000 men defending the city; I do not think that three battalions could have turned the scale. Nor is it true that even these three battalions were very well armed. They had better weapons than most of the Government forces, possibly, but still much inferior to those of their opponents. Moreover these battalions had been hastily thrown together. Some of their members were trained and experienced soldiers, but the majority were labourers or scientists or trade union organisers. To compare them to the Tercio or the trained Moorish forces is quite ridiculous. Moreover the main Franco attacks in the first headlong drive against Madrid came against the Toledo and Segovia Bridges, through the Casa de Campo towards the Norte Station. The Internationals did not fight at any of these points. Then the Insurgent forces concentrated on breaking through the University City grounds to reach the Model Prison and to get into the town at Cuatro Caminos, and here the Internationals fought very bravely indeed. But the Government had already had time to rush reinforcements from Alicante, La Mancha, and the Valencia area, and I think they would still have held Madrid even without the help of the volunteers.

However, this is all very debatable matter and I do not suppose it will ever be possible to bring out actual figures of dead and wounded of Internationals and Republican soldiers or to produce the commanding officers of the various units to give their testimony, for the records have probably gone with the wind as far as they existed and defeat has likewise scattered the participants to the far corners of the earth, or at least those who are not dead.

Many people think that if General Franco had not allowed Yague to turn aside to rescue the occupants of the Alcazar he might have caught Madrid by surprise and have taken it. I do not think so. I think that Franco did not have enough men to assault and take a city hostile to him. Mark those last three words, please. Madrid on Saturday, November 7, had Franco steaming full speed ahead through its suburbs. I do not know exactly how many men he had. His sympathisers said 15,000, Government people said 60,000. These men could have broken through with support from inside. Madrid on that day had lost its Government. Even the chief of police had gone. The censorship had gone and we telephoned virtually what we pleased. The streets were deserted. Every

R

available rifle was being sought out for use to defend the town. Now I cannot believe that if a majority of the people of Madrid had really sympathised with the Nationalist cause they could not have shown their will. Despite much 'purging' of the armed forces there is no doubt that quite a number of army and police officers would have favoured an 'armistice', which is the nice word used in the Spanish War to avoid saying 'surrender'. There were even a few Republican, and at least one Socialist, politicians who had never shown red hot enthusiasm for resistance. As a rule I do not care a great deal for sweeping phrases such as 'the people this . . .' or 'the people that . . .' but this is one case I think where the solid determination of the majority of the people did result in the temporary victory of their cause.

General Franco used most of the six weeks between the taking of Toledo on September 27 to his arrival at Madrid on November 7, in reorganising and preparing his forces for the big attack. He received Italian light tanks, with their crews, of course; there was German artillery pulled by motor tractors. Many thousands of Moors were brought over to replace losses. His air force had been strengthened by at least fifty or sixty heavy German bombers for they now came out fifteen or twenty at a time. The Government air force had simply folded up. 'Our last fighter plane goes up at dawn to-morrow,' Colonel Hidalgo de Cisneros—the enterprising young aviator who smuggled Prieto out of Spain in 1934 and now head of the Republican Air Force—told a friend of mine one night in October. The Government had hopes, for Russia had announced in London her intention of interpreting the Non-Intervention Pact with the same degree of latitude as taken by Germany and Italy, and planes were on the way. Russian tanks arrived in October with a few drivers and they were used in the Government counter-offensive to try to check Franco at Torrejon de la Calzada and to hit him in the flank at Seseña, near Aranjuez. At Seseña, the militiamen did not co-operate and the tanks went on alone. I think four were burned with their crews inside. I think they were all Russians. But there were very few of these tanks and the Italian tank detachments—we learned that they were Italian because they 'captured' Mr. Henry Gorrell of the United Press who ventured too near the scene of action and as he spoke Italian he was able to speak to the crews of the tanks which captured him—backed by Moors, simply raced across the country. Franco was on top of Madrid before the capital had time to do more than improvise a few hasty defences.

In August a number of architects prepared a plan of elaborate defences of Madrid. It was turned down by the Giral Cabinet with the explanation 'that to commence defence works near Madrid would upset the people and have a defeatist effect. . . .' Until October, work was going on on a new Underground Railway tunnel in Madrid and new tram-car lines were being laid down in the Calle de Principe. In the last six or eight weeks many so-called lines of defence were built but they were primitive in the extreme. Men, women and children went out on Sundays in thousands and toiled and dug.

But in open country the Franco forces, with air strength which Sr. del Vayo in an interview told me outnumbered the Republican force by twenty to one, and superior tank, artillery and other equipment, not to mention co-ordination and good staff work, could go where they would. They could have encircled Madrid, I think; although I do not know if they could have besieged it effectively with the number of men at their disposal.

The people of Madrid had every reason to be demoralised when they found Franco at their gates. President Azaña had departed on October 19 for Barcelona. It was rather a bad business because although he was right to move from Madrid it seemed to be rather sudden and a foolish Press communiqué saying that he 'had arrived in Barcelona to continue his visits to the fronts' was ridiculous because he had done practically nothing of this kind. I think he had paid one solitary visit to a quiet spot on the Guadarrama front since the war began. It looked sadly as if he had left the capital without the matter as to where he should go and when and under what conditions being properly arranged.

The Government was just adding to its number by including four Anarchists, Federica Montseny, Juan Peiró, Juan

Lopez and Juan García Oliver to bring the Anarchist Federation (F.A.I.) and the Anarchist labour organisation (C.N.T.) into the Popular Front, when Franco arrived before Madrid. The re-shuffle took place on November 5 and on November 6, Sr. Largo Caballero left for Valencia in the evening. Other Ministers left during the evening and night. Del Vayo, Foreign Minister, took leave of Mr. Ogilvie-Forbes before going but there was no immediate communication to the Diplomatic Corps as a whole.

Sr. Largo Caballero left General José Miaja in charge of Madrid. Miaja was not well known; he was just one more of Spain's four hundred Generals. He had been War Minister in that brief Cabinet of Martinez Barrio on the night of July 19-20. Later he had taken charge of the forces attacking Cordoba. Miaja had two grown sons, and his wife and several smaller children, in prison in Franco Spain.

He and General Pozas, chief of the Central General Staff who was at Alcalá de Henares, were left sealed envelopes with instructions to open them next day, Saturday. But they decided to open them at once and found instructions which I believe called on them to hold the town if possible but if not to withdraw towards Tarancon. I cannot, however, vouch for these instructions for I never got first-hand confirmation. I think that the Republican Government did not want to involve Madrid in the horrors of fighting unless it was clearly possible to defend the approach to the town.

CHAPTER XXX

MADRID IS SAVED

D own by Toledo Bridge the shells shrieked overhead in swift succession and the whining struck terror into my heart. In the whole war I never experienced such a situation, namely that shells whined overhead in large numbers without my having some general idea as to where they were coming from and going to. I neither heard the roar of the guns nor the explosions of the shells, or at least I could not distinguish them in the general din. I think they must have been shells from guns somewhere near the University City which were of considerable calibre and firing on the communications of the advancing Franco forces.

This was Sunday morning, November 8, and most of the British and American newspapers appearing on this particular morning had already described 'the last hours of Madrid'. Telephoning to London the night before to the office of a great Sunday newspaper, I had been dealt with very efficiently by a smart young news editor who when I had described how the Franco troops were attacking the suburbs across the river and how Madrid was quiet, had come to the phone and told me crisply: 'I say, Buckley, do you know that your copy does not tally with the other information we have on Madrid?' I apologised. What could one say? 'I say, where are you speaking from, are you actually in Madrid?' I had to say that I was, and in the centre of Madrid at that. Our smart young man was upset. He said: 'This is really very strange, we have it quite definitely that Franco's forces are now fighting in the centre of Madrid. Of course, I am not suggesting——' At that I hung up and left him to it. Five minutes later I had already thought up at least four good crisp replies guaranteed to devastate that news editor.

But I soon forgot about him because shortly afterwards a friend of mine from Paris spoke to me over the phone; an experienced correspondent who had spent four months in Franco Spain. His comment was: 'Ye gods man, what are you waiting for? Clear out of Madrid at once. Do you know that the Franco people look upon you foreign journalists in Madrid as a most obnoxious crowd of Reds and that you may be treated very roughly?' I knew that one of our number, a veteran correspondent in Spain and the most respected of the journalists there, had received a message from responsible sources in Burgos saying that he would be shot if he were caught in Madrid. The argument used was that a foreign correspondent who stayed with the Reds must expect to be treated as if he himself were a Bolshevist, no matter what his personal record or that of his paper might be. Yet until I had heard this anxious voice of my friend from Paris who knew the Franco people intimately, I had not felt that I was in danger. That morning a number of journalists had already left. There was a good deal to be said for leaving. We none of us thought that Franco would try to take Madrid; we all expected encirclement and a siege. There would be possibly more scope for a correspondent on the outside of the siege than cooped up in the city. I felt thoroughly nervous. If anyone had offered me a lift to Valencia I would have gone like a shot. I asked the British Chargé d'Affaires, Mr. Ogilvie-Forbes, whether he had any cars going to Valencia. He had not and he said crisply that it was nonsense to go away. I and the other journalists would be quite safe whatever happened if we took the shelter he offered us in the Embassy. I was depressed and very upset.

Yet down by Toledo Bridge talking to old Colonel Mena, who must have been well over sixty and who had fought gallantly all the way back from Toledo, I saw a sight which made me very ashamed of my petty worries about myself. Going up into line were long files of civilians. They had no uniforms. Just ordinary suits and a rifle slung anyhow over the shoulder. Most of the rifles were aged and I should say were nearly as unsafe for the man who fired as for the enemy. Some of the rifles had not even a bandolier and their owners had improvised one with string. Each man was given a handful of cartridges which he had to carry as best he could. Most of them had pockets in which to stow them but a few who wore overalls had to carry them in their hands.

They were just men called up by the trade unions and the political organisations to fight for Madrid. Many of them did not even know how to handle a rifle. On my way back into town I passed a news reel theatre which normally was open all day. I asked if the show was to be as usual. The girl at the cash desk was not sure. One of the operators had gone to fight but the other one was awaiting orders. It seemed that there were only a limited number of rifles. If the second man was told to stay at his post then, of course, the show would go on. At the Gran Via Hotel, half the waiters had gone.

Believe me, those were the men who saved Madrid. It was not General Miaja, nor the International Brigades. There were those two critical days of November 7 and 8 when the situation hung in the balance. It was the courage and sacrifice of the Madrid people which alone held the feeble lines which separated Franco from the city. Many of them died, unknown and unsung. Tram-drivers and café waiters are not personages whose names make news. Of those who were known, there was Emilio Barrado, one of Spain's best sculptors. He went down with a group as 'political commissioner' to give what the Americans call 'pep talks' to the men. He told a friend of mine that in the first few days the men could only be given fifty cartridges to last them twenty-four hours. Supplies did not run to more. These men had no sanitary services, no regular food supplies, often they had neither trained officers, nor non-commissioned officers. Yet they held the pick of the Nationalist Army, the highly trained Tercio, the well-disciplined Moorish corps, the fanatical Carlists from Navarre. They just stayed doggedly in the positions in which they were put and fired their rifles blindly at the foe, when they could see him. The Franco troops too showed great heroism. Time and again they hurled themselves down these suburban and slum roads running through a strange mixture of poverty and well-being from Carabanchel into Madrid. Many units of the Tercio were virtually wiped out. They tried to force their way through the Casa de Campo down to the Norte Station. Yet everywhere the defenders refused inexplicably to give up ground. And the Government artillery reinforced with some new guns and although probably outnumbered by at least four or five to one, nevertheless was able to batter down very effectively on the attackers. The artillery chief could see the whole battlefield from his post at the top of the Telephone Building and could 'dial' his batteries which were perforce all in or near Madrid now.

Now a strange new life began for us, and for Madrid. Before there had been occasional air raids, but on the whole there was relative quiet in Madrid and one could sleep and eat in nominal comfort. Now we were living at the front with the roar of artillery and trench mortars rarely silent for long and with machine-gun and rifle fire sounding on a still night as if it were in the next street. And the Nationalists were brutal when checked. It was then that they commenced to bomb Madrid ruthlessly with five-hundred pound and even one-thousand pound bombs. Shells burst intermittently in various parts of the city, although scarcely ever in the quarter near the Castellana where the various embassies and legations were for the most part situated or in the Arguelles sector where most of the homes of the aristocracy and middle class lay.

On the night of November 17 I was buying a newspaper from the old man who sold papers on the Gran Via with supreme indifference to shells or bombs. It was a dark night with drizzling rain from low-hanging clouds. Suddenly from above came that unpleasant 'whur-whur-whur-whur-whur', which is caused by the propeller placed on the rear end of heavy bombs in order to keep them as far as possible in an upright position so that the nose will be the first to strike. Before I could take shelter or even lie down, there came a shattering explosion from the Carmen Market about one hundred yards away and flames shot up. Here indeed was a nice answer to those comfortable prophets who assert that bombing cannot be carried out by night if there are clouds. I think the clouds were little more than low-hanging mist and that the bombers were able to get their bearings fairly well, probably by signals from the Franco lines or possibly from lights in the streets for no one could cure the motorists of using their lights.

That was about nine o'clock. Until 2 a.m. we knew no

peace. They came again and again. Even the solid Telephone Building trembled as the great bombs knocked down buildings or tore caverns in the ground. They rained down thousands of incendiary bombs. The city seemed to be ablaze. In the Puerta del Sol, a bomb ripped open the entrance to the Underground Railway killing a score of shelterers. Those who managed to escape and rushed out into the open found a new danger from falling glass from windows broken by the explosions. A friend of mine who was there saw a piece of glass decapitate a man as he ran to what he thought was safety.

The Prado Museum was hit although not badly. Next day eighty unexploded incendiary bombs—these are often small affairs not weighing more than one or two pounds and they are dropped in bunches—were picked up around the National Library. The Savoy Hotel, where one used to get the best meal in Madrid, was gutted. A house near the Telephone Building which was eight stories high was ripped down as if by a giant hand. Its occupants and those in the cellar were buried under hundreds of tons of masonry and I do not know if they were ever recovered. The fire brigade had 300 calls in five hours. Long rows of houses were ablaze. These were the old houses with sloping roofs covered with slates or tiles and with wooden rafters underneath. The liquid calcium burning with a white flame trickled down to the rafters after the bomb had exploded on the roof and set these ablaze. Five great buildings in the Puerta del Sol were hit by both kinds of bombs and were burning for days before the fires were completely extinguished. In that central square alone at least £2,000,000 worth of damage was done. How many died we never knew exactly. One raid ran into another and figures overlapped or were given out in a confused fashion. Madrid municipality took the view that the number of killed and injured were 'secrets of war'. The Government was in Valencia. About all we could do was to go to the Morgue and count the poor battered remnants of flesh lying there on the marble slabs. The spare limbs which did not obviously fit anywhere were put in a box. I think that at least 300 were killed and probably 1,500 wounded in that five hours gruelling of the night of November 17 and probably 1,000 would be a moderate estimate of the civilians killed by bombs during the month of November.

All Madrid seemed to be on the move. People whose homes were bombed had to find new shelter. Those whose homes were near the front line had to go somewhere else. Out in the Rosales district near the University City the bombing was terrific. Great nine-story houses were wrecked with amazing accuracy by the big German Junkers, the Ju-52, three-motor, rather slow, bombers which did most of the destruction of Madrid. Bombs did strange freaks. One went straight down a lift shaft, stripping away lift and stairs and killing everyone in the cellar. Those who stayed in the flats were unhurt, but isolated. Fire escapes had to be brought to get them down. Everywhere were people on the move, carrying their pitiful little bundles. The hospitals, filled to overflowing, were in turn bombed. Children who had lost their parents hunted tearfully through the streets. The Underground stations at night were jammed with refugees so that one had to pick one's way over sleeping bodies when one got off the train. A little grey-haired old woman who worked at the Telephone Building told me her tale of woe. She lived near Toledo Bridge with her daughter and the two children of her daughter. The husband was in the militia. Seventeen shells had hit the house in which they lived. But they went on living there. Each day she had two precarious trips from the Telephone Building to her home. She said she could find no other place to take her daughter and the children. Yet neither she nor any of the other working-class people with whom I spoke ever suggested surrender. They were terrified, they hated the war, but they thought that their cause was the right one and were prepared to fight.

One day I was at the Morgue counting, as usual; moving along among the rows of naked bodies, some peaceful and apparently unhurt, others blasted out of all recognition, when the doctor in charge began to talk to me. He was completely overwrought by the ceaseless work and with his hands joined he pleaded with me in the most passionate tones to do something to make Britain help the Republicans against this wrecking of the town by German bombers. His voice trembled, tears ran down his cheeks; I have I think never seen a man so completely in the grip of emotion. I hated myself as I assured him with as much conviction as I could put into my voice that British opinion would change, that the reaction to the ruthless bombing of Madrid would be very great. I got away as best I could. But that day I did not eat any lunch.

For me it was not just the emotional question. For me, the fall of Madrid meant a blow to the British Empire. Here in the University City was the front line for us, not just for the Spanish Republicans. I felt this conviction passionately. For long hours I debated with myself as to whether I should join the International Brigades. But I had not sufficient courage in my convictions to do this. Our modern Democracy in its education conveys to youth singularly few convincing reasons as to why he should die to save it. There was also the element of physical fear. The chances of death were big. My body is not of a robustness calculated to survive long exposure, lack of food. I think now that I was wrong. It would have been better to have joined up, feeling as I did.

The emotional wave hit me occasionally, but only in gusts; when I was in the Morgue, or when I watched those poor mangled bodies being gently withdrawn from under bricks and dirt by sobbing relatives.

About the end of November a parliamentary commission came out to investigate conditions as the result of an appeal made to the House of Commons by Sr. Alvarez del Vayo, Foreign Minister. The members were: F. Seymour Cocks (Socialist), J. R. J. Macnamara (Conservative), W. F. Crawford-Greene (Conservative), D. R. Grenfell (Socialist), Wilfrid Roberts (Liberal), and Wing-Commander A. W. James (Conservative).

It seemed strange in this weird Madrid to find a typical cross-section of the House of Commons appear on the scene. Seymour Cocks, handicapped by lameness was bluff and jolly, always ready with a good story, anxious to get into the danger zones. Macnamara was youthful, tall, elegant. Crawford-Greene was apt to bark questions and was very precise when troops paraded in front of the commission. Grenfell was active, in his element, organising this, that or the other. Wilfred

Roberts, gaunt, an intellectual type and, like Grenfell, an eager organiser with much tact. Wing-Commander James spent long hours measuring the depth of holes made by bombs and asking all kinds of technical questions.

Their cicerone was singularly ill-chosen in the person of Margarita Nelken, a fierce and imposing woman, a kind of Lady Astor in reverse, Member of Parliament for many years and always quick to criticise and attack. The Socialist Party had sighed with relief when she departed after some stormy discussion and the Communist Party found her a turbulent new recruit. However, her uncompromising manner and directness made her useful in some situations. This was not one of them. She was determined to show the M.P.'s the damage which had been done to Madrid and she literally took them by the nose and dragged them from one wrecked house to another until they cried for mercy. This was also a waste of time because one bombed house looks very much like another bombed house.

On their return to London many of the parliamentarians did much good work of a humanitarian character for Spain and their presence at least saved the centre of Madrid from any devastating bombardments for ten days or so. Germany in those days was very careful not to offend British opinion too openly. Hitler knew that he might still need to use Britain to help him to attain necessary positions for the beginning of real operations against ourselves and France, and the Spanish adventure was cloaked over as much as possible. The Germans themselves have since proclaimed to the world that after many hundreds of technical men from the Army had been sent during the first four months, finally 6,000 experts were sent at the beginning of November. There must also have been at least three or four thousand Italians there at the time.

All my impressions of those days of November and December in Madrid are blurred and confused. Perhaps in years to come I will be able to sort out my impressions more clearly. But I doubt it. My colleagues and myself lived at such a furious pace. Madrid had suddenly become the focus of world interest. The world was on the rebound after the expectation of an easy triumphal entry by Franco. The seventy or eighty special correspondents, many of the world-famous reporters, who had gathered in the Franco territory to report the fall of Madrid and, presumably, the winding up of the Spanish war, were dispersing and our dispatches of Madrid's resistance had to fill the columns which they had been all set to fill. So weary were we that even our shake-downs on the hard wood floor of the large room in the British Embassy where countless distinguished feet had trodden at many a score of receptions, seemed like heaven and the heaviest bombing raid could hardly wake us. For a few weeks we continued to sleep at the Embassy. We all believed that some night General Franco would, under cover of darkness, hurry ten thousand men up to the front lines in the University City, which were little over one mile from the centre of town, and make a fierce attempt to break through into the town and regain his prestige, which had gone down sharply.

We were a small and happy band working in friendly co-operation. We were mostly young; somewhere between twenty-five and thirty-five. The exception was the veteran correspondent of the *Times* in Spain, Mr. E. G. de Caux, and we all benefited much by his experience and counsel. I remember when we were all sure that Franco would either break into the town or surround it, Mr. de Caux one day after scanning the Franco lines with powerful glasses from a vantage point which enabled us to see well into Franco's rearguard, said: 'I see no masses of troops moving there, Buckley, which could enable General Franco to take Madrid. A city of one million inhabitants cannot be taken by a handful of soldiers. Franco will need many more men to take Madrid; a great many more men.' He proved to be right.

There was Geoffrey Cox, of the *News Chronicle*, an alert little New Zealander with a penetrating eye for the truth hidden in the background which the successful reporter must have. Sefton Delmer, huge, burly, cosmopolitan, of Irish-Australian blood and born in Berlin, thought out carefully every word of his short but graphic word-pictures of Madrid which he telephoned to the *Daily Express*. Stubbs Walker, of the *Daily Herald*, showed an exquisite taste in dressing-gowns and pyjamas and was our only casualty having to fly to Paris to hospital to have a wisdom tooth, which had grown the wrong way, extracted. Jimmy Oldfield, always dapper and immaculate, educated us in the phraseology of American news agencies by telephoning from our mantelpiece phone such opening sentences as: 'Oldfield's wire opener,' 'Oldfield's early morning special,' 'Oldfield's freshener . . .' for he is on the staff of the Associated Press which turns out a huge volume of wordage daily for the American newspapers and the handling of news becomes standardised and rationalised, that is as far as such an uncertain substance as news can ever be rationalised, under these circumstances. For instance a 'freshener' is a new introductory paragraph, or paragraphs, which will give a new angle to a story already sent; so that the American newspapers which often turn out an edition each hour of the twenty-four can bring a story already used up-to-date, or up-to-the-hour perhaps one should say. This system has, of course, its disadvantages as well as its advantages. The reporter may be tempted to over-play some small incident in order to secure the 'freshener' which otherwise was not in sight. Still I prefer the huge newspapers of America. To report even cursorily the events of the world to-day the reporters must have a huge volume of space for their stories. Even the largest British newspapers have to cut and prune the news too much. The result is that situations pop out unexpectedly at the reader which were not in the least unexpected to the experienced reporters on the spot, but which they cannot explain day by day as the situation develops because their papers have no room.

British readers, I think, ask too much of their newspapers. They want them printed on good quality paper; they do not want to pay enough. They prefer to skim over a series of short, highly condensed reports rather than to read carefully one or two stories. Yet it is a rather sad reflection that one can read very often in the *New York Times*, for instance, more news from the Empire than in a British newspaper. That is not the fault of the newspapers. They would be only too delighted to publish thirty-page or forty-page dailies with long daily reports from Australia, South Africa, Canada. But such newspapers would cost more and they would have to be printed on the cheapest of paper.

It is, you see, imperative for the conduct of a great Empire that statesmen, financiers, merchants, should be able to have reliable and accurate information on happenings in the whole world each day. You may argue that nobody can read a newspaper of forty pages. There is no reason why anyone should. Suppose your interests lie in politics you would read the political section. If you wanted news of Greece, India, Brazil, you would turn to the appropriate section. But it is so important that correspondents should have room to write not only of sensational happenings but of the daily events in these countries. Naturally our great dailies such as the *Times* and the *Daily Telegraph* already carry large quantities of foreign news. But in my opinion it is still not enough. They can still only skim the surface of the day-by-day events of the world. The *Daily Telegraph* devotes a column each day to news from the Empire, that is to say of the daily events of life there as distinct from the actual sensational news which may come also from there and which goes in the general news pages. This is a fine example. But just think what a vast difference it would make to the co-operation and understanding within our Commonwealth of Nations if the co-operation and comprehensive help of the people of Britain made it possible for every London newspaper each day to devote an entire page to news and articles from Canada, New Zealand, from the West Indies, Australia, Kenya, South Africa. Think of the quickening of contacts, of the arousing of interests. You, the British public, no longer have even the excuse of distance. Why, one can fly to Australia in a week now. Ye Gods, can't you shake your interest for a while from cricket and tennis and cheap novels and cheaper magazines and not-so-good films and think of the thrill of re-making our Empire into a progressive and great Commonwealth with Blacks and Whites using the great gifts science lays at our feet to build mightily and splendidly? The world lies at our feet; money, brains, science, youth are ours. We could rebuild our Empire into the greatest landmark of civilisation in one hundred years' time.

Well, I had better come back to earth. I know that I am supposed to be writing about Spain, about Madrid at the end of 1936 to be precise; about this Madrid which battled mightily and splendidly with every man's hand against her.

Abroad, Democrats and trade unionists held meetings and collected money. Poor folks in Antwerp and Aberdeen gave money they could ill afford. But what did that avail when not only Germany, Italy and Portugal were giving full support to General Franco but also many important financial concerns in Britain, France and the United States. A friend of mine, a charming member of the Spanish nobility, was at this time busy in Franco Spain organising the distribution of petrol. He said that they had now even established petrol pumps in small villages which did not possess them before the war. Yet Franco had no money, no resources, for all the gold had been stored in the Bank of Spain in Madrid.

Mr. Harold G. Cardozo, who was *Daily Mail* correspondent in Franco Spain for more than one year, wrote in his book *The March of a Nation*: 'The Madrid Reds had to pay in gold to Russia for every gallon of petrol sent to Valencia and Barcelona, while the Nationalist Government was amply supplied with petrol on credit. This was due to the fact that intelligent financiers had realised that the Nationalists were going to win and that the Nationalists would pay very early in the conflict. In other words, Nationalist credit was good and the Red Credit was bad.'

I used to feel rather ashamed in those dramatic days of Madrid to see the huge headlines and profuse thanks accorded to Britain or some other country where Democrats had collected a few thousand pounds to help the tortured capital. Yet in some discreet office in London, Paris or New York a few men would meet and after a discussion perhaps of minutes, accord General Franco a credit of maybe one hundred thousand pounds and no word of that would ever appear in any paper.

Our financial circles as our governing circles, you see, give so little thought to Empire safety. Their whole future existence depends on it, but wishful thinking pushes the alarm signals of intelligence into the background. These otherwise astute men of the City love to dream of a fine new Europe full of Dictators who will all spend their time suppressing Communism and clipping the wings of the Soviets and who will never, never even dream of turning their gaze on the overflowing wealth of the British and French Empires. It is a strange political mirage which lures from the path of safety otherwise sober men of judgment.

Sooner or later, possibly before this book is in print, possibly in five years' time, whole nations will be undergoing the torture that Madrid underwent in 1936 because in this world all sins bring their punishment. And sins of omission can be even worse than sins of commission. If the captains of our Empire head the ship into a region thick with dangerous shoals and rocks then we know what to expect.

CHAPTER XXXI

A COUNT IN GAOL

O NE morning I was sitting in the salon of a very charming and quite youthful Countess when there was a loud knocking at the door. The butler came back and announced: 'The Police!' I felt slightly nervous. I did not know much about the Countess or her family and if this turned out to be a centre of espionage or something like that the results might be most unpleasant for me as well as for them. It turned out, however, that the police were just looking for spare rooms in which to billet a tram-driver and his family whose home had been wrecked by a bomb in Cuatro Caminos. The Countess showed them several spare rooms at the back of the huge flat, which occupied the whole of one floor of a large house, and the tram-driver decided to go back and fetch his family at once.

This excursion of mine into high society had been brought about by friends of mine in London who knew the Countess from the days when she and her husband had mixed a good deal in international society in Biarritz, the Côte d'Azur, Paris and London. She told me that she knew King Edward VIII quite well and I dare say that was true. Her trouble now was that the Count was in gaol and her London friends had asked me to try to get him out.

After a great deal of trouble I managed to get the police to give me details of the charges against him. There were I suppose some twelve or fourteen thousand people in prison at that time, November 1936, and it was not easy to find out who was in which gaol and why. The police charge against him was that he had belonged both to the Clerical Party and to Falange, had subscribed liberally to both parties, and in general had been an active worker for Right-Wing causes. I was inclined to disbelieve some of this. I had been to see the Count in gaol and found him a rather uninspiring husband for such a pretty and energetic wife. He seemed listless and uninterested in life. Perhaps this was the effect of gaol. I also knew Spaniards who knew the family and they assured me that this particular family although rich in blue blood had a Liberal tradition. At any rate I pulled all the strings I could think of to try and get at least a provisional release, but without result. At this time, with Franco smashing Madrid badly every day with bombs and shells, the authorities hardly felt like showing great indulgence to prisoners. In fact there had been a recurrence of irregular shootings. On several mornings dead bodies were found on the Ronda de Atocha. It was reported that over three hundred prisoners who were being sent by the Government away from Madrid had been seized by the Anarchists at Tarancon and all shot. I think that the report was true. I am not quite sure as to the numbers. But among those killed was, I believe, poor Ramiro de Maeztu, a charming old man personally, although a fanatic in politics who used to write some tremendous articles against the Left in *A.B.C.*

The Countess, unlike the rest of her family who seemed to be in the depths of depression and resigned to any fate, was full of activity. When I finally reported that I could do nothing whatever, she only smiled and said: 'Well, never mind because I have the whole thing practically fixed through the Anarchists. Now, what I would like you to do is to see if you can get him into the British Embassy for protection when he is out. Because although the Anarchists think they can smuggle him out, he will of course be arrested again if the police run across him.' The Anarchists were playing a strange role in this war. In the first days they had murdered and butchered savagely. An acquaintance of mine in the police force told me how time and again he or friends of his had had to intervene practically at pistol point to prevent the Anarchists taking out and shooting some perfectly innocent person. They could be terrible with that blind passion of the illiterates with all the hatred of a feudal régime burned into their souls by centuries of sufferings and without leaders or a programme capable of turning this hatred into something more or less constructive, as was the case with Socialists and Communists.

The Junta, composed mainly of very young men, which was now controlling Madrid, had a number of Anarchist members and prisons were under Melchior Rodriguez, an Anarchist.

I sounded a lesser official at the Embassy about shelter for the Count. But it was, as I expected, quite impossible. The British Government was rigid in the extreme on this point. Our Embassy and the American Embassy shut their doors firmly against refugees. Most of the others did not. I am not sure that we were right to be so firm as we were in the first months. Afterwards, there was a slight change in our policy. It seemed to me that shelter could have been given to people whose lives were in danger and who had not actually done anything to warrant this menace. Some Embassies had sheltered Army officers known to be implicated in the Franco revolt, or at least the Republicans claimed this. This was unjustifiable, but there was a case for some laxity in the first months and until the Republicans were able to organise some kind of regular police force.

It is a sad reflection on human nature to see that now, in the summer of 1939, General Franco is having very serious trouble with the Chilean Government because they refuse to hand over sixteen Republicans who took shelter in the Chilean Embassy in Madrid when the town fell to the Insurgents. Well over 20,000 people were sheltered in Madrid diplomatic buildings while the Republic governed there and their position was respected despite the fact that many were very active Franco supporters.

One night as we were returning to the Embassy about midnight, we suddenly ran into a police cordon and heard shots and a general uproar. The police were raiding the 'Finnish Legation' situated just across the way from the British Embassy. Mr. Ogilvie-Forbes had given permission for the police to go through the home of the British Consul in order to take the 'Legation' defenders in the rear. This 'Legation' contained four hundred people, all Spanish subjects; even the 'Chargé d'Affaires' was a Spaniard. The Finns had all left early in the trouble and had put a Spaniard in charge who with the credentials left to him had managed to impose himself on the authorities as being the 'Chargé d'Affaires'. He had taken two other blocks of flats where he had some five or six hundred further refugees. He charged anything from £50 to £200 admission and then six shillings daily for food. The Right-Wing people inside defended themselves when the police made the raid, hence the shooting. One man was severely injured.

Life was not made easier for the British Pressmen by the appearance of the International Brigades. Inquiries as to whether this person or that had been killed were hard to answer in such a turmoil and with troops spending much time in the firing line and shifting about a great deal. The son of Rear-Admiral MacKenzie was 'killed' so emphatically by a Press report that a memorial service had been held before he finally turned up alive and well; and what a fine young fellow he seemed to be. Esmond Romilly, youthful, pale, venturesome, in keeping with the best traditions of British aristocracy, gave us a great deal of trouble as being 'the nephew of Winston Churchill'. Up to the end of December there were only two small groups of Britons in action, about half a dozen with the XIth Brigade, attached to the French section, and about a dozen or fifteen with the Germans of the XVth Brigade. Romilly was with the latter.

One day I was seated on the bed of a young Scot who had been wounded, not too badly, and was in the great ward of the Palace Hotel. There were about 300 people in this place which was formerly the banqueting hall where great political feeds were held and you got hors d'œuvres and roast chicken and ice and bad champagne and coffee just as sure as the sun rises, no matter whether the Party concerned were Left, Centre, or Right. Now it was full of pain and the operations were going on behind a screen only and the Spaniards do not use anæsthetics the way we do and would never think of giving more than a local injection for the purpose of chopping off a finger or something like that, so you could hear a lot of screams.

Then suddenly in came Romilly and three or four others and began to tell their tale to the man in the bed. They had been caught near Boadilla del Monte to the west of Madrid and only five were left alive of the dozen who had gone out. Arnold Jeans had been killed. A queer man whom I had met twice. Very cultured and polite, Jeans seemed to have no place whatsoever in war. A refugee from the Russian revolution, he was from Finland, I think, he came to England. But he was expelled by the police. He returned on a false passport. Later he apparently made friends with Communists and helped to sell the *Daily Worker* in Manchester and elsewhere. Lorimer Birch was dead too, I believe he was an educated man and a scientist. Several others were ex-soldiers and had had, I am afraid, some acquaintance with the inside of gaols. But they too had died gallantly. These details I learned later. Romilly happening to glance up in the midst of his story to their Scottish comrade and seeing me there, flew into a passion: 'What is this damned reporter doing here, eavesdropping?' he raged. 'Get away; clear out!' This was obviously not the moment for me to explain that I had merely dropped in to give some cigarettes to the wounded man and I slipped away. I remember that the hardy young Scot who made light of his own wound had tears trickling down his face as he heard how his seven friends had died.

Afterwards I met the passionate young Romilly and there was no ill feeling. I got him a Christmas pudding from the British Embassy. It hurt me terribly to have to leave him at the gate while I went in. But he could not enter for he was in uniform. The British Embassy, you see, was barred to men who risked their lives for the defence of our Empire and for the cause of democracy. The young Germans and Italians in the opposing ranks were heroes to the men in charge of their nations and those who survived took part in triumphal parades because they had helped to inflict a bitter blow on Britain and France.

There were all sorts and sizes in the Internationals; idealists, good-for-nothings, and some half-way between. But by and large they were heroes in the way they fought. Their weapons were bad, discipline was hard to obtain, they spoke a dozen different languages and few of them any Spanish. They worked miracles by sheer heroism. The Germans were the best. They were political refugees who had for the most part tasted the sadistic terrors of concentration camps and then the bitterness of exile. Death meant rather less to them than to the Englishman or the Frenchman. The Italians too were good. They had a Garibaldi battalion under Captain Pacciardi, a nice quiet-spoken lawyer who had lived many years in Paris after escaping from Italy where he had been a member of some very moderate Republican organisation.

I should like to say that as far as I came into contact with the International Brigades, and particularly the British section, I could find no truth for the assertion so often made abroad that mercenaries and adventurers predominated. There were a lot of very fine and cultured men among them. I never met John Cornford, but he had quite a reputation as a writer. I met such people as Tom Wintringham, Ralph Bates, Malcolm Dunbar, Hugh Slater, Esmond Romilly, Mackenzie, and many others who bore the lie to these accusations. Nor is it true that Jews were in a majority; there were relatively few in the ranks but they fought very gallantly. I remember meeting a very charming young Jew, son of a wealthy Frankfort family, in a Madrid hospital where he was lying with a bullet in his lungs. I wish I could remember his name.

Franco battered blindly against Madrid's defences until the middle of January without success. Recently I was rather amused to read a German officer, General Sperrle, writing in *Die Wehrmacht*, special Spanish number: 'Our bombers had the mission of blasting a way into Madrid and of demoralising the town in order that the Franco troops could break through. But it was impossible to get the troops to follow up the lead we gave them.' After the middle of January Franco changed his tactics, realising that it was in open country that he had everything to gain with his small, highly-trained, well-equipped and well-officered units, supported by ample foreign aviation. tanks and artillery. So he devised plans for encircling Madrid.

CHAPTER XXXII

ATTEMPTS TO SURROUND MADRID

THE last head-on attack of General Franco's forces against Madrid took place early in January 1937. After that he turned to attempts to surround it. He tried to do in February what he could perhaps have done in November and now he failed.

In three months and despite continuous and fierce fighting at Madrid, the Government forces had changed greatly. It had been possible to organise regular units with reliable officers who had had experience of fighting; not on a large scale but in a small way. They had received tanks, artillery, machine-guns from Russia and elsewhere. Aviation had come from Russia. The first morning the small snub-nosed biplanes (chatos, they called them) and the thin monoplanes (moscas), which seemed to move across the skies in jerks, had come on the scene at Madrid, people had gone on the roofs and cheered and wept and waved their handkerchiefs. That was early in November. The aeroplanes were Russian but of American design, of the Boeing type. There was also a light Martin, two-motor, bomber which was used a good deal, but they never had many heavy bombers. And they were always without exception heavily outnumbered by their opponents.

One morning, it was about February 9, 1937, I lay in a ditch near the Arganda Bridge on the main road from Madrid to Valencia and a few stray bullets whistled by. The Insurgents had made a great drive, starting February 6, to reach the road and thus cut the main traffic artery along which Madrid's food, and war material, were flowing. The night before they had claimed to have reached the bridge. But they were still about two miles away and their machine-gun bullets were spent when they arrived. But they could shell it; this they did, however, with light artillery which did not wreck the bridge. Some of our colleagues, Irving Pflaum of United Press, and Herbert L. Matthews, of the *New York Times*, actually drove across without their car being hit. I decided not to attempt it. The risk was considerable. My driver was a married man with a family and it seemed rather unnecessary to run the gauntlet to prove something which had already been proved. Up on a flat-topped hill above the Jarama lay hundreds of Government soldiers, a wonderful target for the Nationalist bombers. They had fought bravely to check the advance made by a force reported to be about 80,000 strong, with good storm troops of Moors and Foreign Legion, German tank-drivers and machine-gun sections, not to mention German aviation, artillery and anti-aircraft defence.

The Nationalists were full of enthusiasm. Malaga had fallen on February 8 to the new Italian Divisions which had arrived in recent weeks. Well-equipped divisions under their own officers and staffs, with their own equipment including transport, communications and feeding arrangements, and with first-rate modern war material, it was not surprising that they broke easily through the half-armed, primitive militia forces defending the Republican lines. They also had the help of German aviation operating from Spanish Morocco and Italian and German naval units.

The Republicans on their side not only had not sufficient materials nor a properly organised Army but they also suffered from the poor leadership in the War Ministry. Caballero, who in office turned out to be very stupid and obstinate, was not a great success as War Minister and his Under-Secretary to whom he left the military details was General Asensio. A party of British journalists who tried to go to Malaga when the attack was made on the town, found the main road obstructed between Almeria and Malaga because a bridge had been damaged by rains and not repaired. Apparently nobody was interested in this detail. Moreover, supplies being sent from Valencia were dumped in Almeria by lorry-drivers who said that that was the end of their responsibility. The lorry-drivers of Almeria said they had no transport available to forward the materials. There was no one on the spot to co-ordinate and command. Lesser officers, party politicians, trade union men, did miracles of organisation. But it was not enough. Probably Malaga could not have been saved but, as at Toledo, with just a little organisation from above the loss could have been minimised very greatly.

There is a fine account of happenings in Malaga both before and at this time in *My House in Malaga*, by Sir Peter Chalmers Mitchell, an excellent book by a calm and cultured Englishman.

Nevertheless, Malaga was on the whole a piece of luck for the Republicans because its taking did not affect the war greatly either way and this adventure by the Italians kept a well-equipped body of men busy down there while the Franco forces were trying to cut off Madrid. It is difficult not to believe that there was not some rivalry here. Franco and his German friends were anxious to show the Italians that they could stage just as good a show at Madrid as was being done on the Andalusian coast. With Italian help in the attack on the Arganda Bridge there seems no doubt that a big triumph would have resulted for Franco. The Government was hard put to it and the launching of 50,000 new men under their own officers and with good equipment could hardly have failed to turn the scale.

Despite the fierceness of the Franco efforts to reach Arganda Bridge, the Spaniards held solidly. The Nationalist commander-in-chief, I think it was General Aranda, swung his attack lower down in order to drive across at the main road many miles south of Arganda. They smashed across the River Jarama and headed for the small village of Morata de Tajuna which lies about half-way between Arganda and Aranjuez and is about five miles west of the Madrid-Valencia road.

So the famous Battle of the Jarama developed. And I think that here the help of the International Brigades was decisive. At Madrid they arrived too late but here they arrived in the nick of time. Even without them the Government might have managed to have dammed the gap before the Franco forces reached the main road; that is an open question. But here there was a wide open gap, the handful of Spanish troops had broken and it was the men of the 11th and 15th International

Brigades who closed this at tremendous loss. It is not hard to judge the tempo when one considers that of 400 Britons of the English Battalion, not many over fifty were left in action one week later. Fortunately, just when they were so decimated and exhausted, the Americans of the Abraham Lincoln Battalion arrived.

When General Aranda struck across the Jarama about February 10, after his direct attack on the Arganda Bridge having failed, there were I think somewhere about three or four thousand men of the International Brigades rushed into action, some from Madrid, others fresh from the organising centre of Albacete. It is difficult to know numbers because no records were kept, as far as I know, and battalions in the Spanish Army, of which the Brigades formed part, varied greatly in strength from the theoretical 600 men. Generally they had not more than 400 and often 150 or less. So that if someone told you that four battalions had arrived at such-and-such-a-point, one still did not know if 2,400 men had gone there or 500.

The first Internationals to go into action on the Jarama were the Italians under Pacciardi near Arganda Bridge. The well-known Italian anti-Fascist leader, Nicoletti, was with them and seemed to be very plucky, sharing the dangers with the men.

The Germans under Walter, a Pole, I think, went in near the White House, which became famous, as did the 400 British under Captain Tom Wintringham, a frail-looking little man with great courage and much interest in military matters. The Franco-Belge Battalion was also there and the Dimitroffs, made up of Serbs, Bulgars and a variety of nationalities. Somebody told me once that there were twenty different nationalities in that Battalion. How the commander got anything done is a mystery to me. General Gal, a Hungarian, I think, was in command. He was, unlike most of the Brigade officers, a stickler for discipline. According to Captain Wintringham, who has written a book dealing almost entirely with this battle and a grand description it is (it is called *English Captain*), Gal was rather fond of calling on his men to make dramatic stands and to 'hold-on-at-all-cost', but on the whole he seems to have done a good job. Major George Nathan, an immaculately-dressed British officer who always appeared shaved and with a clean shirt amid the most exciting events, was on the staff of General Gal. He was killed in July 1937 in a silly fashion while resting behind the lines. He did not realise that some planes overhead were going to bomb them and sat calmly on a tree trunk. A bomb fell alongside and killed him outright.

The Government was usually tolerant enough to the foreign correspondents but on this occasion it closed down firmly against the issue of any passes to the front. This could be understood, for the enemy if it had known of the very thin and wavering line which was holding on the Jarama might have made a still extra effort to break through. We managed to avoid, however, this effort to keep us in the dark and with old passes and a small amount of lying a group of us managed to get up close to the White House. This building was a farm which stood on a hill-top just at the point where a road running from Morata de Tajuña to San Martin de la Vega, down in the Jarama Valley, crosses the road running from Arganda Bridge to Aranjuez via Chinchon. I had been over the road several times in peace-time on happy Sunday-afternoon excursions. The Nationalists had crossed the Jarama and climbed the hill-side up to the White House. They only needed to push another half-mile through the olive grove which crossed this flat-topped hill and then they would have had Morata at their mercy beneath them. So the fight raged for possession of this plateau which was almost completely covered with olive trees.

Sefton Delmer, of the *Daily Express*, knew Ludwig Renn, the tall, bespectacled German writer and former officer of the Prussian Guard who was on the staff of the XVth Brigade, and also Gustav Regler, another German writer, who was a political commissioner in the Brigade. We found them both seated under the olive trees on the edge of the plateau along with Major Hans, who commanded the Brigade. Hans was a tall, heavily built German aged about forty, with a quick friendly smile and an intelligent interest in war and life. What his background was I never found out. He said that as his family was in Germany his name could not be used so he was always just 'Hans'. He had spent some years in Mexico and had been in Russia. I think he was a Communist but I never found out for certain. However, when I first met Hans sprawling over maps in this olive grove there was nothing friendly about his smile. He hated the sight of us there and did not trouble to hide his thorough suspicion of our persons and of our motives for being up there. Fortunately, Renn and Regler talked him out of his desire to see us bundled straight away back to the rear. Without any enthusiasm he allowed Regler to take us up to the artillery observation post just behind the Republican front line—a front line which merely consisted of scattered groups of men dug in as best they could manage it—and we watched the loyal artillery shelling the White House which we could see about a mile away from us through the olive groves.

There was a most awful din and muddle. The Nationalists were firing with light artillery not directly towards us—thank Heaven!—but across us diagonally at Government forces away on the right of where we were lying. For the line wound in and out. It was about as straight as a corkscrew. In the observation post there were five men of different nationality, a Spaniard, a Frenchman, a German, a Pole and a Jugoslav. The artillerymen were Frenchmen of the International Brigades. Somehow or other the orders were given and received over a feeble telephone line, it all seemed very miraculous to me that the shells should hit anything. They were hitting the White House. I should think that there was nobody in such an obvious objective.

From February 10 to 20, a terrific struggle went on in these olive groves, which stretch out for miles on either side. We learned most about the fight just near the White House because by means of our contacts with Renn and Regler we were able to get up there without our passes being in order. We could not risk this with the Spaniards and indeed we had in the first days no contact with the British either, for they were sticklers for passes being in order and, unfortunately, some of them were rather apt to take a deliberately offensive tone towards what they described as 'bourgeois journalists'.

This did not apply, of course, to men like Nathan and Wintringham. So the world learned more about the tremendous struggle at this point and on the shoulder near the White House known as Pingarron Hill—I never quite identified this hill to my own satisfaction—than it did of the rest of the struggle along a twenty-mile front which was everywhere of tremendous intensity and the gallant fight of the Spaniards went by, I am afraid, almost unnoticed. This was not, however, any fault of ours. Regler and Renn were, I think, quite right to give us a chance to see the resistance which was being put up by the Republican forces. We had no chance to learn any secrets and it was invaluable to the Republic to have its stout resistance spread abroad. The censorship would not, at first, let us refer to the Internationals. Naturally this soon was told abroad for journalists were always coming and going and then there were certain diplomatic bags which were not always closed to journalistic copy.

I do not know how many men General Aranda attacked with, but one newspaper report from Franco Spain said 80,000. I should think that the Republic had about thirty to forty thousand men on the front which stretched over some twenty-five or thirty miles from the Madrid side of the Arganda Bridge to down near Ciempozuelos, formerly noted as the site of Madrid's lunatic asylum, where the battle fizzled out. It is hard to explain why the attempt did not succeed. I think that it was perhaps due to the fact that the Nationalists were fighting on three fronts at once. They had, for instance, their aviation divided between the Northern Front, where the attack on Bilbao was going on, the Andalusian Front where the operation on Malaga was afoot, and the Madrid front. In a way this held good also for the Governmentals but as they had so little aviation they solved the problem by having virtually none either in the North or in Andalusia. But this meant that the new air units with new Russian planes, a few Russian pilots, some International pilots and many newly-trained and very good Spanish pilots, had only to meet odds of about two or three to one, instead of ten or twelve to one as had been the case.

The whole advantage of the fight lay with the Nationalist

General. He had good discipline, men under their own officers, well trained Moors. The German machine-gun and tank units were under their own officers. The aviation was properly organised. They had excellent staffs. Nevertheless, apart from the heroic defence put up by the Republicans, probably the chief factor in the failure was the lack of energy and enterprise in the Nationalist infantry units, apart from the Moors, Foreign Legion, Navarrese and suchlike 'crack brigades'. The average Franco soldier did not have his heart in the fight. If these 80,000 men, even suppose that in reality there were only 50,000, had fought as did the Republicans possessing as they did modern equipment and every other advantage, they could not possibly have been stopped by the mosaic of ill-equipped soldiers facing them. The heavy fighting was done nearly always by the few really high-spirited units of the Franco forces. The remainder moved here or there as they were bidden and isolated members might do great deeds, but by and large they were apathetic and the greatest help that the Government forces had for this reason.

The equipment of the Government forces was pitifully bad. Their machine-guns for instance were old Maxims of war-time vintage which functioned only in fits and starts. Their rifles were ancient but apparently they functioned reasonably well.

Of the drama of the British volunteers at the Jarama much could be said. Many of them had never fired a shot before. Over a score were fooled by Franco forces who advanced singing the 'Internationale' and with clenched fists and then pulled out guns before the surprised British, who assumed that the Spaniards were deserting, had discovered this deceit.

Once, the remaining handful under Jock Cunningham, a squat, burly Scot, disappeared worn and weary from the plateau but after being harangued by General Gal they went up again to face an enemy which had not realised the absence of Republicans before it and they marched into line singing with such vigour that a unit of Moors fled at their approach apparently in the not unreasonable belief that they had somehow got well out on a limb into Republican territory if people were casually marching about singing songs.

This gallant body of men without experience and with few arms showed a heroism which Britain can write to her credit. While irresponsible politicians, financiers and civil servants showed no care for the safety of our Commonwealth of Nations, this gallant handful of men gave freely of their blood and very many their lives in an effort to keep it safe. What most of them wanted was probably not so much to save the Empire as to create a better state of things in the world in general and to safeguard that elusive human value known as Democracy. Actually the two can, and should, coincide.

CHAPTER XXXIII

THE BATTLE OF GUADALAJARA

IN Madrid in this spring of 1937 we lived a strange war-fevered life of which much has been written by Ernest Hemingway and other writers.

We ate beans, dark bread and roast mule in the cellar-restaurant of the Gran Via Hotel, providentially installed and inaugurated only a few months before the war commenced. Even there an odd bit of shrapnel would occasionally find its way through the thick glass slabs which, let into the pavement of the street above, forming a ceiling to several alcoves where the more flirtatiously minded could eat in semi-seclusion.

One day we had a delegation of women Members of Parliament which included the Duchess of Atholl and Miss Ellen Wilkinson sitting at one table eating lunch when there was an explosion and a piece of glass came down, without hurting anyone. I went upstairs to see what had gone on and found a man with his interior more or less blown away by a shell which had landed outside the hotel door. I got bits of his inside on my boots and other bits were sticking over the Duchess's car. The funny thing was that he just looked puzzled and not in the least hurt. Poor little man, he probably died before the ambulance got to hospital with his mangled body. Only a few days before, one of the maids who served at table in the upper restaurant of the hotel had been blown to pieces while standing at the service entrance of the hotel. She was waiting for her sweetheart.

Miss Wilkinson superintended the removal from the Duchess's car of the bits of the intestines, which seemed to me rather a nice thought. Not that the Duchess was not very game despite her sixty years. An American correspondent remarked cynically: 'If British men had the guts and understanding of some of their womenfolk, the old Empire would be more sturdy than it is!' That was a bit hard, I suppose. But actually I know few men with such a clear understanding of the danger to the Empire as the Duchess of Atholl showed by her conversation. I was very sorry indeed twelve months later when I heard of her defeat in the bye-election she fought in Scotland; it was sad confirmation indeed of the worst fears that Britain was on the down grade when a great patriot such as the Duchess could be pushed out of the House of Commons. I am quite certain that that news was a tonic to both Rome and Berlin.

I liked Ellen Wilkinson's clear-cut manner. She seemed like a good fighter.

We got all kinds of visitors. One day a delegation from the Second International turned up. I tackled at dinner a much-bewhiskered man whose name was, I believe, Adler. I think he was the secretary of the Second International. He was not helpful to myself and other journalists. The Second International was not tremendously popular in Madrid at the time. Its frequent meetings and collections of money while very welcome at first, palled after a time. The Republic had gold, it could get on without sympathy—and it had no arms for its soldiers. Most Republicans felt that British, French and other Socialists in Europe could have done a great deal more than they did to put pressure on their respective Governments in connection with non-intervention.

The distinguished visitors stayed as a rule at the Gran Via, which was rather quieter than the Hotel Florida. The Florida got more shells. But it had a brighter life, especially during lulls in the fighting. There was one Basque captain who commanded a sector in the University City and who would often spend a night with some friend in the hotel. One could see his orderly seated down in the lounge. If there was any trouble at the front, the officer on duty in the line—a mile and a half away!—would ring up the hotel and the orderly would rush upstairs to interrupt the captain's interlude from trench monotony and rush him off in a car.

There were strange characters who flitted across the hotel scene. There were two Moorish girls, one tall, muscular and plain and the other slender and with a lovely head. They were sisters. Alas, the demon alcohol one night drove the slender and charming Mooress to bite deeply into the leg of a friend of ours. That was quite a night. At a farewell party to some colleagues I found myself—not an expert dancer— doing the rumba with surprising agility with a Norwegian woman journalist, who must weigh a good fifteen-stone, in a small and crowded room; apparently it was a very successful rumba. Another day we found a waffle machine, and even maple syrup, and had a lovely breakfast of crisp, golden waffles which were a credit to their caste.

The fronts were quiet after the Jarama battle simmered down; actually fighting went on in a sporadic way for weeks there. The Franco side was doing itself well at sea. It sank a Government steamer named the *Galdames* and took prisoner Sr. Carrasco Formiguera, a Catalan Deputy, a fervent Catholic and leader of the Democratic Union Party of Catalonia. They shot him, for no particular reason, and one listened in vain for Catholic protests, except for those of the small group of French Catholics, such as Bernanos, Maritain, and François Mauriac.

The Nationalists also captured the Government vessel *Mar Cantabrico* which had left the United States with aeroplanes and other war material on board only a few hours before Congress extended the Neutrality Law in order that the sale of arms to Spain should be banned. This was one occasion at least when the Democracies really did co-operate, namely, on the necessity for not allowing Republican Spain to purchase war material. Naturally, their bans affected General Franco too. And it was, of course, just coincidence that he had no money and no particular interest either in the purchase of arms from Britain, the United States or France. He was getting all he needed without difficulty from Italy and Germany. Can one wonder if there was happiness and merriment in Berlin and Rome? This was equivalent to giving the Fascist Powers *carte blanche* in Spain. Rome and Berlin knew quite well how the Intelligence Service and the Deuxième Bureau must be reporting faithfully the stream of arms and men being landed in Spain from Germany and Italy and at the same time reporting the small quantity of arms which the Government was able to obtain.   No one, I think, can reasonably blame Germany and Italy for going joyfully ahead to secure the triumph of their protégé which would ensure them a friend at one of the most strategic points in the world and a key point as far as the British and French Empires are concerned.   If the Fascists had not seized the opportunity handed to them on a silver tray by the stupidity of the Democracies, they would have been most foolish.

The *Mar Cantabrico* had, I think, been hiding in some Mexican port in order to trick the Nationalist vessels keeping watch for it.   But, here again, the Government worked at a terrible disadvantage because the whole of the immense net of secret service agents kept all over the world by the Germans, —it is probably the best-organised intelligence service in the world to-day—was at the disposal of General Franco in so far as matters affecting Spain were concerned and for that matter the Italian service also could help General Franco.   The latter had no money to maintain anything like an espionage service even over Europe, let alone America, and even if many enthusiastic supporters of the cause were willing to help, that kind of work does after all require a certain amount of knowledge and costs a certain amount of money and of preparation as to the way of transmitting the information acquired.   The Republicans had to rely completely on such service as they could build up.   They possibly got some help from the Russians but I do not think that the Russian intelligence service is anything like so extensive or well-informed as is the German.   So that General Franco could receive quick and accurate information as to ship movements in America, Scandinavia, Turkey, which interested him or on any other aspect of Republican activities.   I mention this because so often one hears the blasé statement: 'Oh, well both sides got equal help.   If Franco was helped by Germany and Italy, the Republicans had the help of Russia and France.' And this, as an assertion of equality, had no foundation. France was doing virtually nothing and Russia was far away and had so many other preoccupations that the help she could give was limited.   General Franco had full and active support from Germany and Italy.   The British Internationals who arrived in Spain had to slip over to France as best they could and then they had to be smuggled across the Pyrenees by night. Many were caught and after a period in gaol sentenced to expulsion from France. This meant that if they still slipped across the frontier after this episode, then on their return from Spain they were liable to a minimum of six months' imprisonment. This was actually inflicted on many.

Ships bringing normal food and non-bellicose material to Government Spain or taking fruit away were captured by General Franco's ships in the Straits of Gibraltar and their cargoes robbed. The Dutch had cargoes stolen over and over again until finally in March of this year, 1937, they sent a cruiser, the *Hertog Hindrich*, to patrol the Straits and convoy the boats through.

The relative calm near Madrid was broken on March 6 when about 30,000 Italians under General Bergonzoli were launched at the Madrid communications from the north-east angle and the Battle of Guadalajara ensued.

The Battle of Guadalajara has been held to prove a great many things. It has been taken as proof that mechanisation of armies must be done carefully, that the Italians are not good soldiers, that aviation can stop an advancing army, and so on. All these theories must be accepted with a great deal of reserve. The actual battle lasted from March 6 until March 23 and it was a tremendous defeat for the Italians. They were reported to have lost 3,000 killed and many thousands of wounded. The Government took about 600 Italian prisoners.

My own opinion is that the defeat arose mainly from a complete misunderstanding of the state of affairs by the Italian officers in command of the expeditionary force, which was what it was for it was Italian from the General Commander down to the last orderly or chauffeur. It must be remembered that the Italian contribution towards helping General Franco had until the attack in Andalusia which had resulted in the capture of Malaga, consisted mainly of air co-operation, and the sending of some tank and artillery units.

The real force of Italian units sent to Spain in the winter of 1936-7 was used first in Andalusia. It had an easy task.

It was opposed only by pitifully under-equipped train-bands, or militia, composed mainly of Andalusian peasants. They probably numbered nearly as many as did the Italians but they had no modern arms, little artillery, few tanks and, I think, only three or four chaser aeroplanes as their entire air force. Naturally the Italian force went through this defence like a knife through butter.

But General Bergonzoli did not realise, and apparently the position of General Franco was not strong enough for him to impose his authority in order to make the Italian General Staff realise the actual conditions, that the situation at Madrid was very different indeed. The Italian force could be expected to do great things because of its homogenity and its fine equipment, but it must expect a rugged resistance. It would meet with artillery fire and aviation attacks, always with the Italian artillery and aviation in great superiority of numbers, but nevertheless, resistance. It would meet units of the International Brigades. It would meet newly organised units of the Republican forces with officers who were ridiculously young and inexperienced but who had a courage and enthusiasm which moved mountains.

The Italians apparently had no conception of all this. Preceded only by light tanks they launched their thirty thousand men with typically Latin ardour and with the rapidity supposed by the fact that the units had been mechanised, or motorised, so that even the infantry were rushed along in big Fiat motor lorries. They simply went down the road to Guadalajara and Madrid just as they had motored most of the way to Malaga.

Doubtless this belief in easy victory of the Italians was strengthened by their first contact with the Government forces. Out in the rugged country near Siguenza, the Republican lines were held almost entirely by groups of the old Anarchist militias. They had not been reorganised to any extent. The front had been relatively quiet since the beginning of the war and life had not been too unpleasant for these militias. They had few arms and little in the way of tanks or artillery. When the Italian machine swept down on them there was indeed practically nothing they could do except run as fast as their legs would carry them. This must have encouraged the Italians in their belief that this operation was just a repetition of Malaga. An Italian station broadcasting Franco propaganda which I tuned in to one night indeed said as much. It recommended the Madrid people to surrender while there was yet time because soon the wonderful triumph of the Legionaries at Malaga would be repeated in Madrid.

I should point out that when I speak of the Republican troops running away there I am only generalising. Actually some of the men, and particularly some Anarchists, did behave very heroically by staying behind and lobbing hand grenades at the advancing tanks. They put quite a number out of action. The few batteries of artillery also fought their way back very tenaciously despite the fact that they were completely overwhelmed. They obstructed the roads so well that the Franco forces only advanced about eighteen miles in two days, which was, of course, an excellent advance but not perhaps quite as big as was expected. They reached, and took, Trijueque, by the end of the second day and were thus about twelve miles from Guadalajara and sixty miles from Madrid. They had also gone down another road to the westward and along another road which went farther to the east. On the latter road they had reached a place called Brihuega, which was about parallel with Trijueque and on a rambling side road which eventually led down to the road from Guadalajara to Cuenca.

The Government had forty-eight hours in which to prepare some kind of a defence before the enemy began to get really near Guadalajara. It ripped out from the Jarama front the Eleventh Division under a young quarryman from El Ferrol with the English-sounding name of Lister. Actually he was very much of a Spaniard—Franco also comes from El Ferrol—and as far as I know has no knowledge of any other language than Spanish except for a few words of Russian. The Germans of the XVth International Brigade under Hans were likewise hurried off and the Franco-Belge and the Italians, but the British and Americans were left to hold the very thin Jarama front line. Other Spanish forces were also sent helter-skelter up the Guadalajara road. Motor transport played a decisive part. The Government had large quantities of very fast and lightly-built American motor trucks and these were invaluable. When I see the heavily-built Army lorries at home I often wonder if those responsible realise that while solidity may have its advantages, nevertheless a lorry that weighs little can go over uneven and soft ground much more easily than a heavy one and that given a good road its speed is so much greater. In these days when it is essential to take trucks off the road and shelter them from planes under trees or in fields, lightness is very important. It also escapes my comprehension why our Army lorries have no cabs, or at the most a waterproofed hood to pull over. Who is the gainer if the driver is left more or less to the mercy of the elements?

By Wednesday night, March 10, when Trijueque was taken by the Italians, the Government had probably some six or seven thousand men grouped near Torija, which is about nine miles from Guadalajara and about three miles from Trijueque. Forces had also been sent towards Hita on the western side and the road from Brihuega was guarded farther south. But the Italian main forces were at Brihuega and Trijueque and the Government was therefore in a good position at Torija.

At this point everything began to go wrong for the Italians. When they began to push gaily on towards Torija on the Thursday morning, they found the way blocked by troops which remained quite unmoved by the heavy bombardment directed on them by the Italian artillery. The tanks went out only to meet heavy fire from the Government batteries and from Government anti-tank guns. The heavy tanks which might have saved the situation either had not been brought or were somewhere else.

The Government turned out every aeroplane it possessed. The weather was vile. There was a fifty- or sixty-mile-an-hour gale. It rained fitfully in torrents. The clouds at times were only a few hundred feet off the ground. It was bitterly cold and snow-showers and hailstones alternated with the drenching rain. But the Republican aviators were superb. They brought the 'halt, the lame and the blind' out of the hangars and converted air liners, old private machines, derelict bombers were sent out. They bombed that road again and again. The chaser planes came down and machine-gunned time after time. The Nationalist aviation hardly appeared. I think the explanation was that the only aerodromes from which chaser planes could work and which were at Soria and somewhere else in that neighbourhood, were in very bad condition owing to the weather. Bombers could be sent from Avila, Salamanca, or other towns, but chasers have only a small petrol supply. Actually, I have no very accurate information in this connection. The Nationalists took care that all foreign correspondents were rigorously excluded from the zone where the Italians were operating because the polite fiction of non-intervention was being maintained. Indeed Signor Farinacci, Secretary of the Italian Fascist Party, had just visited General Franco for the purpose, according to London newspapers, of explaining to the Nationalist leader the reasons why 'Italy had been obliged to put a ban on volunteers for Spain in accordance with its non-intervention commitments'.

All that can be said is for some reason or other the Italian and German aircraft scarcely put in an appearance over the sector for several days. This applies only, of course, to the chasers. Actually they bombed Guadalajara tremendously and killed sixty in one raid alone. But they did not defend the Italian columns. Nor did the Italian staff appear to have made anything like adequate arrangements for anti-aircraft protection of the mobile columns. An ample supply of anti-aircraft machine-guns would have upset the Government attackers very much for even the bombers were flying very low owing to the bad weather conditions. It seems also surprising that adequate aviation fields had not been prepared on well-drained ground for in the hilly country around Guadalajara bad weather could be expected with more or less of a certainty at this time of the year.

The Italian commander floundered. Instead of withdrawing his men to a place where there were good positions he tried to consolidate himself on the flat open country, broken only by a few woods, running between Trijueque and Brihuega.

He piled up artillery and endeavoured to shift the Govern-ment forces lying in the muddy and wet ground in front of Torija. The pretext that the weather defeated the Italians is only true in so far as it hindered their aviation. But the roads were good and not water-logged in any way and the open country although wet had still a firm and stony enough subsoil to make it quite practical to use tanks and to move artillery about with ease. I visited the battlefield both while the fight was on and afterwards and I do not remember seeing a single vehicle bogged owing to soft ground. The main road was fine and wide and with tarmac surface. It was one of the special motor roads built by General Primo.

The Republican men were superb. Half frozen, soaked to the skin, without steel-helmets, waterproof capes or any of the modern equipment of the Italians, they held their ground stubbornly.

Sefton Delmer, Loayza, of International News Service, and I spent some hours at Torija on Thursday, March 11 and we all came back with the impression that the attack had been held. I had a long talk with Corporal Guiseppi Log-gonoro, of the 157th Regiment of the Italian Army. He had walked by mistake into the Republican lines with almost two hundred others. At least it had not been quite by mistake. They happened to have in front of them the Garibaldi Batta-lion of the XVth International Brigade. They had lost contact with their neighbouring unit and on calling out in the dark, they had been answered by a quick-witted outpost of the Gari-baldis who cheerfully assured them: 'Yes, come this way com-rades, we had been waiting for you.' It had not occurred to them that the man who answered them in perfect Italian might be an enemy. The corporal who told me all about this was quite frank about his presence in Spain. He had been ordered to 'leave for an unknown destination' and had come to Spain. He had not, he said, been given any choice. It was simply a military order. The commander of his battalion, Major Luciano Silva, was also caught. He had served through the World War and the Abyssinian War and various colonial campaigns. Such soldiers of experience and long training should, of course, with the material at their disposal, have been able to cope easily with three times their number of Republican troops.

The Government aviators worked tremendously hard. I watched them on this Thursday in question scooting low over Torija back to their base at Alcalá through a blinding rainstorm and with a gale which was so strong that it required real effort to walk against the wind. In fact, of the patrol of five which flew over us, we learned later that only three reached Alcalá. The other two got lost in the clouds and finally landed at Alcazar de San Juan in La Mancha. One of these was 'Whitey' Evans, an American and a fine flier. There were about half a dozen Americans in the La Calle squadron at Alcalá. La Calle is a young Spanish airman of about twenty-eight who is such a brilliant and courageous flier that his men, even very hard-boiled and experienced foreign fliers, adore him. It was undoubtedly due to his courage and leadership that such a brilliant show was put up against terrible weather at Guadalajara. Poor La Calle. The last time I heard of him in February of 1939 he was a refugee in Toulouse Aerodrome, shut up with the rest of his pilots in a hangar and given the food of a private soldier. Undoubtedly to observe one's oath and to fight for democracy is not the way to success in our modern Europe.

Spanish, and a few foreign, pilots flew the bi-plane chasers but most of the monoplanes, which are difficult to fly, were in the hands of the Russians. The bombers were mixed, with more Spanish than Russian pilots I believe. The Government at no time in the war had many bombers. The Martin light bomber, manufactured under licence in Russia, was their chief stand-by.

The Italian attempt to swing round by a westerly route by Hita was checked at Padilla de Hita without much difficulty. It was a small force I think and it was, I believe, composed in part of Spanish forces, the only ones who had any connection with the attack. The Brihuega forces were not seriously menaced but they were obviously afraid to push on so long as the Trijueque people could not make any headway.

Nor did the Franco troops on the Madrid and the Jarama front make much attempt to help the Italians. The Jarama front had been greatly weakened by hastily pulling most of the best forces out of line, yet apart from a few half-hearted attacks the Nationalists in front made no effort to break through. Whether this was because the Franco troops in this sector were really exhausted by the Jarama battle or whether the Italian attempt to score a victory single-handed had been resented and satisfaction was felt at its failure, I cannot say. Correspondents who were with Franco at that time told me afterwards that the failure of the Guadalajara attempt was received with delight by most people in Nationalist territory and that officers even held dinners to celebrate this.

In the little town of Torija, there was feverish activity. I met the commander of the XIth Division, Lister, for the first time. Of moderate height, bulky with a big head and a heavy ponderous voice, this thirty-one-year-old quarryman now facing an Italian field force with well-trained officers and soldiers, made a good impression. He had a Russian in plain clothes, a thin, pale-faced and most unmilitary-looking individual as his 'adviser'. And the chief commander was General José Miaja. The tactics were planned by Colonel Rojo, Chief of Staff to General Miaja. But it was Lister who had actual command in the field. I had never heard of him until the Jarama battle. He was an active trade union organiser who had worked several years in Cuba and had fled from Spain after the 1934 revolt taking refuge in Russia for a year where he apparently had had some military and doctrinal instruction. I do not think that the amount of military instruction he could have gained there without knowing the language and in such a short time could have been very great.

He was one of the officers of the 'Fifth Army' Corps founded by the Communists in Madrid in August 1936. It was called that because Madrid had four Army Corps stationed there normally. In the Jarama as chief of the XIth Division— the Communists had dissolved the Fifth Army Corps and the units had been reorganised in the regular Army—he made a fine showing on Pingarron Hill and farther down in the direction of Ciempozuelos and it was obvious that at least one good officer was in the making. At Torija he was in charge and did a fine job of work.

As the Italians continued to flounder and as the Franco forces in other points in the Centre Zone made no effort to come to their assistance either directly, which would have been difficult, or by attacks on the Government lines at other points, which would have been easy, the Republicans decided to attack and on Sunday, March 14, the mixed Spanish and International forces drove forward and took Trijueque amid tremendous fighting. I was up there the next day and Trijueque was still being shelled by the Italians. My progress through the town consisted mainly of much standing up and lying down. The small town was in a terrible mess as a result of fierce bombardment from both sides. It was a magnificent victory, for the Republican troops had, it must be remembered, just come almost straight from the fiercest battle of the war, the Jarama, whereas the Italians had had one month's rest since taking Malaga which had, in any case, been a light task. Among those who helped to take Trijueque were Gustav Regler, who rode in on a tank, and Ludwig Renn, the German writers who really set an excellent example for the intelligensia of the world. Renn's real name, by the way, is Arnold Vieth von Golessenau, and he comes of an old aristocratic family from Saxony. He had been sent to gaol by the Nazis for thirty months in 1934 because of his Left-Wing sympathies, and he had left Germany after his release.

Sunday was the sixth day of the attack and General Bergonzoli had had plenty of time to reorganise and to ask for help or to change his plans. But apparently no inspiration came to him for he still continued to fight desperately over on the eastern wing near Brihuega. The Government forces resisted all his attempts throughout a week and then once again counter-attacked and swept over the plateau and down into Brihuega, which lies in a hollow. This time the Italians broke. This was on Friday afternoon, March 19. They simply fled, with relatively little rearguard action, until they were beyond Yela. On the main road they went back to somewhere between Ledanca and Algora, so the line went back to not far from where it had been when the offensive began.

Among the papers captured after this collapse was a message purporting to be from Il Duce and which rang true although it was denied. It said: 'I receive on board the yacht *Pola*, on the way to Libya, the communications on the great battles now in progress.

'I follow the course of the battles with a firm spirit, because I know that the impetus and tenacity of our Legionaries will triumph over the resistance shown by the enemy.

'To crush the international forces will be a great triumph and also of political importance. Let the Legionaries know that I follow hour by hour their activities, which will be crowned by victory.'

This message had been sent to divisional officers as an order-of-the-day by General Bergonzoli.

The Duce hastily cut short his tour of Libya and hurried back to Rome to take charge of a situation which was far from pleasant for him.

The last time I visited the front, March 23, things had quietened down except for odd skirmishing on a line which was slowly coagulating again. The weather was better with a high 'ceiling' and some sunshine. The Government was in no position to pursue the Italian troops any longer for its men were dead on their feet. As I have pointed out, they had been rushed over straight from the Jarama. The countryside was simply littered with coats, capes, gas-masks, helmets, even boots. The last phase had obviously been a 'sauve-qui-peut'; a complete collapse. One could tell that because there were very few corpses.

I do not think that one can draw any very definite conclusions from the battle. The Italian officers had completely misjudged the situation, had split up their already small force, were not co-operating with Spanish forces who would have known the country and who in any case could have warned them of the resistance the Republican forces were capable of. The staff work was poor and pride obviously led them to attempt to go forward when they were in such a muddle that their only course was to withdraw for reorganisation. It seems to me silly to decry the Italians as soldiers because of this. We have seen that the Garibaldis, who were about three or four hundred strong only, fought magnificently. And all I hear of the Italian Army is that it is improving day by day out of all recognition. More than anything the battle was an example of what the Republicans could do when they had even a minimum of arms and some kind of a decent break. Credit is also due to the Government forces in Asturias and near Cordoba who made determined attacks in order to draw enemy fire and prevent the dispatch of local Franco forces for use against Madrid.

I do not think that the blame for the failure can be attributed to the mechanisation, and motorisation—two separate phases—of the Italian forces, although possibly the deficient handling of the fast-moving units was due in part to lack of experience by the officers in charge in using these kind of units. It must be remembered also that the magnificent motor transport services improvised by the Government alone made it possible for the Republicans to concentrate a small army so quickly in position to block the Italian advance. The Republicans even moved their artillery by motor-lorry, or at least the lighter pieces—and they hardly had any heavy ones. Each gun was hauled aboard a four-ton, light, pneumatic-tyred lorry; the crew went aboard as well and, if necessary, a gun could be firing one day in Madrid and next day be in position on the Teruel front, 300 miles away. This system saves the gun the bad shaking it receives when towed behind a lorry or a tractor and also means that artillery can be shifted at at least twice the speed as when a tractor is used.

CHAPTER XXXIV

NEW TACTICS

A FTER the Battle of Guadalajara, General Franco and his allies changed their tactics very decidedly. They turned their backs on the main Government forces and took what must have been a very difficult but was a supremely wise decision to confine operations to clearing the northern areas in the Basque country, Santander and Asturias which were still held by the Republicans.

This took them until the end of the year 1937. Bilbao fell on June 19, Santander on August 25 and Gijon on October 22. I do not propose to record this struggle because I saw nothing of it and I only know the details I read in the Press. A good book on the defence of Bilbao is *The Tree of Guernica*, by George L. Steer.

If the Republicans in the Centre Zone had been able to obtain arms easily this chance offered them to organise would have been highly dangerous to General Franco, but during 1937 the noose was drawn still more tightly about their throats from without. If General Franco and his allies had not known that they could make it virtually impossible for the Republicans to obtain arms in any quantity near at hand and that they could prevent those from afar from reaching Spain, they could not have taken the decision they did.

The North was unimportant. It was not strong enough to constitute a serious threat in General Franco's rear and it would have automatically collapsed if the Government forces had been defeated in the rest of Spain. The North was merely a diversion which offered certain success for General Franco's small. well-armed forces with their overwhelming equipment of tanks, aeroplanes and artillery. There were, I think, three chaser planes defending Bilbao against at least 150 or 200 chasers and bombers used by the attackers. The Government could not send chaser planes there because the direct flying distance was too long. They tried to send some via France and for this they just needed permission to refuel at Pau Aerodrome. The French refused this, removed the machine-guns from the planes, and sent them back to Barcelona and even at this there were vigorous protests from Franco supporters in France and Britain that the planes were not impounded. This at a time when German ships full of planes and tanks were being unloaded without any particular concealment at Pasajes and the Italian ships escorted by war vessels went by Gibraltar to Cadiz to unload their war materials there!

It was impossible to send much material to Republican Spain by sea, for the example of the *Mar Cantabrico* stood out large. That boat had seventy aeroplanes on board destined for Bilbao which all fell into the hands of General Franco. The Franco blockade along the coast was very tight. That the Republicans of the North could resist for so long was a remarkable performance.

Nevertheless it must have been a great wrench, considering the strength of Spanish pride, for General Franco to give up all hope of any immediate victory and to settle down to minor operations in the North while the business of starving out and strangling the main Republican forces went on. It was a most un-Spanish way of doing things. But it was supremely clever. Its success, of course, depended entirely on the attitude of France. France was not supplying arms, but it was essential that she should not only continue to do this but that she should also resolutely refuse to allow Russian arms, or arms from other nations, to pass through into Spain. Arms from Russia, the main source open to the Republicans, if they came by sea had to pass through the Mediterranean where they could easily be taken care of by Franco or his allies. The *Konsomol* had already been sunk, and several other Russian ships captured and impounded. But if the arms could be landed at Bordeaux and sent overland then there was not much that Franco and his allies could do for they were still not quite bold enough to sink ships in the North Sea and the English Channel.

If France had permitted this then the whole position in Spain would have been changed, for with ample arms the

Government could have built up a fine army very rapidly which would have menaced General Franco from the rear. He could not place a large army in the field; he was not sure enough of the average conscript. If the Government had obtained arms then the battle was lost for him unless Germany and Italy decided to really take the gloves off and send in whole army corps of trained troops with full equipment in order to meet the Republican challenge and we may assume that neither of the totalitarian powers was anxious to do this because the expense would have been enormous and it would have upset their military preparations for the really big fight ahead of them. Moreover the effect on Britain and France of the moving of army corps of crack troops with their full equipment to Spain might have caused some international friction.

It was rather ironical that non-intervention, which was attacked with such fury in the Franco newspapers, was the real weapon by which the Republicans were to be slowly starved into submission and kept without the essential and most elementary supplies needed to put up an effective resistance.

The removal of the actual pressure of attack also led to developments in Republican Spain. Behind the scenes there was a struggle going on. The Anarchists had after their first and wilder moments of ruthless and indiscriminate murder settled down into the role of economic racketeers on a large scale. The industry of Barcelona which should have been a great help to the Republicans, was not pulling its weight. It must, of course, be taken into account that this industry is in great part concerned with textiles and chemicals and patent medicines and suchlike and that there are no blast furnaces at all there and very few iron foundries. It was not, therefore, an industry which offered unlimited prospects for the manufacture of war materials. But it could have done more than it did if it had not been for the reckless social experiments which were going on; high wages were being paid, hours reduced to thirty-five or forty per week and the reserves built up over years were being extravagantly wasted by the committees in charge of this, that or the other works. Even apart from this, in every walk of life the uncertainty and erratic behaviour of the Anarchist political groups and labour unions was so erratic as to make the sorting of order out of chaos a most difficult task. Actually, the Anarchists were not strong. I dare say that the C.N.T. (Confederación Nacional del Trabajo), their labour organisation, had some 2,000,000 members but great masses of these were much more inclined to an orderly solution. The political side, the F.A.I. (Federación Anarquista Iberica) was very small and although its numbers were never revealed I should doubt that it ever exceeded 10,000 members.

But there were wheels within wheels which caused the Anarchists to find support in high places. Caballero definitely appeared to support the Anarchists and he seemed to play them off against the Communists. It was not until the former stepped over the bounds so far that they initiated a revolt in collaboration with the P.O.U.M. (Partido Obrero Union Marxista) in Barcelona on May 1, that various of the Socialist leaders felt that the moment had come for a 'show-down' and Caballero was overthrown and replaced by Negrin.

The May revolt was a very nasty affair which if General Franco had not already firmly initiated the new programme of attacking only in the North, might have given him a chance for a quick break-through on the Aragon front. Actually I think only one division left the line in the direction of Barcelona and that was speedily disarmed by the remainder of the forces but Barcelona itself was in the hands of Anarchists and their friends of the P.O.U.M., who were labelled as Trotskyists although they denied this with vigour. The Government rushed up 6,000 troops from Valencia by motor trucks under General Pozas and the movement found so little support in Barcelona itself that it fizzled out within a week.

The majority of the Anarchists had no connection with the *putsch* and the Ministers in the Cabinet representing these forces, such as Federica Montseny and Garcia Oliver, rushed to Barcelona to help to quell it. It was the work of a small ultra-Left group of the Anarchists and of the P.O.U.M. who were led by an intellectual named Andres Nin. I dare say there were other forces at work too, one imagines that the hand of Franco agents could not be missing from such a helpful movement. Nin was arrested and taken to Madrid, where he disappeared from gaol. It was said that he was shot by the Communists. He was never seen or heard of again. The other leaders were tried in Barcelona when I was there and they were given minor sentences which were nominal. One of them named Escuder appeared to be the chief figure. But the Government made the mistake of trying to prove that these people were German and Italian agents instead of simply charging them with treasonable revolt.

I met a group of people, mostly foreigners, who shared the views of the Left-Wing Anarchists (if one may be permitted such a definition) at a cocktail party held some time after the *putsch* at the home of a foreign consul in Spain. One of them was Emma Goldman, the veteran American revolutionary. She was explaining that the revolution in Spain was over; that the Government had become reactionary. Her description of the Republican Government made it seem to be a tremendously conservative and reactionary affair.

I think myself that the Barcelona *putsch* was the work of a few ultra-Radical intelligensia, who profited by the weakness of the Catalan authorities under President Companys and the tolerance of Caballero, to break out into an open revolt which was doubtless fanned and aided by other forces with an interest in creating trouble. The Catalanists were very weak. They were loyal to the Republic; they wished to defeat the attempt to restore the old Centralist Spain. But they were good Liberals without any constructive programme. They allowed the Anarchists to run amok because they had not the strength to hold them in, but the real truth, and what was worse, was that they themselves had no programme. They wished a great many things, most of them laudable. They had no plan for the realisation of these wishes—a fault which so often afflicts Liberals and not only in Spain. In fact if it had not been for the sudden growth of the Catalan Communist Party, the P.S.U.C. (Partido Socialista Unificada Catalana), and its allied trade union force of the U.G.T., it is possible and even probable that Catalonia would have dissolved into complete chaos between the irresponsibility of the Anarchists and the weakness and futility of the Esquerra, or Catalan Left.

Caballero fell on the Catalan issue on May 16, 1937, and he

was replaced next day, May 17, by Dr. Juan Negrin, his former Finance Minister, and with Don Indalecio Prieto, his former Minister of Marine and Aviation, now adding the War Ministry to his other two portfolios.

The overthrow of Francisco Largo Caballero, the man who had been the acknowledged leader and champion of the working classes in Spain, was one of the most dramatic, and tragic in so far as the personal aspect was concerned, incidents of the war. The Catalan incident had only been the deciding factor. The actual cause of his fall went much deeper.

It seems strange that while Caballero was being described abroad as the 'Red Leader' and his Government frequently referred to as a 'Communist Government', he had actually been waging a strong battle against the Communists behind the scenes. In this he was influenced not only by personal pride but also by Don Luis Araquistain who was his intellectual guide and who had no use whatever for the Communist Party.

Caballero, early in 1936, had fought Prieto on the issue of electoral collaboration with the Communists and he had won and carried through an electoral alliance. But that was in the days when the Communists had not a great deal of power in Spain. They had at that time I think about 10,000 members. The Communists had suffered from internal strife until about 1933 and had not even numbered hundreds. Then after 1934, the active efforts of the International Red Aid to bring succour to the persecuted Leftists and the shelter given in Russia to several hundred refugees had given the Communist Party a start; but at the beginning of 1936 it was still a minor factor.

This was not the case by July 1936. During that period it increased its members to, I believe, over 100,000. This was due, as I think I have pointed out before in this book, mainly to the lack of initiative of the Republicans. The Socialists, who although out of power had no direct responsibility, nevertheless also failed to give a lead. But Caballero who in January 1936 was fighting even his Socialist Party friends because he wished an alliance with Communism, by June 1936 was already expressing his dislike and annoyance at the union of Socialist

Youth and Communist Youth organisations into a joint movement. He did not mind collaborating with a weak Communist Party but he was very frightened when it became
strong and a potential rival to the Socialist Party.

Caballero's plight was a sad one. In theory, he was a Marxist but in actual practice he was a good slogging trade union
leader whose whole life had been far too much occupied with
the rough and tumble of trade union organisation and ordinary politics for him to have acquired any very deep culture.
His ideals were noble enough; he wished to improve the lot
of every working man and woman and he had devoted his life
to that end. He had never lived in luxury or ostentation; his
whole life had been clean and open for the world to inspect.
But virtues do not compensate for lack of knowledge or capacity and the war showed that he did not personally, nor did
his Party as a whole, have the talent for leadership and for
facing new situations as did the Communists.

This was in a way reasonable enough. The Russians had
gone through a civil war. In twenty years they had perfected
an organisation of a Party destined to lead. The Spanish Communists could draw on all this wealth of knowledge. By their
organisation and their 'cells' they could get things done and
move public opinion. The Army officers liked the Communists because of their discipline. They obeyed orders and discussed them, if necessary, afterwards. The Fifth Army Corps
of volunteers raised by the Communists proved to be indis-
putably the best, and it formed the backbone of the new
Army. The Communist slogans for economic organisation, for
the defence of Madrid, for the reorganisation of the Army had
an uncanny way of putting into language easy to understand,
things which inarticulate masses felt deeply about and wanted
expressing.

If Caballero had been more flexible in his ideas he might
have bowed to the inevitable and pacted with the Communists.
By allying the two parties under Caballero all the mature
soberness of the Spanish Socialist Party could have been maintained with the useful addition of the new ideas and valuable
methods of organisation which the more youthful people in
the Communist Party could have contributed. Instead, he

chose to fight them. Not openly, but under the surface a steady battle went on.

This attitude of Caballero was approved by most of the Socialists but only up to a point. Prieto felt strongly about this too but he also felt strongly about the Anarchists who were constantly throwing a spanner into the works.

Prieto, who was in very close touch with Negrin, had been, or so it was said, in large part responsible for the new organisation of the Carabineros, the customs' police. Numbering some 14,000 before the war, they had now been brought in Government Spain up to some 40,000. They all had smart green uniforms and the very best of equipment, they had steel helmets, good thick overcoats, the best transport and were in fact a very much looked after force. The major part was kept at the rear. They guarded all Ministries and formed a kind of bodyguard for the Government in general. They were formed in no small part from former Socialist militias and the officers were in great part either Socialist or Republican or former Army officers with no political leanings. The never-expressed idea behind the corps was that it should be a strong Socialist bulwark in case the Communists either before or after the war should try a *coup d'état*. It was for this that it was built up and cared for.

Among other things the Carabineros had no political commissioners.

But despite the mistrust, and in part envy, felt by the Socialists for the Communists the feeling grew that Caballero was going too far. It was one thing to have the Carabineros as a reserve against the Communists but to tolerate the Anarchists up to a point where they could carry out a *putsch* was going too far. Moreover, Caballero had not proved a success in the War Ministry despite the success of the Republican arms during the last months of his stay in office. This did not outweigh general criticism at the lack of haste in the reorganisation of the Army, dislike of the Under-Secretary for War, General Asensio, who finally had to resign because of charges of neglect in connection with Malaga, and much friction between Caballero and his fellow-ministers who found him intractable. Finally they joined forces with the Communists and overturned him. Prieto put Negrin in as Premier because he preferred to work behind the scenes himself but he was generally believed to be the strongest man in the Cabinet. Actually it did not altogether work out this way. The Anarchists refused to come in without Caballero and the new Cabinet was composed of three Socialists, three Republicans, two Communists, one Basque, one Catalan.

Throughout the war the Socialist Party never recovered from the blow of this split in its ranks. When the war started the Socialist Party had made the mistake of closing its doors at once and although this had as its object the exclusion of new-comers anxious to take shelter in its ranks, the result nevertheless had been that many quite active young people had gone to the Communists. So the Socialists remained with the some 80,000 members who belonged in its ranks when war began while the Communist roll swelled and swelled. I think they reached about 300,000 by the end of the first year of the war. At least this was the number they claimed.

I never had much chance to come into contact with the various Communist leaders but Dolores Ibarruri was certainly a woman of character. I heard her speak many times in Parliament. I was present at that last session of Parliament when, so it is alleged by the Nationalists, she was said to have shouted at Calvo Sotelo: 'You will never speak again in this House!' I did not hear her say this. She may have said it because there was a fine old uproar that night. But even if she did I really do not think there was anything premeditated about the death of Calvo Sotelo.

Undoubtedly Calvo Sotelo was much involved in the forthcoming *coup d'état*. Herr von Goss, who was the representative of the German Official News Agency (D.N.B.) in Madrid before the war, has written, since Germany made her participation clear, in *Die Wehrmacht*, special issue on the war in Spain published in June 1939: 'Calvo Sotelo was the man who had the mission of organising and utilising the forces of Falange to the best needs of the nation.' But I think there is no doubt that his death was decided on the spur of the moment by the furious policemen who gathered around the corpse of Lieutenant Castillo who was murdered in such a cold-blooded way by the gunmen of the Right.

Dolores Ibarruri, born in 1903, was a Basque girl of humble parents who became a servant. She married an Asturian miner and had, I think, four or five children of whom all but two died. She somehow or other got into politics and into the Communist Party. By 1933 and 1934 she had already become well known as a speaker.

After many fruitless efforts I managed to get an interview with her in Valencia in May of 1937. On the day of the interview I went into the Communist headquarters in Valencia. It was a Sunday morning and very still and very hot. The girl at the door wrote me out a chit which said: 'An Englishman to see Dolores.' That got me by the sentinel at the foot of the stairs. I climbed three or four flights. In an ante-room, a secretary came out. He was just one more secretary to a politician. 'I am very sorry but Dolores Ibarruri is very busy. Please write out your questions and they will be sent back to you with the answers,' he said. I objected wearily that an interview done in that way was no good at all. He went into an inner room. After some delay, he motioned me in.

Sitting at a desk was 'La Pasionaria'. It was a simple white-washed room. Very clean, very cool. The desk was clear. So were the walls. There was a handkerchief smelling of eau-de-Cologne on the desk. She sat there a woman of thirty-five, tall, well-built, arrogant; one hand on the desk. 'What do you want to know?' she inquired in a sharp and most unfriendly voice. I managed to get her talking. She plunged into her theme. I was, I think, quite forgotten. She was angry. she laughed, she pounded on the table, she frowned, as she unfolded the story of the fight of the Spanish people. Three-quarters of an hour later I walked downstairs with my head going round in rings. She had given me as furious and intensive a speech as if she had been addressing the meeting.

But what a woman! She was, I think, the only Spanish politician I ever met; and I think I know most of those who have any call on fame during this generation, and she is the only one who really did impress me as being a great person.

She has more character in her little finger than Azaña in his whole body. Mind you, I do not say that all she said was right or that she had not made mistakes. All I am saying is that she has a dynamic character and one which left its mark on even a hard-boiled reporter such as myself who for years has taken down the more or less uninteresting banalities of politicians of various countries.

I never spoke to any other of the Communist leaders. José Diaz, who was Minister of Education, seemed a very alert and capable person. He was very young; about thirty-five. Uribe, the Minister of Agriculture, was apparently the theoretician of the Spanish Communist Party. He did a pretty sensible job as Minister of Agriculture. For instance, the peasants of the Province of Valencia, that is to say one of the richest in all Spain, were stopping cultivating because of the capricious ideas of the Anarchists and Socialists who insisted on making co-operative farms. Now the peasants on the *huerta*, or plain, of Valencia—wonderfully pictured in Blasco Ibanez's novel *La Cabaña*—did not want to co-operate. They said that now the land was theirs and that each would in future be his own proprietor. This may have been all wrong according to Marx but that was the way it was. They were furious when the Anarchists came along and insisted that their donkey, or plough, or small herd of goats, belonged to the community. Uribe came along and took the side of the peasants. He formed them into an association and provided them with co-operative facilities for buying fertilisers and for the sale of their products but each man remained master of his own plot. This suited the peasants, but the Anarchists and Socialists attacked the new movement bitterly and said that 'the Communists were admitting into their ranks all the most reactionary peasants of the Province of Valencia'. Which may have been true, but for the issue of the war the important thing was that food should be produced in large quantities and this was done.

It was not only in this that the Communists were helpful. They worked day and night and they tried to advise their people. For instance, suppose a man who had been chief clerk in an office now found himself in charge of the whole business of some important company as a result of the disappearance, or imprisoning, or murdering, of the rightful chief. If he were a Communist he could turn to the Party at every issue for advice as to what he should do. But if he were a Socialist or a Republican he would have to rely on his own ideas or those of friends because they did not set themselves out to meet and face every new situation. Socialists and Republicans worked very hard on some things and did wonders but they always tended to be a little wishful in their thinking.

I had a long talk one day in the Baviera Restaurant in Valencia with Luis Araquistain, the publicist and one-man 'brain trust' of Largo Caballero. There was still some passable sherry to be had, which facilitated our talk. He made some really amazing statements. He said: 'We are as much opposed to Communism as we are to Fascism; we will not see Spain under the yoke of Moscow.' I asked him to explain how Moscow was going to obtain control of Spain, considering the geographical obstacles in the way. Even supposing the case that the Communist Party succeeded in obtaining complete control of Government and nation, it would still, presumably, be composed of Spaniards and although there might be some Russian influence it seemed to me that it would be very difficult for Russia to impose any particular line of conduct not approved of by Spaniards as a whole. He was very vague about how this control would be imposed, but he was quite sure that it would be clamped down.

The talk only confirmed my impression that Caballero and his friends were suffering from a very bad case of jealousy. It was, of course, horrible for them after having led the working-class movement for so many years to find themselves on one side. But they had not been big enough to re-shape their outlook.

Russia had, of course, every interest in saving the Republic but I do not think that apart from a natural desire to see the Spanish Communist Party as powerful as possible and to spread its ideas as much as possible, the Russians had any idea of making Spain into a subject state of their own and I fail entirely to see how they could have done so at such a long distance.

A good deal has been written about Russian activities in Spain during the civil war but I certainly did not see any numbers of Russians about either in the police force or as private persons, except for the diplomatic staff, a few journalists, and a few military advisers. There were also a number of aviators and tank experts from October 1936 for some time until most of them were gradually replaced, but all of these latter kept very much to themselves. Indeed all the Russians did, the Russian journalists hardly mixed at all with their foreign colleagues. I never spoke to Michael Kollzoff, of *Pravda*, who was out there for over a year, although I saw him quite a number of times. Towards the end of the war I met his wife in Valencia, a very highly-strung and quite pleasant person. Also later in the war a Russian woman journalist whom we knew as 'Bola', her full name was Boleslavskaya and she also was on the staff of *Pravda*, became a popular figure in the journalistic crowd at the Majestic Hotel in Barcelona by her high spirits and amusing conversation.

I think there were probably a good many less Russian agents in Republican Spain than there were of Germany and Italy, who wormed their way into the International Brigades and many other places and who appear to have been able to supply on some occasions General Franco with more accurate information than his own services could give him from Government Spain. At least I heard it said that Italian secret agents gave Franco full details of the preparations for the Battle of the Ebro in July 1938 but that he did not act on these and as a result was caught sleeping.

CHAPTER XXXV

CORONATION INTERLUDE

ON Coronation Day I sat in a shop-window in Oxford Street like any tailor's dummy and watched the pageant of Great Britain roll by me. It was an illustrated page of history, but of past history I felt. Wonderful indeed, but rather of yesterday than of to-morrow. Too many magnificent guardsmen and kilted highlanders of rare physique, no tanks, no motorised corps, only a few aviators—on foot. Many rajahs indeed, but where were the representatives of the rank and file of the natives? Where was the youth of the Empire, white and black?

Perhaps the change had been too sudden. It was only relatively a few hours before that I had left Madrid after ten days of the steadiest shelling we had during the war. The shelling was, I know, light. I do not suppose that it exceeded 2,000 shells even on a bad day. But even 2,000 shells dropped at intervals on the main streets of a town where 900,000 civilians and a considerable number of soldiers are living as much of a normal life as is possible, do upset life. The dead I suppose never went over forty or fifty in a day with perhaps two hundred wounded.

My last day had been quite unnerving. When I went to obtain the safe-conduct to leave I heard the shells bursting. It just sounded as if someone were dropping heavy weights in the room upstairs. I took the Underground and when I came up the steps at the Banco de España Station I met a few people hurrying down, but without undue excitement. The Madrid people had rare nerve. On reaching the top, I saw the reason for their hurry. Near the entrance lay a man without a head. I do not know where his head was. It had been cut off as cleanly as if with a razor. Just beyond lay, very still, a girl, her silken-clad legs twisted queerly. Beyond her another woman lay in a crumpled heap. I suppose I should have gone out to make sure they were dead, but instead I dived down into the shelter of the Underground and only came up when there had been silence for a while and people began to move around. As far as I could see the Franco troops were using anti-aircraft artillery to rake the Calle de Alcalá, Gran Via and other main streets.

All day long the fire kept up. About five o'clock in the evening I went by Underground to the Telephone Building to send my last story before leaving. I hated to leave the safety of the station below ground. But just in front of me were two girls of about eighteen years. One obviously did not wish to go out, the other was very firm. She said: 'I came down here to buy stockings on the Gran Via and I am going to do it, General Franco or no General Franco!' And out she went followed by her weaker friend. She strode up towards the Gran Via steadily and without hurry, although the road and footpath were littered with fragments and dirt from explosions. That was the kind of fantastic spirit one found among the Madrid people. I trotted along behind her encouraged by her example but listening intently for a whine. Fortunately, there was a lull but I could see in two hundred yards at least twenty or thirty new hits made on houses since the morning. At the Telephone Building. which now had I think about 160 hits, there was a tarpaulin just inside the door. It covered what was left of two girls who went out of the Building and just walked into a shell. There was not much left and that was not nice to look at. This sadistic kind of shelling did General Franco a lot of harm. It was directed so deliberately on busy streets. There were munition factories, the Mint for example, which were not as far as I know touched by a shell during the whole war. Presumably because such buildings were felt to be needed after the war. One frequent custom was to shell the Gran Via just after eight o'clock at night when the final performance of the cinemas ended and crowds came out. In a civil war these tactics were bad because they turned against Franco considerable numbers of petite bourgeoisie who were sitting on the fence or were not very happy under the Republic.

I left at five o'clock in the morning with a shell coming over about every minute still and motored off to Valencia with John Lloyd of Associated Press in a sardine-box of a car with a shrivelled up mummy of a driver whom we called 'Homen Sapiens'. It seemed incredible, and lovely, soon to be motoring over a glorious spring landscape with the sun shining and birds singing and we stopped at a wayside cottage and had fried eggs and wine with fine rough country bread. Life felt good indeed and I realised how the soldiers who live through battles find so much good to say of a soldier's life. Safety, after danger, provides an undoubted thrill. But in my case it lasts a very short time indeed.

Paris, in a brief passage through, gave me the blues. London deepened them. I suppose the truth is that I was worn out. I dined here and there. I went to a night club on Regent Street and saw strip-tease with a rather charming girl stripping herself completely naked before a small crowd of rather bored spectators. Frankly, it all seemed rather decadent. In coming through Valencia I had gone to a variety show during which the main object of the spectators was to induce the girls to take off as much as possible in the way of clothing. It was an uproarious, lusty affair with yells and shouts and broad humour and coarse jests. It was gross, but in a healthy way. In London, of course, the class of people was completely different, but it all seemed somehow obscene and cold. There was nothing red-blooded about it.

I had never before seen full-scale pageantry in London. Never before seen the Guards swing down *en masse* with their bands, the gigantic bagpipers with their swinging kilts, and the officers and personalities of the Empire in all their finery. Nor had I ever seen so many people faint in such a short time. They keeled over like ninepins. Sometimes the ambulance men were kept at the double for a long time. There seemed to be a big sprinkling of 'C 3' citizens here. Nor was there much snap to the crowd. A loudspeaker gramophone played 'Land of Hope and Glory' and a few things such as that but scarcely anyone joined in. In my shop-window we had a radio and could follow proceedings and the broadcasting was at times really bad. A gentleman who sounded as if he had been unearthed from a London club and was still only half awake told us: 'The carriage is waiting for Their Majesties. There is a tremendous crowd in front of the Palace; yes, a really enormous crowd. Er, well, yes, it is quite surprising the great crowds that are here . . .' It was really very bad and uninspiring.

I watched Mr. Stanley Baldwin. 'Good old Baldwin! Hurray for Baldwin!' shouted the crowd as the heavily-jowled face looked out through a coach window. I wondered what he really thought about Spain, if he himself realised actually what non-intervention meant. There was not much time for thought; the heavy carriages rolled past swiftly. I liked the look of the King, he was pale and worried in aspect, so like the majority of his subjects. I wondered what he thought of Spain, what he was told of Spain by those around him.

Soon it was all over and the rain was pouring down and great crowds were kept standing and got soaked because the police kept the side streets barred while the troops who had lined the route were marshalled into long columns. They could quite well have been marched off in small detachments. So authority was happy and had its sweet will and hundreds of thousands received an extra and unnecessary drenching.

I was very unhappy as I went back to my hotel. It seemed to me that it should all have been so different. The parade should have been twentieth century; it was definitely nineteenth century. There should have been tanks, and motorised artillery, and clouds of planes overhead and troops in service dress with the most modern equipment. And the people of the Empire seemed absent. There should have been groups, tableaux if necessary, with the young whites and blacks from the world over who form part of the Commonwealth indicating the progress and vigour of their lands. The King and Queen should have been in open motor-cars so that people could see them well. Hollywood does all this old traditional pageantry well enough, or better. This is the twentieth century and we either lead to new fields or we and our linked people will be pushed aside and new leaders will come up. Time does not stand still. Tradition is good; to build on. But you must go on building to suit the new times. The useless and obsolete must go, be ruthlessly ripped aside.

Most people, I found, had little interest in Spain. The Left-Wingers supported the Republic and their political opponents attacked it. But the mass of the people were indifferent.

A distinguished British diplomat who knew Spain well was harangued by a friend of mine on the subject. My friend pointed out the tremendous danger to the British and French Empires if Spain were even slightly hostile to them. The diplomat answered: 'There is a great deal in what you say, old man, a very great deal indeed. But you know the essential thing to remember in the case of Spain is that it is a civil conflict and that it is very necessary that we stand by our class.'

Few indeed of our politicians, civil servants, diplomats, were frank enough to say this openly. But how many of them also forgot or overlooked the safety of their Empire because they were thinking too much of their class, too much of the necessity for squashing Communism and too little of the grave dangers looming up to imperil the existence of Imperial Britain?

CHAPTER XXXVI

ADMIRAL RAEDER SHELLS ALMERIA

ONE morning I found myself having breakfast in the pleasant town of Murcia. It seemed strange to be in a Spanish town which had never been bombed during the whole war. While we breakfasted we heard a fanfare of trumpets. Now, we thought, at least we will see some evidence of the war even down here. But no. It was only the local bandsmen advertising next Sunday's bullfight.

A queer backward town is Murcia surrounded by a lush, well-watered plain where oranges and vegetables flourish under the semi-tropical heat. Its massive cathedral was shut. The roads through the town were vile. Illiteracy was as high as eighty per cent there, I believe, until the Republic came.

I was only passing through the town on my way to Almeria to get the story of the bombing of that town by the German 'pocket battleship' *Admiral Scheer* on May 31 by way of reprisal for the bombing of the sister-ship *Deutschland* in Ibiza Bay on May 29. There had been twenty killed aboard the *Deutschland* and seventy-three injured, of whom six died. In Almeria there were twenty-four killed and about one hundred injured. Apparently the *Deutschland* was lying in the Ibiza roadstead about 200 yards from the quay. Two Republican bombers came over. They said that the ship opened fire on them with its anti-aircraft guns. The Germans say that they did not fire and that the bombing was unprovoked. The Republicans argued that the vessel had no business there, which seems to be true. The Ibiza area was patrolled by the French non-intervention vessels and the *Deutschland* should not have been in this area nor should it have been in port. The regulations were that the non-intervention vessels stay outside territorial waters. The incident took place on the Thursday and on Monday morning, May 31, 1937, the

Deutschland and four German destroyers appeared off Almeria and proceeded to shell every part of the town in a systematic bombardment which lasted nearly one hour. Admiral Raeder, later commander-in-chief of the German Navy, commanded this attack on a practically defenceless town.

I had set out from Madrid by slow and haphazard means, The authorities were quite unmoved at the spectacle of Sefton Delmer and myself trying to obtain some kind of transport to go to Almeria. Our chief press officer, a woman who was an Austrian Socialist émigré, was engrossed in a passionate romance with a Spanish colleague and was deaf to our appeals for transport. Delmer and myself finally departed perched insecurely on top of a loaded motor lorry, grilling in a fierce sun. But the lorry broke down when only twenty miles out. Finally we managed to find an old taxi driven by an antique driver who sat up stiffly to his wheel like a horse-cab driver and who when night came on stopped, preferably in the middle of the road, when he saw lights coming in the opposite direction even if they were five miles away.

By Thursday morning I had reached Murcia having shed Delmer en route and picked up a versatile American photographer and lecturer named Russell Wright, who was excellent company and who told me much about the facts of life in the United States. According to his version it seemed to be a country for hard living and good loving.

Nowhere in Europe have I seen a land so grim as that to be met with between Murcia and Almeria. It is parched in the extreme. You can drive twenty miles and see no sign of life or sign of green stuff. Houses by the wayside are old and derelict, sometimes abandoned, with the roof fallen in. The trees have all been cut, the goats have torn up the roots of the grass. Sun and erosion have done the rest. Great irrigation schemes would be needed to make this land bloom again and they would have to be combined with re-afforestation plans. It is impossible to be cheerful amid so much neglect and abandon.

Long before we got to Almeria we saw groups of people camped on the countryside; refugees who feared further bombardments. The town itself was crowded, nevertheless. It looked more warlike than it was because of the mounds of earth thrown up where shelters had been dug. Later, a foreign diplomat who visited the town was unkind enough to say that I had mistaken these mounds of earth for damage done by German shells 'of which he could see very little'. The Civil Governor gave me a secret policeman to take me around the town. He was a thin spare Andalusian, an Anarchist, and in ordinary life, clerk in a shipping office. But he was indefatigable. He took us right to work and walked us up streets and down alleys until nine o'clock in the evening when darkness fell. At five o'clock in the morning he had us out again. The damage was not easy to see, but it was extensive. One big shell alone from the *Deutschland* had caused the roofs of about fifteen cottages to collapse. If you drove down the street past them you would not have noticed anything. I visited and kept note of seventy wrecked houses, including the British Consulate. I estimated that there were about seventy others completely wrecked, about one hundred badly damaged and a further hundred slightly damaged. In all about 8,000 people were homeless. The *Deutschland* and its four accompanying destroyers had shelled the town steadily for nearly one hour. One huge shell which stood nearly as high as my shoulder had gone down into a refuge and had not exploded. The only answer made had been by a futile and ancient shore battery which was no danger to anyone. They were not able to land a single shell anywhere near the German avengers.

I suppose that this business of shelling a virtually undefended town has been done by other navies before, including our own, but it does seem to be pretty horrible and hardly heroic.

While in Almeria, I saw a funeral of one of the injured who had died. Behind the coffin walked a big number of working men; the victim was apparently some trade union leader. all looking rather clumsy and out of place, dressed in their best and clumping along behind the hearse. Looking at their worn faces and gnarled hands I wondered how it is that so few people care how much the working masses suffer. Even in Britain where they are as well off as anywhere, how many working-class families are able to live decently and comfortably with their health thoroughly cared for and a reserve for a rainy day and old age? I should imagine that the percentage is very low. How many people buying a suit are interested as to the wages paid those who sold it or made it? Or who, crossing the ocean in a luxury liner, takes any particular interest in what kind of accommodation or pay the stewards and stokers get? We would not cut Mrs. X dead if we knew that her new motor-car had been bought by profits made through lowering salaries in Mr. X's workshop. Once we have sufficient to eat and drink ourselves and can safely salve our consciences by an occasional subscription to a hospital, we care little indeed for the fate of the rest of the world. Civilisation, indeed! I imagine the average African tribe has more social sense of responsibility towards its members than we mortals who like to think of ourselves as shining specimens of the 'Civilised and Progressive Twentieth Century'.

The *Deutschland* dead were buried at Gibraltar in the presence of the Governor, General Sir Charles Harington, Rear-Admiral Evans of H.M.S. *Cormorant* and Rear-Admiral Wells of the *Arethusa*.

The war in the North was not hindered by the death of General Emilio Mola, one of the most intelligent of the rebel Generals, but not I think really great either as a strategist or a leader of men, on June 3 when the aeroplane in which he was flying flew into a hillside between Valladolid and Burgos. On June 19 Bilbao fell. On July 6, the Republican forces launched an attack on the small town of Brunete, a road junction a few miles from Navalcarnero and about fifteen miles west of Madrid. If the attack could have been pressed hard enough and have reached out to Navalcarnero or the road from Navalcarnero to Madrid, then Franco's forces lying before Madrid would have had their flank threatened.

Lister's XIth Division, now part of the newly formed Fifth Army Corps of the new Republican Army, was given the most difficult task. It had to march by night through about twelve miles of enemy territory and take Brunete by surprise while other troops mopped up the rear. Considering that the offensive had been the talk of Valencia cafés for several weeks, it is surprising that it could be a surprise. Nevertheless, it was and Brunete fell. Then ensued a terrible battle under a burning July sun. The Insurgents had plenty of reserves near at hand and they were able to send aviation from the North immediately. The British of the International Brigades helped to take Villanueva de la Cañada in a terrible all-day battle. Many were killed and hurt. I saw many of them in hospital. One man who gave us a name which obviously was not his own, had been hit in the spine. He was about twenty-three and a Cambridge graduate. He did not know that he had no chance of living and he talked eagerly enough about his enthusiasm for the fight. He asked us to read to him, so that he could listen to it, the order of the day issued to the Brigades on the eve of the attack and which he thought was a fine piece of writing. For once in these days of national disgrace, I could feel proud of my country. We still bred men who would give up good careers and easy lives to die for an ideal.

The battle ended about July 25, it had drawn the Nationalist aviation from Santander for some days, but it could not save it nor could it break the ring around Madrid. Santander fell on August 25. The Government forces showed that they were capable of carrying out a business-like attack but they had not the artillery, tanks or aviation in sufficient quantities to make serious inroads on the well-defended Franco lines.

The Republicans in the centre zone naturally felt that they must do something to aid their fellows in the North. But I think the Brunete battle was a great tactical mistake. With the blockade of Spain becoming more and more severe they should have husbanded every piece of material to meet possible attack.

CHAPTER XXXVII

IN CAUX-SUR-MONTREUX

ONE of my weaknesses when I have some leisure is to buy all kinds of reviews and weekly papers and to browse through them. I had an orgy of this when I got to Geneva. I spent the whole of August 1937 in Switzerland, all because I ran into a British woman doctor at El Escorial whom I had never met before and whom I have never met since. She knew some of the other journalists I was with and while we were having some drinks she said to me quite suddenly: 'How are you feeling?' 'More or less all right,' said I, 'except that I can't eat because of the heat and I have lost ten pounds in weight since the end of May.' She said wisely: 'I thought as much; now take my tip young man and get yourself a good rest or you may regret it.'

Geneva in August seemed a foretaste of paradise, after the Battle of Brunete. The air was so cool and clear. I lay in an easy chair on a balcony of the Hotel de Russie and watched a steamer come in with its gay lights and a band playing. Yet only a week before I had been lying on the parched ground of a gulley way back behind the lines talking to the British boys who were at rest. The Internationals were now mixed with Spanish troops because they were getting killed off too fast. But they were too weary even to fraternise just then. They had been at rest for over a day but everybody lay stretched on the ground unless he had something important to do. People did not even talk much, partly because most of them did not care much to talk to a 'bourgeois journalist', and partly because they were just all in. I met Jock Cunningham, a square, short, burly young man full of energy. He has, I think, quite a revolutionary record. But apparently he had done a very good job in command of the British battalion and showed both leadership and courage. Hugh Slater was there too, a fair and polished young man who had spent some months in Spain as a reporter during the early part of the war and who had now come back to fight. He had been arrested in France on his way through and had served two weeks in Perpignan Gaol and had been expelled from France because, you see, the authorities of the French Republic suspected that Mr. Slater was going to fight in Spain. In charge of two Russian anti-tank guns, Slater had done brilliantly in the Brunete battle.

From Geneva I moved to Caux-sur-Montreux where indeed, in the words of Rupert Brooke, 'there was peace and holy quiet there'. From my balcony I could look down to the lake three or four miles below and the air was so still that the thug-thug of the engines of the lake steamers could be heard. Here I should have read about lovely, restful things but mostly I picked my way through my mass of newsprint, or read solid books on such subjects as 'the defence of the Empire', or international politics.

Do you ever read the *Commercial Motor*? Or the *Motor Cycle*? I find them fascinating. *The Universe* and the *Catholic Times* interest me naturally, as I am a Catholic. But it depressed me terribly in that August of 1937 to see the way in which they supported General Franco. Even allowing for the priests killed, there still was a case for the Republicans. The *Saturday Evening Post* has some good time-killing yarns but I do not care for its political articles. *Cosmopolitan* or *Colliers* have some better stuff in them. I do not like *Time* very much now, but I used to like it. At one time I thought its jerky, telegraph, style good and it has indeed revolutionised the manner of presenting news in a short pithy standardised style. But I find that it gets boring by endless repetition.

I also picked up in Geneva a monthly I had not seen before, called *Physical Culture*. I did not buy it for the nudes, believe it or not. If I had been feeling that way about things I would not have isolated myself on the top of a Swiss mountain. I was just too weary to care much about women. But this review did not, as it happened, specialise, as do most of those kind of papers, on lavish photographs of the maximum of beauty in the minimum of dress. Under the guidance of one Bernarr MacFadden who apparently is getting on in years but is still full of pep, this paper set out some ideas as to breathing deeply and eating the right kind of food, not over-eating, getting exercise, and keeping the bowels clean, which seemed to be pretty good. I took a shot at filling my chest rather more energetically and, I am writing with one hand and clutching the wooden leg of my desk hard with the other hand, I have not had a bad cold from that day to this. It may, of course, have nothing to do with doing a little deep breathing each day. But I used to have a lot of colds up to then.

I tried a little fasting, as recommended, but with less success. After cutting out dinner and next morning's breakfast and walking briskly down to Montreux I found my head reeling and had to hurry to a restaurant on Montreux's cosmopolitan high street and get a beefsteak.

Another interesting weekly out of my pile was *The Aeroplane*, edited by Mr. C. G. Grey who has the most unorthodox ideas imaginable. You would hardly expect to find in a technical weekly on aeroplanes and the people who use them, lively talks about 'our blood brothers of Western and Central Europe' but Mr. Grey will tell you all kinds of things like that. His fervent defence of the Franco cause made me feel pretty bad at that time. I believe Grey has now resigned and been succeeded by Major E. C. Shepherd, aviation correspondent of the *Times*.

Besides all this varied fare I read every day the *Times*, because one has to read the *Times* to keep careful track of things British and things foreign, and the *Daily Telegraph*, because it carries more straight news than any other paper and keeps a balance, and the *Daily Express*, because it is the smartest piece of editing in Fleet Street, and the *News Chronicle* because it writes a lot of sane things and sticks up for a lot of causes which I think are good causes. When I am in England I also take the *Daily Worker* because that little paper has guts and even if it is apt to present its stuff with too many demagogic qualifying adjectives—it seems to have improved somewhat of late—it still says many things which other newspapers do not and which it is important that Britain should know. But in Caux-sur-Montreux I could not get the *Daily Worker* because, apparently, some Swiss cantons ban all

Communist newspapers. This does not apply to Fascist organs and you can buy, or you could then, the *Volkischer Beobachter* or the *Corriere della Sera* without let or hindrance.

I did not read any more papers, except *Le Temps*, which I do not like but which one must read and especially its leader, because that was quite enough. When I am in a big-hearted mood I sometimes read all the London dailies which is really the only satisfactory way of covering the day's news, but it takes three or four hours to do this seriously.

So many things were clear up in Caux when one lay on a mountain side with only the cattle bells breaking the silence and one read the Press slowly and carefully. The Republic was being strangled, very slowly it is true, but deliberately strangled. Scarcely a day went by that some ship was not sunk in the Mediterranean.

Here is a list noted by myself from the Press and which probably misses quite a few:

August 7: British tanker named *British Corporal* and French steamer bombed in Mediterranean.

August 13: Fine new Spanish motor-ship *Ciudad de Cadiz* sunk by submarine off Gallipoli.

August 14: 13,000 ton Panama oil tanker set afire by shelling from Nationalist cruiser between Sicily and North African coast.

August 17: Spanish steamer *Adecoa* escaped into French port after chase by destroyers apparently belonging to Italian Navy.

August 18: Spanish ship *Armuru* coming from Russia to Republican Spain sunk off Gallipoli.

August 24: London steamer *Noemiejulea* carrying phosphates from Tunis to Barcelona, bombed 20 miles off Spanish coast.

August 31: Russian steamer *Timiryazeff* bound for Port Said with coal from Liverpool torpedoed and sunk off the Algerian coast.

August 25: British tanker *Romford* bombed.

September 2: British tanker *Woodford* sunk twenty-five miles off Spanish coast while proceeding from Valencia to Barcelona, by submarine painted grey and carrying no identification marks or flag. The *Woodford* was flying the flag of the non-intervention agreement to show that she had a non-intervention officer on board.

September 6: British tanker *Burlington* bound from Batum to Cartagena with 7,700 tons of oil on board was seized by Nationalist cruisers while approaching Palmero to take aboard her non-intervention officer. The Nationalists took her to Palma, emptied the oil and turned her loose.

Naturally, the insurance rates on all ships going through the Mediterranean soared, international shipping business was seriously interfered with and the British Government managed to draw up the Nyon anti-piracy agreement of September 15, together with France, Greece, Turkey, Russia, Bulgaria, Jugoslavia, Rumania and Egypt. Later, Italy agreed to take part in Mediterranean patrols which were to look out for submarines not proceeding on the surface which it was agreed would be sunk at sight unless they were in certain waters used by the various navies for practice purposes.

This indiscriminate sinking of ships all over the Mediterranean, which had happened before in the case of two Russian and a number of ships of several nationalities, nevertheless hit the Republic a tremendous blow. With the ships and their cargoes went not merely millions of pounds but also in some cases the necessary arms and in others such vital supplies as petrol and fuel oil or food. Now, prices to carry goods to Spain went up to fantastic figures. The insurance alone on some small tramp steamer would be several hundred pounds a day. Such arms as could be bought had to be bought in clandestine fashion for the most part, at high prices for bad material and under all kinds of incredible difficulties. The honest buyers often did not know much about war material and the dishonest ones as likely as not went off with the money. Not only that but the lives of such men were often in danger. A diplomat told me how a buyer of arms went to Prague on behalf of the Republic. He had not been there long before he received warnings from German agents of the Gestapo that he would be killed if he did not leave.   And he had to go, even from a city which in those days was the capital of a Democracy.

The German arms went to Pasajes or Bilbao in big German steamers where tanks, aeroplanes in sections, were unloaded without any very great secrecy.   Other boats unloaded at Vigo. The Italian ships were usually escorted by units of the Italian Navy and went past Gibraltar with their colours flying to Cadiz.   The Republican Government would then publish a long list of these boats loaded with arms which had come from Germany and Italy but nobody took any notice.   The naval vessels of the various non-intervention patrols would only intervene if a non-intervention officer aboard a ship reported an infraction of the regulations.   As the German and Italian ships which carried arms did not take an observer on board, there was no way of insisting that the non-intervention patrols should intervene.

I only remember one such case, although there may have been others, and this was when a German non-intervention officer denounced that a British boat, I think the name was the *Stancroft*, was carrying aeroplane engines.   A British destroyer promptly came and took the boat under escort to Gibraltar where the captain was tried.   There was a tremendous fuss all about some twenty aeroplane engines which were not even complete and which were being taken from Barcelona to Valencia.   Yet as I say, at least two or three times a month, ship loads of stuff for General Franco could steam by Gibraltar where the responsible people must have known exactly where they were going and what they had aboard, but not a finger was lifted.   And yet there are still people who talk suavely of 'both sides got more or less equal help'.

The Franco people insisted that the submarine which was sinking ships so neatly was the C 3.   All the submarines had remained in Republican hands but the C 3 had been sunk off Malaga.   The Nationalists claimed that they had raised it and put it into operation.   But they never showed it to anyone. Nor did the descriptions of the submarines which were sinking ships tally with that of the C 3, nor was it explained how the C 3, a small submarine, was able to cruise so far away as Galli-poli.   Since then, of course, the more or less certain suspicions that they were German or Italian submarines working from the Dodecanese Islands have been confirmed and panegyrics have been delivered to the sailors of the totalitarian States who took part in this 'crusade against Communism'.

On the frontiers also there were non-intervention officers since about the end of April of 1937, who looked at all the trucks and lorries passing in and out of Spain and made sure that no arms went by. So the situation was practically perfect for General Franco. He could receive all the arms he needed without any danger or trouble whatsoever while the Republicans could only get an occasional cargo through by sea and nothing at all by land.

I am not going to give here a complete history of non-intervention because so much has been written about it, but it was a disastrous thing for the Republic and fatal for the safety of our Empire route. When we did take a stand to stop the rampage of indiscriminate torpedoing by 'unknown' submarines it was, alas, merely because trade was being badly interfered with. Empire considerations had no part. We stood by, and by much omission and a little commission, aided in the strangling of the Republicans who could not otherwise have been defeated in the field except by the intervention of large and new expeditionary forces from Germany and Italy.

One thing I loved in rainy weather up at Caux was to watch clouds being 'born'. Down in some glen thick with pines I would see what would look like a wisp of steam, then it would grow very rapidly until a fine baby cloud was evolved and would float away down or up the valley and take its place with the masses of clouds. I suppose the explanation was that currents of cold air came down into warm and damp valleys. But up to then I had often wondered where clouds began their foot-free, careless existence.

CHAPTER XXXVIII

PRIETO AS WAR MINISTER

THE period from the end of July 1937 until the capture of Teruel on December 22 was not particularly fruitful for the Republicans despite the fact that General Franco continued to devote his attention entirely to the North, which campaign virtually ended with the fall of Gijon on October 22.

The Republicans tried another offensive after Brunete, namely, an attack in the direction of Saragossa from the South-East. They captured Belchite on September 5 and the front lines actually came up to within ten or twelve miles of the Aragon capital, but despite heroic work by the International Brigades and the Spanish troops it was a hopeless task. They could succeed brilliantly for just the three or four days it took Franco to rush the motorised artillery, anti-aircraft batteries, tanks and shock troops from the North and to transfer more aviation to the new field of action and then they would face once again a position of technical superiority which they had not the weapons to deal with successfully. The only successful role they could possibly hope to play was that of defence but there was, of course, the factor of morale to be considered and naturally the Republican troops who fought so bravely in the North expected that the efforts should be made to draw the fire of the Franco forces away from them.

An attack on Teruel had actually been planned for the end of September in conjunction with another offensive from Guadalajara which was to be a big effort to drive the Nationalists right back towards Saragossa, but the chief of staff of the Republican forces slipped across to the enemy lines only six hours before the action was to begin, taking with him copies of all the plans and instructions. Luckily his absence was discovered in time and troops were hastily scattered from the concentration points and munition dumps moved so that when at dawn the enemy bombers came over *en masse* the damage they were able to do although serious was not catastrophic in character. Actually that chief of staff probably did the Republic a very good turn because it definitely had not the means with which to carry out such a large-scale operation and it would almost certainly have been a bad failure.

The Republic had its back to the wall as far as supplies were concerned. For one ship which got through from Russia, one or two would be sunk or captured by the Nationalists or their allies so that the sea route became impracticable. The land route was impossible because the French frontier was tightly closed. Don Indalecio Prieto, the plump and solid War Minister, dedicated all his efforts to making as much war material as possible. This was very difficult in view of the relatively few engineering industries in Government territory, but a great effort was made.

On October 31 the Government moved from overcrowded Valencia to the more roomy Barcelona in order to carry out this new scheme to manufacture war supplies on a large scale. Only a few days before they moved, on October 22, one of their best vessels, the *Cabo Santo Tome* of 12,000 tons, was sunk off the Algerian coast. One of Sr. Prieto's first measures there was to suspend the forty-hour week which Catalonia still kept in force. In order to prevent this new scheme of making weapons at home from being successful the Nationalists began from now onwards systematic bombardment of the ports of Valencia and Barcelona in order to hinder as far as possible the delivery of raw materials necessary to make armaments. On October 5 it was announced by the Rome correspondents, and not denied, that Bruno Mussolini, son of Il Duce, had joined the bombing squadrons stationed by the Italians at Palma de Mallorca for the purpose of attacking the East coast of Spain.

There were, of course, secondary factors to aid in the lack of Republican success in the battlefield and one of these was the fact that Don Indalecio Prieto was not a good War Minister, he was far too much of a politician. He appeared to dislike the system of 'Commissars' or Political Commissioners introduced into the Army under Largo Caballero at the end of September 1936. These Commissioners were supposed to explain to the men why they were fighting, to look after their comfort, and to lead them in every way by example. 'First to advance and last to retreat,' was the motto of the Corps of Commissioners which was headed by Julio Alvarez del Vayo. The idea is not, of course, a new one. Political delegates played their part in the French Revolution but as they had had a big role in the Communist Revolution in Russia, naturally the Spanish system was an adaptation of the Russian one. The Communists had adopted the system most enthusiastically in Spain but the actual ranking Commissioners were divided up fairly equally between Communists, Socialists and Anarchists. They got quite good pay, a battalion Commissioner had honorary rank as Major and so on; the Chief Commissioner had honorary rank as General, and they received pay corresponding to these ranks.

There was some friction between Commissioners and officers but I never found it very great. Actually some such institution was indispensable. A newly formed Army with no tradition, always very much under-officered and with very defective administrative services, had to have some kind of man whose job it was to smooth out all the difficulties which are eliminated by the smooth organisation of a regular standing army. Not only that but in a civil war the men need a good deal of explanation on the question of exactly why they are fighting. It is one thing to be able to tell a man that he must die to save his country from invasion. It is very different to ask him to fight masses of his fellow-countrymen. Best proof of the pudding was. however, the fact that those units in which the Commissioners were most active were the best fighters.

Prieto did not abolish them, but he tried to annul them and he tended to fill the leading posts with Socialists or Anarchists or Left Republicans.

Apart from the fact that he studied everything from a political point of view, Prieto suffered from a secondary drawback that he was not surrounded by good men and that he dealt with every minor detail personally. For instance, every application for a pass to visit the front was studied personally by him and signed by him and as these passes were only valid sometimes for two weeks. sometimes for a month, the amount of work involved alone in dealing with the constant claims of some fifty or sixty regular and visiting correspondents was not inconsiderable. He had a secretary named Cruz Salido who stolidly referred everything back to his chief and was a most exasperating person to have to deal with.

The fact that Prieto was a nice fellow personally makes it rather hard to criticise him. He was a good executive but very slow, stolid and cautious and with not a great deal of background. He was the kind of man to make an ideal second-in-command to a person who could dominate him. He disliked extremist measures. In his speeches he always took a very orthodox and gloomy view of the situation and would almost invariably say: 'No matter what happens or who wins, our economy is ruined for twenty years to come.' In view of the tremendous resource and latent energy being shown by Spaniards in the war I could not help feeling that this tremendous, unleashed effort would make its presence felt in peacetime also.

Major C. R. Attlee, Leader of the Opposition in the House of Commons, who, accompanied by Philip Noel Baker, M.P., and Miss Ellen Wilkinson, M.P., came to Republican Spain in December 1937, to have a look at things for himself said in a newspaper interview that the fundamental key to victory was the amalgamation of the Anti-Fascist Parties.

This would have made a great difference and would have had a very stimulating effect on the mass of the people. But here again the mistrust and jealousy of the Communists was the chief hindrance. This party was so active that there is no doubt that it would have played a leading part in the new united organisation. The gap was too wide and the majority of the Republicans and the Right-Wing Socialists would not even consider throwing in their lot with the Communists. The Anarchists also were not enthusiastic but they might have been amenable. With a strong united party and a really energetic programme much more could have been done.

Another strong objection, however, was the possible reaction in France and Britain to a union which might be considered as a step to Communism. This objection was advanced most strongly both by Republicans and many Socialists. But actually as Britain and France were definitely not helping the Republic and by their share in non-intervention were indeed helping very efficaciously to bring about its end, there did not seem much to lose by risking the drawing of their displeasure by such a political union. Of course, all the parties were amalgamated to a certain extent in the Popular Front, but this never became an active executive body. It was just an expression of co-operation and agreement on a general programme.

It was particularly hard lines on people like Prieto who struggled tremendously to keep the Republic on moderate lines that they were not rewarded by any help from the Democratic Powers. The gradual decline of the Socialist Party in the last eighteen months of the war was due in great part to the turn of popular support from it to the Communist Party in view of the attitude of the Democracies. For instance, Prieto by his efforts which for a time greatly restricted the powers of Political Commissioners never as far as I know ever got the slightest advantage out of this from abroad. In British diplomatic circles one would hear that Prieto was 'a stout fellow', or the French would enthusiastically describe him as 'le seul grand homme de la République'. But that was as far as it got.

At this time Manuel Irujo, a Basque leader and Minister of Justice in this period of autumn 1937, was rounding up all the Anarchists and Trotskyites who had most distinguished themselves by murders in the first days of the military revolt, and thus causing great consternation in Anarchist circles.

There was every chance even at this late date that Britain and France by taking a firm line to restrict German and Italian intervention could have helped the moderate Republicans to win and thus have ensured the safety of our Empire routes. But nothing was done. The pretext was always advanced that any such effort to ensure this would mean a world war; a most highly contentious statement and even if true merely raises the question as to what future exists for an Empire which is not willing to take the risk of war in order to safeguard her imperial integrity, which one cannot repeat too often is not guaranteed when a hostile Spain is in a position to menace our lines of communication. It seems to me that any Empire which is not ready at any instant to go to war to check any threat to its security, might just as well acknowledge that its days are over.

I was very curious to meet Attlee, whom I had never seen. Negrin's secretaries were not helpful; they rarely were. By gate-crashing the Prime Minister's guest-house—he had a house adjoining his own residence and office which was used for distinguished visitors—I found the party rather lost and abandoned. Dr. Negrin, who was out of town, had so far not come to receive his guests and they were being allowed to 'rest', but as they had come to Spain to see things a 'rest' from three in the afternoon until nine o'clock at night seemed needlessly extensive.

I found Mr. Attlee very quiet and very sensible but he did not strike me as being a strong man. He personally understood the situation fairly well. He said that he thought that not just Socialism or Democracy, but the safety of Britain was involved here in Spain. However, I could understand that he had a difficult team to drive and many an honest and stolid trade unionist such as Caballero in his own ranks, which rendered it impossible to do more to help the Republic. He saw the British Internationals and gave permission for the battalion to be given the honorary title of 'Major Attlee Battalion'. But one felt that he too was gripped by a feeling of impotence and helplessness and that little could come in a practical way of his visit.

Actually he had to face a vote of censure presented in the House of Commons by Mr. W. S. Liddall, Conservative Member of Parliament for Lincoln. This Member charged him with having betrayed his promise, which it was necessary to make to the Foreign Office in the rare cases when a visa to visit Spain was granted and in which the applicant pledged himself not to take sides. The House did not take a serious view of the matter.

A remark of Earl Winterton, Chancellor of the Duchy of Lancaster, at a Manchester meeting at this period is I think worth recording in view of the attitude shown, which was not untypical of that adopted by some people in high positions. He asked his audience: 'What business is it of the Leader of the Opposition who wins in the merciless and indeed frightful Spanish civil war?' I think that 'indeed' is charming.

It is also worth recording that the League of Nations early in October, on the third of the month to be precise, rejected a very mild proposal that the League father a scheme to withdraw foreigners fighting in Spain. Britain and France voted in favour but the proposal was rejected by thirty-two to thirty. Even in Geneva, the Berlin-Rome sympathisers could sweep the board. Later, Spain was ejected from the League Committee by the same pro-Fascist group.

However, all this takes us away from the actual happenings in Spain and the attack on Teruel, which is a bleak town if ever there was one; it is a sort of Spanish Buxton. It stands on a small hill in a basin surrounded by blunt hills nearly all of which are treeless. In normal times Teruel always scores by having the lowest temperatures of any other important town in the country each winter. It is about sixty miles from Valencia with its pleasant climate and its orange groves. It is also famous for a legend of two lovers. The poor boy, so the story runs, loved a rich man's daughter. He was given a certain length of time in which to make a fortune. He achieved this, but arrived just a little late and only in time to see his loved one married to another. He killed himself and the girl died of grief before she was possessed by her husband.

The unsentimental Spaniards have evolved a popular couplet which says:

> 'Los amantes de Teruel
> Tonta ella y tonto el!'

That is to say:

> 'The Lovers of Teruel,
> She was stupid and he as well!'

There is a grandeur about this town perched on the top of a low hill, alone in this desolate terrain. It is a lovely sight seen on a winter's evening with the sun setting and the hard, surrounding landscape bathed in a soft, rosy glow. I knew something about Teruel for I had Spanish friends there. It is the capital of a very poor province, although there is richer ground in the direction of Saragossa. It was tremendously reactionary as far as I could find out. My friends certainly were. As soon as I got into Teruel I tried to find them but the first man I asked said to me very curtly: 'My God, you have strange friends, young man.' I found out that my friends were all in the Seminary where the Nationalist troops were resisting.

The Government lines had been near the town since the first days of the revolt. They occupied the heights of the Puerto de Escandon, about six miles from the town. The lines were even nearer round about Valdecebro to the North-East. The town was shelled occasionally and had been bombed, although not very much I think.

The operation was begun by a very neat and well executed cutting off of the town by Major Lister who repeated similar moves done at Brunete and Belchite but this was on a major scale. The attack made, I think I am correct in saying, at three o'clock on the afternoon of Friday, December 17, started a battle which raged almost unceasingly until Teruel was re-taken by General Franco on February 22. The first step, made in broad daylight, consisted of sending troops across country from Valdecebro to beyond Caudete but without taking either this town or Concud and then sending part of the troops due south along the crest of the great rolling hill known as the Muela de Teruel (the tooth of Teruel) until they met another detachment coming up from the Republican front line near Villel. At seven o'clock in the evening Teruel was surrounded completely in a large circle which contained probably some 15,000 troops who had not yet come into action and probably about 20,000 civilian inhabitants.

How it had been possible for the Republicans to bring up at least forty or fifty thousand fresh troops, with all the corresponding equipment, to this front without the Insurgents finding this out remains one of the mysteries of the war. Their own and their allied spy systems either did not work or their warnings were disregarded. The weather when the attack was launched was terrible. It snowed almost the whole of the first day and all the roads were ice-bound. The Republican troops had to perform miracles to move their materials forward.

The officer responsible for the Teruel attack was the

commander of the Eastern Army, Colonel Juan Hernandez Sarabia, formerly in command of the Presidential Guard and once War Minister for a brief period. He was promoted to General after the capture of Teruel. A mild-mannered little man he was always most pleasant to deal with but I never got the impression that he was a very efficient soldier. The strategy of the move had been planned by General Vicente Rojo, former teacher of strategy at the Toledo Infantry Academy and the man who had been General Miaja's chief of staff in Madrid throughout the defence of Madrid and later in the Battles of Jarama and Guadalajara. His handling of the situation at Guadalajara had been exceptionally good. Personally, he was very modest and retiring.

Whether the Republic was wise to carry out the Teruel operation at all is, of course, open to much debate. My personal opinion is that it was a great mistake for the Government to waste its few arms on attacking. It would have been much wiser to wait and let General Franco do the attacking. Time was also valuable to the Republic for fortification and for reorganising the troops but although much had been done, Sr. Prieto did not appear to give this aspect sufficient consideration. Teruel was not necessary from a point of view of prestige because there was no serious collapse of morale in Republican ranks and there was little help to be obtained abroad with or without prestige. Such help as was received came almost entirely as a result of the expenditure of good gold from the Bank of Spain.

I have heard it said that Sr. Prieto wished after the success at Teruel to negotiate an armistice. Personally, I doubt this very much. But it is nevertheless possible. Just as Sr. Prieto did not, I think, understand at all the political situation on his own side and the necessity for radical and decisive changes in the previous policy of the Socialist Party, it is quite within the bounds of possibility that he did not realise at all that the situation in Franco Spain also had undergone an enormous change since the first days and the wide implications of this change.

As I have pointed out earlier in the book, the help given to General Franco by Germany and Italy was not just a question of arms. General Franco would have had no chance of success without their immediate help after the outbreak and the encouragement and assistance given in the preparations for the *coup d'état*, but once he had gained control of a substantial part of Spanish territory he found himself attached to the carriage of a very powerful new movement destined to change completely the course of European history.

Spain indeed presented a strange spectacle after two years of war. Nationalist Spain comprised an Army Dictatorship linked with a newly-developed Fascist Party while the other side was under the control of Liberals and Socialists with a strong Communist Party as its greatest measure of support.

Some superficial observers described one side as Fascist and the other as Communist and in view of many similarities between these two régimes wondered what the Spaniards were fighting about anyway.

In my opinion it was not correct to describe Franco Spain as 'Fascist' or Republican Spain as 'Communist', even though one had a huge party with a totalitarian programme and saluted with the outstretched arm and the other had most of its factories, and even whole branches of industry, controlled by workers' committees.

The revolt of 1936 was not a Fascist revolt. Falange was a very small party prior to July 1936, and its leader, José Antonio Primo de Rivera, was in gaol. Some politicians such as Don José Calvo Sotelo undoubtedly aided in its preparation, but by and large it was the Army which arranged and carried out the coup. And the Army remained in control. The fact that Falange had hundreds of thousands of members and assisted greatly in the conduct of the war and in the organisation of civilian life behind the lines did not give it supreme power. General Franco had replaced Primo de Rivera as leader. When one of the principal figures of Falange, Manuel Hedilla, objected to the policy which was being followed by General Franco, he was tried and exiled. Although all national enterprise was subject to control during the war, there did not appear to be any steps taken which could permanently affect the owners of industry or of large areas of land. The Clergy regained much of the power they had lost under the Republic and Cardinal Pedro Segura, the ascetic and fanatical cleric who was Primate and who was expelled from Spain by the Republic, returned, not as Primate of Spain but as Cardinal Archbishop of Seville.

I have not made much comment on Franco Spain in this book because as I did not go there I do not think it fair to write about it. I hope that some other writer will some day give us a full description of that part of Spain during the war. But I have made a slight exception here for the sake of contrasting the two régimes.

It seems to me that General Franco may not find it any more possible to build up a Fascist régime of a permanent character on feudal foundations than the Republic found it possible to superimpose a Democracy on such a base. There are, of course, many kinds of Fascism. The Nazi régime with its iron control over agriculture, industry and commerce leaves little freedom to the trader. Such Fascist régimes as that of Senhor Oliveira in Portugal and General Metaxas in Greece on the other hand give considerable latitude to private enterprise. I was able after I left Spain to discuss the situation there with an intelligent and quite highly-placed functionary of the Nazi Party and he gave his opinion to me that General Franco could only succeed if he could make his movement one dependent on mass support. He thought that this would not be very easy in view of the repression of the workers by such violent methods as were employed in the first months.

The success of the régimes in Germany and Italy has been due to the skill with which they have gained control of the national economy without perturbing it too greatly and thus diverted the maximum of national effort to forward the aims of those in charge of the régimes. In both cases the use of radical methods such as those employed in Russia and by which the space from feudalism to a totalitarian State with all property in the hands of the nation was cleared in a single leap, would obviously have only brought ruin and disaster. Neither Italy nor Germany were feudal States but were already industrialised nations with considerable experience of government of a more or less democratic character.

In Republican Spain, in contrast to Nationalist Spain, industry was not merely under State control but it was being actually administered mainly by committees of workers and higher employees. This, as I have pointed out elsewhere, was not due to any wish of the Republicans in control. Quite the contrary in fact. It arose from the fact that most property owners went to live abroad or in Franco Spain when the revolt broke out, while others were killed or imprisoned. Of those who had no political antecedents and were able to, and cared to, stay on, few were friendly to the Republic. So workers and employees took over plants and offices and peasants took the land in many cases because there was no one at all to take charge. The Republic, therefore, did have the opportunity to start the reconstruction of a new Spain from the bottom upwards in the event of winning the war.

This was, I think, a situation which Sr. Prieto did not understand. He was, of course, not alone in this. President Azaña and a great many responsible people in Britain and France also did not see how rapidly the whole face of Europe was changing nor how this fact affected General Franco radically. The only thing he could possibly accept was unconditional surrender.

In the Europe of 1937 we already had in full swing what one might best call a 'rebel capitalism'. That is to say that two nations at least, Germany and Italy, were so tired of their position of economic inferiority *vis-à-vis* Britain and France that they had organised themselves and were arming themselves to reach a position where they could force a re-distribution of economic riches, or at least this was their intention.

I should also record the fact that Franco achieved a diplomatic triumph by the arrival in Salamanca of Sir Robert Hodgson on December 16, 1937, as Chief Agent of Great Britain to Nationalist Spain. It was announced in London not long afterwards that Sir Henry Chilton, British Ambassador to Madrid, who had established himself at Saint Jean de Luz, just near the Spanish frontier, shortly after the civil war broke out, would go on leave. He had already passed the age limit. So Britain now had a Chargé d'Affaires in Barcelona—Mr. Leche, who was shortly afterwards promoted to the rank of Minister as a sop to the Republicans—and an 'Agent' in Salamanca.

CHAPTER XXXIX

TERUEL FOR THE REPUBLIC

S AD little Teruel with its some 14,000 inhabitants and five
or six thousand soldiers which had suffered already the
anguish of shelling and bombing for one and a half years, had
also suffered from the 'white terror'. The Left estimated about
2,000 of their people shot, but this probably was an exaggeration. Certainly some hundreds had been shot according to
all the evidence available. One shooting had apparently taken
place in the Plaza de Torico in the presence of hundreds of
people. Women also had been executed. A Republican
Councillor told me that of seven Republican Councillors only
he and another one had escaped death; these two had managed
to cross the lines to Republican Spain.

I went into Teruel twenty-four hours after the first troops
and kept my eyes open for corpses on the outskirts of the town.
I only saw one, a thin little man dressed in black, maybe about
fifty. Some people standing near said that he was 'a Fascist'
who had been shot.

On the whole every effort was made to avoid reprisals. The
population streamed out of the town by back roads while
inside fighting went on around the Civil Governor's office, the
Bank of Spain, the Convent of Santa Clara and the Seminary
where in all maybe some 4,000 people were shut up.

For over two weeks I stayed up there watching the drama
of this little mountain town which had suddenly become a
world name. Each night I motored down to Valencia to
telephone to London. I was in Teruel the day they brought
out the governor of the local gaol and along with him the spy
he used to have among the prisoners—who were nearly all
political and therefore Left-Wingers—and the spy was crying
and the governor dirty and unshorn and indeed a tough-
looking piece of work, bawled him out and called him a coward
for crying. I found a shop where they had seven hundred

346

hams and two soldiers were on guard. The owner was a nice little fellow; we smuggled his youngest son aged fifteen into Valencia in our car as if he were a journalist. I suspect that he had been a member of the Falangist Youth but he seemed a nice kid and we were glad enough to do a turn to the father who gave us a good deal of useful information.

Then there was Christmas Eve and the staff of a brigade asked us to supper in a tumble-down barn with a big wood fire. What nice young fellows they were, few of them over thirty; nearly all university students or clerks who had now been trained as officers and were full of enthusiasm. The troops provided a rondalla, or choir of guitar players and singers in the Aragonese fashion, who played and sang magnificently. There was a young Swiss with them. He had been brought up in Spain where his parents had a business, but he had of course no need to do service. He thought it a good idea to strike a blow for Democracy. Despite good wine and singing I was sad, for these boys were so earnest and out beyond the Pyrenees who cared about them? Paris would be in the whirl of the reveillon, champagne, balloons, concertinas, kisses. London would be asleep preparatory to great trencher feats the next day.

As I lay rolled in blankets in a car before I fell asleep I wondered where I should be next Christmas Eve and whether the world would still be sloughed deep in its egoism, those who have, greedily feeding, indifferent to the hunger and misery around them in the world. Two thousand years, nearly, since Christ was born and even to-day who follows His teachings?

At first there was little danger at Teruel—if one kept away from the strongholds where the Insurgents were holding out —but soon Franco massed for counter-attack. Fiat chasers raked the roads with machine-guns. Huge Caproni and Junkers bombers appeared in the sky with dawn and were still there when dusk fell; as one flight unloaded, another one would be coming up with fresh bombs. The Franco counter-offensive began about December 28 in a furious attempt to drive down at Teruel from the North and West and reach the town.

Report had it, I have no idea with what extent of accuracy, that Germans and Italians were against the idea of counter-attacking but would have preferred to have gone on with steady preparations for the vast spring offensive planned, instead of milling around a town which strategically was not of great value to a weak opponent such as the Republicans were.

But it must be remembered that General Franco had his own problems. He must by this time have had considerable debts not only to Germany and Italy but in London, New York, Paris where he received credits to buy petrol and other vital necessities. As he must continue to be able to rely on credits against the belief that he would eventually win, it was very necessary for him never to admit defeat and during the war on more than one occasion he sacrificed purely military considerations to political ones.

New Year's Eve was grim beyond measure, the Insurgents hurled their best troops forward in a tremendous effort to smash their way through. The Government forces stood their ground like heroes. Despite a gale which in the afternoon developed into a roaring blizzard, the Nationalist aeroplanes bombed and machine-gunned without cessation until all visibility went soon after three o'clock. I stayed up on the Puerto de Escandon, above the town around which shells were falling thickly, for the Insurgents had their artillery so far forward now that they could shell behind the town, and make the trip in and out highly unpleasant. Soldiers flocked past. Assault Guards with sub-machine-guns turned them off the road and ordered them to prepare camps. But actually there was no collapse although it looked like it. These men were mostly from fortification units which had been working on the other side of Teruel and had had to retreat.

Down in the valley, although we only heard of it later, a shell had hit a car containing our 'opposite numbers' on the other side and Mr. Edward Neil of Associated Press, Mr. E. R. Sheepshanks of Reuter's and Mr. Bradish Johnson, Paris correspondent of *Spur*, were killed. Mr. Harold Philby of the *Times* was injured. The Nationalists were so sure that they had the town and indeed the snowstorm gave them a magnificent opportunity to take the Government troops by surprise, but the Republican defence was so good that the attackers desisted when only little over two miles away. That must have been a great disappointment with their 4,000 supporters resisting so near and yet they could give them no help.

The icy gale blew for two days and snow was four feet deep in drifts before the blizzard eased. It was several days later before a passage was cut and normal communications with Valencia restored. Six hundred vehicles had been blocked in one long jam half-way up from the coast. Sefton Delmer and myself went down to Teruel to see how things looked and I, at any rate, had my heart in my mouth. The Nationalists were kind and did not shell or bomb us on our way in although the trail of dead mules on the ice-bound road leading into the town told its own tale. But inside that town there were plenty of things happening. Bombers hovered the whole time and bombed the outskirts steadily. Chaser planes swooped down every once in a while and machine-gunned the streets. Sporadic shells from the Nationalist batteries landed. Around the Seminary and the adjoining Santa Clara Convent there was the devil's own inferno. Green-clad, unshaven carabineros who had been fighting fifteen days without rest, hurled bombs down into the cellars of the buildings, both of which were complete wrecks. Those below fired back with rifles. From a church tower we looked out over the countryside and had the front pointed out to us, very little over two miles away. The Nationalists had taken part of the Muela de Teruel, but their impetus had failed at the critical moment and they did not make even the outskirts of the town. Government planes dashed across and bombed the Insurgent lines and scurried away chased by angry pursuit planes. Puffs of black smoke from the German anti-aircraft batteries filled the air.

It was nearly all up with the defenders. Sr. Prieto had insisted that so far as possible the people within should not be harmed and this had greatly slowed up the attack for it excluded drastic measures with really big mines and meant slowly driving the people back and back from one building to another until they could not move. This had happened now for the Seminary was a heap of ruins and there were about 1,700 in the cellars of the Santa Clara Convent with a

349

wrecked building on top of them and, so I understand, no water. There were about 3,000 also in the Bank of Spain and an adjoining building. On January 3, the Civil Governor's office had fallen and those within had escaped to the Bank of Spain. On January 7, Lieutenant-Colonel Rey d'Harcourt, the senior Nationalist officer, surrendered. All those within were evacuated. Teruel was now completely empty except for the Government soldiers and they resisted there stoutly until February 22.

Rey d'Harcourt was viciously attacked as a coward and traitor by his own side, but it is difficult to see what else he could have done with 2,000 civilians, old people, women and children, under his care and neither food nor water for them. I saw their position just before they emerged and as I pointed out higher up, they were literally buried under ruins with Government soldiers on top of the ruins. They would all have been dead long before February 22. Poor Rey d'Harcourt met a sad end for he was, along with Bishop Anselmo Polanco of Teruel and some sixty other prisoners, shot, apparently by Anarchists, near the French frontier while being brought towards France during the final days of resistance in Catalonia.

For six weeks a fierce battle raged before the Nationalists finally managed to drive the Republicans well back from the mountains to the north of Teruel and so free their communications. The International Brigades who had not previously been used, Sr. Prieto wanted this to be an 'all-Spanish effort', were thrown in including the Washington-Lincolns, the Mackenzie-Papineaus (Canadians) and the Major Attlee Battalion (British). Many British lost their lives up in these hills in fighting which was never properly reported because of the difficulties of reaching the scene and of moving from one sector to another.

One thing worth pointing out, I think, in considering the Battle of Teruel is that the very strict instructions issued by Sr. Prieto to the effect that as far as possible the defenders and the refugees inside the buildings which held out for nearly three weeks should be taken alive and that ruthless measures should not be adopted, made the defence of the town tremendously difficult from a military point of view. This arose from the peculiar situation of Teruel which is perched on a hill. Communication with Valencia is from the southern part of the town over a bridge which passes over a deep and wide gully. The other main road which runs from Saragossa to Cuenca does not actually enter Teruel but runs along the Valley of the Guadalaviar (a contraction of the Arabic for White River; the same river is called the Turia lower down and plays a great part in watering Valencia's fertile *huerta*) which runs along the western edge of the town.

Consequently this road was under complete domination from the people in the Seminary and Santa Clara, even when they were downstairs for the ground shelves down precipitately at that point, and these buildings are on the western edge of the town. They could fire with rifle, machine-gun or trench-mortar on to this road and on to the branch road running down from the Valencia road.

So the troops in Teruel had no road communication whatever either to the North or South or in front of them. If, for instance, Colonel Leopoldo Menendez commanding the troops in the town, wished to send a piece of artillery to a position on the Muela de Teruel, say at two miles from his headquarters, this gun had to travel back to Puebla de Valverde, then across a villainous mountainous road through precipitous country to Vilel, then up the Cuenca-Saragossa road back to the Muela. About seventy miles in all! The same held good for the North. Valdecebro could only be reached by a very bad road from Puebla de Valverde and the northern sectors of the Teruel front such as Alfambra were supplied from a road running inland from Tortosa. It was an incredible situation.

General Hernandez Sarabia, who had his headquarters in a train which was pulled considerately into a tunnel near Mora Station, must have had enormous difficulties in moving supplies and in keeping communication with his men and in organising the defence of the town, which it must be understood had to be organised from the two wings for the people in the town could only move backwards towards Valencia, they could not go forward or sideways. All this could have

351

been avoided, of course, if the Government forces had gone ruthlessly forward and concentrated numerous batteries on the buildings or placed large mines underneath, for the town had a labyrinth of underground passages. Fire or tear gas might also have been employed if really drastic measures had been decided on.

I motored 4,000 miles in one month while covering the Teruel story. I started off with a chauffeur who had been a grocer in Santander and had had his own little shop and delivery van. He was an excellent driver and an intelligent man. He was a Left Republican and he told us the tremendous fight he and his fellow Leftists had had to prevent the military groups from seizing Santander on July 18, 1936.

Later we got another driver, a pale youth of twenty-one who was a most fervent Anarchist. As part of this creed he never drank alcohol, smoked or had carnal relations with women. At least so he said. He certainly never drank or smoked. His spare time he spent in reading involved tracts by Bakhunin and Sorel. He had been some months as an infantryman on the Aragon fronts but had returned to Barcelona because 'the mountains gave him neurasthenia'. Despite his many virtues he knew very little about driving a car and in some of our more exasperated moments we often said coarse things about the apparent effect of abstinence and chastity on this remarkable product of our twentieth century.

One day up at the railway station on Puerto de Escandon I met another curious Anarchist. He was the sole caretaker of this station abandoned since the last train went through to Teruel on July 18, 1936. He was a railwayman from Valencia and his father before him had been a railwayman. He had come to this front in the first hectic days with the Columna de Hierro (Iron Column) of ill fame, a brigade of Anarchists formed in Valencia. Its first members, it is true, had an unpleasant experience; they set off for Teruel with an apparently loyal Major of the Civil Guard and 200 of his men with a view to preventing the Franco supporters who had taken Teruel from advancing towards Valencia. When they got to Puebla de Valverde, about twelve miles from Teruel, and while they were resting, the Major suddenly shouted 'Viva Franco!' and he and his men overpowered the rest. Many escaped but the Civil Guard executed seventy or eighty of those who did not get away.

Nevertheless the Iron Column themselves proved to be a most undesirable lot. They looted from the peasants and murdered the priests in the villages. Once, one of their members who was a professional criminal with a nick-name such as Seven Fingers or something like that, was shot by the police in Valencia. Whereupon the Iron Column left the Teruel front with armoured cars and machine-guns and went to the funeral. The Valencia police and the local Communists also went to the funeral and there was quite a little shooting during which sixty were killed, or so I heard. Most of them were from the Iron Column. Not much was heard of them after that. But this lone Anarchist railwayman up at Puerto de Escandon thought that those were 'the good old days'. He said: 'I left the Army when they commenced to introduce all this nonsense about discipline and saluting officers. That is not revolutionary freedom. Without libertarian ideals one cannot win a revolution.'

Somebody should really write a book about this Anarchist phenomenon in Spain. Its real cause, as I have pointed out before, is illiteracy. The only leader of repute the Anarchists produced during the war, they shot themselves. This was Buenaventura Durutti, a Catalan of Andalusian origin I think. He led the Anarchist forces on the Catalan front in the early days of the war but he became tired of the thefts and murders of some of his men and after various warnings he rounded up twenty or thirty of the worst offenders and executed them, 'pour encourager les autres!' After that he seems to have been much mistrusted by the Anarchist school and when he came to Madrid with a relief column in November 1936 he never moved without a bodyguard of about a dozen who walked with their fingers on the triggers of their sub-machine-guns in the best tradition of Hollywood gangster films. But apparently they were not quite quick enough, for one night on leaving some Anarchist gathering near the University City front he was shot dead. It was announced that his death was caused by a stray bullet from the front but the overwhelming impression was that he had been murdered by his own people.

The Anarchists who took Cabinet posts proved of little talent. Federica Montseny, a plump little bespectacled Barcelona 'intellectual', had a good chance as Minister of Health to do some useful social work but she did not appear to leave any particular repute when she and her fellows left the Cabinet along with Largo Caballero in May 1937.

CHAPTER XL

FRANCO WINS THE BATTLE OF ARAGON

G ENERAL FRANCO gave his opponents no rest after Teruel fell on February 22. By a remarkable 'tour de force' in two weeks he prepared and delivered a series of smashing blows all along the Aragon front from the Pyrenees down to Montalban, that is to say over a front of at least 150 miles, possibly more, for the fronts wound in and out so much. There were three principal attacks launched on March 8, namely, from Huesca, from Saragossa towards Lerida and Barcelona, and from Saragossa down the Ebro Valley towards the sea. This latter was aided by another attack from Montalban down towards Teruel.

The Republicans were completely taken by surprise. Their best troops were completely worn out after the terrible struggle at Teruel. They appeared to have scarcely any artillery or tanks with which to replace the material lost at Teruel. I myself saw units going into action in which not half the men even had rifles, let alone machine-guns or hand-grenades. The only branch which showed some relative strength was in the air where they still seemed to have some planes despite Teruel, but I do not think that this number exceeded 150 bombers and chasers when the Aragon offensive began and they could certainly count on having at least 500 opposing planes to deal with and also an efficient anti-aircraft gun service to face. The German anti-aircraft artillerymen who served in Spain, according to the German official figures since published, numbered 128 officers and 4,717 non-commissioned officers and men. The Italians and the Spaniards of the Nationalist Army also had their A.A. units, so the Republican aviators could rely on meeting trouble almost anywhere they went.

The main offensive was directed towards the Mediterranean and it was a hard proposition to face for here were two purely Italian and two mixed Italo-Spanish Divisions under Italian officers. These forces had apparently not been used in the Teruel fighting, or if they had it had only been on a few occasions. At any rate they appeared on the Aragon front fresh and with, of course, complete armament. They had a good staff, plenty of light tanks which were invaluable once the front had been broken. The Littorio and the 23rd of March Divisions were entirely Italian as far I could learn, while the Black Arrows and the Blue Arrows had some Spanish privates in the ranks. This meant a force of 60,000 fresh, well-equipped shock troops backed by magnificent artillery and aviation services. The commander-in-chief was named General Berti and the second-in-command, General Mancini. General Gamabara was chief of staff.

The blows were dealt with such accuracy and *élan* that within relatively few days the Republicans had lost 1,600 square miles of territory and their front in the whole of Aragon and up in the Pyrenees simply crumpled. Because even where troops resisted bravely they almost invariably had to retreat because they were outflanked by the collapse of neighbouring sectors. The Eastern front collapsed as if made of cardboard and the Eastern Army almost melted away.

The moral effect was terrific coming as it did right on top of the fine fight put up at Teruel which had given the Republicans the feeling that they now had a grand little army. Which was true, in parts. Only three days before the attack was launched Barcelona had been greatly elated by the sinking of the 10,000-ton Franco cruiser *Baleares* by three Republican destroyers, the *Admiral Antequera,* the *Lepanto* and the *Sanchez Barcaiz.*

The Republican fleet under a Basque named Admiral Luis G. de Rubieta had somehow or other managed under cover of night to slip out to sea and catch the Franco fleet sailing along on some mission or other. The Government force was composed of the cruisers *Libertad* and *Mendez Nunes* and the Second Destroyer Flotilla. The Franco ships were the cruisers *Baleares, Canarias* and *Almirante Cervera* and some destroyers, how many I do not know.

Usually it was very hard for the Republican fleet to contact with the Franco ships for the latter had very active and very useful help from their Italian and German allies. The minute Republican ships left their base at Cartagena they would find a German or Italian destroyer cruising along in their wake, observing their movements and reporting them. And there was nothing they could do about it. Once when the Franco ships were taking an active part in the capture of Malaga the Republican fleet went out to meet them. Don Bruno Alonso, Political Commissioner to the Fleet, said afterwards in a statement to the Press that they saw several cruisers which seemed to be of the same type as the Franco vessels they were looking for. The ships had no colours flying. For several hours they went after them in a mad chase until suddenly the others slackened speed and as they came into full view hauled up their colours. They were Italian naval units.

But on this occasion the Republicans had luck on their side and at 12.45 a.m. on Sunday, March 6, the Franco cruisers suddenly found themselves in the unhappy position of being completely broadside on to three Republican destroyers, which immediately let loose their torpedoes and swung away untouched by the shells from the Franco cruisers. The *Baleares* was hit amidships and there was a great explosion. The Republicans, satisfied with their coup, headed back to Cartagena.

For some reason which I have never seen explained anywhere the other Franco ships did not go to the rescue of their shipmates. I only have the Republican version, for if any explanation of how the battle was fought has been published by the Nationalists, I have not seen it. But the Republicans definitely said that the *Baleares* was accompanied by the *Almirante Cervera* and the *Canarias*. It seems unlikely that the *Baleares* would have been sailing between the Island of Majorca and the East coast of Spain quite alone. Possibly the other Nationalist ships imagined that they were badly outnumbered and disappeared at full speed in one direction while the Republicans were steaming away in the opposite direction.

The British acted the part of good Samaritans and the destroyers H.M.S. *Kempenfeldt*, under Captain R. R. McGrigor and H.M.S. *Boreas*, under Commander J. W. M. Eaton, which were on non-intervention patrol duty, came to the spot and picked up some 400 men of the crew of 1,100 which was aboard the *Baleares*, according to an Insurgent statement. They reported the ship ablaze and in a sinking condition. This was at 4.30 a.m. Apparently they went away to transfer the men to the *Canarias* which was returning to the scene. While they were transferring the men, a good many of whom were injured, Republican bombers came over and let loose their cargoes. No great damage seems to have been done, but Able-Seaman G. G. Long of the *Boreas* was killed and four British naval ratings were injured.

Nobody actually seems to have seen the *Baleares* sink. The Republican planes looked for it far and wide all during the day. The Republicans thought that they had hit the *Canarias*. When the planes next day saw the *Canarias* they assumed that she must be in a bad way and that she was being abandoned. They took pictures which were flown to Barcelona and shown to the Press by Sr. Prieto himself, who was so pleased that he dropped his usual attitude of hostility towards journalists and offered us champagne. Naturally I and other people said that the ship in question did not seem to have much wrong with it. Vice-Admiral Buiza, chief of Prieto's naval staff, assured me that it was probably badly holed amidships and that the cloud of smoke coming out of the funnels was from an internal fire and not from the furnaces. So I and the rest of the Press wasted a great deal of time and money getting pictures to London which really only showed the *Canarias* taking survivors aboard from British destroyers.

This left the Government with the cruisers *Cervantes* and *Mendez Nunes*, twelve destroyers, six torpedo boats and five submarines.

The Nationalists had the cruisers *Canarias*, *Almirante Cervera* and *Navarra* (this latter was being built when the war commenced and was completed with German technical aid), two destroyers, five torpedo boats, four submarines. Where these submarines came from was not stated. They had none when war started.

Nor was the identity of the destroyers very clear. Later, works on naval strengths announced that they were Italian destroyers which had been sold to General Franco. I wonder what would have happened if Soviet Russia had 'sold' some naval units to the Republicans; there would have been a fine fuss. But nobody, except the Spanish Republicans, seemed to find it abnormal that Italy should supply Franco with destroyers. Since then, of course, both Germans and Italians have publicly praised the work done by their naval units, including submarines, in the active part of the Spanish War.

The sickeningly unfair part about it all was that the Government if it had only to face General Franco alone could easily have dealt with his fleet and have put it out of action for the Republicans were in great preponderance. In this way the Republic could have permitted its vessels to come and go unmolested to Russia for supplies and it could have blockaded Majorca and Ibiza and have caused them to surrender. The very active intervention of the German and Italian naval units throughout the war made it impossible for the Republicans to move in the Mediterranean. The Republicans were hemmed in on every side.

The Nationalists had lost the *España*, sunk by a mine in April 1937 and one or two smaller craft sunk. The Government lost the battleship *Jaime I* by an internal explosion in Cartagena Harbour, June 1937, the cruiser *Libertad* damaged by a torpedo and out of action for some time, destroyers *Ciscar* and *Fernandez* sunk in the North and submarines C 3 and B 6 sunk.

Anyway we soon had more than enough to keep us busy without bothering about the Spanish Navy. Not only had we the ticklish job of trying to find out where the front was; if there was any. But to add to our troubles the Nationalists gave us a dose of the tactics suggested by General Douhet, an Italian General now dead, who had the notion that wars could be won in future by tremendous aerial bombardments which would paralyse the enemy rearguard.

Barcelona had already had a taste of heavy bombing of the centre of the town for about 100 people were killed on January 25, 1938, and five days later on January 30 the sabbath calm of Barcelona was disturbed by a vicious attack by Italian squadrons from Majorca which killed 350, including eighty children in a building used for infant welfare purposes. On January 25, bombs hit the gaol, full of Nationalist prisoners.

On Wednesday night, March 16, the Italians began the 'Douhet test'. The first raid came about 10 p.m. From then onwards at roughly three-hour intervals we were raided seventeen times until the last raid took place at three o'clock in the afternoon of Friday, March 18.

The death roll was about 1,300 dead and something over 2,000 injured, as far as I could find out.

I did not find it so trying as many experiences at the front, but I think this was due to the fact that there was such a tremendous amount of work involved in getting the news and dispatching it that one had hardly time to be afraid. Still, I was more than thankful when it ended. It was a ghastly and piteous thing to see. One house had bits of human flesh plastered on its façade; in one street a bomb did such thorough work that I saw the Red Cross men scraping up what was left of human bodies with newspapers. As for the morgue, that is better left to the imagination.

I was only three hundred yards away when the bomb fell which tore down four great buildings in a couple of seconds and which we all believed was some kind of marvellous new weapon of death. Actually it was proved afterwards that what happened was that a bomb of 100 pounds weight dropped on top of a motor-lorry loaded with two tons of T.N.T. destined for a munitions factory. So it was not surprising that 'things happened'. But it really was ghastly. That one raid alone killed, I believe, over 400 people. It took place just at two o'clock when all the offices were closing for lunch and the streets were crowded with people going home.

The people of the town were terrified and tens of thousands went out at night to sleep on the hills. But I do not think there was any real panic or that the experiment came near to breaking their nerves. The resentment and hatred born of such a cruel attack did much to offset the effect of terror. One of the lighter sides of the whole affair was when in the middle of a raid an arms' salesman who was down in Barcelona trying to sell, I think it was aeroplane parts, to the Government, came up to me and swore violently 'that he would never sell a single arm in his life if he ever came out of this experience alive'.

On the Friday morning the Government instead of relying on A.A. guns of which it only had about a score or thirty where it needed some hundreds for adequate protection, brought back some squadrons of chasers from the front and commenced to keep a permanent patrol in the air. This soon discouraged the attackers but in any case the reaction abroad was so strong that it would hardly have been good policy for the attacks to have been continued by General Franco.

I think that the experiment showed that even when used by an immensely strong opponent with complete domination of the air against a very weak opponent, as was the case in this 'Douhet test', it still did not give good results. Naturally, it can be argued that it was a very small-scale test. The bombers did not usually number more than nine, although I think they once or twice had fifteen. But they had on the other hand no intense anti-aircraft fire to meet and they could come into the town from the sea without any lengthy warning being possible. Even if much greater numbers of bombers were used in a modern war between Great Powers, the defences would nevertheless be on a much greater scale.

Nor do I think it would be easy to find again such favourable psychological conditions for a 'Douhet test'. These people knew that practically the hand of every nation, except distant Russia and in a platonic rather than practical sense Mexico, was against them. The front had crumbled completely and General Franco's troops were advancing as much as ten to twelve miles in one day. There were not sufficient arms to meet this attack. The Government was in part in favour of peace negotiations. The mass of the people were definitely undernourished and not obtaining sufficient food. That they did not panic seems to me a tremendous tribute to their belief in the righteousness of their cause. They had every reason to despair but they refused to yield and in the Europe of 1938 it was pleasant indeed to meet courage and conviction allied with democratic principles.

The same night that the series of raids began I saw a procession of some thousands trudging on foot along the

Paseo de Gracia. The people massed up near the Presidential Palace at Pedralbes where President Azaña was presiding over a Cabinet Meeting. The word had gone around that the Republicans were proposing an armistice. Apparently, the idea was that a proposal should be made, using the British or French as intermediaries, that the Government surrender and that Franco also resign and that a neutral Cabinet presided over by Professor Besteiro or some such personage should take control of Spain. That, at least, was as near as I could find out the idea behind this move of the Republicans.

The Communist and various other groups organised the demonstration to show their determination to go on with the war. The Anarchists and some Socialists took part, although next day the Anarchist Press got tangled up in knots in complicated efforts to explain that while it approved of the end sought for by the demonstration it must be understood that it could not possibly have given official approval to a move sponsored by Communists. Rumour had it, and this I cannot confirm, that a Republican Minister gazed out on the silent mass of people outside the Palace gates and at last said with relief: 'Thank goodness, here come the Shock Police!' But the Shock Policemen also formed part of the demonstration! Finally, and apparently after acrimonious discussion, it was agreed that the war should go on and that Dr. Negrin should receive a delegation of the demonstrators and reassure them to this effect.

This reaching for the moon, or pathetic hopes of an armistice which never had the slightest chance of becoming reality from the hour the conflict started until the end, was endemic with some of the Republicans. As I have pointed out, they had not the slightest grasp of the realities in modern Europe. They could surrender, which meant death for thousands, prison for tens of thousands and the sponging of hopes for a progressive and democratic Spain for years and perhaps for generations. But there was no other alternative.

I am afraid Professor Besteiro when in his stately and dignified manner he represented the Republic at the Coronation of George VI also built up hopes in Britain of the possibility of an armistice. Mr. Eden received him. Now Mr. Eden should have known better than to believe that an armistice was possible in Spain, but it is not unlikely that Don Julian Besteiro told him things that he, Mr. Eden, wished to hear. Sr. Besteiro also saw M. Blum. Possibly he also told M. Blum things which that gentleman liked. I am afraid that Professor Besteiro with the greatest sincerity in the world and the best of good wishes, misled both these statesmen. Frankly I do not think Besteiro understood either the Fascist position or the situation of the Republic. A good deal is spoken of Señor Besteiro's faith in Madrid and how he stayed on there with the people of the former capital. This reflects great credit on him but I do think it should be made quite clear that this did not necessarily mean that Sr. Besteiro was in close and intimate touch with the mass of the people in Madrid. In the most critical days of Madrid I never saw or heard of Señor Besteiro taking any prominent part in any effort to aid or encourage the Madrid people. I never heard of him visiting those who had lost their homes and their parents and friends in air raids, nor addressing gatherings, nor helping in hospital work or relief work. He may have done it. But I lived through all the tense days of Madrid's agony and I never saw or heard of much activity by Sr. Besteiro. Later, Professor Besteiro became chairman of a Junta for the Restoration of Madrid which directed the cleaning up of débris caused by the bombardments and linked this with plans for a complete changing of the face of Madrid after the war. But I never heard of him being very active in this connection and indeed this planning anew of Madrid seemed somewhat premature. No, Professor Besteiro seemed to me to be one more example of so many in contemporary Europe of how it is possible to be superlatively honest, devoted to one's country, highly cultured, and yet to live completely outside the soul of one's nation. Europe is moving with devastating swiftness to new shapes and so many people are as bits of flotsam in the backwaters spinning idly in the backwash of the current.

The people of Spain by instinct felt the situation more accurately than did many of their leaders. So the armistice idea was shelved, for the time being.

Back came the lines from positions which had been within sight of Saragossa, which had nearly surrounded Huesca, which had been near Jaca. In the Pyrenees and in all Northern Aragon, communications are few and far between and the capture of one crossroads may mean the key to hundreds of square miles. Many troops and civilian refugees were cut off and made their way over the snow-clad mountains into France, suffering terribly from cold and exposure. At least 10,000 crossed that way and one division, the 43rd, under Colonel Beltran, made something of a name for itself by staying for some weeks in the mountains defying attacking parties until their food and munitions ran out and they had to retreat into France. It said a great deal for the tenacity of the average soldier that when 4,000 who escaped to France were questioned individually by the French authorities as to which side they wished to return to, only 168 volunteered to go to General Franco.

Those days were horrible. Down the roads came streams of refugees, their belongings piled high on mule-carts. Then would come the Nationalist planes and bomb and machine-gun, leaving dead peasants and mules in pools of blood. I watched the fight for Lerida which lasted a week thanks to the really plucky fight put up by one of the more picturesque figures of the Republican Army, Valentin Gonzalez, better known as 'El Campesino'.

He was a swarthy, powerfully built, olive-complexioned man from Estremadura, aged about 40. He was of peasant origin but actually I think he had served several years in the Navy and had been trade union organiser and agitator. He had the strangely magnetic eyes of a madman. He first distinguished himself at Guadalajara. He was a Communist. I visited the Shock Division he commanded while it was at rest at Alcalá de Henares in December 1937 and his men were really good. Training was excellent, discipline good, quarters clean. I had the impression that possibly more than to 'Campesino' this was due to his second-in-command, a young university student of about 26 named Medina, who was a dynamic youth and was learning to be a good soldier.

'Campesino' and his staff were the last to leave Teruel. In fact the Franco forces surrounded the town and could never explain how he got away. Apparently he and his officers left the town by dark and crawled through the enemy lines to safety.

He and his men had been sent back to Madrid for rest and reorganisation after that gruelling fight, which only ended on February 22. On March 26 they were on the Catalan front and were thrown in to try to save Lerida and for one week they fought a really gallant fight. There were no fortifications outside the town; a key position like this had been left without even a trench in front of it. The only saving feature was that the bridge over the River Cinca at Fraga, noted for its figs and about eight miles west of Lerida, was blown up by the retreating Republicans and dams were opened up in the Pyrenees which made it difficult for the Nationalists to press forward; in fact they got half an army corps across and then could not keep them supplied for several days until a pontoon bridge was installed. I saw 'Campesino' one morning in his headquarters in the cellar of a bank, just alongside the bridge leading to Barcelona. He said that he could hold on 'if he received artillery and tanks'. He did not. He was nearly killed when a Nationalist plane dropped a bomb on the bridge, which was mined. Not only did the heavy iron bridge fly through the air but the explosion caused the bank building which was just alongside the bridge to collapse on top of 'Campesino' and his staff. He was not badly hurt but he never shone much after that incident and indeed I think that he was nothing more than a good guerrilla leader but without the capacity to handle any large unit of men. Once they took away his second-in-command, Medina, and gave him a division of his own, Campesino was lost. Towards the end of the war he was living in retirement without any command. Some people said that he had consumption. I heard just before the war ended that he was in Madrid but I never heard what happened to him.

Lerida fell on April 3 but the hard fight there was of value. It gave the Government time to reorganise. As I was coming back from Lerida on the last day I picked up an engine-driver who had come up to drive away any locomotives left but had found that they had all gone. He was a stolid veteran of about sixty. I asked him what his politics were. He said in slow measured tones: 'I have no politics. I know nothing about them. But what I cannot understand is why people who themselves had so much in life should have risen against we who had so little.' Never, I think, have I heard the Spanish case presented so clearly and so accurately.

April 3 was indeed a black day because Gandesa fell also, and this small town was not only an important strategic point but the advance there had been of such a fashion that the International Brigades had been struck a terrible blow. Three hundred of the Americans of the Lincoln-Washington Battalion were killed or taken prisoner and 125 Britons of the Major Attlee Battalion were taken prisoner and many killed and injured. The Germans likewise suffered severely.

This particular incident was a very bad example of the lack of competent staff officers to co-ordinate the various forces and even allowing for the work which pressed on the War Ministry at the time I still think that General Rojo and his assistants incurred rather heavy responsibility for what happened.

I and Dick Mowrer, of the *Chicago Daily News*, had been over this front only a few hours before Italian forces led by light tanks made a swift movement up towards Gandesa cutting off some eight or ten thousand men. About two miles west of Gandesa the road forked. One road went on to Alcañiz and the other turned right going to a place called Maella and, I think, finally to Caspe. Now at dusk on the night of April 2 the Italians managed to make a cross-country attack and reach the Alcañiz-Gandesa road not far from the cross-roads I have mentioned. Alcañiz had been lost some days before but there were still Republican troops up in that direction. These were now cut off from Gandesa and had to retire towards Tortosa, regaining the Alcañiz-Tortosa road which runs, lower down, along the right bank of the River Ebro.

Now up on the road towards Caspe were about 10,000 men including a large part of the International Brigade. They had fought sturdily and now held at a steep ridge. We went up and saw their position was good. As we came back we gave a lift to two refugee women and several children, plus a goat which the women assured us was house-broken when Dick rather raised his eyebrows at the idea of a goat coming aboard his Ford. The women had walked all the way from Belchite. That town had been in Franco hands until September 1937 when it was recaptured by the Republicans and these two women, they were sisters, had had their heads shaved for they were supposed to be Socialists. Their brother was shot. Now as Belchite had again fallen to Franco they had slipped away, anxious to escape coming again under Franco rule.

As we motored down beyond Gandesa we met the Lincoln-Washingtons and I think some of the Major Attlee Battalion but I am not quite sure, as we were in a hurry to get back to Barcelona to file our stories and we drove past quickly. They were walking up to the front. They were dead beat and walking in two long files one on each side of the road carrying their equipment, hand luggage, and rifles. It was a tremendously impressive picture. Hardly looking up, they trudged steadily. A few glanced enviously at us. One could feel that they were saying: 'How nice to be a reporter and slip off back to Barcelona every night and have a bath and eat decent food and see women.' But mostly they were not looking up at all. Granted that some of them were adventurers, as a whole they were a good lot of boys. Here they were going steadily up into battle, to a front which hardly existed, with no staff to direct operations. Some had come from the ends of the earth to fight for something they thought was a good thing. As I have stated above, three hundred of these Americans were killed or wounded or made prisoners.

They had simply trudged along the road, past the cross-roads and had seen a number of light tanks stationed on one side of the road ahead. The commander, I think it was Bob Merriman, an American, sent one of his men up to ask the officer of the tanks to tell them where headquarters was. The answer was a hail of lead from the machine-guns on the tanks. They had walked right into the enemy vanguard. Most of them were captured before they even knew what had happened.

The men up the road to Caspe had no escape except across country and the confusion was tremendous because the Italians came up the road from Gandesa behind them so that they could not take either the road going back to Mora de Ebro or the road from Gandesa to Tortosa. Some hundreds of them got across country to the Ebro. But there all the bridges had been blown up and even most of the boats on the right bank burned. So for those who could not swim, the swift-running and flooded river had no escape. Many were drowned, as exhausted and in some cases wounded they tried to swim the Ebro. Others hid for several weeks, thanks to the help of friendly peasants and finally got down to the river's edge and got across. Colonel Kopic, Commander of the XVth Brigade, escaped along roads already occupied by the enemy, in an armoured car.

One of the difficulties of the Republicans was, of course, that they had no observation aeroplanes with wireless senders and with receiving stations near the front to get the reports. They simply lacked the equipment for this kind of thing. The Franco forces had excellent German observation air services with good photographers and they could easily observe all Republican movements.

But in this case the complete lack of any kind of elemental staff work to prevent the XVth Brigade and other forces from digging themselves in along the Caspe road when they were in imminent danger of being completely isolated was bad and reflected little credit on the Central General Staff under General Rojo.

On April 5, new hope came to the Army with the news that Indalecio Prieto had resigned. For some weeks his leadership at the War Ministry had not been of an inspiring character. There was a slight re-shuffle of the Cabinet with Negrin taking National Defence as well as premiership. The labour unions were again represented, this time the Anarchists by a man called Blanco and the Socialists by Gonzalez Peña. the trade union leader who found himself at the head of the movement of 1934 in Oviedo. There were eleven members in the new Cabinet, namely: Four Republicans, three Socialists, one Communist, one Catalan, one Basque, one Anarchist.

The Army appeared to take a fresh lease of life. The trucks along the road flew Republican flags. The troops began to hold here and there. The Franco troops also were apparently beginning to feel the strain of a month of progress. Balaguer, just north of Lerida, went on April 6 and that was disastrous because the cable lines bringing the chief electric current supplies for the Catalan industrial zones and especially Barcelona came down through here from Tremp, Camarasa and Capdella. In any case, however, these places themselves were soon taken. Tremp was captured on April 8. That left Catalonia without the current necessary for lighting, train services, munition works. The old small steam-generating plants had to be put into work again. There were cable lines running to Andorra and the French frontier where supplies were available—but no one wished to supply current to Spanish Republicans.

CHAPTER XLI

ENRIQUE LISTER

A PRIL 8 was a pleasant spring day, sunny and warm. Dick Mowrer and I were sitting on the floor of a barn in a village just near Cherta on the road from Alcañiz to Tortosa. Here for four days Lister and his men had been holding the Italians who were fighting furiously to break down to the coast and to cut Republican Spain into two parts.

I was eating a piece of very nicely braised meat and drinking good local red wine and reflecting over many things while a few yards away Lister was sitting at a telephone talking to Tagueña, one of his young officers, and who had charge of one sector of the defence at Cherta. In the first place I wondered where a quarryman like Lister ever learned to appreciate the importance of good food. He had a cook who had been with Wagon-Lits restaurant cars before the war and in the various times in various retreats in which I managed to pick up a meal at Lister's headquarters I do not think I ever had a bad one.

Then I looked at Lister sitting at a field telephone with his heavy face impassible, his voice, ponderous, monotonous: 'Yes, but where are they attacking? No, get your map! Got it? Now where are your tanks? All right, then if you move your tanks along the road a few hundred yards you'll catch them neatly. Never mind if there are planes overhead, follow that map! Do you see the wood on the right of the road at kilometre 17? Send your tanks there now. Shoot yourself? Don't talk nonsense. Get the tanks going. I'll be up soon.'

Tagueña, whom I had seen once or twice, was a big young man with glasses and a very intellectual appearance. He had been a leading figure in the Spanish University Students' Union. Now with half a division he was doing most of the work in holding up the crack Littorio Legionaries commanded by skilled professional officers. His men had scarcely slept in three weeks.

I wondered though why a quarryman should be giving orders to a youth of the middle class with a university education. Apart from an elementary school education and self-acquired knowledge and the year he spent in Russia, Lister had never had time to get much learning. Yet here he was handling the remains of an army corps with coolness and considerable skill. There was a fat and pudgy Russian officer there to advise him. But he was sitting talking to a big buxom blonde girl who was his secretary. All the Russian officers had Russian women as secretaries, who went everywhere with them, and I dare say that was wise. A good deal of Franco's information came from women who got hold of Republican officers, or at least so I was told. But I do not think the Russian really helped Lister very much, except to keep him from making any too obvious military error.

That Lister had natural talent was obvious. Despite his lack of education he naturally imposed himself. At table he could lead the conversation, he could impart such information as we reporters could reasonably have but without giving away things which might have been of value to the enemy.

He had got his chance thanks to Communism, thanks to his training in the Communist Party. Now I wanted to know what was wrong with Democracy that we too could not turn out men like this. At home we hear a great deal of Democracy, we frequently assert that we prize it more than life. Yet today we have few leaders of merit despite our endless millions spent on education, our great schools and colleges, our universities. Why is not Democracy turning out leaders to help us face our troubles? Why is it that only Communism has concrete programmes, training to lead? What have we done with Democracy?

All these questions and many more ran through my mind as I sat on the floor of the barn. I found no answer; I have still no answer. Every day our country, our Empire, swings to and fro on its course, practically without helmsman, swung hither and thither by the waves instead of forging through them.

When an air raid was over we went back to Tortosa, or in the words of Willie Forrest of the *News Chronicle*, 'the town that was Tortosa'. Tortosa had been a deserted town for three weeks now. After a few raids which killed forty or fifty each time, the inhabitants left. Now two or three times each day the Italians came from Majorca and bombed the town heavily, a fact which merely inconvenienced the few soldiers in the town and any passing transport.

When we crossed the big iron road bridge in the morning there had been a very smart little sentry on duty. He stood alertly at his post in a new uniform. He was cleanly shaven. I said to Dick how neat he looked. When we came back the Capronis were just going away. On the bridge was just a mangled red heap. Somewhere there was, I suppose, a mother wondering where that boy was and not guessing that he looked like nothing human any more. But the bridge was not damaged. It would have needed very big three- or four-hundred pound bombs to wreck a bridge like that. They only did it just before the Italians finally outflanked Cherta, then their bombers came over, about twenty of them, and chain-bombed the bridge, that is to say, coming over three at a time. It took them several hours before they knocked it out. Even then they did not hit the old road bridge. The railway bridge had been hit several weeks before and partially damaged.

All the time Tortosa was being bombed to pieces there was very heavy traffic through the town. This was due partly to military transport, partly to the rush of French motor trucks which were going down to Valencia in hundreds to pick up loads of oranges. They came in with good francs, changed them into Republican pesetas at fancy figures, bought oranges at more or less usual peseta prices with these pesetas and then sold the oranges in France at a very handsome profit indeed.

On April 15, Franco took Vinaroz and the road to Valencia was cut and Republican Spain divided into two. The advance in Catalonia had roughly ended against the natural boundaries formed by the Rivers Ebro and Cinca and the line ran up to the French frontier west of Seo de Urgel. The attack was now continued along the coast southwards towards Castellon de la Plana and Catalonia was left in peace.

About this time the French suddenly decided to open the frontier and to allow Russian, and I think some American, material through in transit. I do not think the French themselves supplied anything. But it was all the Republicans needed. They could get arms from Russia, provided they could be consigned to France and then transported overland.

The gesture, was, of course, done with dramatic tardiness. With the rapid-fire artillery, anti-tank guns, tanks, machine-guns, rifles, that now poured in for the few all too brief weeks before some time in June the frontier was again hermetically sealed, in Republican Spain six weeks earlier, the sweeping March break-through by General Franco would never have occurred. Or at least only in much smaller proportions. A ridiculously small number of anti-tank guns could have held up those Franco tanks which raced here and there with complete impunity because there was no artillery or anti-tank artillery to stop them.

France gave this very grudging and tardy, indirect aid when the already weak Republic was cut into two parts and Catalonia had lost its electric power. One could hardly blame the Spaniards for feeling bitter.

CHAPTER XLII

ON VALENCIA, JOURNALISM AND OTHER MATTERS

GENERAL FRANCO continued his push southwards from the Tortosa area during May, June and July of 1937 but without great success.

The district known as the Maestrazgo which stretches inland for at least fifty or sixty miles between Tortosa and Castellon, is a dreary mountainous region full of legends of the Cid and a very backward peasantry, where there are any inhabitants at all. One can drive twenty miles without passing a village or even a hamlet in this desolate area.

A Madrid journalist named Alardo Prats wrote an interesting book in 1932 in which he described an annual festival in this region where the 'devil was cast out of bodies'. It was more pagan than Catholic, according to him, although a shrine was there. All kinds of sick people were taken there and the 'casting out of the devil', according to Prats, took place in a dark cave where old women, who were the local wise-women and midwives of the region, took the victims in hand and gave them a very thorough body massage, driving the patient into a state of excitement which was much more fleshly than spiritual.

In this region the Government forces were under Colonel Leopoldo Menendez, a career officer and a brother of Captain Arturo Menendez, who was police chief in 1933 when the Casas Viejas incident took place and who was caught by the Nationalists in Saragossa when the Franco revolt occurred. They shot him. Colonel Menendez had been in charge of the troops in Teruel and had made a good show there.

But the real reason for the slow progress was the fact that the Government had some supplies, not much but still enough to enable the forces to stand wherever they found a good position. Then the Franco mobile forces had to find a way to pass this obstacle and so wasted much time. So that although Franco took Vinaroz on April 15, he did not take Castellon until June 16, that is to say, it had cost him two months of hard fighting to advance sixty miles along the coast and to clear some hundreds of square miles of rugged hinterland which were of no particular value to anyone. Castellon was necessary because so far General Franco had no harbour of any importance on the North-West Mediterranean and he needed the Port (known as the Grao) of Castellon, several miles from the town.

I flew to Valencia in July to cover a fierce attempt by the Nationalists to break down towards Valencia from Teruel. The Government forces along the coast had fought them to a standstill at about twelve miles from Sagunto. Batter away as they would it was impossible to break through here without heavy loss because the great Sierra de Espadan comes nearly to the sea and the Government forces were in well fortified positions between Nules and Sagunto. This coast position was held by one of those incredibly young Government officers. His name is Duran. He comes of a prosperous middle class family, is a musician and a composer and was engaged in the cinema industry in quite a good position before the war. In this July of 1938, he was, I think he told me, just thirty. He was one of the very few lucky ones to escape from the Centre Zone after Madrid surrendered and he managed to reach London.

It was a great tribute to this defence that General Franco had to launch a new attack on Valencia from the Teruel area which was over fifty miles from Sagunto in the hopes of being able to push right down the Teruel-Sagunto road and so out-flanking and inutilising the strong coast defences. This attack from the Teruel area began July 15 and lasted with great intensity until about July 23.

As far as war reporting goes, the covering of this attack was about the most pleasant of any I had to do during the Spanish War. We usually got back from the front about three o'clock in the afternoon. We ate, wrote our dispatches and sent them off by radiogram to London and then we would pile into the station wagon which the foreign correspondents had at their service and off we would go to swim at Perello. This meant a

375

lovely ride through the Valencian 'huerta', which is much like a richer and more colourful Dutch landscape with pleasant windmills here and there to add to the illusion already fostered by the water-ways for irrigation.

Out at Perello, where the British Consul, Mr. W. J. Sullivan, and the American Vice-Consul, Mr. Woodruff Wallner, had their homes, we would go to the home of the latter. We would swim in the choppy, refreshing Mediterranean, lie in the sun, then go back to the house and have a warm shower and then a whisky. It seemed unbelievable as one floated peacefully on one's back in the sea and looked up at the blue Mediterranean sky, to think that only a few hours before one had been lying in a ditch with bombs crashing not far away and the stink of dead bodies and dead mules everywhere.

In the old days the lot of a foreign correspondent was a good deal different from present conditions. He tended to follow the army of the side he was reporting and to send back telegrams through military channels. Often he was himself a military expert. In the Spanish War, at any rate, conditions were very different. Everything depended on speed. One raced out by car in the early morning, hastily gathered a rough outline of the situation at the front, and then raced back to a large town again in order to write a dispatch and either telephone it or telegraph it to London. None of us ever lived out with the armies and few of us were, I think it is correct to say, military experts. Brief, staccato messages to-day tend to replace long and more leisurely dispatches explaining at length principles of strategy, although of course these still have their place in some newspapers but rather as an occasional retrospective summing-up of some military operation than as a regular daily feature.

I remember one evening several of us lay on the warm sand at Perello after a hard day at the front and discussed the degree of fear we felt when in the actual scene of operations. We very rarely, of course, went to the front lines. Our dangers came from long-distance shelling and from the constant bombing and machine-gunning of the roads behind the lines. The risk was actually not very great. I had no hesitation in saying that I always felt highly nervous when getting near the front.

Nor had I any shame in confessing that when I lay in some field and watched bombers coming towards the point where I was lying and heard the 'whur-whur-whur' as the bombs came speeding down, was I ever anything but thoroughly frightened. Even more terrifying, I think, is being machine-gunned. You know that a bomb must practically fall on top of you in an open field in order to hurt you. But it is only rarely that any shelter against machine-gunning can be found when one dives haphazard from a car with the planes coming over and minutes or even seconds in which to throw oneself into the best shelter available.

To find an ideal correspondent for jobs such as Spain is a hard task for any paper. On the one hand someone with a constitution like an ox might be suggested in order to stand the physical exertions involved. But then again people with fine muscles and tremendous resistance do not always have the quick emotional reflexes that a modern journalist must have. Unless he has an active mind constantly at work, a good imagination in order to think out the possibilities arising from any sudden change in events, a sense of the dramatic so that he reacts emotionally to big happenings and can write of them graphically, he will not be suitable.

I found, for instance, that when I was feeling physically very fit I was more nervous at the front than if I was tired. That seems the wrong way round, but I know that it was so. Of course, there has to be a limit. If one got really run-down then one was no use. It seemed to me that occasional indulgence in the way of wine and women tended to counter-balance the daily emotions of fear and anxiety in the case of the average kind of man. Some people can stand a long period of combined mental strain and abstinence. But others crack if they have no relief.

The drive from Teruel down to Valencia undertaken on July 15 was one of the bad mistakes of General Franco and he paid dearly for it. The Government estimated that he had 20,000 casualties in eight days. That is probably an exaggeration. but he probably had 15,000 which was a lot for the Spanish War. This drive was mainly in the hands of Italians. The Littorio, the 23rd of March and the Blue Arrows were among the Italian forces there. The Blue Arrow Division consisted of Spaniards and Italians under Italian officers. Then they had a most fearsome array of artillery; Government officers estimated about 600 pieces of the Italian and German artillery and about 400 German and Italian aeroplanes. The beginning was not unlike Guadalajara. The weight of some seventy or eighty thousand crack troops crashing down armed with magnificent equipment was too much for the thinly-held Government lines. They crumbled away. The Nationalists pincered Sarrion and took the town on July 15.

Mora de Rubielos out on the right flank of the Republican lines was taken, but not before a very gallant force of Carabineros who had been holding out against tremendous odds for weeks there managed to escape when they were almost surrounded. The Insurgents broke down the left flank over in the Sierra de Toro. This was very brilliant work on the part of the Nationalists because that is wicked country. They operated with small groups of men who specialised in cutting off Government posts, for in that country there were no lines, just strong posts here and there. They were possibly helped by the fact that the militia in that district consisted in part of the remains of the old 'Iron Column' which I referred to earlier.

I went more or less over the Government front line on July 16 and things looked terrible. Everyone was falling back rapidly. The aerial bombardment was simply terrific. Not only at the actual front, but villages twenty miles from the lines had been knocked half into ruins so that the inhabitants had fled and they were completely deserted. It was one of the most savage and ruthless bombings I have known and what the Nationalists hoped to gain by it I do not know. That is unless they thought that there were reserves in these far-back villages. Picturesque old Segorbe was in a terrible mess with one of the buildings of the main street in flames. Despite this fact a group of girls were collecting scrap iron and loading it on to motor-lorries in order to take to Valencia to convert into war material. The women really were fine on many occasions such as this. Their courage and calm in the face of great danger was unbelievable.

The only comforting sight was that of a line of rather useful looking fortifications running from in front of Viver right across to the Sierra Espadan and which more or less blocked the Insurgent path.

I do not know who designed those fortifications but what a good job they were there. They enfiladed every useful road or track along which the Nationalists could press. They had real dug-outs, made by architects who evidently knew the kind of dug-out needed to stand 1,000-lb. bombs.

By July 18, those lines were manned. The Italians and Spaniards continued their impetuous rush apparently convinced that they had the militiamen 'on the run'. What a mistake they made! As they rushed ahead they were literally mown down. It was sheer slaughter for a war where the relative small numbers engaged naturally kept down the casualty figures. The Nationalists were, of course, prepared for some resistance. They brought up their guns and then they pounded those fortifications with World-War intensity. I do not know how many shells a minute fell. All I know is that we would sit on a hill-top for hours and watch the endless cloud of smoke as a wave of shells broke all along the line which was not much over twenty miles long. Then the bombers would come and unload and go back for more and return. It seemed unbelievable that anyone could live any more on those ridges. Yet every time this infernal barrage stopped and the Nationalists charged furiously towards them, the machine-guns rattled away furiously from these battered ruins. Then would come more hours of strafing, more bombing. The bombers could come as low as they liked, the Government had no anti-aircraft guns at all on that sector. And as the bombers came protected by enormous numbers of chaser planes, sometimes there would be nearly one hundred machines in the air at once, there was, of course, no danger of their being attacked by the handful of Republican chasers which existed on this front.

By July 23 the defenders were still holding bravely and the attackers were really fought to a standstill. Good fortifications plus some machine-guns had decisively stopped a magnificently equipped force which had a superiority of at least six or eight to one in artillery and aviation and more than that in tanks, machine-guns, anti-aircraft guns and such accessories to the fight.

If only the Government had had a really good General he would almost certainly have tried to get down some more artillery and other equipment from Barcelona and have hoped that the Italians and Spaniards would attack again.

But unfortunately the Republicans did quite the opposite. They launched the Ebro attack. They meant to save Valencia, just when Valencia was saving itself very nicely at tremendous expense to the enemy. What was still more impressive was the fact that there were no Internationals or even Spanish 'shock troops' in the Valencia defence. It was just first-rate fighting by the troops of the area, reinforced from Madrid and magnificently led by Colonel Menendez. He had a staff of young officers whose names I do not remember. One was, I think, Matallana. Another had a Catalan name and was very good indeed. These were young men in the late twenties or early thirties who had been trained during the war, mostly at the Military Academy in Barcelona.

General Rojo did not seem to have grasped the fact that a tank or a piece of artillery was of relative importance to General Franco. If it was lost, another was sent from Germany or Italy to replace it. But for the Government a piece of material was almost worth its weight in gold.

If it had not been for the somewhat pretentious taking of Teruel, it is very doubtful and indeed I think one can say practically certain that General Franco would not have succeeded in breaking through to the sea in April. Because although the troops could have retreated at the first shock, once they had artillery pounding the advancing troops and knocking out the armoured cars and tanks they would have held. It was lack of even a minimum of material which made it impossible to organise a resistance for several weeks. Now with the frontier hermetically shut, they were still in a strong position in Catalonia . Any Franco attack would receive a very warm welcome because they had some stores of arms from the weeks up to the end of June when the French opened the frontier. But to use up these arms on an attack was a thing only to be done in the direst of dire emergencies.

This definitely was not one. On the contrary, General Franco and his Italian allies had met with a fierce resistance and had probably lost in casualties well over twenty per cent of the attacking force while the others were exhausted owing to the intense heat, lack of water, and furious pace of the battle.

Perhaps if General Rojo had been on the spot instead of being in Barcelona, he might have understood the situation better. General Franco was up to his neck in a very bad fight of which he was getting much the worst. Now his opponents offered him just the chance he must have been waiting for, namely, to fight over in Catalonia and deplete that slender store of arms. Of course, if France again opened the frontier this strategy would fail. But the almost continuous closure of the French frontier with Catalonia had so far been the main card in ensuring the victories of General Franco.

I am afraid that both General Rojo and Dr. Negrin succumbed a little to the temptation to take advantage of having a small army on its tip-toes to fight, good material and a chance to make a sensational advance into the enemy lines. Mind you, I think that they really were genuinely preoccupied with saving Valencia. As neither of them was in Valencia they could not appreciate the fact that there was for the moment no need to save Valencia.

General Franco, naturally, at once dropped the expensive and unsatisfactory attack on Valencia and went back to Catalonia to fight the Ebro attackers. So the battle for Valencia ended as suddenly as it had begun, having shown what the army in the Centre Zone was capable of if it had only a few arms and good fortifications. The way the men fought down there was a revelation to me. They were very proud of the fact that they, Spaniards alone, were successfully fighting a professional army composed in part of Italian regular troops, and they ingenuously thought that this would make an impression in London and Paris.

Actually, of course, it was not in the long run highly important whether this battle or the other was lost or won because the Republic was not only 'on its uppers' with regard to war supplies, but food was becoming scarcer and scarcer, not only in Catalonia but in the whole of the central zone. Madrid had been on semi-famine rations for months. The war was being lost because of the blockade set up by the Nationalists, and as has now been openly confirmed in public statements in Germany and Italy, with the help of naval units and the aviation services of those countries. This blockade would not, of course, have been of such great importance if non-intervention had not sealed the Catalan frontier. Food could, of course, be brought in by land to Catalonia. But the transport arrangements were not good enough to permit the wholesale shipment of really big quantities of food by road and rail from France. Non-intervention was Franco's best ally.

When I arrived in Alicante on my way to Valencia early in July I found the wrecks of four British ships in the port. They were the *Maryad, English Tanker, Thorpehaven* and *Farnham.* The first three had been sunk on moonlight nights by a lone bomber who would come in low—Alicante had only a couple of anti-aircraft guns which were no menace to the raiders—choose his victim and sink it with a bomb launched from five or six hundred feet up. A number of other ships had been damaged. The centre of Alicante which had no war factories of importance or any real objectives had been murderously bombed on several occasions. On May 24, 300 people were killed. The next day, seventy. I just arrived in time to see the forty-first raid of the war.

In Valencia, I lost count of the raids. There were three or four wrecked British vessels in the harbour. There were usually two or three raids a day there.

During the whole war there were, I think, about twenty-seven British ships sunk outright in Republican ports and about 170 badly damaged. The French had thirteen sunk and forty-two damaged. Most of this damage was done on the East Coast.

Some of the bombing of ships was done by 'dive bombers', of which the type most in evidence was the Junkers Sturz bomber, Ju 87, with which the Germans claimed after the war was over to have sunk a number of vessels. The light, fast, single-motor plane of this type can carry a 1,000-lb. bomb under the fuselage. It dives at its object, using wing flaps to brake the descent and allow aim to be taken. The advantage of a machine such as this is that it can swoop in below the range of the bigger anti-aircraft guns. One of this type once swooped over Barcelona and landed a 1,000-lb. bomb in the centre of the steam plant for generating electricity for the city. The bomb did not explode and this plant indeed survived serious damage throughout the war despite scores of raids on it. But such bombers seem to give fairly good results against ships such as merchantmen which have no A.A. defences. I do not think that this dive bombing is very accurate; for otherwise the Franco forces would have used them more than they did for shelling bridges and suchlike vital points. Their chief use seems to be against some large and bulky object which is not provided with anti-aircraft defence.

Barcelona up to July 3, 1938, had had ninety-one raids and 2,000 lives had been lost. It was remarkable the way in which the port workers carried on despite the endless bombings. They showed great heroism. Many of them were old men. Very many were killed or badly injured, but those who remained carried on. In some cases the work of discharging should have been done quicker. Democracy has its drawbacks; I remember one investigation showing that no less than twenty different organisations had a say in the control of the port of Barcelona alone. But all that still does not erase my memory of the patient courage of those labourers who day by day risked their lives under terrible conditions.

The Republicans could, of course, have gone in for reprisals. Burgos was within easy bombing range from the Madrid front. But Sr. Prieto adopted the policy of no reprisals. I think he broke this once, early in 1938 when Salamanca was bombed as an answer to some particularly bad bombing of Barcelona. But by and large from about autumn 1937 onwards I do not think that there was any serious bombing of large towns away from the lines in Franco Spain. I think the policy paid. People whom I have since met who went through the war in Franco Spain have told me so, at least. I am sure neither the Franco people nor their advisers realised the fierce hatred engendered by those cruel bombings of civilians, which happened only too often, as apart from the more or less legitimate bombing of the ports. That hatred will last many years, it may have strange results in time to come. Sooner or later most sins come home to roost.

When I said that the bombing of the ports was 'more or less legitimate' I referred to the fact that according to international law Franco had no right to attack foreign ships engaged on legitimate trade in Spanish ports. Actually this international law was made before the days of aeroplanes. But that was no excuse. A zone could easily have been made. The situation was, I am afraid, that we were not interested in stopping this bombing to the extent of taking strong action. Such action would not have been difficult. Franco was getting credits for petrol and other essentials in Paris and London and a few gentle hints in the right quarters from the British and French Governments could have made things most awkward for the Generalissimo without a single voice being raised in anger or a single war-like or aggressive measure being taken. Such things can be arranged behind the scenes; when the party concerned so wishes.

I met many of the officers and crews from these ships which came to Spain. Some of them were just out for the money, but many of them too stuck it long after they needed to and showed great courage and desire to help a cause which as Englishmen they thought was right. Some members of the crews were non-British; that applies to many a fine liner sailing from Britain. I often felt a renewed hope in Britain and comforted after seeing the quiet courage of many of these merchant marine officers.

One of the most flagrant bombing cases I struck in the whole war was one at the small port of Gandia. This charming little port belonged to a British company. It was under the management of a Mr. Edwin Apfel, a British subject who was always to be found at his post at the port, bombs or no bombs, and, even in the July heat, always with his bowler hat firmly fixed on his head.

On July 27, the British steamer *Dellwyn* was sunk in the port at Gandia under particularly bad conditions. It was the only steamer in there. There was nothing in the dock sheds except some fertiliser. The *Dellwyn*, which I believe belonged to 'Potato' Jones, of Bilbao fame, had a cargo of coal on board destined for some gas factory. You could, if you liked, imagine that it would be used for a munitions factory. But coal was allowed under non-intervention. There was a control officer on the ship and it flew the control flag. Now a big Dornier seaplane of the type which came along the coast regularly from the German base at Pollensa on the Island of Majorca, came every night for five nights and always at dusk and dropped bombs around the *Dellwyn*. The pilot did not secure a direct hit and sink her alongside the quay until the fifth night. Nothing could have been more deliberate. To make matters worse, from the point of view of prestige, there was during the whole of that time a British destroyer, H.M.S. *Hero*, which was at the service of the British Consulate in Valencia, anchored half a mile off the port and the whole crew every night had to sit and watch while one of their own country's ships was slowly destroyed against all international conventions by a German seaplane.

CHAPTER XLIII

THE TOLL OF HUMAN SUFFERING

Two facts became clear as autumn of 1938 wore on. The first was that the defence of Valencia and the Ebro attack showed that the Republic had created at least the nucleus of a first-rate army. The second was the fact that Republican Spain was reaching a level of semi-starvation. In other words one had good soldiers with few arms and less food.

I had visited Madrid in July 1938 and found conditions really bad. People were living on a few beans and a small portion of bread as their daily ration. The railway branch line which linked it again to Valencia via Tarancon and Torrejon de Ardoz was finished in August but that did not help matters much because there was not much surplus food in Valencia once the town itself had been supplied and an army of about 400,000 in the Central Zone catered for. People had literally shrunk. There was little complaining, but obviously this could not go on indefinitely.

Barcelona was not quite so bad, but people were not very far from starvation conditions. Good work was done in relief in Madrid by the Scottish Ambulance Unit under Miss Jacobson which had a 'porridge kitchen' in Madrid's main street under the kilted Miss Jacobson herself. There was a Geneva committee under a Swede, Hr. Malcolm de Lilliehook. The latter made a report to the League in 1938 in which he said that most of the 2,400,000 children under fourteen in a population of 12,000,000 in Government Spain were under-nourished. The Society of Friends did great work. They formed a Friends' Service Council in September 1936 with Mr. Jacob in charge in Spain. There were also several American organisations. A canteen organised by Mr. Kendall Park and his wife in Barcelona with the aid of other British residents did sterling work. The International Red Aid furnished large sums subscribed from abroad. Trade unionists in various countries gave large sums for relief. I believe the British trade unions gave something like £200,000. This, however, is an early figure and it is possible that they exceeded this before the end of the war.

Even with all this aid, conditions were terrible. The incessant bombings of the ports destroyed many cargoes before they could be discharged; it was hard to get ships to come to Spain. The cost of a single ship was fantastic. Many ships were seized or sunk at sea, although after the Nyon Agreement of September 1937 this fell off a good deal. Nevertheless as all the ports could be bombed daily if necessary, the destruction done was so great that traffic was very effectually hindered. Some food could be brought in by rail through Port Bou. The other line, through Puigcerda, had been virtually put out of action because it was adapted for electric service and there was now no current for it.

The trains going out from Barcelona were jammed to suffocation. People climbed on to the roofs. They were going out to tramp the countryside. Rather than money they had to take soap, sugar, coffee and other things the peasant needed. Slender girls could be seen staggering along country lanes with half a sack of potatoes triumphantly on their backs. Then, after perhaps five miles' walk to a station, they must fight their way on to a train and perhaps have to hang on to the step. Then probably when they got near Barcelona some Nationalist plane would come in from the sea and bomb and machine-gun the train and the poor people would have to fly panic-stricken for shelter in the countryside.

The pace was terrible. Night after night people lost sleep because of the incessant air raids. Sometimes the alarm would sound four or five times in one night. It might only be a single plane cruising around, but nevertheless those who lived near the port or near some point frequently bombed would have to dash downstairs and take refuge.

War material could only be turned out slowly under these conditions. Every time there was an air raid, the workers had to go to the shelters. There was not sufficient electric current and even some important factories could not work all the time. Coal had to come in through the bombed ports. The horses and carts bringing it from the boats were sometimes blown to pieces. Scrap metal likewise had to come in through the ports.

Explosive materials had to be smuggled in as best they could. One small port often used for this was Vallcarca, on the rocky Garraf coast and about twenty miles south of Barcelona. Some small steamer, often British, without the benefit of a non-intervention officer, would slip out from Oran or some such port. If it got safely to Vallcarca, aeroplanes would immediately take up a patrol overhead and the unloading of the few hundred tons of T.N.T. would be rushed through in a few hours by soldiers. Within eight or ten hours the ship would be on its way again. But the shells had still to be manufactured in Barcelona. Compare this with the munition ships which sailed easily from Genoa or Hamburg loaded with shells and bombs and proceeded without let or hindrance to Pasajes or Bilbao or Cadiz or Malaga.

A staff officer whom I knew well told me that during almost the whole Battle of the Ebro something went wrong with the supply of shells for trench mortars and the Republican mortars were simply silenced except for a brief space when they captured some Franco munitions which fitted their weapons. Aeroplanes were being built under these difficult conditions. But the parts had to come in in ships which ran the risks of all ships and some parts had to be built in Spain.

A minor detail perhaps but one which had a bad effect on health was the lack of soap. Such fats as existed locally were required for the Army and for munitions and the Government had, of course, not sufficient gold to go on purchasing unlimited quantities even of necessary materials.

The reserves of gold, silver and bronze of the Bank of Spain were 2,951 million pesetas on February 8, 1936. This at the par rate of 20 to the £1 totals some £147,000,000 but owing to the fact that neither the peseta nor the pound was on a gold basis it is not easy to say the exact equivalent. The amount of British sterling given for a given weight of Spanish bullion would depend on the exact price of gold at the moment when it was put on the market.

In addition to this amount, the Government also confiscated large quantities of valuables and securities belonging to people considered hostile to the régime. Later in the war it called on people to surrender all gold objects and valuables in order to eke out the existing gold supplies. So many more tens of millions of pounds must have been added. The amount of sterling obtained from orange and other exports during the war could not have been very great.

Expenses were, of course, enormous. As I have pointed out earlier just the insurance alone on a small tramp steamer in a Spanish port would cost over £100 a day and in ports such as Valencia it was nothing uncommon to have a dozen ships in at a time. Sometimes it would take three weeks to unload a ship.

I had a feeling that towards the end of 1938 the Government if not actually short of money was beginning to foresee a possible shortage in the future. I can quite well believe that £200,000,000 could easily have been spent in two and a half years of war with the necessity for paying the most extravagant prices for such war material as could be got and much of it sunk or captured by the enemy even at that. I heard reports of possible negotiations for a loan abroad. So far the Republic had done extremely well. It had managed to fight for over two years without incurring any debts abroad. This was, of course, most important politically because it meant that Spain was not in any way bound to any other state by indebtedness.

I have never seen any clear data as to the extent of General Franco's debts. He, of course, started the war without any gold reserves as these were all in the Bank of Spain in Madrid. He collected gold from private people and took over at least temporarily gold holdings and foreign currency possessions belonging to citizens in his territory. After the war I saw a quotation from a Rome newspaper which indicated that he owed Italy about £100,000,000 but I cannot say if this tallies with reality in any way. He must, perforce, owe very considerable quantities of money not only in foreign currency but also in blocked pesetas which he credited to foreign firms operating in Spain. These must run into enormous figures.

Nevertheless the Franco peseta was always worth a great deal more than the Government peseta despite the fact that the former had no bullion behind it whereas the Government money, at least in the early part of the war, had a much better gold coverage than has the note issue of many European countries to-day. The Franco peseta was changed officially at about fifty and 'bootlegged' at rates down to 90 or 100. That, at least, is as far as I have heard from people who were on the other side.

The Republican peseta was, in autumn 1938, being changed officially at about 100 to the £1 and 'bootlegged' at from 300 to 400 within Spain and at about 500 to 600 outside Spain. Note circulation in the whole of Spain when the war began was about 5,000 million pesetas and this increased within Republican territory alone to about 7,000 million towards the end of the war.

This semi-inflation was due in Government Spain to the very high rate of Army pay and in industry. A private soldier received ten pesetas daily in Republican Spain as compared with about 0.50 centimos in the Franco Army. There was any amount of money in circulation and people just wandered into shops and asked: 'What have you got to sell?'

But the increased note circulation was not sufficient to explain the fantastically low value of the Republican peseta outside Spain. This was due in part to the fact that large numbers of people who left Republican Spain smuggled out big quantities of notes which they sold for what they could get. It is possible also that the Franco authorities, who annulled the former currency and replaced it by a new one, placed some of the notes abroad for what they could get for them. Whatever the explanation may be, the fact remains that one could buy unlimited Republican pesetas outside Spain at very cheap rates.

The main explanation is, I think, the general opinion in international financial circles that General Franco would win. If hopes of a Government victory had appeared then the Republican pesetas would obviously have represented an excellent investment. The fact that among people 'in the know' in financial circles the Republican peseta was looked upon as so much worthless paper was in itself highly significant. Money may not talk, but it listens very carefully and usually in circles where those who speak have reason for their statements.

Throughout the war indeed the outcome depended almost entirely on London and Paris. A decision in these capitals to take strong measures to stop Germany and Italy from open intervention, or even the mere granting of permission for war material purchased elsewhere to pass freely over French territory in order that the Government also could receive its materials without let or hindrance, just as General Franco was doing, would have changed the situation in Spain overnight.

I am sorry if I harp on this subject. But it was such a ghastly experience towards the end of the war to watch a people worn-out, hungry, with the whole world against them, fighting tremendously and with great courage. I used to see a great many people. I travelled by train, in trams, by car. I talked to soldiers at the front, to Franco supporters, to diplomats, to workmen, and the firm impression I got was that throughout the war, until the end, the mass of the people were solid in their desire to fight for their independence and for the future of the Republic as opposed to feudalism. Their courage and efforts were not in vain. No sacrifice like that ever is. They put up a fight which to-day may seem lost but which marked a solid creative effort which cannot be pushed away or hidden. It stands there. It may be shrouded over for a time, but that is all.

This admiration did not prevent me from feeling sorry for people who had had relatives murdered and who had lost everything. Or for the people who were in gaol. I once started on a tour of prisons but before I had seen more than half a dozen the March offensive of 1938 took me back to reporting the war. By and large the prisoners were not badly treated, although there were a few black spots which did the Republic little credit, such as the ill-fated steamer *Uruguay* which had 400 political prisoners on board, shut up down in the holds in the port of Barcelona which was being bombed steadily by the Nationalists. In the earlier parts of the war there was a great deal of ill-treatment of prisoners and use of third-degree methods. But I do not think that there was much of this towards the end of the war. After General Franco entered Barcelona in January 1939 some torture cells of a very elaborate character were discovered but I doubt if they were used at least during the last year of the war when I was in Barcelona. At least no report of their existence came my way. The police could hardly have killed everyone placed in them and some report must have got out to Franco supporters and to relief workers and foreign diplomats who were doing much to help the Franco prisoners and to secure exchanges and releases. I went to several trials by the 'People's Courts' which were composed of one magistrate and two civilians and which tried cases of disloyalty, treason and suchlike. They seemed reasonably fair if somewhat hasty.

The human suffering everywhere was so terrible that it seemed incredible that there should be no glimmer of light anywhere. One would stop on the street to speak with some widow whose husband had been shot in the wild days of Barcelona in the summer of 1936 and she would be anxious to know how far Franco had advanced; how long it would be before 'her side' came to Barcelona. Then one would go to one's hotel and the chambermaid would come to ask what news and whether the Republicans were doing well. Her two brothers had been murdered in Pamplona by the Falange because they belonged to the Socialist Youth organisation.

Things seemed simpler at the front where it was just a fight between soldiers. Yet even there the fearful inferiority of the Republicans in everything except man power was so overwhelming that it was inadequate to try to regard it as an equal struggle.

Actually a much more mature Army could have been proud of the Ebro offensive. It is no joke to launch an attack across a river which is well over one hundred yards wide even at its narrowest, in the sector where the offensive was made. The Ebro runs swiftly even in summer and its sides are steep owing to the speed of the current and considerable difference between summer and winter level.

The Ebro offensive was launched on July 25; I think it was on the night of July 24-25, when the Republican vanguard swam the deep river and in hand-to-hand fighting overpowered the surprised Franco forces. Pontoons were quickly built, supplies and the mass of the troops brought over and forty-eight hours later the Government forces occupied a series of hills and mountains running from Mequinenza where the River Segre joins the Ebro down to below Miravet, more than forty miles away. Their deepest penetration was near Gandesa where they were about twenty-five miles from the Ebro. Their position was rather like that of an unstretched bowstring with the Ebro as the bow behind them.

There was an attempt made to cross lower down at Amposta near the Ebro delta. I think this was only intended as a diversion in order to prevent reserves down there from being rushed higher up and also to draw reserves and supplies from Castellon to this point. It was a costly effort carried out, I think, by Frenchmen and Germans of the International Brigade who were holding the lower Ebro sector near the coast under Major Hans. Burgos reported that 300 were killed, 100 drowned and 350 made prisoner at this point. But higher up success was complete.

The battle lasted nearly four months until on the night of November 14-15, the Government withdrew its last forces back across the Ebro.

How it was possible to prepare boats, pontoons, bringing up some 200 guns, and 50,000 men, is just as inexplicable as was the success of the surprise attack at Teruel. Even just a few machine-guns manned and in the right place could have stopped the attack. For the Republicans it was a brilliant achievement and it was carried out almost entirely by military leaders who were 'amateurs' in the sense that few of them had ever been to a military academy.

The commander of the field army attacking was a quick dynamic little 'Madrileño' named Juan Modesto Guilloto and generally known as Colonel Modesto. He had had some military experience in that he had been three years in the Tercio, or Foreign Legion, and had reached the rank of corporal in that corps. A woodworker by trade he had been active in trade union activities and had escaped to Russia after the failure of the revolutionary general strike of 1934. There, like Lister, he had received the kind of military and general training given to foreign revolutionaries. Lister commanded the Fifth Army Corps which held the southern half of the conquered sector and the northern part was held by the Eighteenth

Army Corps commanded by the youthful Tagueña who fought so gallantly against the Littorio, holding them up for nearly two weeks at Cherta during the March offensive.

The actual operation, as I have explained earlier, seemed to be highly unwise but the responsibility for this rested on General Rojo and on Dr. Negrin and the Cabinet as a whole which must have taken the final decision. At least the men in the field carried out their task brilliantly.

One of the comforting things about the Ebro battle in these days when people easily predict the 'wiping out' of this city or that in a few days of air offensive, is that the Government statistical services worked it out that it cost nearly 500 tons of bombs, on an average, to destroy one pontoon bridge. This, incidentally, supposes a cost of £200,000 or thereabouts. The Franco aviators did their hardest. They came over from dawn until dusk, again and again. Sometimes it was impossible to move a single vehicle across the river by daylight. An observer one day counted over 160 Nationalist aeroplanes in the sky at once. The Government anti-aircraft guns were few and far between and their chasers were not strong enough to attack the main bodies of bombers which often flew twenty or thirty together accompanied by fifty or sixty fighters. Yet even with such a guide as the river, experience showed that a very tiny fraction of the bombs rained down hit a bridge. Republican forces increased the bomb wastage by hanging long stretches of cloth across the river. Apparently this gave the effect of a bridge from above for the Nationalists showered down bombs on these dummies. Modern bombers have gained enormously in speed but this has cost something in accuracy for it means that the bomb must be released so much earlier and hence wind has a greater effect and any slight deviation caused by movement of the plane as the bomb leaves is accentuated. This does not matter in bombing a town but it does in an effort to hit such a small object as a pontoon bridge. This was seen also at Tortosa where weeks of bombing were necessary before the road bridge was badly hit and even then the old road bridge just alongside was never put out of action.

The bridge builders who worked and lived in this inferno were wonderful. The Nationalists opened many dams higher up the river and several times succeeded in sweeping away all the pontoons and temporary bridges.

In the four months of battle I think the Government lost about 10,000 killed and some 50,000 injured. Nowhere in the whole war was such heroism shown by the Government forces who often had to endure the most fierce attacks with the knowledge that they were virtually cut off except for an iron railway bridge near Mora de Ebro.

A serious loss in the middle of the battle was the withdrawal of the International Brigades who were fighting in the Thirty-fifth Division under Lieut.-Colonel Medina. The Internationals had already been much diluted with Spaniards and the inflow of volunteers had been stopped. The Fifteenth Brigade, which included the British and the Americans, had had a Spanish commander since June when Colonel Kopic had been taken away.

There were in Spain altogether, as certified by the Commission sent down by the League of Nations, just over 12,000 volunteers and probably about 5,000 were actually in the front line on the Ebro when Dr. Juan Negrin announced to the League of Nations that Republican Spain would unilaterally withdraw all foreign volunteers on September 21, 1938. They were taken out of line on September 28.

This was a quixotic gesture which received little publicity because the world was watching Prague, not the Ebro, and it was just two days before Mr. Chamberlain went to Godesberg on the Rhine. Taking them out of the line weakened the army on the Ebro and deprived the Republicans of its toughest shock force.

Barcelona gave them a wonderful and dignified send-off at the farewell parade on October 28. It seemed, somehow, like the beginning of the end. The same day Ramón Franco, the aviator and brother of General Franco, was killed in an aviation accident near Palma de Mallorca.

CHAPTER XLIV

DR. JUAN NEGRIN

PEOPLE of the 'intellectual class' rarely seem to feel much at home in a situation which is revolutionary even though they themselves may have helped to create the state of affairs existing.

The leading figures of the Spanish intelligensia such as Don Salvador de Madariaga, Don Ramon Perez de Ayala, Don José Ortega y Gasset, Dr. Gregorio Marañon, Don Miguel de Unamuno, all of whom by their literary efforts had helped to overthrow the Monarchy, came very little into the limelight during the war. Unamuno was, I think, the only one in Spain during the war and he, as far as one could learn, criticised both sides lustily until his death aged seventy-two in Salamanca on December 31, 1936.

I suppose this situation is in a way understandable. Blood must naturally be repugnant to people whose whole interest turns on the finer and more pleasant aspects of culture and civilisation.

Yet the man who played the leading role in Spain during the greater part of the war although not a leading 'intellectual' came definitely from the intellectual classes. Dr. Juan Negrin was to me the most interesting figure of the war. Here was this bluff, hearty Canary-Islander with a gargantuan appetite, fond of life in all its aspects; a man who had the greatest contempt for politics and who had secured election twice to Parliament without making a single speech to secure election as far as I could learn—he certainly never did in Madrid although he may possibly have done so in his native Canary Islands where he was elected once—suddenly at the head of a people fighting for its existence. I used to ask myself: 'Why?'

One can of course take a simple line and say: 'Why, the man is a Marxist and he has simply been faithful to his ideas. . . .' But I do not think that Negrin is a revolutionary. I have known Dr. Negrin since I first went to Spain in 1929. I was not an intimate friend of his, I have never been to his home, but I used to see him regularly at the Italianos Bar in Madrid where there was a gathering of cultured people from the liberal professions who sat and drank beer together each evening.

Negrin, curiously enough, considering the role he has played in the war, has had a completely German education. He went to Germany aged about twelve and stayed there until he was twenty-five or twenty-six. That was in pre-War Germany for Negrin was born in 1889.

His father is, I believe that he is still alive, a Canary Island landowner and Negrin had been able to enjoy a good education. In Madrid during the Republic he was secretary of the University City and largely responsible for its erection. He also occupied the chair of physiology in Madrid University and had a private commercial laboratory for medicinal analysis. He has three fine sons.

In the five years that Negrin was Member of Parliament before the war, he never so far as I know made a single speech except on one or two occasions when as chairman of the Finance Committee of the House he had to answer questions. 'Thank God I am not a politician and that I have no intention of ever becoming one,' he told Parliament when he was Premier during the war and had to make a speech on the policy of his Government.

Slightly over medium height, square-shouldered, heavily built with a face half masked by large horn-rimmed spectacles, Dr. Negrin has a dynamic capacity for work. He might say good-bye to his friends at four o'clock in the morning but at 8.30 sharp he would drive up to his office at the University City in his car. He lived a most irregular life. He could be found lunching at four o'clock in the afternoon and sitting down to a really heavy dinner at 10.30 in the evening.

My chief impression of him was his strong pity for human suffering. He would look at the newsboy from whom he was buying an evening paper and say: 'Having those eyes treated, sonny? No? Well go to Dr. So-and-so at such-and-such a clinic and give him this card and he'll see that you get treated right away.' Or out in the country, he would stop in small villages and talk to the peasants, look in at their miserable homes, peer behind the easy mask of picturesqueness which veils so much disease and suffering in Spain. Before leaving he would slip some money or a card which would ensure free medical treatment into the hand of the woman of the house. That was Negrin as I knew him.

When the military *coup d'état* took place in July 1936, he was one of the relatively few middle-class people who were whole-heartedly with the Republic. When most people, even those who believed in the Republic, who had some kind of social position, drew back horror-stricken at the murder of hundreds of victims without trial and at the expropriation of property and the mob law which reigned in much of Republican territory, Negrin was busy at the front organising medical supplies and hospitals in the Guadarrama and even ordering and helping the militia forces too. It was thanks to the efforts of a handful of men such as himself who did miracles in the way of organisation that General Franco did not push right up to Madrid in the first days of the war. Those who were too horror-stricken to wish to help, even if they sympathised, overlooked the fact that horrible as was the murder of people in Madrid and Barcelona, it was nevertheless being fully equalled by the slaughter of Left-Wing supporters all over Franco territory. A resident of Seville remarked plaintively several months later to a British visitor: 'I suppose one really had to kill off all the Communists, but it did seem to me going a bit far to shoot all the Republicans as well.' The murders were an unfortunate feature of both sides, but I think Dr. Negrin and the other middle-class figures who stood by the Republic were right to fight for it and to defend it in the knowledge that not to do so meant the triumph again of the forces which had ruled Spain with such unhappy results during recent centuries. This was going to mean the end of the Republic and all that it stood for.

Negrin became Finance Minister in the Caballero Cabinet of September 1936. He was organising the evacuation of Talavera de la Reina towards which Franco's forces were advancing rapidly when he was told that he had been made a Minister. In May 1937 he was put into power as Premier to succeed Caballero, largely thanks to the influence of Prieto. In April 1938 after the collapse of the Aragon front, Negrin took over National Defence as well and from that time until the end of the war he was the undisputed leader of Republican Spain.

Yet it would never have been true to say that he was a dictator. If he had been, his work would have been enormously simplified. He had to deal not only with his own Cabinet, but also with the Catalan Government under President Companys. Thus once the Cabinet was in Barcelona and he managed to get his own Ministers to approve some measure, if it affected the local life of Catalonia at all then he had to persuade the Catalans also to accept it.

Negrin stayed in power not only because of his great capacity for organisation but because he had the full support of the Communists and because his own group, the Socialist Party, was so divided that no opposition to him, although often apparent, ever succeeded in uniting the factions which disliked him.

As the war went on the Socialist Party became more and more lost in a maze of contradictions and internal quarrels. Caballero, surrounded by his small clique composed of Luis Araquistain, Rudolfo Llopis, Ricardo Zabalza, Wenceslao Carillo, sat in chagrined retirement. They flirted with the Anarchists but the latter felt the mass pressure of their trade union members, which was against Caballero and in favour of Negrin, too heavily to be able to join forces. Don Indalecio Prieto led another clique. Then there was the trade union sector led by Ramón Gonzalez Peña. I think Peña himself had some sympathy for Caballero but most of his unions did not. Still another clique rallied around Don Julian Besteiro who remained in 'splendid isolation' in Madrid.

Students of the history of our days will doubtless find much scope for investigation and speculation as to the failure not only in Spain, but also in Germany and Austria, of powerful Socialist Parties led by intelligent men and with good organisations to give a constructive lead to the masses dependent on them. The Spanish Socialist Party has, of course, far and away the best record and it did resolutely fight both in 1931 and 1936 but it still was not pulling its full weight. In autumn 1938 Caballero, Besteiro and Prieto, who were the three chief figures of the Party, were all in retirement. Not one of them had any important post.

Although he did not have much following within the Socialist Party, I think one of the clearest heads they could boast of was that of Don Julio Alvarez del Vayo. Born in 1891 and consequently forty-five years of age when the Spanish War commenced, Vayo like Negrin had had a German education although this was confined to two years at Leipzig University, but during the War and afterwards he lived many years in Germany as representative of *La Nacion* of Buenos Aires. Of medium height with a slouching walk, slow speech, a Castilian and aided by a good knowledge of German, English and French, Vayo had a deep knowledge of international affairs acquired by years of work in Berlin and Geneva. He married a Swiss woman, Frl. Gra of Zurich, whose two other sisters were married respectively to Sr. Araquistain and Sr. Viñuales, an ex-Minister.

Vayo's situation was rather peculiar. He had become Foreign Minister under Caballero and had done excellent work. In addition to being Foreign Minister he was the Chief Political Commissioner of the Army with the rank of General until Prieto edged him out of this post in autumn 1937. Vayo resigned when Caballero went out in May 1937 but came back again when Negrin reorganised his Cabinet without Prieto in April 1938. I think Vayo understood the situation better than any other of the Socialists.

In presenting the Republic's case to the world I think that Vayo did all that was humanly possible. That his arguments received such little attention in London and Paris was due to a lack of desire to comprehend them rather than to any flaw in the arguments or in their presentation. In this work he was well backed up by Don Pablo de Azcarate, Spanish Ambassador to the Court of St. James during most of the war. I think it stands very much to the credit of Sr. Azcarate that he gave up an excellent post with the League of Nations to become Ambassador.

Negrin was greatly handicapped by the chaos within his

own party. It meant that he had to take decisions himself which should really have come after pondering the matter with the other responsible Socialists. Instead of being able to pick out a score of reliable party members to occupy posts of importance, he had to rely on a miscellaneous collection of people of all kinds of views. His own staff in the Premier's office were nice people but utterly inefficient. His Under-Secretary, Sr. Prats, made some lamentable blunders which upset the Catalans on more than one occasion; he would forget at gala receptions to have the band play the Catalan 'Els Segadors' as well as the Republican anthem.

The result was that Negrin himself took on a huge mass of executive work which snowed him under. He tried to do everything himself with the result that even most important things were apt to be sadly neglected. He should have had a good man to help him in liaison work with the Catalans. Actually Negrin was controlling not only the Premier's office but also War, Navy, Aviation, War Industries and, to all effects, Finance. For the Finance Minister, Sr. Mendez Aspe, took few decisions of importance without consulting Negrin, whose Under-Secretary he had been while Negrin held the Finance portfolio until April 1938. Trouble with the Catalans caused the representative of Companys's Left Catalan Party to leave the Cabinet on August 17, 1938. This was due to Catalan offence at what they considered was the arrogant behaviour of Negrin.

The people who supported Dr. Negrin through thick and thin were the Communists. They were towards the end of the war far and away the most powerful party with, so they claimed, somewhere well over 300,000 members. But this was only a fraction of their real strength for they predominated in the United Socialist Youth which I think boasted some half a million members. It also had a juvenile organisation, the Pioneers. Then there was the International Red Aid Society which claimed to have over 100,000 subscribers in Madrid alone and a women's organisation as well. In addition the Communists had by now a great deal of strength within the trade unions through a society known as the Group of Revolutionary Socialists. They controlled directly or indirectly a great many newspapers. They probably had quarrels but if they did they kept them to themselves and their leaders such as Dolores Ibarurri, José Diaz, Jesus Hernández, Manuel Uribe, were all relatively young people who gave a tense and active leadership.

All this was tremendously important. If Negrin, for instance, wished to mobilise more men and to have them replaced by women he could get the Communists to give the word to their people to prepare for this. Immediately thousands of meetings would be organised all over Spain. In factories, in the fields, throughout the land propaganda for this idea would be spread. I just give this as an example. Negrin's own party did not have an organisation like this.

The Army liked Negrin. He was quick, alert, ready to comprehend. He would dash out to the front to talk over operations with the officers on the spot. He did much to reorganise it, but this did not remedy the lack of arms nor was he able to overcome many political difficulties within the Army. There were immediate complications if an officer of one party received undue promotion without those belonging to other parties receiving consideration. The Anarchists, Socialists and Republicans were particularly jealous of the Communists and tended to club together to prevent any increase of influence of the latter. When Lieut.-Colonel Juan Modesto was made commander-in-chief of the Ebro Army, Lieut.-Colonel Juan Perea was given charge of the new Army of the East, which defended the zone from Lerida to the French frontier. This was because Perea a career officer and not, I think, an Anarchist himself, had always been associated with the Anarchist militia, a column of which he commanded on the Somosierra front in the first days.

The Republicans had remained in a comatose state throughout the war. Although individuals had done great work, as political forces they had been little in evidence. The only two parties of importance, Left Republicans, led by Sr. Azaña, and Republican Union, under Sr. Martinez Barrio, had both been so to speak decapitated before the war began by their respective leaders becoming President and Speaker of Parliament. Sr. Martinez Barrio himself did much useful work in addition to being Speaker of the House. For instance, when the International Brigades were being formed at Albacete he took charge of that town and brought order out of chaos. Later in the war he took charge of all relief work. But few other Republicans showed much initiative or talent for leadership. The Catalan Left Party showed the same lack of spirit and the same complete lack of constructive leadership.

The Catalans were particularly bad because they allowed themselves to be intimidated by the Anarchists and despite their own strength they failed consistently to make any effort to lead the people who were only too anxious for a programme, for constructive work.

And, at the risk of boring by repetition, I must emphasise how much we Democratic nations of Europe were to be blamed for all this. Spanish Republicans, I use the word in its political sense here and not as a general term embracing those in Republican territory, and most of the Socialists, failed because Democracy failed them. They could not borrow ideas from us, because we had none. The only Democracy really dealing energetically with its problems at the time was the United States of America under President Roosevelt, but the gap between ancient Europe and the young, virile United States with its gigantic resources and unbounded energies is too great for solutions to be transferred easily from one to the other.

Here was Spain groping desperately to find a smooth way from feudalism to twentieth-century mechanised economy. We, instead of being tip-toe and alert, ready and eager to help, were buried in our little lives, anxious to have our little house and our little car. Our supreme egoism in the face of need, our failure to make Democracy something constructive, and not just an insurance of the status quo of a small fraction of the peoples of the world who can afford to live on a decent standard of life, is not only a shocking blot on our record. It is something we shall pay for terribly and with our own blood.

CHAPTER XLV

A CLOSED FRONTIER AND A CRUMBLING FRONT

I T was bitterly cold outside. We had skidded over an icy, snow-bound road to the small country church in England where Midnight Mass was being said. Now I was sitting in the warm little Church listening to the sermon of the Parish Priest and going back fourteen years to the last time I was in this Church on Christmas Eve. Then I was an altar server; now I was a recently-married man of thirty-five just back from a war.

The Parish Priest in his words referred to Spain. He said: 'We hear so many conflicting reports from one side and the other in Spain that we scarcely know what to believe. All we can do is pray that the great suffering of that unhappy nation shall be alleviated.' That was fair enough and I think it represented the cross-cut of Catholic opinion in England. Unfortunately, it was not the position adopted by the Catholic Press of Britain nor by some rather prominent Catholic figures, I could not help thinking.

I reflected too that such figures of Catholic Spain as Gil Robles had not joined the Franco ranks. Robles was living in Portugal.

And I wondered about Catholicism and I thought about a book by William Teeling which I had just read and which I had liked so much. It seemed so strange that Christ who thought so much about the poor and the humble and who virtually said that they were the only ones who would reach Heaven should now be represented as being on the side of tyranny, repression. If Christ were alive now, I thought, I am sure he would be on the side of the Spanish Republic. The murdered priests and nuns? Yes, but would not Christ have wanted to know if this Church in Spain had been doing its duty? Would he not want to know if it had been fighting the cause of the poor and the oppressed? If it had not, then cruel as its punishment had been it would at least be explicable.

It is so easy to be on the side of power and wealth, I thought. But Christ from what we know of his life was never on that side of the fence. It seemed funny that two thousand years later anyone who felt for the poor, who wished to see poverty and misery abolished and the good things of the world extended to all, should be looked upon as anti-Catholic.

Twenty-four hours later I was on my way back to Barcelona because General Franco had repeated his tactics of the spring and after the tremendous Battle of the Ebro he had struck again and quickly.

At dawn on December 23—zero hour had been fixed for December 15 but a blizzard had caused postponement—the great offensive was launched with the Italian Littorio Division in the spear-head and some 200,000 troops in movement. Luck, or treachery, gave the Franco forces a great send-off. At the point they crossed the River Segre, south of Lerida, were Carabinero forces. I have pointed out before that these forces had a certain autonomy, had no Political Commissioners and tended to have a large Socialist element among them. Some of the units were good, but others were very bad indeed. This one was of the worst. After the first few shells the officers in command got into their cars and drove away. The bewildered troops broke and within a few hours General Franco's forces had swept through and outflanked the whole neighbouring Segre line which likewise had to pull back.

The usual remedy was adopted. Lister and his Fifth Army Corps were thrown in to hold the breach and from Christmas Eve until January 3 they held the Italians on hills behind the Segre which were crowned by the village of Castelldans.

Until I got back I had not realised how bad the situation was. I knew the frontier was closed but it was always possible that the Government had been lucky and had slipped through a few good cargoes of arms. Then again I was deceived by a strange conviction that although Britain and France heartily disliked the Republic they would, if they saw that it was collapsing completely, step in. I never could believe that we would let our Empire routes be endangered without making some effort to save them. I had realised by now that influential people in London and Paris, who had fairly strong opposition from other influential people but which was not strong enough to change the direction of governmental policy, were quite prepared to see the Republic smashed and General Franco established because they looked upon the Republic as 'red' and General Franco as representing 'law and order' and they imagined that by a loan or two all question of Axis influence could be eliminated. There were strong and clear-sighted men in London and Paris who despite wealth and conservative politics did not share the predominating view and wished above all to make sure that our Empire was safe. This view was represented in politics by Mr. Churchill and Mr. Eden, but they and their supporters were in a minority.

It seemed that there were some hundreds of pieces of artillery in Marseilles, considerable quantities of machine-guns and other material. But there was no way of moving the stuff by sea, the only way the French would allow it to leave the dock sheds. Marseilles was full of spies and any ship which left would at once be a prey to air attack and to pursuit from the Franco and allied ships. This material was Russian, so I was told. There were also many scores of aeroplanes some, I think, Russian and others I believe were American.

But that was all in Marseilles or Bordeaux. Out at Castelldans I and Herbert Matthews and Willie Forrest found Lister with his Army Corps headquarters in a cave about a mile from the front line holding on grimly while the Italian troops in front battered furiously against his positions. The air was full of Nationalist planes. The Franco guns thundered mightily and were only faintly answered by the few Republican guns. Lister, usually polite and communicative, swept by black and grim as the craggy hillside where he had been holding out for eight days, with a dry 'Buenos dias!' His chubby-faced Political Commissioner, Santiago Alvarez, was more communicative. We did not need telling that things were bad. Shells were dropping all around. The second-line troops were huddled against a ditch only a quarter of a mile from headquarters. The Italians had been held by a tremendous effort but now there was a tremendous push down towards the southern flank nearer Borjas Blancas. We ran through a barrage of shells, found our car had luckily escaped damage, and raced furiously down a terrible, shell-pitted road and through the now completely deserted village of Castelldans. We passed through the wrecked town of Borjas Blancas which the Nationalists had literally 'plastered' with bombs, to no particular purpose for it had been completely deserted for days. No one was going to stay in a town which was slowly being pounded into dust. Then we stopped for lunch and how good a sandwich and a glass of wine tastes when you have just been mixed up in some shell-fire. As we sat and ate we could see shells dropping on the road we had just come down. That night, it was January 3, Castelldans was lost and the next day Borjas Blancas and Artesa de Segre both went and that was all very bad for these towns were important road junctions.

By now we were all specialists in covering retreats and not easily impressed by the streams of refugees, the weary soldiers filing back, the chaos and confusion. But we soon saw that this time things were very grave indeed.

The officers who knew us spoke freely enough. Up in the mountains defending the approach of Valls and Tarragona young Tagueña over lunch told us: 'We have an average of one or two machine-guns for each battalion. We have twenty-eight guns for the whole Army corps. At one time two were functioning only. The men work miracles. The fitters repair the guns in their positions. But they are falling to pieces. Yesterday a tank was set on fire by an incendiary shell. It was towed back by another tank. The charred remains of the crew were taken out, it was disinfected, repaired and to-day it is in action again.' It was the same tale everywhere. Nothing like enough machine-guns, scarcely a single anti-tank gun, the artillery few in number of pieces and all worn out from the tremendous usage they had received on the Ebro.

It was a situation nobody could do much about. There is only one way to silence hundreds of enemy guns and that is to pound them back with artillery. You cannot hold tank and armoured car columns which raid here and there tire-lessly unless you have artillery or anti-tank guns. You cannot stop an enemy who advances from twenty points in broken country unless you have sufficient machine-guns to rake the countryside with.

The only thing that General Rojo can be reproached with is that he had not foreseen the situation. It might have been possible during the lull of a few weeks after the Ebro battle to have slipped up from Valencia a few guns and some quantities of machine-guns and some of the best troops from down there. Destroyers racing from Valencia to Barcelona on dark nights could generally get through without trouble and by this means a good deal of men and material could have been taken from the Central Zone. Naturally this would have weakened that area in case of attack, but a risk had to be taken somewhere and by doing nothing at all disaster came.

It might also have been wiser instead of fighting desperately up near the Segre after the line had broken to have pulled back to the moderately good line of defences which ran across country from south of Pons through Bellpuig down towards Montblanch. This would have meant giving up some hundreds of square miles without a fight. But the defences would at least have been manned by fresh troops and with such weapons as they possessed. Actually I do not think there was anything like sufficient material available to stop the Franco forces even at the fortified line, which was, of course, in no way a Maginot Line but just a series of trenches and machine-gun nests on the commanding positions.

General Franco attacked on a front of over fifty miles from Pons down to Mezquinena. Down by the Ebro he threw in cavalry under General Monasterio but I do not think this played a great part in breaking through the Government forces down there. The Republican forces hardly used cavalry at all during the war. General Franco had more opportunity because the Government forces did not have the machine-guns and the chaser planes which to-day make the life of the cavalry a most unpleasant business. Except in guerilla warfare in broken country with plenty of cover the horse has to-day little chance of remaining alive. The man can take cover but the horse is not so adaptable and remains an excellent target for even a distant machine-gun or a swooping chaser or attack plane.

Spain with a battle front of almost 1,000 miles for a considerable part of the war and most of which was but thinly held would have seemed to have offered more scope to cavalry than most wars. The Government had the idea of arming the cavalry with light machine-guns for raiding work or for mobility in defence but I do not think they ever found that this worked very well. Wherever there was heavy fighting there were masses of Franco bombers and chasers and once the sky is full of aircraft it is a bad lookout for cavalry.

General Monasterio had one fair success and that was about February 5 or 6 of 1938 when the final drive on Teruel was being made. The Government forces were strongly entrenched in the Sierra Palomera to the north of Teruel. But the Franco forces managed to break a gap higher up and to rush in General Monasterio's cavalry so that they swept down to Perales and took the forces in Sierra Palomera in the rear. But mostly the cavalry was used to 'clean up', as the operation was described, areas already passed by the front line troops; a very minor role indeed. I remember once when I was down in Valencia in July 1938 and the small town of Nules was taken by General Franco. After a tremendous bombardment lasting five or six hours his troops charged and took the town which was a mass of ruins as a result of aerial bombardment and which was only held by Republican outposts. They then threw in cavalry in an attempt to keep the Republican front moving back, but just at that moment as the cavalry charged, up came a patrol of Republican chaser planes and swooped down on the enemy. The cavalry broke and fled and was not seen again on that front. The day of cavalry is definitely over except perhaps for some particular task in wild and uninhabited lands.

I think that General Gambara, who I believe was in charge of the Italian forces during this advance, deserves particular credit for the way in which he handled his mobile units. It was a complete vindication of the mobile unit as such because allowing for the disarmed state of his opponents, these were nevertheless good enough soldiers and tough enough to have held their own against infantry attacks. They would have been forced back but not, I think, overwhelmed if they had not had to deal with these mobile units which moved swiftly here and there and continually outflanked positions which were being held with tremendous courage by the Republicans.

One day in the Ebro battle when the Government forces were retiring—this withdrawal by Lister was I think one of the best things he did in the war, he retreated for two weeks without losing a single whole unit, pressed by much stronger forces and for the greater part of the time with only one single bridge, the iron railway bridge, because even the dam tops near Flix and near Benifallet were flooded over and yet he finally took back the last of his men and all his material—I discussed the situation with Lister. He said: 'The Italians worry me more than anything else.'

I asked him how this was and he explained: 'They have in reserve a number of mobile units. These units not only work in conjunction with tanks and armoured cars but the men in them have a very high proportion of automatic rifles or light machine-guns. These forces can be moved speedily in any direction and they have a tremendously high fire capacity. My men are tired; those divisions are fresh. If they are suddenly thrown in against me, I shall be up against it.'

They were not thrown in, except for the light tanks, armoured cars, motor-cycle machine-gun units and suchlike, in the last part of the Ebro battle. But they were the spearhead of the advance through the whole of Catalonia and my impression was that, even allowing for the weakness of their opponents, they did a first rate job of work. They, the Italians, afterwards claimed that their units took 18,000 of 40,000 prisoners taken altogether, and that they captured 151 villages or small towns and six large towns. I do not know if they included Barcelona but I think they arrived there at least as soon as anyone else and they were first into Tarragona, I think, which was the second biggest town.

I wish I knew more about the organisation of the Italian units such at Littorio—all-Italian—and the Green Arrows, Light-Blue Arrows, and Black Arrows—these units had some

Spanish men and officers incorporated—as they were used in this advance because it would provide valuable data as to the right proportion of motorised infantry, tanks, armoured cars, motorised artillery suitable for use in a land such as Spain.

These units must I suppose have totalled something like 40,000 infantry with another fifteen or twenty thousand men engaged in the armoured units, artillery, transport, reserves. Of this I have, of course, no proof because so far as I know no figures have been published. The Italians admitted some 5,000 casualties and claimed that about half these were Spanish members of their units.

I am not, of course, forgetting the fact that other units of General Franco's forces fought very well, notably the Navarre Divisions. But the fight was generally the heaviest where the Italians were. Almost all the way from the Segre to Gerona, where the Italians were retired in view of the fact that the fight was over and that it was desired to play up a little to French susceptibility, the fight was a duel between Lister's Fifth Army Corps and the Italians under General Gambara. They fought at Castelldans, behind Montblanch, near Vilafranca del Panades, on the Llobregat, behind Barcelona.

For instance, despite furious battering in the rugged mountains behind Valls, Tagueña could not be moved by the Franco forces thrown against him. He had to retire and march all his men out because Valls was lost from the Montblanch direction and he was threatened with being isolated.

The mobility of the Italian artillery was particularly impressive. They had, so it was said in Republican circles, about 400 guns, all tractor-hauled. The Germans were reported to have about 100 heavier guns. Then there must have been some Spanish batteries as well. I do not think that the Republicans from Lerida to the coast had more than sixty serviceable pieces when the battle started and all of this had been worn out in the Ebro battle. I do not know how many tanks the Italians used, I was told they had some 200 Whippet tanks, then there was a considerable number of German Mercedes tanks. The Government had very few. They used the Soviet medium-light tank which gave remarkable service and indeed had so impressed our military experts at Russian manœuvres several years ago that we have introduced into the British Army a similar model. The Government forces had special motor trucks which carried these tanks. They fought very well indeed in the withdrawal from the Ebro salient in the autumn fight across the Ebro and did brilliant work in covering the retreat. The Government even used them by night to cover withdrawals. The tank men were all Spaniards since early on in the war when a few Russians were sent out. They were speedily replaced by Madrid taxi-drivers who showed time and again exceeding gallantry in fights in which they were always in great inferiority. I am only guessing from what I saw, but I should think that at the most there were not more than thirty of these in good fighting condition when the Franco attack was launched on December 23.

I do not intend to follow this retreat step by step. Tarragona went on January 15, Barcelona on the twenty-sixth.

Too late, General Rojo had tried to bring up men and some material from Valencia. The boats got through all right but it was not men, it was guns that were needed. Men from the ages of 39 to 41 were called up on January 12 and then on January 15, conscription was announced from 17 to 55. I should think that this was done in order to prevent disturbances in the towns by Anarchists. From a military point of view, the measure was disastrous. The men thus mobilised clogged trains and other transport; they could not be trained; they had to be fed; there were no arms for them. Actually I think only those up to 45 were called.

Funny the things one remembers; there were four steam rollers which I first saw retreating at about two miles an hour near Valls. I last saw them about two weeks later chugging away near Caldetas, on the Catalan coast, eighty miles from where I first saw them and heading steadily for France. Then there were two soldiers whom I saw on several successive days and who were very solemnly 'escorting' a cow to the rear. Instead of hurrying it one would go in front and steady its pace if it showed signs of speed. Obviously the two warriors cherished this job beyond measure. The cow seemed very pleased; she was a fat and comfortable cow who seemed to have survived the lean war years with more success than most animals.

Barcelona when I left was grim beyond all belief. The people had suffered too much; now everything was lost. The streets were still, except for trucks and cars piled high with baggage which took the road towards the frontier, which was jammed with a mass of cars. People spoke in whispers. It seemed as if they could not really believe that all was lost even though the guns were roaring not far from the city and the last thirty-one hours there had seen eighteen air raids. Mostly on the port, where I think some thirteen British ships lay wrecked.

CHAPTER XLVI

PARLIAMENT IN A DUNGEON

I T was clammy and cold down in the dungeons of the great sprawling Castle of Figueras on the night of February 1, 1939. But it was quite clean. The walls were whitewashed. There had been prisoners there, people of the Right. Before that there had been many others. In 1934 it was crowded with lesser known people of the Left and before that on many occasions these cellars had served as gaols.

It is hard for a prisoner to escape from a dungeon. It is also hard for a bomb to get in, if the dungeon be deep enough, and these were pretty deep. This latter consideration predominated on this particular winter night.

Spain's Parliament met here, as the Constitution ordered, on February 1. A sad Parliament indeed. Its election which proved a triumph for Left Spain against tremendous odds in February 1936 had plunged the country into blood and disaster. I had been at its first session, also at the last one before the war. There had been gatherings in Madrid, then it was Valencia—in the lovely old Lonja made gay with marvellous tapestries—and then it had been up in the old Monastery of Montjuich and another in Sabadell in a savings bank; a hunted Parliament indeed. Hunted, as the will of the people of Spain was hunted; an expression of a Democracy which was the soul of a people but which was vague and inert, incapable of constructive expression.

The Speaker, Diego Martinez Barrio, sat at a table draped with the Republican colours. There were sixty-two Deputies there out of 473. Negrin spoke, reading most of his speech; he is not an orator. He made three conditions for peace. These were: (1) A guarantee of the independence of Spanish national territory. (2) A guarantee for the Spanish people to be able to choose their destiny. (3) A post-war guarantee against persecution engendered by the fratricidal strife. Other orators supported him. There was no opposition. There was something very like death down there. I whispered to the Russian writer Ilya Erenburg who stood by me: 'This place is like a tomb.' He answered sententiously: 'My friend, this is the tomb not only of the Spanish Republic but also of European Democracy.' The awful thing about it was that I felt that he was right.

All day long we had sat in Figueras expecting to be bombed. But the raiders did not come. Next day they came and killed over sixty; this town was jammed with refugees. We had sat in the Government censorship office with the very brave staff who stayed on in a fragile house exposed to frequent day and night raids when they all could have gone over the frontier twelve miles away without any difficulty. It is nice to meet brave people, even amid such heroism as one saw on all sides there, and Sr. Quiroga Pla, and Aurora Riano, and others of that staff certainly behaved excellently.

But it was not only in the dungeons of Figueras that I felt that I was watching the twilight of European Democracy as we know it. It was across the frontier in France where the icy truth hit me like a blast from the North Pole.

Many times I grumble at my work and express the wish that I were a boot-black instead of a reporter. But that is just a pose. Actually every reporter loves to feel that he is right up against the moving finger which is writing history. But there is one story that I wish that I had never had to cover. And that was the entry of the refugees into France.

To-day I wish it were a nightmare that I could forget with the new day and wash away with cold water.

The first wave of what developed into a mighty stream totalling in the end over 400,000 refugees hit the small frontier town of Le Perthus on Sunday, January 30. The road was jammed solidly with farm carts, motor trucks, ambulances, mule carts. The French would let no vehicles across; hence the jam. A wild report had gone around that Franco had taken Figueras and people stampeded across the frontier.

Rain streamed down in solid sheets. At first everyone was allowed across. Then M. Didkowski, Prefect of the Pyrenées Orientales Department, reversed the order. All soldiers must return; women and children could stay but no more must enter for the time being. It is only fair to say that the Spanish Government had asked for all soldiers to be sent back. Franco was still a long way from Gerona, let alone Figueras. But the panic-stricken mobs did not know this.

The order was carried out ruthlessly and hundreds of wounded men also were driven back. Only stretcher cases were allowed to stay. I stood at the frontier line with Brigadier A. L. M. Molesworth, of the International Commission of the League of Nations, whose hard work for the British members of the International Brigade did him great credit. He died in retirement at Tavistock on August 30, 1939. He watched the scene in amazement as the Garde Mobile herded these wretched wounded back across the frontier. Many staggered; they were starving; many had limbs covered with gangrene; they were being pushed out with night coming on in a deluge on the cold foot-hills of the Pyrenees. The nearest village, La Junquera, was over two miles away and had already 20,000 refugees jamming every house. Brigadier Molesworth said to me: 'My God, Buckley, they can't turn out wounded men like this!' He went up to the Major in command who answered curtly: 'Sorry, General, we have our orders.'

I went down into La Junquera and found the military commander, a fat man with one arm. Twelve babies had died during the previous night from exposure. There were scores of sick; many hundreds of wounded. When I went back over the frontier I saw a dead man being carried across. He was an aviation officer, editor of an aviation review, who had caught pneumonia out in the rain.

Then back to Perpignan, a lovely French Catalan town with much character. But to-night it was pouring rain and up there in the hills the heart of a nation was bleeding. Surely Democracy could not be completely deaf; surely the people of the whole neighbourhood must turn out to help these stricken Spanish Republicans; surely churches, cinemas, theatres, must be opened for them, soup kitchens started, hundreds of doctors and nurses be brought from all over France. Surely Britain too, another Democracy, would lend its hand, rush over helpers, money, food, field hospitals.

But in Perpignan the cinemas were full—of spectators. The streets were crowded—with well-fed, well-dressed, citizens taking their evening stroll. In the cafés and dance halls the concertinas droned away, ta-ra-la-ri-ra-la-la-la-la. . . .

I wondered bitterly what this scene would be like if Perpignan were German and fellow-Fascists were in trouble on the frontier. I could imagine how everything would be organised, how the ambulances would rush here and there, how the S.A. and the S.S. and Hitler Jugend would speed to the scene.

There were many who helped. The Prefect and his staff did, I think, all that was in their power and all that they were allowed to do in view of orders from Paris. They got a few doctors to the scene—pitifully few; the wounded in the Fortress of Bellegarde above Le Perthus were lying on a stone floor on straw. Socialist organisations did something and the women of Le Perthus were splendid and ran a canteen. International helpers also were there, including the tireless Mrs. Field, an American woman who worked literally night and day to help to feed these poor people. The Catholic Bishop of Perpignan issued a declaration asking Catholics to help. But the result was not apparent in all places for two relief workers whom I know went to the Catholic Chapel in Le Perthus and asked if women and children could not at least be sheltered there out of the rain for one night. The sister of the priest refused. She said her brother was away and without his permission she could not allow this. Against this one must set the example of the Parish Priest of Prats de Mollo who not only threw his church open to the militia-men but suspended the usual early six o'clock Mass each morning in order that they could sleep longer.

A few days later France threw open the frontier to all, and the Republican Army and tens of thousands of civilians poured into France. It was a generous gesture of France. Although quite what else they could have done I do not know. They could hardly have manned the frontier with machine-guns and prevented anyone from crossing. I seem to remember that in 1914 well over half a million Belgian refugees crossed into Holland; they did not want to live under German rule. And Holland quickly organised relief and treated them well.

The Spanish Republicans were admitted to France but their treatment left almost everything to be desired. I watched the whole scene day by day and I am only too anxious to give credit to France where this is due but I must report what I saw. Literally scores of thousands were herded into 'camps' which were nothing but open spaces near the sea shore, swampy when it rained and swept by a blinding cloud of sand from near-by dunes when the sun shone. There were few huts. It was difficult to say which was the worst, Argelès or Saint-Cyprien. The men, and some women, burrowed holes in the sand to sleep in, there was no proper water supply, only brackish evil-tasting water which produced a state of dysentery among those who drank it, food supplies were not properly organised for weeks; after several weeks wounded were still uncared for. Women and children were hurried off here and there in batches throughout the length and breadth of France.

The camps were guarded by French Senegalese, coloured troops, who were given rubber clubs and by the Garde Mobile. At Saint-Cyprien there were French Spahis who rode their magnificent horses with dash and flourished their sabres in the air for no reason at all.

One month after the war had ended in Catalonia, people who in normal life were respectable middle-class lawyers and doctors or university professors were living like primitive animals in burrows in the sand, unkempt and under-fed, with no shelter from the torrential spring rains. Foreign welfare workers were hindered in their efforts to alleviate suffering. The Press was rigorously forbidden entry to the camps.

The whole episode depressed me terribly not just because of its local aspects but because of the wider implications. Surely for Britain and France to have catered properly for 400,000 refugees should not have been an impossibility. Here again, Democracy could offer no solution. Surely there are hundreds of useful works waiting to be carried out. Why not have offered the stronger refugees work in ripping down great parts of our cluttered, unhealthy London and re-building it. France has no fortifications along the Pyrenees which now became potentially a totally hostile frontier; she could have set the men to work.

Once again it became so clear that we do not face facts. We let our chaotic economies creep along like ungainly fat slugs after a shower of rain. We were tremendously worried about the Prado pictures. What a fuss about the Grecos and the Goyas. International experts hurried down. The whole world was excited about the rescuing of some 600 *chef d'œuvres* of Spanish and Italian art which were being guarded near Figueras after their long odyssey. But we cared nothing about the soul of a people which was being trampled on. We did not come to cheer them; to encourage them. To have taken these half-million and cherished them and given them work and comfort in Britain and France and their colonies, that indeed would have been culture in its real sense of the word. I love El Greco, I have spent countless hours just sitting looking at the Prado Titians and some of Velazquez's works fascinate me, but frankly I think it would have been better for mankind if they had all been burned in a pyre if the loving and warm attention that was lavished on them could have been devoted to this half-million sufferers. Better still if we had hearts big enough to cherish both, but since apparently we have not, it would at least have been a happier omen if such drops of the milk of human kindness which we still possess could have gone to the human sufferers.

Yet while men well known in Catalan and Spanish cultural life in addition to tens of thousands of unknown persons were lying exposed to the elements and an average of sixty persons a week were dying of sickness and disease among the refugees in and around Perpignan, the art treasures left for Geneva in 1,842 cases on February 13; they were well protected from rain and wind. Women and children and sick and wounded men could sleep in the open air, almost uncared for. But the twenty trucks of Prado pictures had great tarpaulin covers and the care of a score of experts.

CHAPTER XLVII

THE END OF A REPUBLIC

I REMEMBER very many years ago when I was a small boy, watching an unpleasant scene in a farmyard where the farmer was trying to kill a duck. This duck wanted to live and when its neck was nearly severed by a knife it managed to twist itself free. It raced around the yard with its wings outspread and leaving a trail of gore. Boys tried to knock it out with stones and others tried to catch it and missed and then tried to daze it with sticks. It was really horrible.

I remembered this incident in the last days of the Republic from February 10, when the war ended in Catalonia, until April 1 when General Franco proclaimed the end of the conflict in all Spain.

The Republic was young, not quite eight years old. She did not want to die. The German Republic of Weimar managed to reach the age of fifteen. Austria's Republic attained twenty years and the Czech Republic one year more. The Czech Republic too was in agony now in this spring of 1939 but it was a bloodless affair, or relatively bloodless. Only the Spaniards went down struggling to the last gasp.

After Catalonia fell Dr. Negrin flew to the Centre Zone with all his Ministers and inspected there the possibilities of resistance which were small not only because there was scant material but also because the people were on the edge of sheer starvation and for over twelve months they had been separated from the Government and from the political leaders with the natural consequences arising from lack of any active leadership. Nevertheless there were still 500,000 men under arms and that is a number to reckon with.

The *putsch* by General Miaja, Colonel Casado and Professor Besteiro which overthrew the Negrin Government and seized power on March 5 may have had the best intentions but it was doomed to bring even worse disaster to the Republicans. By putting up a stout front there was always the hope that at least it might be possible to cover a retreat from Madrid to the sea of those civilians and soldiers who wished to escape. The fleet was still in Cartagena. General Franco had never shown any particular objection to the active Leftists escaping. This saved him a great deal of trouble and with the Government forces retiring on Valencia it is possible that he would have allowed many thousands to get away by sea and here indeed there would have been a magnificent opportunity for us to have indulged in humanitarianism.

The Communists, and many others I think, resisted this piteous attempt by Miaja and Casado to secure terms which General Franco had told them over and over again could not be given. He had always, throughout the war, spoken with crystal clarity. He had said: 'Surrender!' Miaja and Casado shot a number of people including Lieut.-Colonel Barcelo. I happened to have met Barcelo in Toledo and, such is the irony of fate, he was at the time rather in disgrace because it was felt that he was not quite loyal enough to the Republic. Now he had been shot as a Communist.

Nor can I see any excuse in the pretext of Miaja and Casado that they were faced with a Communist régime. There was very little communistic about Dr. Negrin's Government which had just one Communist Member. It was true that just before the *putsch* Dr. Negrin reorganised the Army and created 'mobile shock units'. That in the centre was to have 50,000 men and to be under Lieut.-Colonel Modesto, who was promoted to General, and command of similar forces in Estremadura and Andalusia was to be taken by Lister and Francisco Galan, who also were to be promoted to the rank of General.

These men were, it is true, all Communists. But they also were the best soldiers which the Republic possessed. When they had fought their way back from the Segre and the Ebro to the Pyrenees not one of them said: 'Enough!' All of them flew at once to the Centre Zone to continue to fight. I do not see how the placing of such men in command could in any way be interpreted as a Communist move towards domination of the Centre Zone.

It was inevitable that chaos should come. Perhaps for the

sake of those who collect facts, it might be worth putting down the names of those who composed this ephemeral 'Government' which would only fight against fellow-Republicans. They were: Prime Minister, General José Miaja; Defence, Colonel Segismundo Casado; Foreign Affairs, Professor Julian Besteiro; Interior, Wenceslao Carillo; Justice and Propaganda, San Andres; Commerce and Labour, Val; Finance, Marin; Education, del Rio.

I do not know who Val, Marin and del Rio are. I do not think that history will worry much. Carillo is a Caballero supporter of the Socialist Party. San Andres is a man of the Left Republican Party.

Of those who fought to suppress the Communists who rebelled against the new 'Government' it is worth noting Lieut.-Colonel Cipriano Mera, commander of an Army corps on the Aragon front and who was the leading 'Anarchist officer' in the Republican Army.

The people were in any case fought out; gallant Madrid could not have stood much more. Two years of hunger, bombardment, feverish work, had exhausted everyone except the soldiers who had at least obtained such little food as was available.

The new 'Government' gave orders for the arrest of Dr. Negrin and his Ministers. They escaped by aeroplane from their headquarters near Alicante while troops were on their way to seize them. Dolores Ibarurri (Pasionaria) and some others who were being sought also got away by plane. Lister got away but I never heard what happened to Modesto and Taguena.

The naval base at Cartagena was even more chaotic than most places. There, first a Franco revolt upset things, then an attempt by the Negrin Government to suppress this collapsed in the midst because the Negrin Government was overthrown. The fleet sailed off and interned itself at Bizerta, Algeria. I had been down in Cartagena in the previous August and had been surprised to find how much attention was paid to appearance. The sailors looked very smart indeed, and as for the officers in white duck in the summer heat they were just too elegant. The fleet had come very much under

Socialist control. The chief Political Commissioner was at first Amador Fernandez, who was secretary to the Asturian Miners' Union in 1934. Later he was substituted by another Socialist, Bruno Alonso. His second-in-command was a nice, studious, melancholy young Socialist with a Czech wife named Gines Ganga—an extraordinary name which I always thought must be a pen-name but which he always used—and who was a warm supporter of Caballero. There never was much the Navy could do, but under more enterprising leadership it might in the end have done something to ferry away the thousands anxious to leave and not have sailed away on its own. However, this was perhaps an inevitable result of the chaos produced by the manœuvres of the new 'Government'.

The Miaja-Casado régime had as sad a fate as even the most pessimistic had forecast. It finally sent an envoy to Burgos. But General Franco continued to say, as usual: 'Surrender!' On March 26, he ordered Madrid to surrender under threat of bombardment. On March 29, the Nationalists marched into the town.

Very few got away. Valencia, Alicante and all the principal towns collapsed almost immediately and the retreat of those who wished to escape was cut off. Colonel Casado escaped on a British destroyer and was taken to Marseilles and from there he left straight away for London.

The Democracies who had been so anxious that no more blood should be shed in war, showed no perturbation whatever at the fact that thousands of people whose life was in danger, not because they had murdered anyone or robbed a single thing in their lives but just because they had fought for the progress and independence of their land, were left to face at the worst a firing squad and at the best a concentration camp. We made no attempt whatever to get people away who wished to escape. Sr. Besteiro stayed behind. He was sentenced to thirty years' imprisonment in July of this year, 1939.

On April 1, General Franco declared that the war was over. The totalitarian régime presided over by himself now controlled all Spain. The Republic was dead.

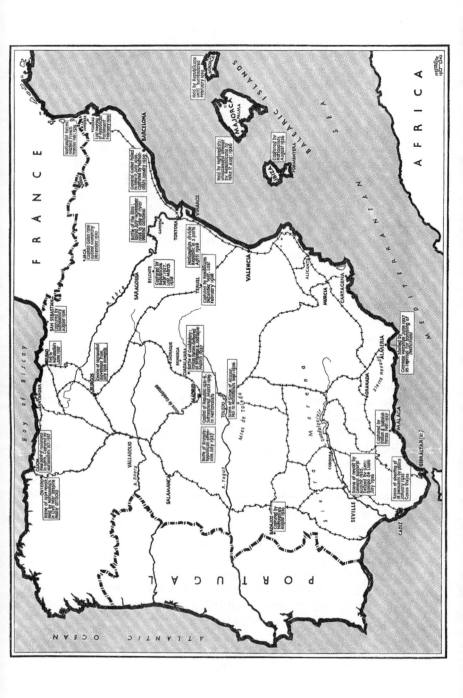

INDEX

431